Race and Rights

EARLY AMERICAN PLACES

Early American Places is a collaborative project of the University of Georgia Press, New York University Press, Northern Illinois University Press, and the University of Nebraska Press. The series is supported by the Andrew W. Mellon Foundation. For more information, please visit www.earlyamericanplaces.org.

Race and Rights

Fighting Slavery and Prejudice in the Old Northwest, 1830–1870

DANA ELIZABETH WEINER

NIU Press
DEKALB

Published by the Northern Illinois University Press
DeKalb, Illinois 60115
First printing in paperback, 2015

Portions of chapters 3 and 4 previously appeared as "Anti-Abolition Violence and Freedom of Speech in Peoria, Illinois, 1835–1848," *Journal of Illinois History,* 11 (2008): 179–204.

Library of Congress Cataloging-in-Publication-Data

Weiner, Dana Elizabeth.
Race and rights : fighting slavery and prejudice in the Old Northwest, 1830–1870 / Dana Elizabeth Weiner.
p. cm.
Includes bibliographical references and index.
ISBN 978-0-87580-457-6 (cloth : alk. paper)
ISBN 978-0-87580-713-3 (pbk.)
ISBN 978-1-60909-072-2 (electronic)
1. Antislavery movements—Northwest, Old—History—19th century. 2. African Americans—Legal status, laws, etc.—Northwest, Old—History—19th century. 3. African Americans—Northwest, Old—Social conditions—19th century. 4. Race discrimination—Law and legislation—Northwest, Old—History—19th century. 5. Northwest, Old—Race relations—History—19th century. 6. Northwest, Old—History—1775–1865. I. Title.
F484.3.W45 2013
305.80097709'034—dc23

2012037642

The Jacket image is from the painting, *The Underground Railroad* (1893 Oil on Canvas, 52 3/16 x 76 1/8 in) by Charles T. Webber.

For my parents

Contents

Acknowledgments

This book is all the richer thanks to the support and help of scores of wonderful people. The research for this project began when I worked with an inspiring cohort of supportive faculty as a graduate student at Northwestern University. From the outset, Stephanie McCurry has shared her formidable intellect and excellent advice. Susan Pearson was instrumental in the development and guidance of this project. Her insights have been vital. These scholars' ideas and those of Josef Barton, Steven Hahn, and Amy Dru Stanley have immensely enriched this volume through our many years of working together. At Northwestern, I would also like to thank the Departments of History and African American Studies, particularly Henry Binford, Paula Blaskovits, Suzette Denose, Marsha Figaro, Krzys Kozubski, Kate Masur, Dwight A. McBride, and Michael Sherry.

In the process of researching this book, I have accrued a multitude of intellectual debts and benefitted from numerous sources of financial and professional support. The staffs at the Wilfrid Laurier University Library, the University of Arizona Library, and the Northwestern University Library, especially their interlibrary loan departments, fulfilled my most outlandish requests with essential promptness. Chieko Maene and Pam Schaus showed me the wonders of mapping software. My many research trips were funded by generous sources and aided by dozens of able archivists. These important grants included a Wilfrid Laurier University short-term research grant; a Wilfrid Laurier University travel grant; two travel grants from the Northwestern University history department; a

Northwestern University graduate research grant; a Bentley Historical Library research fellowship, Michigan Historical Collections; a Price visiting research fellowship, William L. Clements Library, the University of Michigan; a Frederick Binkerd Artz summer research grant, Oberlin College Library; and a King V. Hostick Award from the Illinois Historical Preservation Agency and State Historical Society. More recently, my thanks go to the Wilfrid Laurier University Office of Research Services for a book preparation grant. On the publishing side, it has been a true pleasure to work with Mark Heineke, Susan Bean, Tim Roberts, and Gary Von Euer at Northern Illinois University Press and the Early American Places Series in the production of this book.

I have been blessed with welcoming and inspiring colleagues. From my time at the University of Arizona Department of History, my particular thanks go to Karen Anderson, Michael Bonner, Ben Irvin, and Katherine Morrissey. My colleagues and friends at Wilfrid Laurier University have improved my life, my writing, and my teaching. I much appreciate their encouragement and support, especially Blaine Chiasson, Darryl Dee, Richard Fuke, John Laband, Joyce Lorimer, Amy Milne-Smith, Darren Mulloy, Susan Neylan, Chris Nighman, and Eva Plach.

I have also been fortunate to have friends and fellow historians who carefully read segments or all of this work and offered incisive comments. At Northwestern, the United States History Dissertators' Group and the Center for African American History Dissertators' Group were enormously helpful, especially Tobin Miller Shearer, Mshaï Mwangola, and Katy Burns-Howard. Astute and encouraging feedback also came from Adam Crerar, Jana Measells, and Peter Jaros. Frank Gaugler, Jenn Q. Goddu, and Deborah Van Seters shared their writing expertise and excellent ideas. Vibrant discussions of scholarship at the Society for Historians of the Early American Republic annual meetings have included valuable comments from David Brodnax Sr. and Christopher Waldrep. Finally, my deep thanks go to the two readers for Northern Illinois University Press for their critiques and advice. Any errors that remain are my own.

The comfort and camaraderie of friends near and far can never be overestimated, especially given the solitary nature of the enterprise of writing history. Thanks go to my fellow travelers Francois Barthelat, Debs Cane, Anne Dabrowski, Nancy Deutsch, Sarah Dugan, Cari Ishida, Karen O'Brien, Vandna Sinha, and Chantal Sudbrack for sharing the joys and trials of graduate school with me. We are now so dispersed, but I will never forget the years we had together in Evanston and Chicago.

Across the United States, dear friends including Sarah and Dave Cohen, Kimberly and David Hawkins, Laura Mack, Molly Steinbauer, and Jackie and Lucas Silacci have provided this itinerant researcher with respite. Canada is my home now, and I am thankful for many thoughtful conversations and relaxing times in Kitchener with Lesli Ann Agcaoili, Chip Bender, Antoinette Duplessis, Wendy Janzen, Mary Jo Megginson, Juanita Metzger, Judith Nicholson, Linda Quirke, Tanya Richardson, and Leandra Zarnow.

I am lucky to have a massive extended family that has ever supported my long journey into academia. Thank you to the Mathesons, the Weiners, the Goulds, and the Litins. My parents, Bob and Elaine Weiner, have always encouraged me in everything, not least my loves of history and reading. Their assistance to me is immeasurable. I treasure their love and their faith in me, and memories of all of the wonderful places we have seen together. I dedicate this book to them. My brother, Eric Weiner, has been my friend and ally from our days of digging mud holes in the backyard to the present. Thanks to him, Kyra Weiner is a happy addition to the family. Most of all, Tim has brought so much joy and so many streams, trees, and chili peppers to my life. I thank him for his optimism, new perspectives, patience, and unflagging love.

Introduction

When I drew up the Ordinance, I had no idea the states would agree to the article prohibiting slavery.

—NATHAN DANE TO RUFUS KING, JULY 16, 1787

From the moment the Continental Congress created the Northwest Territory in 1787, the region was at the front lines of debate over the meaning of race and rights in the new nation. After over a year of squabbling between northern and southern delegates in the Congress, Nathan Dane of Massachusetts took over as leader of the Committee on the Western Territory and pushed through the Northwest Ordinance. A compromise measure, Article VI of the ordinance stated, "there shall be neither slavery nor involuntary servitude in the said territory." As an inducement to the southern delegates, it only applied to the lands east of the Mississippi River, south of the Great Lakes, and west of the Ohio River, and contained a fugitive slave clause permitting southerners to retrieve escaped slaves from the territory. The Congress approved the measure on July 13, 1787.[1]

While many of the delegates regarded the ordinance as having settled the issue of slavery in this new Northwest Territory, they may not have realized either the extent to which slavery already existed there, or, as Dane suggested, quite what they were getting into.[2] In reality, the ordinance left the way open for considerable debate over slavery's status in this region. Subsequent residents and lawmakers of the Old Northwest struggled to mold the provisions of the ordinance to their own purposes. Many people who already owned slaves retained them and claimed the law only forbade them from bringing more slaves into the region.[3] They clashed with abolitionists, advocates of African American rights, and

MAP 1. The Northwest Territory. Map by Pam Schaus.

the Free-Soilers who wished to keep slavery out of future new states. With the Northwest Ordinance, the Continental Congress introduced rather than settled a struggle over slavery and race relations in a region whose national prominence would only increase over the next century. In the process, they set the precedent for continued disputes about the relationship between the growth of the nation's territory and the future of slavery, including that institution's ability to expand to the west. This quarrel escalated with the extension of the abolition movement into the Old Northwest in the 1830s.

In the Old Northwest from 1830–1870, a bold set of activists fought against local and distant racial prejudice. These reformers ranged from antislavery lecturers and journalists to African American leaders of the Black Convention Movement. This book is about these women's and men's expansive efforts to eradicate southern slavery and its local influence in the racist milieu of four new states carved out of the Northwest Territory: Illinois, Indiana, Michigan, and Ohio. These states comprised the central battleground over race and rights in antebellum America, in a time when the social meaning of race was deeply infused into all aspects of Americans' lives, and when people struggled to establish political consensus. The Old Northwest in its entirety encompassed those four states, as well as Wisconsin and a portion of Minnesota. This study omits the youngest states in the region, Wisconsin and Minnesota, for in the other four states in this period activism was more vibrant and violence against reformers was widespread.[4]

Antislavery and anti-prejudice activists from a range of institutional bases crossed racial lines as they battled to expand African American rights in this region, one with its own bleak history of limiting civil liberties by race. They formed associations, wrote publicly about their local racial climate, and gave or hosted controversial lectures. In the process, they discovered that they had to fight for their own right to advocate for others.

* * *

As race is a central concept in this book and one that scholars often debate, it is essential to define how it is used here. This book treats race as an ideological construction, particular to place and time, as do many scholars today. Race in the early United States was the product of deliberate human efforts to shore up white supremacy in law.[5] Racial categories are formed through historical processes, through laws and human action, and are social creations rather than immutable facts.[6] This historical understanding of race as constructed underlies the book's analysis, but nonetheless, throughout the text, the term *race* and references to racial categories will not be written in intrusive quotation marks, except in cases of actual quotations.[7] Quoted material retains its original format, including spelling.

In contrast to historians' current understanding, the majority of antebellum Americans considered race a problematic fact, and one that they should apply to others to evaluate their rights. When most of them read in an individual the signs of blackness, the meaning they assigned to African ancestry justified discriminatory treatment. This is racism, a national problem, and also one that was particularly pervasive in the

Old Northwest. It underlay support for the "Black Laws" and opposition to abolition in this disputed area. In its most extreme form, racist logic utterly dehumanized African Americans in their contemporaries' eyes, and justified holding them as property, as chattel slaves.[8]

Among most of the activists in this study, race was no less real than it was to their foes. The important distinction they made related to its meaning, for they thought individuals merited equal rights regardless of their race, not because the category of race itself was without concrete reality. When they opposed prejudicial treatment, most did so because they believed such distinctions were immoral, not because they thought that race was a fiction. A few of them, both those who identified as white and African American, advocated perspectives that, to modern eyes, appeared to foreshadow the view of race as a social construction.[9] Regardless of their perspectives on race, all of these reformers faced substantial obstacles to their efforts for change.

The racist character of the Old Northwest meant that the fight against slavery there became but one facet of a larger rights struggle. While this is a history of activism, in a broader sense it is also a history of how reformers in the region understood the law and shaped new conceptions of justice. The ideas of civil liberties these agitators developed represented a key shift in Americans' views of rights, an expansion that to date historians have overlooked. By the 1830s, the law was an instrument of oppression in the Old Northwest, as seen in the "Black Laws" that limited African Americans' status there. Race-based legislation was well entrenched at the state level across the region, and federal law provided no relief.[10] While "Black Laws" existed elsewhere in the North, here they were at their most extreme.[11] In these four states, white supremacy penetrated politics and public life, as did the local and national history of slavery.

Looking at these states as a region reveals the impact of bias that these stalwart reformers—white as well as African American—faced when they disturbed the deep-rooted racial order. In the legal debates their bold actions catalyzed, Old Northwest activists claimed they deserved freedom from the violence their activities, including violations of gender and racial norms, elicited. In the process, they developed innovative strategies that pitted state and federal rights against one another.

Old Northwest activists drew on the language of rights in a period when people questioned and changed the very meaning of the term. They and their contemporaries developed many new ideas of rights, and interpreted older sources such as the Declaration of Independence in new,

MAP 2. Old Northwest towns and cities, with dates of statehood. Map by Pam Schaus.

egalitarian ways.[12] Antislavery and anti-prejudice reformers adopted the term "inalienable rights" for slaves' claim to the fruits of their labor, for African Americans' entitlement to rights more generally, and for their own right to express their grievances.[13] These arguments were essential in the Old Northwest, where the region's ambiguous relationship to slavery and to African American freedom contributed to local turmoil. There, people fiercely debated the racial limitations of rights.

While the Old Northwest was notably hostile to African Americans, they still had many allies in these new territories and states; indeed the region had a dedicated, active cadre of advocates against slavery and for racial equality. The Old Northwest environment shaped the nature and local efficacy of their activism, organizing principles, beliefs, and goals. Although communities throughout the region fostered outspoken foes of slavery and proponents of African American rights from 1830 to 1870, their struggle is a little-understood aspect of activist history. In Illinois, Indiana, Michigan, and Ohio, reformers pressed their antislavery and anti-racist agenda in the face of intense opposition.

In the Old Northwest, networks of activists across dispersed communities took controversial direct action against prejudice and slavery. The focal towns of this study are mostly small, like Noblesville, Indiana, and Pontiac, Michigan. In these places, free African Americans represented a tiny, beleaguered minority that often worked with sympathetic whites across racial lines to improve their circumstances.[14] Many community studies of reformers focus on the Northeast, especially its cities, but this did not reflect the experience of most Americans, who resided in "rural settings or small villages until the Civil War."[15] While African Americans faced discrimination, and anti-abolitionists lived throughout the region, the ever-growing and increasingly diverse populations in the cities meant that activism there had a much different dynamic than in smaller places. Instead of focusing on the growing cities that disproved the Old Northwest rule, this is a study of reform as it affected most people at the local level. Activists sought to influence the small communities of this region that they believed would define the future of the young nation as it grew. For these reasons, the oft-neglected Old Northwest states, so vital in the eyes of antislavery organizers, are essential to understanding the history of racial politics in antebellum America. The extraordinary agitators of the region were determined to face down slavery in its hostile borderlands.

* * *

Both local and national reformers used antislavery and egalitarian policies to pursue racial liberation in the Old Northwest, despite the antagonistic environment there. Local women and men who embraced the battle against slavery and for African American rights encountered formidable, often violent, resistance. The fight in this region differed from contemporary northeastern struggles, and even in recent accounts of reform there historians have minimized the extent to which its marginalized, dispersed combatants boldly faced community opposition for decades.[16] Other scholars of antislavery, in treating the Old Northwest as a remote, fragmented outpost of the northeastern agenda, have missed the fundamental fact that the trials of transforming this region shaped local activists into unusually dedicated reformers. Whether as newspaper editors or meeting attendees, for decades Old Northwest agitators displayed an extraordinary commitment to social and political change, regardless of the personal cost.

The region had become a stronghold of political antislavery by the 1850s, and increased in prominence as the nation approached the final battle over slavery in the political and ultimately the martial realms. The region's activists found that rising national tensions brought their reform activities even more opposition, for the political parties feared anything that increased sectional divides. What Old Northwest activists had been facing for decades—intense and inescapable clashes over slavery—became the national experience. As sectionalism increased, the political universe shifted, and the whole country confronted difficulties in establishing political consensus similar to those with which Old Northwest people had long struggled. Out of these conflicts, the Republican Party rose to prominence, and the Civil War began.

The status of African Americans in the Old Northwest remained precarious even after the nation's four years of bloody civil war. Indeed, even into the era of the Reconstruction amendments, many people there only reluctantly accepted the race-neutral extension of political and social rights. While all four states had ratified the Fifteenth Amendment by February 3, 1870, African American men subsequently had trouble exercising their right to vote there. In the Old Northwest, they could not always implement the privileges the law guaranteed them on paper. African Americans nonetheless tried to do so, and did not do this alone. While Old Northwest reformers who sought to improve African American rights were always a tiny minority, their actions prove that racial politics and antiracist activism in the region deserve a closer look.

* * *

Who were these Old Northwest activists? They were a diverse group that represented a range of occupations, religions, and backgrounds, from Quaker entrepreneurs to fugitive slave farmers. Local firebrands were not necessarily professional rabble-rousers, and many in fact were homegrown grassroots agitators who lacked simple, cohesive identities. Whether they were from southern pro- or anti-slavery communities, reform-rich western New York, or New England, as they forged their communities, Old Northwest rights promoters attempted to blend their ancestral cultures with those of their fellow citizens.[17]

These activists' agenda—to abolish slavery and the "Black Laws"—was bound up with the central problem of the Old Northwest in that era: building community in a region undergoing dramatic transformation. Agitators and their foes fought over who would mold and who could participate in local politics, culture, and public life, in a time when none of these questions were settled. They crafted reform communities and alliances that linked their distant towns. These networks arose out of the mutual values and risks of activism in these activists' unreceptive climate.[18]

* * *

This book has a thematic structure that also follows a rough chronology. It opens with the context essential to understanding the challenges of activism in the region, but quickly moves in focus to the 1830s when reform began to take root in the Old Northwest. The necessary background of agitation there includes both the early activist history and the many obstacles to racial equality in the region.

Activists' strategies to improve the status of African Americans in the Old Northwest were broad and shifting, for the region's reform climate in many respects worsened over time, and these advocates needed to accommodate its changes. As neighbors to the institution of slavery who lived under restrictive "Black Laws," these champions of equality claimed that they must combat what they saw as slavery's local influence. Beginning in the 1830s and continuing through the 1850s, these activists put fighting the "Black Laws" and the fugitive slave laws at the center of their project to transform the region. They paralleled the national antislavery effort by opposing local racial prejudice, and matched its most radical claims. These stalwarts fought biased laws with a range of integrated and African American-only strategies, and used tactics that included direct action, the press, and petitions. In their critiques, Old Northwest activists refused to embrace binary racial categories, and they questioned the significance of subjective differences between races that most of their contemporaries took for granted. Concurrently, local African American advocates articulated an independent vision of a more just nation as they used the Black Conventions to fight the "Black Laws" and prejudice more generally. The movement against racist laws was an integral component of the larger rights movement in the Old Northwest.

Indeed, Old Northwest antislavery and anti-prejudice activists fought a protracted struggle to secure the liberties they needed to reform the region. Americans' conceptions of rights were in transition in the antebellum period, and Old Northwest reformers stretched and molded them to fit their needs. They sought new interpretations of federal and state law to protect themselves from levels of violent opposition unusual even in the turbulent antebellum era. The anti-abolition violence they encountered lasted into the 1860s, substantially longer (and more frequent and severe in nature) than other historians have previously argued.[19] Local activists invoked the freedoms of assembly, press, and speech to defend their vital political tools of meetings, newspapers, and lectures.

Old Northwest antislavery organizations strove to secure freedom of assembly, a right that people closely contested at the local level. As they gathered in their communities, they catalyzed conflicts over social control. Both women and men were central to this work, and they created mixed-sex and women's organizations that held meetings, petitioned, and published articles and tracts that argued against slavery and prejudice. In their towns, women formed a significant, outspoken activist subset. Antislavery societies in the region remained viable through the Civil War, and their operations encompassed still more sweeping efforts for rights.

Freedom of the press in the Old Northwest had a troubled history. Reformers in the 1830s and 1840s found that as they strove for change, this inserted them into controversies over publishing about slavery and race. Newspapers built the antislavery and anti-prejudice community in the Old Northwest, for organizing in these sparsely populated states would have been impossible without press freedom. Champions of this right thus articulated broad and compelling arguments about its merits. Women in the region regarded press freedom as essential, and were unusually active advocates of it and journalists. Both female and male reformers expanded contemporary understanding of press freedom as a guaranteed right, and debated the anti-abolitionists who used violence and economic pressure to suppress them. Their persistence in transforming this especially difficult activist region—and their demand to use newspapers to join together across the miles—meant that their claims enlarged extant definitions of freedom of the press. Old Northwest reformers' public struggles showed rights advocates across the nation their particular local obstacles to activism and the antislavery message, and exemplified for their peers the dedication that they needed to change the country's picture of race and rights.

Itinerant lecturers who traversed the Old Northwest from 1830–1861 were essential to local activists' struggles for rights, particularly freedom of speech. These traveling women and men fought against formidable resistance in order to expand and secure the liberty to speak. Many communities emphatically rejected lecturers whose gender or racial identities compounded the provocation of their unpopular message. Despite this, with both large-scale lecture tours and brief local jaunts, people such as Josephine S. Griffing worked to build an antislavery public sphere for a diffuse population. Itinerant lecturers, both local and from the East, worked symbiotically with local supporters, and both were necessary to spreading the abolitionist message over these four challenging states. For their part, local supporting activists willingly gave them aid. They also violated gender norms with such actions as women's physical defense of male speakers, as in 1856 in Pontiac, Michigan, when a group of women protected Aaron M. Powell and Richard Glazier after a contentious lecture. Particular flashpoints in this free speech battle included the growth of political abolition and sectionalism, both of which led to increasing threats to lecturers' freedom of speech and often their personal safety. The actions of Old Northwest antislavery speakers, and the responses they elicited, unmask the consequences of rights struggles in this hotly contested region. Since theirs was an exceedingly unpopular cause, reformers experienced serious repercussions for their meetings, including violence and ostracism. Such consequences were of long duration in the Old Northwest, for its culture strongly resisted change to its racial mores.

* * *

By the 1850s, African Americans in the Old Northwest had gained few of the rights that they and their allies sought. Improving the region's racially discriminatory legislation remained a major focus of reformers' energy, and the increasingly harsh nature of fugitive slave legislation outraged them. They denounced the laws as unjust and vowed to continually resist them, along with slavery, which they still fought ferociously. While aid to fugitive slaves had formed an essential part of the local reform mission since at least the 1830s, its importance intensified with the passage of an enhanced fugitive slave law in September 1850. The new Fugitive Slave Law piled additional legal repressions onto the extant local "Black Laws." Activists fought back with a range of tactics; African Americans continued to meet in Black Conventions, and they and their white allies also used direct resistance, vigilance committees, and state personal liberty laws to weaken the law's new federal muscle. African Americans in the Old Northwest felt in the 1850s that their rights were increasingly precarious, and they and their collaborators realized that their fight for equality was far from over.

For Old Northwest activists, the Civil War ushered in an exciting sense of potential change. Debate over the "Black Laws" grew ever louder during the war years, as reformers sought to seize this moment to improve the lives of African Americans, and their opponents fought such developments with equal passion. The war escalated local fears of partisan discord, and party and sectional loyalties became reactionary bludgeons to stifle social and political transformation. Activists fought on, and secured some expanded rights in the war era, although the long sought-after emancipation failed to guarantee equality for northern African Americans, any more than it did for their southern brethren and sisters. White supremacy remained entrenched in these states, as exemplified in their residents' foot-dragging over ratifying and enforcing federal laws that expanded African Americans' rights. The uneven history of the Fifteenth Amendment's ratification in 1870 concluded an era of struggle for the rights of both free and enslaved African Americans in the Old Northwest. Nevertheless, African American men in these four states continued to have extensive difficulties in securing the vote, even after the ratification of that amendment. This is just one sign that many people in the region consistently lacked the will for equal rights, even when the letter of the law so dictated.

Old Northwest activists, whether African American or white, sought to eradicate both slavery and racial prejudice through their quotidian conduct and their reform activity. As progressive agents, they collaborated for the full racial, social, and political equality of African Americans, and aimed to create a more just society through the interconnection of ideas and social practice. They demonstrated this uncompromising devotion as they faced ostracism, financial ruin, and physical danger, but remained singularly committed to enacting egalitarian principles. Even as activists' opponents sought to destroy them, they found solace in their ideals of transcendent morality and universal human rights.

1 / Activist Taproots: Place, Reform, and the Quest for Unity

Antislavery and anti-prejudice activists believed they must mold the Old Northwest according to their ideals of a virtuous community. This was an immensely difficult mission. When he toured the region in 1841, antislavery lecturer Dr. Erasmus Hudson faced down abundant challenges. These included numerous anti-abolitionists who tried to silence his meetings, but he remained determined to continue. In a letter at the time, Hudson asserted that he must work on in the region, and claimed that the nation's "hopes . . . are in this great Western Valley; and if they are disappointed, our country will be filled with sorrow and confusion." To him, only diligent reform organization could save these deeply flawed "great western States."[1] Collaboration among activists thus held the key to changing their society and their nation.

* * *

From the 1830s, the Old Northwest grew in importance in many reformers' eyes as their desire to clean up the nation expanded. Passionate advocates increasingly spread ideas about the region's potential influence and the need to remove its substantial problems regarding slavery and race. The Old Northwest was far from isolated, and over time reform there moved toward the center of the broader movements against slavery and prejudice. Local activists' efforts to change the region were thus a subset of their larger struggles. While it was evident to Old Northwest rights promoters that their locality was critical, eastern abolitionists also saw this area as significant beginning in the 1830s, well before its growing economic importance and centrality to national politics converted more Americans to that opinion in the 1850s and 1860s. In Hudson's vision and that of many like-minded people, they undertook a crucial struggle to determine the culture of the Old Northwest.[2] This quest motivated agitators there for decades.

Reform shoots in the region sprung from rocky yet fertile soil, and their conditions of growth are vital to understanding these movements' struggles and successes. It is essential to learn more about the people, the debates over race and rights they incited in reform and politics, and the initial development of organizations in the region. The place of the Old Northwest and its rights climate both shaped the struggle for change there and made it necessary, because the racism endemic there necessitated strong efforts to fight it. Many of the obstacles Old Northwest activists faced actually brought reformers together, and people with different approaches often collaborated.

The Old Northwest context explains much of the diversity of the movement there, for bold antislavery and anti-prejudice activists faced a largely antagonistic population in the region, and one that had a great deal at stake in excluding both African Americans and abolition. The ratio of slavery's opponents to its supporters minimized institutional competition. In effect, local antislavery people often proved willing to collaborate with allies of any stripe, even when their creeds differed, and their societies had more harmonious operations there relative to the East.[3] Even as they sought out the unity required to organize effectively, these activists nonetheless fought forces of division in this fractious region.

The people of the Old Northwest offered substantial resistance to reformers' goals. In many ways, at the same time as these agitators broadened their base, hostile forces in their communities continually undermined and divided them. Chief among these obstacles was local opposition to advocates' message. This had several sources, but most important among them were the political parties and people who depended on slavery economically. The region's racism and its dispersed settlements also increased the challenges of activism. All of these hardships—resistance to reformers' and African Americans' freedom generally, racism, and the logistics of antislavery organizing in this difficult place—are developed throughout the remainder of the book. Exploring the place and the forces that unified and separated these tenacious Old Northwest activists provides context for understanding their efforts and the culture they sought to transform.

* * *

When early nineteenth-century white Americans viewed the varied landscape of the Old Northwest, they beheld its potential for financial opportunity, and perhaps even riches. The land appeared to them ideal for profitable agriculture, and appropriately linked by water (and later canal and rail) to southern and eastern markets. There, fortune seemed to await the industrious, and the region's incoming prospectors and settlers refused to allow people they viewed as racially inferior to interfere with this vision. This economic orientation shaped the settlers' interactions with the indigenous inhabitants there, and by the 1830s the white migrants had legally and militarily driven most of them out to secure these territories and later states for westward expansion.

The settling process was a labor intensive one, and for some migrants to the Old Northwest, particularly in Indiana and Illinois, slaves seemed the ideal solution to their various work needs, the Northwest Ordinance's prohibitions be damned. Others believed local slavery would diminish the value of white men's toil. Overwhelmingly they agreed, however, that as white men their claim on the Old Northwest was paramount, and they had little interest in sharing its potential and actual bounties with African Americans or others at all, and certainly not on equal terms. This perspective, along with their diverse origins, contributed to widespread aversion to reforming the Old Northwest and its race relations.

The people who settled the Old Northwest presented activists with both support and challenges. These relatively new states—populated by migrants from across the East and the South with disparate views on race relations—lacked regional cohesion about slavery and civil rights, and even consensus within each state. To take Ohio as one example, by the late eighteenth century its residents originated in such varied places as Virginia, New England, the middle states, and France.[4] A majority of the initial settlers of southern Illinois, Indiana, and Ohio, and some Michiganders had southern origins and exclusionary (and often proslavery) opinions, while New Englanders and New Yorkers made up the plurality of those who migrated to the central and northern portions of the first three states and to Michigan.[5] Not all former New Englanders and New Yorkers held antislavery views, however. Over time, the population became even less homogenous, including larger numbers of immigrants and more easterners who often lacked interest in sharing the region's economic opportunities with African Americans.[6] Activists' organizing efforts in this unsettled climate catalyzed debates about slavery and over the racial boundaries of social and political rights. These accompanied and expanded the nationwide movements to address those issues.

* * *

Anti-racist and antislavery activism in the Old Northwest grew out of a national reform context that dated back to the eighteenth century. Then, African American easterners like Richard Allen and Prince Hall were among the first to advocate immediate abolition and to inspire activists across the nation. Free African Americans saw and decried the indisputable connection between the obstacles to their own full citizenship and their enslaved brethren's condition. They protested against the colonization movement that sought to send them out of the United States; claimed full American citizenship; and directly demanded civil rights, including the vote. These calls paved the way for later egalitarian arguments, including those that Old Northwest activists made.

Beginning in the 1820s, African American militancy, accelerated by the anticolonization struggle, grew in intensity. The writings of David Walker, Maria Stewart, and later, Henry Highland Garnet provided important intellectual and rhetorical background for the awakening to radicalism.[7] In the early 1830s, a new cohort of white reformers with a growing interest in opposing slavery and racism emerged, as a result of several factors: egalitarianism; the Second Great Awakening's religious revivals and moral reform crusades; and the print, market, and democratic revolutions. They began to perceive the limitations of colonization and early abolition strategies, and to take up immediate abolition along with their African American allies.[8] An expanding corps of activists fought slavery even as, over time, the institution itself gained ever more vocal supporters, who themselves built on a long-standing intellectual heritage that justified slavery and its associated discrimination.

As the movement against slavery expanded, ideological divisions increasingly cleaved eastern organizations. These tensions transformed the first major American abolitionist association, the American Anti-Slavery Society. Founded in 1833, it provided the chief northern antislavery voice until its schism in 1840, which resulted partially from disagreement over women's right to vote and to take leadership positions in the society. The antislavery movement then split into what historians usually describe as three factions: the Garrisonians/immediatists, the evangelicals, and the political abolitionists.

The fiery *Liberator* editor William Lloyd Garrison led the innovative Boston-based American Anti-Slavery Society. Contemporaries also called this group the immediatists, and eventually, the "Old Organization." Beginning in the early 1830s, their peers deemed them radical for their opposition to electoral politics and their advocacy of controversial causes: immediate abolition, racial equality, women's suffrage, and anticlericalism. They promoted a "come-outer" position, wherein they argued people should resign from corrupt churches, political parties, and other associations and only join groups that had become "purified," as they said they had done.[9] They eschewed violent means by advocating nonresistance, argued that partisan politics was necessarily corrupt, and espoused the indirect means of moral suasion as the only true method to fight slavery.

The second main antislavery faction was the smaller, moderate evangelical one. Frustrated with the immediatists' anticlericalism, the evangelicals founded the American and Foreign Anti-Slavery Society, colloquially known as the "New Organization."[10] These people worked within established religious and political institutions, and kept moral suasion as their fundamental principle. They disdained the other causes the American Society took up, and never obtained much of a foothold in the Old Northwest. They overlap somewhat with the third faction, the political abolitionists (themselves often religiously motivated), and over time, the distinctions between them blurred even more.[11]

Old Northwest reformers, like other antislavery people, operated in a world where politics and debate about affairs of state deeply infused all aspects of life. Even those activists who favored anti-political immediate abolition found that they could not avoid the reach of politics and disputes over reform techniques. Antislavery struggles and those for rights in the Old Northwest were inescapably linked with partisan politics. Whether they debated the appropriateness of immediatism versus political abolitionism, or fought to promulgate a particular antislavery agenda, politics permeated the Old Northwest and influenced activists' freedom to advocate for slaves and free African Americans.

This was of course particularly true for political antislavery advocates, who beginning in 1840 successively organized through the Liberty, Free Soil, and Republican Parties, and used direct electoral means to combat slavery. Each of these political parties found substantial support in the Old Northwest (relative to the region's population).[12] While that was true, the area's tendencies toward unity influenced its reform structure, in that the political/immediatist division, as well as those between African American and white abolitionists, women and men, often did not apply in the Old Northwest.[13] Local organizers took the movement's larger national disputes in new directions and were less factionalized. This rendered them all the more threatening to their antagonistic contemporaries.

The major parties, reflecting the general opposition to abolition in the population, viewed the antislavery third parties with fear. While the Liberty and Free Soil Parties were minor players in antebellum politics, they nonetheless raised the specter of disorder for mainstream politicians as they, to varying degrees, insisted on discussing abolition, slavery, and race. The Liberty Party in its early years shared many of the immediate abolitionists' anti-racist goals and was outspoken on these issues. By 1842, most of its members had shifted their emphasis away from rapid emancipation and equal rights and toward an argument that slavery hurt whites.[14] In contrast, some individual Liberty activists, male as well as female, bucked this trend and advocated racial equality.[15]

For their part, the main political parties had ample reason to avoid debating touchy, divisive subjects related to race, and unsuccessfully sought to avoid them. Mainstream partisans delicately balanced upon the blurry line between the North and the South even as, over time, that task neared impossibility and as the political parties became increasingly sectional. Many Old Northwest Democrats and Whigs tried to prevent third parties like the Liberty Party from wooing antislavery voters.[16] This explains much of their hostility toward any racialized discussions in the region. In the 1830s and into the 1840s, the Democratic Party's main agenda was national unity, with a pro-southern slant. It was moderately permissive on slavery in order to court voters in the South, which perpetually risked antagonizing its northern supporters.[17] Northern Democrats' views on race were complex, for while they often had racially biased views, these differed in many cases from actual pro-slavery positions. They opposed "social equality" and resisted offending southerners, but this did not mean they necessarily favored slavery.[18] By the late 1830s, southern Democrats increasingly influenced national policy formation, and over time the fragile alliance between the party's northern and southern members broke down even more.[19]

The national Whig Party, while less permissive toward slavery, nonetheless had a firmly entrenched ideology of white racial superiority, and most of its members attempted to evade antislavery ideas and their potential for discord. Formed in 1833, the Party remained viable only as long as it convinced voters that its agenda substantially differed from that of the Democrats.[20]

Clearly, while some political antislavery people were willing to engage with slavery and race to a degree, the major parties proved recalcitrant. Both parties exploited opposition to abolition and African American rights to expand their share of the electorate.[21] This made activists' fight for these causes all the more difficult in the Old Northwest, for as they sought to reform the nation's racial mores, they directly confronted a political system stacked against them. Importantly, this balancing act also helps explain both Democrats' and Whigs' willingness to use violence to stop activists from organizing, as was particularly common in this region, whether they had political affiliations or not.

Throughout this turbulent era, as the political antislavery parties gained in strength, all of the major political parties fought hard to maintain dominance over the Old Northwest, which fed anti-abolitionism there. Many partisans could not get past the view of abolitionists and antislavery political parties as posing a divisive threat. While these four states differed, in all, the major parties feared losing power, even in places where no one disputed their dominance. The turmoil in these states helps explain why some Whigs joined the more overtly anti-abolition Democrats in suppressing Old Northwest activists, since their electoral position was particularly vulnerable. Reforming activists and politicians offered not only competition to the mainstream parties, but they also stirred up polarizing topics that the latter wished to keep quiet.

The Whigs were particularly strong in Ohio, while the Democrats were more successful in Illinois as well as in Michigan and Indiana in most years before the mid-1850s. The Democrats had a firm hold over the Michigan presidential elections from statehood in 1837 until 1856—except in 1840—and over the governorship (except in 1839) until 1855, when the Republicans took over. Liberty and Free Soil strength there also cost local Whigs some of the small ground they had gained.[22] In Illinois, the Democrats exercised overwhelming political control from the 1830s until the 1850s.[23] The Indiana Democrats steered the presidency and governorship for most years between 1828 and 1869, with a brief period of Whig strength in the mid-1830s. After 1860, the Republicans took the reins there, too. In Ohio, the Whigs obtained the majority, for the Democrats only maintained sway from 1828 until 1832 and from 1848 until 1852. After 1856, the Republicans predominated across the region, and by 1860, all gubernatorial and presidential elections in these states went Republican.[24] In this period, these rivalries and shifts in local politics mean that the major parties, accordingly, had substantial motivation to oppose antislavery activists of all stripes, and many were comfortable using violence to do so.

At the same time that the major parties aimed to avoid the glaring issues slavery and race raised in the Old Northwest, the antislavery political parties grew increasingly moderate. Beginning in 1848, at varying paces across the Old Northwest, the Liberty Party—with its stronger antislavery stance—dissolved, and the Free Soil Party arose in its place. This party and its successor, the Free Democrats, united former Liberty Party advocates with ex-Whigs and Democrats, along with other previously apolitical foes of slavery.

Despite some significant overlap in leadership with the Liberty Party, this new party had a less racially progressive agenda; it mainly opposed the extension of slavery. It neither pushed tenaciously for emancipation nor fought the Fugitive Slave Act of 1850 with much vigor. Some abolitionists strongly opposed the Free Soil Party's weaker racial justice mission.[25] While its vision of racial change was limited, the party nonetheless argued that slavery was a "moral evil," a position that differed markedly from both the Democrats and the Whigs.[26] The Free Soil Party did far better at the polls than its predecessor, earning 12 percent of the total vote in 1848. Its disruptive impact in that election reaffirmed for the Democrats and Whigs the need to avoid stirring up these sensitive subjects; if anything, the diminished radicalism of antislavery politicians made them more threatening to the party faithful, rather than less so.[27]

Over the course of the late 1840s and early 1850s, the positions of the Democrats and Whigs converged to a degree, most notably as they sought to hold the nation together with measures like the Compromise of 1850. This compromise further polarized American political discussion, and its fugitive slave provisions proved incredibly divisive in the Old Northwest.[28] For the next few years, the Free Soil Party retained varying degrees of popularity across the region, but had lost most of its limited support by 1851.

In the remarkably roiling 1850s, the arguments that activists made against slavery, and increasingly against slaveholder power, began to exert some sway over politics. The Whigs and Democrats failed to maintain national unity in the face of immense sectional pressures. The Kansas-Nebraska Act and the fatal conflicts over sovereignty and slavery that ensued in Kansas proved too much for the already fracturing parties to handle, and the Whigs collapsed.[29] The Republicans, the most effective of the antislavery political parties, emerged in 1854, and the Democrats began to divide even more along sectional lines. This new party continued in the Free Soil Party's moderate trajectory.[30]

The birth of the Republican Party was closely tied to the Kansas-Nebraska Act and sectionalism more generally, both of which had persuaded many northerners that they must take more aggressive action to defend their interests against the extension of slavery.[31] The Republicans argued for free labor's economic and social superiority over slave labor, and emphasized slavery's threats to white privileges. This brought the institution's indisputable relevance to the attention of the northern public. Free labor ideology's perspective that slavery's territorial expansion endangered white northern workers' fundamental right to "economic independence" contributed to escalating sectional conflict in the 1850s.[32] In the Old Northwest this was a persuasive argument for a varied constituency, and one which pro-southern government decisions, like that in the Dred Scott case, also affirmed.[33] The Republicans' distinctive—and moderate—ideology so effectively melded personal and sectional interest with morality that the party overcame its numerous political obstacles and rose to electoral triumph in 1860.[34]

The political situation in the Old Northwest enormously influenced this complex society, for there, antislavery and anti-prejudice reformers had their friends as well as their foes, their allies as well as their opponents. They drew upon a range of organizing methods, including both the sacred and the secular, to build their own following. Churches led the way into reform work for the myriad activists who were religious and had spiritual motivations.

* * *

Religion added to Old Northwest activists' tools and tensions, for both local and national churches also helped shape the landscape of reform there. As residents of a highly religious milieu and moment, antislavery people commonly believed that their faith meant they had a duty to change their society. The Second Great Awakening had converted many; these people had embraced its message that they must remove the nation's sins before Judgment Day.[35]

Old Northwest abolitionists tended to cluster in several religious traditions nationally known for opposition to slavery. Quakers, or the Society of Friends, were prominent reformers in all four states, but especially in Indiana. The Presbyterians and Congregationalists had particular support in Illinois, Michigan, and Ohio. The Methodists especially found many supporters among the antislavery people in

Illinois and Ohio, and the Free Will Baptists did so in Michigan and Ohio.[36]

Even as sections of particular evangelical strength within each of these states were more receptive to abolition, nonetheless for many devout Old Northwesterners, the road to publicly opposing slavery was rough.[37] While religious ideology could motivate antislavery work, churches could hamper activism. The Friends of Indiana, among others, encountered serious obstacles to their reform actions. Beginning in 1841, their state leaders refused to allow antislavery lecturers into their meetinghouses. The orthodox national leadership of the Society of Friends argued that abolition was divisive, and that their members should not mix in organizations with people outside of the faith or with non-Friend leadership. For over a decade, they had experienced splits both nationally and locally, including the departure of the so-called Hicksites in 1827 and 1828.[38]

Some in the Society of Friends took a strong stance against their religious body's refusal to work directly against slavery. Consequently, in Indiana approximately one hundred antislavery Friends left the denomination to form a new Yearly Meeting of Anti-Slavery Friends, at Newport in February 1843. The split there was at least in part motivated by events during the Society of Friends' Yearly meeting in nearby Richmond, Indiana, in 1842. A group of antislavery Friends led by Hiram Mendenhall had presented a petition to visiting Whig politician Henry Clay, asking him to free his slaves. Mendenhall was a Quaker who had migrated from North Carolina, and a Whig at the time.[39] Clay refused the petition, outraged that Mendenhall dared to publicly approach him about this controversial issue.[40] Local immediate abolitionists believed that many of Clay's Richmond supporters proved they were excessively moderate on slavery, and too willing to follow the Whig party line. Other events aided that impression, for at that same 1842 meeting, the Society expelled four Friends—Benjamin Stanton, Jacob Grave, William Locke, and Charles Osborn—for their abolitionist activities. This was but the latest development in an evolving controversy among Friends concerning the appropriateness of uniting with other causes.[41]

As late as 1847, Richmond's orthodox Quakers treated the visiting Hicksite lecturers, Lucretia and James Mott, as pariahs.[42] Pennsylvania reform powerhouse Lucretia Mott had previously visited the town in 1841 with her fellow lecturer, Vermont-born Oliver Johnson. Her visit there in 1847 was part of a larger tour; she also lectured in several Ohio towns, along with African American speakers Dr. David J. Peck (of

Philadelphia) and Frederick Douglass.[43] Even if Richmond did not welcome the Motts, other Friends eagerly embraced the fight against slavery, and the membership of the Anti-Slavery Friends ultimately grew to about two thousand, roughly 10 percent of the total number of Indiana Friends. The orthodox Friends eventually took up a stronger antislavery position, and the denomination consequently reunited in 1857.[44]

Old Northwest activists belonged to and tried to clear a number of other Protestant denominations of their association with slavery. Many chose to work within their existing religious bodies, but others called for separatism, as was common among immediatists. The Illinois State Anti-Slavery Society made a "come outer" statement on October 24, 1843. They argued that duty obligated antislavery people to leave the "Episcopal, Baptist, Methodist, [and] Presbyterian" denominations due to their stance on slavery.[45] By the mid-1840s, the Congregational Church in Illinois opposed slavery, and demanded that its ministers share this stance.[46]

In the Old Northwest, antislavery organizations also frequently encompassed members of multiple churches. In the antislavery convention at Granville, Ohio, in 1838, Quaker, Baptist, and Methodist clergymen all addressed the crowd.[47] The Michigan Anti-Slavery Society combined strong Quaker, Baptist, Methodist, and Presbyterian influences in the 1830s and 1840s.[48] On the national level and in the region, Congregationalists had an easier time condemning slavery than did Presbyterians and Methodists; the former church had little presence in the South and its leaders usually governed it locally. When the Methodists divided in 1844, the Wesleyan Methodist faction emerged and took on slavery, as did some of the Baptists the following year.[49] This denominational diversity continued in later years, and many of these reformers had sweeping visions of how they must change their society, which extended to its consumer products.[50]

* * *

Much as activists tried to reform churches they saw as sinful, they also sought to eradicate what they saw as the immoral aspects of the economy. Old Northwest direct action against slavery included the free produce movement, the effort to replace slave-tainted goods with ethical products. Since abolitionists knew that southern ties contributed to racism and anti-abolition, they tried to separate themselves economically from the institution, from the 1820s through the 1860s. These reformers claimed that they must combat the slave economy, and sought to deny slaveholders financial support by refusing to buy the products of unfree labor. Cajoling others to join them, the organizers of a free labor convention for Ohioans and Indianans in 1842 argued that they must take action to create change: "It is not sufficient for us to develop correct principles; we must endeavor to put them in practice. We must be willing to *do* as well as *say*, or we shall effect nothing."[51] Despite the movement's financial failure, this practical antislavery method proved that activists in the Old Northwest went to considerable lengths to avoid worsening the situation of slaves.[52]

These advocates' moral choices were enmeshed in the new market economy's economic developments and depended upon its exchange of commodities. The free produce movement was an effort to mold the market to fit the conviction that all workers had a right to be paid for their labor.[53] Its champions politicized economic behavior by making purchases the basis of an argument about free labor and universal rights. While the movement failed, such abstention did incremental good, both for slaves and for the people who bought free produce.[54] Free produce supporters learned they could use consumer movements to transform the context and the nature of discussions of the economy; they further claimed that purchases could create social change and advance an egalitarian agenda. Many individuals closely linked such activism to their work with antislavery societies.

* * *

Whether directed outward at visitors or inward at transforming their own towns, Old Northwest activists enthusiastically participated in abolitionist and anti-prejudice institution-building, beginning in the early 1830s. The region soon witnessed an explosion of action against slavery, the varied and visible fruits of local organizers' labor. The daily work to overturn slavery and prejudice presented reformers with physical, intellectual, and logistical challenges that they faced together, sharing their strength. Linked by their travels, letters, and newspapers, women and men in Illinois, Indiana, Michigan, and Ohio relied upon each other and upon their eastern compatriots to build their activist base. Their actions demonstrate that the region's antislavery struggle, while different, was inseparable from national battles. The Old Northwest was both central to the larger antislavery cause, and important for how it changed the national picture of abolition. The massive opposition and adverse legal climate they found gave local organizers a unique stance on activism, and focusing on the Old Northwest made the antislavery enterprise appear all the more daunting. These activists, from ordinary residents to leaders, from individuals to organizations, typically hitched their star to larger national bodies and agendas, but also differed from them.

While fighting slavery was difficult for reformers across the nation, it was particularly so in the Old Northwest, where the environment presented them unusual challenges that warrant closer investigation. The context in which Old Northwest antislavery reformers worked made them stand apart from those of the East in the duration of their activism, in the work they did, and in the possession of fewer rigid distinctions between antislavery groups. While largely overlooked by previous scholars, local and state organizations (including those that advocated immediatism) remained robust in some areas as late as the 1840s, and some even until the Civil War, in the very era when nationally oriented political abolition was on the ascent.[55] The growth in political abolition did not necessarily entail immediatists abandoning their former organizational techniques, at least in the Old Northwest. Despite political abolitionists' presence and increasing strength in the region over time, they did not, as historians have argued, monopolize the activist scene in the Old Northwest from the 1840s onward.[56] Antislavery people used a variety of strategies to push their agendas in this tense environment. Old Northwest women and men formed societies that advocated both political and immediate antislavery, with widely varying levels of interest even within individual states. This diversity contributed to the strength of the larger national antislavery movement. The immediatists' most obvious stronghold (relatively speaking) in the region in the 1840s was Ohio, but nonpolitical strategies remained viable elsewhere, even as the Liberty Party gained ground.[57] Both male and female activists made substantial contributions to this burgeoning, vibrant Old Northwest antislavery movement from 1830 to 1861.

* * *

Old Northwest people who opposed slavery and prejudice felt compelled to ally for change, and this was a mixed-sex endeavor from the beginning. As the region began to organize, women were the abolition pioneers. Their activism is an essential piece of the larger puzzle of Old Northwest opposition to slavery and prejudice. In early October 1832, five years prior to Michigan's statehood, the women of Lenawee County organized the first antislavery society in the Michigan Territory, and the first female society in the Old Northwest, the Logan Female Anti-Slavery Society. Antislavery propagandist Elizabeth Margaret Chandler was the main catalyst for this development. This devout Quaker activist dedicated her short life to slave liberation and other reforms, using both newspapers and organizations. Raised in Philadelphia, Chandler was active in the local Female Anti-Slavery Society. In 1826 she began writing acclaimed articles on a range of rights issues for the *Genius of Universal Emancipation,* a newspaper in Mount Pleasant, Ohio.[58] In 1830, Elizabeth and her brother Thomas moved to Lenawee County, where she pursued her activism and editing from her remote location, and contributed to the *Liberator* beginning in 1832.[59]

Chandler argued that antislavery labor was a Christian necessity, regardless of where people lived. To take proper action, all people, but especially women, needed to form societies and directly combat slavery. She took as a given that women opposed "sin" and favored moral reform.[60] Chandler enacted her convictions in 1832 when she co-founded the pioneering Logan Female Society, which affiliated with the American Society upon the latter's formation in December 1833.[61] Chandler died after a brief illness on November 2, 1834, at the age of 27.[62]

Chandler was but one of many Old Northwest propagandists for the cause. With their writings, meetings, and actions, she and a cohort of less famous people in Illinois, Indiana, Michigan, and Ohio led the way into social reform for legions, but women found her particularly inspiring. From 1832 to 1855, women's participation in the antislavery and anti-prejudice movement blossomed nationally, as the movement itself grew. In those years, women organized more than 200 female antislavery societies in the northern states, and in no place were they so closely linked with broader organizations as in Michigan.[63]

After Chandler, both women and men took up abolition; in her own state, antislavery organization experienced its first of two peaks in the late 1830s. The Michigan State Anti-Slavery Society (Michigan State Society), a mixed-sex society, formed in the autumn of 1836. This group and the lecturers they hired organized 17 societies across the state in their first year, and favored immediate abolition as their main strategy at least through 1839.[64]

While each state soon debated antislavery tactics, Ohio's activists were particularly outspoken and prolific. The history of Ohio antislavery organizations reveals a stratified fate superficially similar to their eastern counterparts, although still less factionalized. The Ohio Anti-Slavery Society (Ohio Society) first met at Zanesville in 1835, and initially followed the tenets of the American Society, including avoiding the vote. However, some Ohio activists took up politically oriented activism soon after the society's formation, and this foreshadowed later local debate.[65]

This society exemplifies how Old Northwest organizations were willing to consider multiple reform methods. In 1837 they promoted newspapers, and raised money for their own operations, the American Society, and African American schools.[66] Concurrently, from 1835 to 1836 women organized twenty female societies across Ohio.[67] The founding of new societies continued throughout the 1830s and went on for decades.

As is logical given the greater extent of racism there, Indiana—Ohio's western neighbor—had a more troubled history of antislavery organizing. Despite the presence in the early 1830s of antislavery pioneers Levi Coffin and Charles Osborn, reform proceeded slowly in Indiana, with the first society against slavery forming in 1836.[68] In September 1838, the Indiana Society held its founding meeting, where it initially resolved to take a politically independent course. At that time, there were still only eight societies in Indiana.[69]

Farther north and west, Illinois activists both witnessed and created turbulence when they moved into antislavery organizations, but nonetheless participated actively. In October 1837 they founded their State Anti-Slavery Society at Alton, amidst bloodshed and turmoil; an anti-abolition mob shot Maine-born editor and minister Elijah Parish Lovejoy the following month, after a period of intense conflict there.[70] By the end of the decade, the Illinois Society encompassed both the political and immediatist strands of abolition, and had come to include at least eight county societies and sixteen local ones.[71]

* * *

In the Old Northwest, the drive toward unity included personnel; activists welcomed all to aid the antislavery cause, as women exemplified when they claimed a substantial role. As antislavery societies organized in this region, most of them displayed a strong interest in women's participation in both mixed organizations and separate female societies, despite the fact that, if anything, it increased their unpopularity among their neighbors. Women enthusiastically and vocally joined both the western Garrisonian movement and the local and regional Liberty Party.[72]

Publicity for new mixed antislavery societies in the Old Northwest often explicitly appealed to women and called for their participation with arguments that all could contribute to reforming the region. On February 26, 1839, the editor of the *Genius of Universal Emancipation* wrote, "Every one—the aged and the young, male and female—may *do something* to aid in pushing forward the good work."[73] In Illinois, mixed and women's antislavery societies cited ideals of women's special abilities that they grounded in a tradition of female activism.[74] In 1840, the Economy Society in Wayne County, Indiana, also opened its membership and leadership positions to both sexes.[75] This pattern continued into Ohio, where at a June 1841 Ohio Society meeting held at Mount Pleasant, the leaders hailed all to join them in membership, and one speaker, Thomas Morris, an antislavery Democrat and former Ohio senator, emphasized the importance of women's action in the struggle.[76] These organizations' willingness to accept women's political aid and identity suggests that the cause was so crucial to its advocates that they sought out support from all available sources.

The unifying tendencies in the Old Northwest antislavery movement also appear in the efforts of planners to facilitate women's activism in the region, for they scheduled meetings in close succession, with audiences that varied by ideology and sex. The Indiana Society met in February in 1840 and 1841, and had concurrent meetings with the Liberty Party.[77] Women were not active as officers in either meeting. This incident aside, women sometimes took leadership roles at the offshoot political meetings that accompanied antislavery conventions. Many women participated in the Indiana Society gathering on November 22, 1841, where both men and women had the same voting rights. The women also held a separate gathering "for their own special action.[78] Women commonly worked in mixed associations throughout the decade, although they rarely attained parity.[79]

Indeed, lest the vision of inclusiveness be overstated, the reality was that in the 1830s and 1840s, in most cases men retained the influential positions in mixed organizations. Among other instances, both women and men attended the Ohio Society's second anniversary in April 1837 in significant numbers, although men had a substantial majority. In leadership positions there, women were only on the ladies' petition to Congress committee, for men held all of the officer, manager, and executive positions.[80] In addition, the Chicago *Western Citizen* never listed women as officers or speakers in Illinois antislavery societies, except in female ones.[81] Despite this limited inclusion, Old Northwest women pressed for involvement throughout the abolitionist movement—including its political strata—and in their own organizations.

This enthusiasm for abolition was evident in the Illinois women's societies as they grew in the early 1840s and played a substantial role in the state's antislavery movement during that decade. In 1843, their expansion began with the founding of the Putnam County Female Anti-Slavery Society on January 30, 1843, and six others soon followed. All but one, Jerseyville, were located in mid-sized towns in the northern half of the state.[82] Women's prominence in the Old Northwest antislavery movement was uneven but notable, and exemplified the diverse cohort of reformers there.

* * *

As Old Northwest abolitionists organized their societies, they worked toward unity by bridging boundaries among different factions. With notable recent exceptions, historians have attempted to divide antislavery people by categories such as "immediate abolition" or "moderate political abolition," by organizational affiliation, or along racial and gender lines.[83] In the process, they have overlooked the Old Northwest, where borders between different types of activism were fluid. Telling evidence of historians' limitations lies in the fact that individuals often changed their allegiances over their life course, and had multiple motivations for their activism.[84] This, along with the violence that they risked and experienced, demands a reconsideration of the abolition movement that recognizes their singularity. Many Old Northwesterners did not neatly conform to either the political or the immediatist abolition faction as defined in eastern terms.[85] The inelastic categories prevalent in many antislavery histories mask activists' openness, which grew out of the Old Northwest reform environment.[86] While political antislavery had obtained a significant foothold by the early 1840s, neither it nor immediate abolition absolutely ruled the Old Northwest. Old Northwest women and men had more options for organization—and for opposition—in their strife-filled realm than did their counterparts elsewhere. They willingly sought allies to enhance their movement's strength.

While many western abolitionists attempted to steer clear of factional squabbling and to ignore the antislavery schism of 1840, this proved challenging. As the national movement split, the Ohio and Illinois state societies became independent, while Michigan affiliated with the American and Foreign Society in 1841.[87] Dr. Abraham Brooke, a prolific Ohio abolitionist, shed some light on local events in a series of letters to the *National Anti-Slavery Standard*. Maryland-born Brooke took up Garrisonian abolitionism in the 1830s, and headed the Garrisonian exodus from the Ohio Anti-Slavery Society. He aided fugitives extensively, worked to form the Western Anti-Slavery Society from his base in Clinton County, Ohio, and hosted abolition meetings on his land.[88] In September 1840, Brooke wrote that the Clinton County Society supported the American Society, and claimed Ohio had an exceptional perspective on "political action," one that was "very much mixed up." There, even people who called themselves "new organizationists" still did not necessarily advocate third party abolition.[89] The next year, Brooke continued to argue that western differences existed, but noted that a number of locals found political antislavery increasingly relevant.[90]

Brooke was correct, in that some Old Northwest activists joined the political fray and made notable efforts to elect Liberty Party candidates in the 1840s. The fairly decentralized Liberty Party made its first foray into elections in 1840. That year, its national candidates, Birney and Earle, found their only substantial support in the Old Northwest in Michigan. On the state level, Whigs, who also still retained much support in Ohio's Western Reserve, dominated the antislavery society there. In Illinois, while a few pioneers advocated the electoral approach against slavery the previous year, the state Liberty Party did not organize until 1840.[91] There and in Ohio, there was little state-level Liberty organization for the election that fall, but the party still won some local offices in both of those states and in southern Michigan.[92]

After 1840, Indiana saw a flowering of both political and immediate antislavery action that welcomed both men and women. In 1840, the Indiana Society voted against supporting the Liberty ticket, but that party's local organization nonetheless had already begun.[93] Opposition to slavery in that anti–African American state remained behind the rest of the Old Northwest, but accelerated in the early 1840s with the founding of the antislavery newspapers the *Protectionist* and the *Free Labor Advocate*.[94] The number of local female antislavery societies also grew there from 1840 to 1842, with the establishment of at least four.[95] By February 1841, the Liberty Party controlled the Indiana State Society, but the possibility of boundary crossing remained, as the 1842 annual meeting of the state society—with its 1,500 to 2,000 attendees—revealed. This meeting harmoniously used both political and non-political abolition approaches.[96] Old Northwest societies, like the one in Indiana, permitted an unusual level of combination of resources across ideological boundaries at their large annual meetings.

Despite such expressions of unity, the Ohio abolitionists nonetheless soon became more divided. Among other issues, the Ohio American Anti-slavery Society (Ohio American Society) split from the Ohio Anti-Slavery Society in 1842, due to dissatisfaction with its moderate focus on political abolition. The new Ohio American Society first met on June 8, 1842, and was predominantly composed of Hicksite Quakers. It affiliated with the American Society and allied itself with many of that group's potentially divisive stances, including its opposition to voting and advocacy of moral suasion, the free produce movement, women's public action, churches opposing slavery, and nonresistance.[97] At that meeting the attendees also requested that some of the American Society's lecturers visit them.[98]

Interestingly, even after the split, the Ohio American Society was not entirely opposed to voting, and remained congenial, exemplifying unity even in the face of growing discord. Brooke, ever willing to be controversial, alluded to this in October 1842, when he anticipated that Ohio American Society members would vote Liberty and eschew Whigs and Democrats. Unlike members of the American Society, they would vote, he predicted, and vote in favor of political abolition.[99] Brooke's was not an isolated opinion, as became apparent when the Ohio American Society met at Cadiz that same month. This was the site of an assault on an early antislavery meeting in 1836, when local residents met immediatist lecturer James A. Thome with an eggy reception. By 1842, Cadiz had changed, for abolitionists had earned the right to hold a meeting there. They resolved that while they were responsible for voting their consciences on abolition, their members had no obligation to take a stance on the Liberty Party, any more than on the major parties.[100] Voting was actually on the table, even for the Ohio abolitionists most like the Garrisonians. Some eventually switched entirely to political abolition.[101] The Ohio American Society retained its overall immediatist orientation when it adopted the more general name of the Western Society in 1846. This change reflected the longtime participation of Indiana and Michigan activists in its reform work.[102] The allegiances of Old Northwest antislavery people varied from place to place and shifted over time.

In Illinois, the Liberty Party began making significant progress in terms of publicity and votes only after 1842, even though a small contingent in northern Illinois had supported it since the party's founding two years earlier.[103] The Illinois Society contained a substantial Liberty Party faction that year, but some members also adhered to immediatism. The umbrella of the Illinois State Society contained both groups, but by 1843, the political abolitionists outnumbered the immediatists.[104] However, as elsewhere in the Old Northwest, in Illinois the division between the two groups was rarely clear-cut. Chicago political abolition editor Zebina Eastman claimed his state was unified, "Antislavery men here were never divided or troubled with the divisions that characterized the East. . . . "[105] The Illinois State Society further demonstrates this boundary blurring. Even as that organization became auxiliary to the Liberty

Party in 1843, immediate abolitionists still retained their membership.[106] Over the next two years, the Illinois Liberty Party gained some small measure of support, polling 3 percent of the vote in the 1844 election. In that state, the party was interracial, and to a larger degree than most, open to both sexes. It grew in strength from 1843 until its peak in 1847, a year before its dissolution.[107]

Until 1844, Michigan remained Liberty's most supportive state in the Old Northwest, but it also retained an immediatist faction throughout the decades. Many who favored moral strategies had little institutional foothold for a time, because the Michigan State Society had formalized its support for political abolition by endorsing it in 1843.[108] Their views were at times puzzling, as in 1844, when the Michigan State Society debated whether third or main parties were their best option. Both sides of this dispute denounced voting, calling into question how locals defined political abolition.[109] The Michigan State Society remained loyal to the Liberty Party while it lasted. Michigan's female abolitionists underwent another upswing in organizational fervor in 1846, when they formed four new societies.[110] This exemplifies how Old Northwest activists maintained breadth in their approaches and diversity in their ranks, for decades.

* * *

Slavery's Old Northwest opponents showed with their quotidian actions that they were quite willing to compromise as they collaborated. For many Old Northwest citizens, the eastern antislavery movement's tendency toward separation and rigid bifurcation had met its limits. They were creatures of their time, nevertheless, and could not entirely escape the moment's tensions. As Old Northwest political abolitionists gained strength, over the course of the 1840s, this eventually shrunk the space available to the immediatists in public discussion, even if it did not directly silence their efforts or stop them. Immediate abolitionists still retained a presence in some places, such as Michigan, until 1861.[111]

In fact, a second peak of immediatist organization appeared as early as the 1850s in Michigan, and the antislavery movement there returned to its former heterogeneity.[112] This contravenes other historians' claims that the Garrisonians had vanished from the region (apart from Ohio) after the rise of political abolition. While the Michigan State Society had fallen apart in the late 1840s and early 1850s, as it followed the Liberty and Free Soil Parties into obscurity and electoral compromise, another state organization had risen in its place. Revived statewide in October

1852 by Lenawee County Garrisonians and the Michigan Central Committee as the Michigan Anti-Slavery Society, it allied with the American and Western Societies.[113] They met monthly and supported the latter's paper, the *Anti-Slavery Bugle.*

Pressure for this new organization came from longtime local immediatists like Thomas Chandler and traveling organizers including Garrison himself, who came to Michigan in 1853 to push the Michigan Society into being.[114] This is but one example of how Old Northwest activists enjoyed the infusion of experienced antislavery leadership easterners provided, while the eastern old guard simultaneously benefited from the movement's expansion into western terrain.

As this Michigan case confirms, from 1832 and continuing into the Civil War, the Old Northwest had diverse antislavery advocates—both women and men—although their respective public presences varied. The Michigan Society held to its immediatist views, for in 1855 it denounced Republicans for being complicit with slavery, and at its October 1856 meeting, the attendees radically disavowed national and local governments for appeasing slavery.[115] The broad approach to reform notable in Michigan characterized this ideologically heterogeneous region through the Civil War. Elsewhere, from 1856 on, the creeds of the Western and American societies increasingly diverged, even as the Western Society remained active until the war began.[116]

* * *

In this region of fiery opposition to abolition, Old Northwest activists heeded their own conception of antislavery factions, and their environment influenced their reform activities. They chose to bond together as they labored in a new universe of possibilities, challenging white supremacy as it became increasingly politically entrenched, and refusing to grant it the appearance of natural fact. This environment was rife with racialized laws and their consequences, and thus the straightforward antislavery fight there also encompassed a struggle against this pervasive legislation.

African Americans and their stalwart allies strongly resisted the northward-reaching tentacles of the slave system. In this seemingly free but very racist place directly north of the slave region, slavery's influence was everywhere in law and social behavior, but its actual presence was limited. As these four states grew rapidly from the 1830s through the 1860s, they became sites of acrimonious and often violent debate over slavery and the rights of their residents. Despite the states' free status and their small African American populations, racial discrimination ran rife, along with anti-abolitionism. The activism of the tenacious grassroots fighters for political and social rights uncovered here reveals that this difficult region always had a counter-narrative to the race riot, the "Black Laws," and the manipulation of racism for political gain.

2 / Scrubbing at the "Bloody Stain of Oppression": A Human Rights Movement against Unjust Laws, 1830–1849

In February 1843, the New Garden, Indiana, *Free Labor Advocate and Anti-Slavery Chronicle* announced the Ohio Supreme Court's ruling that the Ohio Constitution permitted men who officials could identify as "nearer white than mulattoes" to vote. While white abolitionist editor Benjamin Stanton recognized the revised interpretation as progress, he mocked the "discriminatory" powers that enforcing this would require. Stanton worked as a merchant, editor, and publisher while helping fugitive slaves and the free produce movement. With Henry H. Way, a fellow Quaker and a doctor, he edited the *Free Labor Advocate* from 1841 to 1848. The mainstream Friends in town expelled him in the 1840s, and he was very active thereafter in the Indiana Yearly Meeting of Anti-Slavery Friends.[1] In his article, Stanton argued that Ohio's election judges would need a new appliance to carry out these machinations: "[w]ill it not be necessary for some genius to invent a colorometer, by which to determine the claims of applicants to the right of suffrage? But to be serious; when will enlightened men become ashamed of these absurd and odious distinctions?"[2] With this effort to quantify and clarify the fuzzy divisions the Ohio Supreme Court drew among people, Stanton revealed his disdain for legislation such as the "Black Laws" that aimed to fix the arbitrary color line in a particular location.

Both friends and foes of the "Black Laws" recognized that with the two 1842 cases Stanton mentioned, *Parker Jeffries v. John Ankeny* and *Edwill Thacker v. John Hawk*, the Ohio Supreme Court undermined race-based legislation. The court, using precedents from two 1830s cases, argued that election judges had been in error when they denied voting rights to men of mixed race ancestry. Stanton's criticisms hit close to the mark, since even the language of the decisions is itself vague, calling these men "nearer white than black" or closer to white than "mulatto," or in the case of Jeffries, nearer white than "Indian," even as they affirmed their right to vote.[3] The editor's critique of these divisions as having little basis in reality very much resembles the laws' own confusing content.

In vigorous dissents to both of these decisions, Ohio Justice Nathaniel C. Reed argued they set dangerous precedents about the meaning of the word "white," which in his view was far from ambiguous. He said of the Thacker decision that it "violates the spirit of the [Ohio] constitution" which defined the voter as white. To Reed, whiteness was neither a subjective category nor a visual matter; "It is not the shade of color, but the purity of the blood, which determines the stock or race to which the individual belongs." Reed, a strong supporter of the "Black Laws," saw this distinction as crucial. He dissented because he believed the court had begun to dismantle the basis of these laws. Under Ohio law, in his view, nonwhites had "no political rights." He argued that the "Black Laws" were deliberately exclusionary, and that they encouraged African Americans to leave Ohio by denying them rights. In fact, he claimed that the laws' very purpose was to keep those who remained in the state "miserable and degraded." The "Black Laws," he readily acknowledged, were the product of calculated policy choices. To grant any degree of rights to nonwhites, as these decisions had done by "conferring political rights upon all [who had] less than half black [ancestry]," undermined the "Black Laws" and their exclusionary logic. The law thus illegitimately bestowed rights on people whose African heritage, regardless of its proportion, justified their exclusion.[4]

As likely pleased Reed, the "Black Laws" remained entrenched, and in the *Advocate* in June 1848, Stanton and his coeditor, Henry Way, revisited the idea of a "colorometer" to measure race for the purpose of establishing rights. This description was more fully realized than that of 1844, and the imaginary machine churned with internal tensions. The editors envisioned a conglomeration of "white superiority—Black inferiority—slaveholding logic and southern intelligence," melded with slavery's immorality in the "furnace of misrepresentation." These factors vied for space in a medium composed of "southern arrogance, proslavery patriotism, the . . . Black laws, southern chivalry, a northern doughface's integrity, and a political demagogue's moral honesty." The editors added other ingredients to the contraption, including "Calhoun's nullification," mobocracy, and theology.

This whole poisonous concoction was encased in the lofty documents of the Bible, the Declaration of Independence, and the US Constitution. The editors cited religion, ideas about liberty, and the laws of the land as all complicit with slavery's sins, and thus linked. Susceptible to pressures from the South, subjectivity, and lies, this machine could read race in people's "skin, lips, hair, and heel."[5] In this satirical piece, Stanton and Way divulged the forces that contributed to the Old Northwest's strained racial environment. White abolitionists like themselves, their African American neighbors, and their foes—all lived in this veritable pressure cooker.

* * *

These Ohio disputes over African Americans' status and racial definitions confirm that in the antebellum United States it was the states, not the federal government, that set civil rights. In this portion of the Old Northwest, legislators introduced discrimination with their "Black Laws," beginning in 1803 in Ohio, the oldest of the four states. Indiana and Illinois modeled their "Black Laws" on those of Ohio, as did Michigan to a lesser degree. Even as the Old Northwest states influenced each other and crafted similar laws, many of them also drew upon southern slave codes as they limited African Americans' local rights, and excluded and degraded them as ineligible for full citizenship. By 1830, each state had racially biased laws of varying severity in place. While this legislation differed in scope, effectiveness of enforcement, and duration, the "Black Laws" all enforced inequity and impeded both the legal rights and daily individual freedoms of all Old Northwest African Americans.

The sweeping "Black Laws" set the tone for and grew out of the region's racial climate, which varied but was nonetheless unusually inhospitable. While many older states in the North had introduced discriminatory provisions as they abolished slavery, the newer states of the Old Northwest brought them in with their statehood and constitutions, establishing inequality in their founding documents. While the region innovated in the development of racialized law, inequity was a national trend. Between 1800 and 1860, of all of the existing states, only Rhode Island granted African American men suffrage. Among all of the new states admitted in that period, solely in Maine could they vote at statehood.[6] While the national picture was bleak, the Old Northwest was worse, and indeed, it was a particularly unfriendly place to be African American.

Under the "Black Laws," through the 1870s, Old Northwest African Americans lacked most legal rights of public personhood, and the restrictions grew worse over time. Their small communities suffered from extensive *de jure* and *de facto* discrimination.[7] These laws kept African Americans out of the franchise, denied them political representation, prevented them from holding office, and excluded them from the militia. It also fettered them with bond laws, restrictions on marriage choice, court testimony, property ownership, education, immigration, and their right to work. These harsh laws circumscribed African Americans' mobility, and required them to carry freedom papers, as in Illinois, where such documents either proved people's freedom or gave them license to travel farther than ten miles from their place of residence.[8] *De facto* forms of discrimination, including segregation, were also endemic in the biased Old Northwest. The region was rife with racial and political tension, and African Americans encountered bigotry there that extended well beyond the Civil War. This prevalent oppression inspired substantial opposition.

* * *

Old Northwest antislavery and anti-prejudice activists found the racial basis of rights unacceptable, and refused to permit biased legislation to stand uncontested. They thus fought not only to abolish the national problem of slavery but also the local "Black Laws." The tiny African American populations and their white allies wielded abundant weapons, even in this racist region. From the 1830s through Reconstruction, at the height of the antislavery movement and in debates over racial justice in the region, they made equal rights claims that exceeded opposition to the national scourge of slavery and included full citizenship for African Americans. As neighbors to that institution, African Americans and their allies keenly felt its impact. They especially experienced it in the fugitive slave laws, and in the way that northerners supported prejudice by keeping the "Black Laws" on the books.

These reformers employed many methods to convert local and national laws from instruments used against African Americans to tools to secure equal human rights. Whether their weapons for equality were defiant residency, aid to fugitive slaves, the pen, the press, petitions, lobbying, court cases, or the Black Convention Movement, Old Northwest activists proclaimed their human rights vision with their reform work. They constantly pushed for political and social change and resisted race-based legislation, despite the challenges that their isolated location presented. The obstacles they confronted were both substantial and deep-rooted.

The "Black Laws" imposed severe hardships, for at their worst, they contradicted the term "free state" by permitting slavery and indentured servitude, as was legal in the region at least until the late 1840s.[9] Rather than observing the term limits the law mandated, some individuals kept people in bonds after their terms had expired, in a status that closely resembled southern slavery.[10] This was a clear target for activists, who used Article VI of the Northwest Ordinance of 1787 to argue that slavery should have no foothold in these states, and that its framers intended the territory to be entirely free of the institution. While the article stated that "there shall be neither slavery nor involuntary servitude in the said territory," the ordinance had actually made no provisions for enforcing this federal measure within the Old Northwest.[11]

Indeed, while the ordinance appeared to exclude slavery from the region, the new states interpreted it very loosely. It left the institution untouched in the South and enabled Old Northwest people to keep slaves in much of the region for many years. This loophole existed due to lax enforcement provisions and the legal interpretation that the ordinance permitted retaining slaves who had that status at the time of its passage; people thus remained enslaved and indentured there.[12] The censuses from 1810 through 1840 also recorded a few enslaved people in these four Old Northwest states.[13] While by the 1830 census the number of slaves recorded in the region had become very small, the clandestine nature of some of their labor terms means that it is difficult to ascertain how many lived as indentured servants or in *de facto* slavery. The numbers were probably actually higher than recorded, but given the marginal legality of Old Northwest slaveholding, underreporting was likely. These covert, forced-labor arrangements varied from state to state and even within the states; in somewhat problematic places like Ohio and Michigan, slavery was more clearly outlawed than in the more racist neighboring states of Illinois and Indiana.[14] The new laws that Old Northwesterners wrote as they joined the union demonstrate slavery's influence, too.

In the territorial period, at statehood, and in constitutional conventions as late as the 1830s, proponents of slavery sought to introduce the institution into Old Northwest constitutions and skirt the Northwest Ordinance. In the territorial period, Ohioans evaded the ordinance with the complicity of Governor Arthur St. Clair.[15] Nonetheless, later in Ohio the Constitutional Convention of 1802 made only a weak effort to include slavery, and the resultant constitution explicitly barred indentures from thus binding African Americans.[16] Still, the state's "Black Laws" were onerous, and a handful of slaves remained there through 1840.[17]

Pro-slavery people in Indiana and Illinois each made forceful, ongoing attempts to legitimate slavery in their early years. These included resident slaveholders' petitions to the United States Congress to abolish Article VI of the Northwest Ordinance. In Indiana Territory, which initially included what later became Illinois, slavery dated back as early as the 1730s under the French. There, attempts to legalize the institution, including a petition to Congress to permit slave importation, began in 1800 and continued through statehood in 1816. Many slave owners in the territory claimed that the Northwest Ordinance did not apply to them, and kept people in bondage regardless. The effort to include permanent servitude in the Indiana Constitution failed, but it instituted harsh and coercive indentures, which resembled slavery under another name. Laws there originally permitted holding indentured people for life, but eventually the legal codes mandated freeing women at age 28 and men at 35.[18] The Indiana Supreme Court ruled against indentured servitude and slavery in the early 1820s, and the numbers of slaves subsequently sharply dropped.[19]

Slavery was a long-standing institution in the land that became Illinois, for the French had held slaves who worked primarily in agriculture and in salt production there. Slavery continued under the British and subsequently the Americans.[20] Illinois became a territory in 1809, but as early as 1803, it followed Indiana's model of using indentured servitude as a euphemism for slavery, and in other ways closely emulated southern racial law.[21] At statehood in 1818, the new Illinois Constitution protected extant relationships between "master and slave or servant" and permitted incoming southern migrants to bring their slaves with them, but forbade contracting further such relationships. This constitution also kept indentured servitude in place, with the pretext that the servants had consented to their contracts. While the law required owners to grant indentured servants a choice between "freedom" and servitude, these choices were not of equal plausibility or desirability, since those African Americans who chose freedom had to leave the state in sixty days or face being sold as fugitives.[22] Slaveholders who wished to preserve their cheap or unpaid labor force would very likely have coerced them to stay in bondage.

Illinoisans long debated slavery and race relations, and the institution remained in place and had strong supporters in the state for quite some time. For example, a fevered legal battle ensued in 1823 and 1824 over introducing slavery there, and the contest was close. While the antislavery faction prevailed, their victory was far from absolute or immediate.[23] The United States Census of 1840 recorded 331 slaves and over 400 indentured servants as resident in Illinois—the largest number in the region then—and bills of sale indicate that slaveholders in the state continued to sell and transfer African Americans as late as 1848.[24]

In Michigan, African Americans had the highest status out of these four states, but they still faced substantial issues. Michigan had the smallest African American population in the region, but slaves had also been present there since the colonial era, and the institution retained support as it became a territory and subsequently a state. In 1807 in Michigan, as elsewhere, the territorial court ruled that the Northwest Ordinance's antislavery provisions did not apply to people already enslaved in the region before the territorial period began in 1805.[25] Even more obvious proof of the protection of slavery there lies in the fact that children born to slaves in Michigan only gradually won their freedom. Nonetheless, slavery was uncommon, and lawmakers there made less effort to evade the ordinance than did those of Illinois or Indiana. This is evident in the wording of the state's 1835 constitution, which overtly outlawed slavery. Michigan's residents may have felt a smaller economic motive to keep the institution than did those of Indiana and Illinois, but they were far from egalitarian, since they nonetheless still imposed devastating "Black Laws" and segregation, and made few efforts to help African American migrants from elsewhere.[26] In Michigan and the other states in the region, the debates over rights illuminate the deeply rooted local racism.

* * *

Resistance to an expanded and equal African American population in the Old Northwest continued in the early nineteenth century; it was present at these states' founding moments, when they codified the "Black Laws" in their state constitutions. These were moments of immense political and economic transformation that included shifts in republican ideology, the concurrent expansion of the franchise, and the continual equation of white manhood with full citizenship. These changes all inspired and amplified opposition to African American immigration and equality. The debates in state constitutional conventions in the Old Northwest showed the stakes that many of their participants—and by extension their constituents—had in keeping African Americans excluded. Each of the states revisited their constitutions over the years, and for decades opted to keep African American rights limited.[27]

The race-based constitutional provisions attempted to designate an individual's proper social place. While a few of the founders held more egalitarian views, the majority of participating delegates defined citizenship narrowly, and cited landholding, self-sufficiency, and white manhood as necessary ingredients for it.[28] The region's history of slavery and proximity to the institution gave it a tense racial climate. As delegates sought to use their constitutions to create racially homogeneous states, their efforts salved the consciences of men disturbed by the market revolution's social and economic shifts. By excluding African Americans, these men displaced onto others the fears the new market economy inspired with its increasing instability and dependency. They believed that only a society of white men would be sufficiently virtuous to face the challenges of their modernizing times. Delegates' arguments against African American rights centered on concerns that their alleged lack of independence would render them susceptible to the influence of others, and neither qualified nor able to participate in the polity on an equal basis.[29] Ideas about race's meaning thus had far-reaching effects on African Americans' political and social rights.

In seeking to restrict rights on the basis of race, states that crafted "Black Laws" also had to create some means to define racial distinctions in law. Who merited the designation "white" was inconsistent, and changed from state to state as well as over time.[30] Indiana law grew more stringent, as the 1818 law defined people as African American when they had one Black grandparent, and by 1840 the law required only one such great-grandparent.[31] In the 1853 Illinois anti-immigration statute, the General Assembly used the latter standard.[32] Ohio law tried to determine racial identity based on perceptible skin tone, and the legislature originated the term "visible admixture" to articulate this method. As Benjamin Stanton had noted, in 1842 the Ohio Supreme Court weighed in and settled the definition of whiteness as a visual issue, not one of blood. This subjective label meant that the Ohio government treated people of mixed racial ancestry with ambiguity, even as late as 1859, when the state legislature again affirmed the visible admixture rule.[33]

In Michigan, too, the courts weighed in on the definition of race. State law initially allowed for no gradations between African American and white, but some men passed for white (or white enough) in order to vote there.[34] Courts in Michigan also embraced the visible admixture test in 1847 and again in 1866. In the 1847 case of *Douglass v. Farrar*, a Michigan man's preponderance of white over African American ancestry meant that the county court deemed him entitled to vote.[35] Since jurists defined race as a visible marker, the outcomes of their decisions were not always predictable.[36] These subjective standards of racial difference remained legally valid for decades, betraying their supporters' determination to use the legal system to subjugate African Americans. The "Black Laws" had a number of important consequences, and one of the most serious was the impact on the region's demographics.

* * *

When Old Northwest people implemented these staggering legal and social obstacles to racial equality, they aimed to, as Justice Reed had argued, render the region unwelcoming to people of African descent. The "Black Laws" officially designated these states as communities for whites, using exclusionary and discriminatory provisions to maintain African American subordination and keep their local numbers low. Across the region, with these laws legislators intended to minimize interracial interactions, either by forcing African Americans to relocate or by making life so uncomfortable that any of their settlements would be small. Supporters of these laws claimed that incorporating more African Americans into the northern population would diminish the alleged superiority of the white race by exposing it to an "inferior" race.[37]

State legislatures in Ohio, Illinois, and Indiana erected formidable legal obstacles to free African Americans' immigration, and while Michigan lacked an exclusion law, it had its fair share of other discriminatory laws with similar effects. Proponents of the "Black Laws" argued that without these restrictions, unscrupulous owners would bring elderly former slaves to the region. They feared that these freedmen and freedwomen would be unable to work for their keep, and thus become a burden on the community.[38] One "Black Law" that exemplified these concerns forbade slaveholders to transport African Americans into Illinois to liberate them there. With these regulations, legislatures also tried to encourage resident African Americans to emigrate to Africa.[39] Adding to the matrix of discrimination, some wage workers feared labor competition from African Americans, who could only command reduced wages due to racist hiring policies. From the beginning, debates over the "Black Laws" thus used early versions of free labor ideology, often to the detriment of African Americans.

Panic over African Americans' immigration to the Old Northwest inspired specific efforts to control their population growth in the region. These are evident in the earliest "Black Laws," for Ohio passed its first such laws, those aimed at immigration restriction, in 1804 and 1806, and later affirmed them. They required African Americans to provide proof of freedom to enter the state and in order to work, and a $500 bond against becoming a public charge.[40] The bond provision compelled African Americans to have two people willing to pay a bond of $500 to prevent them from becoming a community responsibility. It was not a demand for an immediate cash bond, for the money would need to be paid only if the African American migrant violated any laws.[41] The Illinois "Black Laws," beginning in 1813, restricted immigration and the right to work to proven free men, and appointed "overseers of the poor" to force poor African Americans to move elsewhere.[42] The exclusionary sentiments were of long duration, for Illinois also held a referendum on immigration in 1848, where in a ringing endorsement, 70 percent of voters favored continuing the restrictions.[43]

Indiana had similar laws, for after 1831 African Americans had to provide proof of freedom and to post bond upon entering the state to settle or work there. Quakers and other sympathetic whites joined them in fighting this provision and later such laws. The Indiana Supreme Court upheld the constitutionality of the bond law on three separate occasions.[44] The Indiana Constitutional Convention of 1850 passed a provision that outright banned African Americans from the state. Advocates of equality protested against these provisions, as they had with previous measures. In the 1851 popular referendum on immigration, 83 percent of Indiana voters favored retaining extant immigration restrictions, and to persist in restricting the vote to white men.[45] The 1851 constitution that convention created had a few potentially liberating provisions for African Americans: it reaffirmed slavery's prohibition and banned all forms of indentured servitude from Indiana.[46] Nonetheless, the exclusion message found reinforcement in substantial support for colonization that went as high as the governor's mansion in the 1850s.[47]

While Michigan had no prohibition on African American immigration, its certification and bond laws were themselves stringent, at least on paper. Prior to statehood, the Michigan legislature mandated that each African American prove his or her freedom prior to settlement, register with the county clerk, and pay a $500 bond, for good behavior and to ensure "that he would not become a public charge." As the African American population grew, other Michigan residents expressed their desire to curb this expansion through segregation and colonization.[48] These discriminatory laws had notable, measurable effects on the region's populations.

In one sense, the exclusionary provisions of the "Black Laws" were a success, in that they achieved their aim of keeping the number of

African Americans in the Old Northwest from becoming substantial, even as the region's overall population grew between 1830 and 1870. Their small local numbers nevertheless remained a source of concern for some hostile Old Northwest residents. The United States censuses reveal that Ohio's African American population grew slowly over the decades, from 1.1 percent to 1.6 percent, only slightly exceeding the overall population growth rate. By 1870, it had grown to 2.3 percent. In proportion to the white population, that of African Americans in Indiana remained very small, for it decreased slightly, from 1.1 percent to .8 percent by 1860, but had risen slightly to 1.5 percent by 1870. In Illinois, there was a larger decrease from 1.5 percent to .4 percent in 1860. The number there had rebounded to 1.1 percent by 1870. In Michigan, the number was .9 percent in 1830 and returned there in 1860, with a dip in the intervening decades. It had risen to 1 percent by 1870.[49]

That same data can give a different perspective on the region's population and the effects of the "Black Laws," and indeed demonstrates African Americans' persistence in moving to the region. To take the turbulent 1850s as an example, Illinois, Michigan, and Ohio each experienced substantial African American population growth between 1850 and 1860. In Indiana, where the Supreme Court forbade Black immigration in 1851, the total population grew by 37 percent between 1850 and 1860, and its African American population only expanded by 1.5 percent in that same era. Elsewhere, while the aggregate population of Illinois more than doubled from 1850 to 1860, the African American population increased by 40 percent in that same decade. Michigan's overall population grew by 188 percent in that decade, while its African American population proliferated at nearly twice that rate. In Ohio, the already large populations grew at slower rates than in the other, newer states. Nevertheless, while the overall population grew by 18 percent in the 1850s, the African American population growth rate was much faster at 45 percent. Despite these small numbers and the region's overwhelming hostility and whiteness, the data indicates that African Americans refused to stay away, and indeed, established communities.

This issue is even more complicated, for residents across the Old Northwest often showed little will to enforce immigration provisions scrupulously. The African American population thus continued to grow throughout the antebellum period.[50] It was evident to some of the opponents of the "Black Laws" that these legal decrees failed to suppress African American populations and movement. White itinerant lecturer

Dr. Erasmus Hudson mocked the difficulties of the laws' enforcement while opining that they simply did not work. Connecticut native Hudson was an agent for the Garrisonian organizations, the Connecticut and the American Anti-Slavery Societies, from 1838 to 1849.[51] He wrote from Delaware, Ohio, in February 1842, that the convoluted "Black Laws" made no sense and were difficult to enforce. Hudson credited Ohio's extensive fugitive traffic in part to the ineffectiveness of these laws.[52] In 1843, the Ohio American Society echoed him, claiming that in most situations, Ohioans would not implement the "Black Laws."[53] A similar situation existed in early Michigan, where the "Black Laws" had little support, the required bond was particularly unpopular, and many whites helped protect African Americans against kidnapping.[54] Many African Americans, though well aware of the problems with the "Black Laws" in the Old Northwest and their communities' inconsistent reactions to them, still preferred to move there rather than remain in slavery or its vicinity. They sought to change the region for the better, and used pointed critiques to fight to improve their local status.

* * *

Chief among Old Northwest African Americans' grievances were the ways in which the "Black Laws" deprived them of their right to vote, of political representation, and of participation in civic defense. The facts are clear: the vast majority of African American men in the Old Northwest lacked the franchise until the ratification of the Fifteenth Amendment in 1870, and this bar remained in place even longer in many areas.[55] While African American men in Ohio could vote in elections prior to statehood, they lost this right with the ratification of the state constitution in 1803. With Indiana's statehood in 1816 and Illinois' in 1818, their new constitutions excluded African Americans from the vote, population count, and the militia.[56]

Michigan did not reach statehood until 1837, and implemented somewhat less punitive laws than the other states after debating even more permissive alternatives—including the vote for all men. In May of 1835, as Michigan prepared for this transition, delegates met in Detroit to frame a constitution. John Norvell, the Detroit postmaster and a Wayne County delegate, called for a ban on slavery in the state, which the convention unanimously adopted. Judge Ross Wilkins from Lenawee County tried to take African American rights one large step further. He asked that the convention grant universal male suffrage, but found much antipathy. Norvell asked whether Wilkins intended to permit all men, including "Indians and negroes," to vote. Wilkins replied with a claim that racial identity was ambiguous:

> the term white is not specific...There are men of every shade and complexion, white, sallow, brown, olive, yellow; how will you regulate the shade of him which shall entitle an individual to the privilege of a freeman?...[there were those] who were American born, who were neither Indian, negro, nor of any connexion in color with either of these races, and yet who could not be called white.

As had Benjamin Stanton with his colorometer, Wilkins displayed an early understanding of race as a constructed category, which he used to argue that qualified African American men deserved the franchise. He was not alone in this desire, for Quaker Darius Comstock, also of Lenawee, then the home of the strongest support for progressive racial views in Michigan, agreed with these principles. Despite these efforts, the "Black Laws" took hold in Michigan, with particularly strong support in Wayne County (the home of Detroit).[57] As passed, the legislation reserved the vote and the jury box for white men.[58] By 1860, African American men had the right to vote in only five states in the North—and none in the Old Northwest.[59]

* * *

Despite the substantial hardships the "Black Laws" imposed, many Old Northwest citizens actually were divided about the laws' justice; this mattered, since the legislation relied upon an array of citizens for enforcement. In addition to justices of the peace, community members who included the overseers of the poor, public school teachers, and employers all became potential informants to turn in African Americans who lacked the proof of freedom that entitled them to work.[60] Some communities and counties even created their own local level "Black Laws," which added to the burden of those on the state level. In one such case in 1843, African Americans faced expulsion from Peoria County if they did not "enter into bond with security."[61] Since ordinary people performed most of the work of upholding these laws, activists focused their energy on changing both public opinion and the laws at their source.

While many Old Northwest people ignored the "Black Laws" and sometimes even challenged them, this did not diminish the laws' importance or their demoralizing effect. On the infrequent occasions when people did try to prosecute under the "Black Laws," the impetus often originated in personal disputes.[62] While in most places enforcement of these laws was weak, they nevertheless symbolized white supremacy for many Old Northwest African Americans and their allies for equal rights. They also gave hostile whites a universally applicable rationale to oppress African Americans, commit mob violence, and otherwise badger them.[63] The "Black Laws" created a permissive attitude toward racialized violence; at times African Americans' foes took advantage of their lack of legal status and attacked them, knowing their governments were unlikely to prosecute them. When activists called for repeal, pro-"Black Law" mobs also acted against them.[64]

The provision of the "Black Laws" that ruled African Americans could not testify against whites in court led to a sense of license to exploit and assault them. While Michigan did allow African American testimony, in 1807 the Ohio legislature—and later, Illinois—barred such testimony in court cases involving whites.[65] Indiana's 1816 constitution prohibited African Americans from testifying in court, and their lack of this right exposed them to abuses from unscrupulous whites. On occasion this had serious, even deadly, consequences.

Proof of the extent of these dangers for Indiana's African Americans lies in the 1845 murder of John Tucker in downtown Indianapolis. A drunken crowd attacked Tucker on July 4 and beat him to death. The men in this crowd, which the Ohio *Anti-Slavery Bugle* claimed had 200 members, made numerous bloodthirsty proclamations about their racial motivations for this murder. A mob subsequently chased the antislavery publisher of the *Indianapolis Freeman*, Henry De Puy, for hours, and authorities only arrested one man for the murder.[66] The lack of justice for Old Northwest African Americans living under the "Black Laws" is starkly revealed in the refusal of many witnesses to intervene and in the paltry retribution for Tucker's death. The picture in Indianapolis might have been rather different had African Americans had the right to testify.

Foes of the "Black Laws" acknowledged that the testimony provisions imposed specific problems for African Americans. The lack of this right—as seen in Illinois where the prohibition applied to any people with at least one African American grandparent—was a substantial legal disability.[67] The clause that confined the right to testify against whites to whites gave African Americans little recourse to the legal system. Similarly, Ohio abolitionists also claimed that the testimony law allowed criminals to abuse African Americans. Whether accused of fugitive status or directly attacked, they lacked this right when they faced white opponents in court, unless they had a cooperative white witness who could testify for them.[68] The overt racial basis of Tucker's murder reveals that people's lives could even be at stake with these laws. Despite such incidents and the "Black Laws," many thousands of African Americans came to the region and remained there, flouting registration laws and legal proscriptions, and inciting debate over their place in the Old Northwest.

* * *

The Old Northwest's location and the consequent fugitive slave traffic also inspired the "Black Laws." Many people in the region believed they needed stringent laws to prevent large numbers of African Americans from migrating from the South, across their weak borders. Ohio shared state lines with Kentucky and Virginia (now West Virginia), while Illinois and Indiana bordered Missouri and Kentucky, and Michigan contained several well-known fugitive slave routes from the southern states. The Old Northwest was a way station between slavery and freedom, and the site of both hospitality to runaways and struggles over fugitives. As slaves decided to escape, they educated themselves about their environment and plotted their flight, which often took them through the region.[69] Traveling north, many newly freed and self-liberated people passed through on their journey to Canada from as far as Tennessee and North Carolina, creating significant fugitive traffic, and local people aided them.[70]

The Old Northwest's location meant that race substantially affected individual rights, for even African Americans with freedom papers found that these documents protected them only minimally against the threat of being kidnapped into slavery. This ever-present reality kept many free African Americans anxious and socially subordinated; the combined effects of the "Black Laws" and the federal fugitive slave laws of 1793 and 1850—which forbade aid to runaways or interference with owners' effort to repossess their human property—proved onerous indeed.[71] In addition to their legal challenges, African Americans had to live with the advertisements for runaway slaves and servants that regularly appeared in Whig and Democratic newspapers in the region, and which demonstrated an aggressive presence protecting slavery in nearby states.[72] Clearly, even African Americans who were formally free encountered imposing barriers to recognition of their civil status in the Old Northwest, including the opinions of their many pro-southern neighbors.

Many Old Northwesterners had southern origins or sympathies, especially among those who settled on the riverfronts and along major roads. Southern nativity did not necessarily determine views on slavery, since people had a variety of reasons to leave the South, including antislavery views. Numerous former southern residents nonetheless did engage in economic exchange with their native region and were hostile to African Americans, most likely out of a deeply ingrained bias as well as an interest in preserving these trade relations.[73]

Slavery and transportation had an uneasy relationship in the Old Northwest, particularly since Indiana, Illinois, and Ohio bordered the Ohio and Mississippi Rivers and hosted the national road that extended as far as Vandalia, Illinois, by 1839. From the perspective of slaveholders and their sympathizers, national concord depended on them being able to move through the North with ease—even with their slaves. Article IV of the Northwest Ordinance guaranteed the right of unfettered water travel, and many southerners interpreted this to mean that they and their slaves could pass through the Old Northwest, as many did on their river journeys to the new western slave states.[74] As slaveholders and slave hunters traversed these borders, they demanded local fealty to their property rights. Whether or not Old Northwest people agreed that they should protect slaves as property, these slaveholders' actions gave further proof to "Black Laws" opponents that restrictions on African American rights were no mere southern sectional issue, and in fact were widespread in the North.

* * *

In the face of these many deprivations of legal protection for African Americans, resistance to the "Black Laws" became central to the Old Northwest antislavery and anti-prejudice mission. The majority of these states' residents greeted the prospect and reality of African American neighbors with a hearty rejection of equal rights. Consequently, combating the "Black Laws" was an essential element of activists' broader commitment to racial transformation, and of their refusal to accept the bias infused throughout their political culture and social mores. Their work against the "Black Laws" extended from the local to the statewide level, and from everyday activities to overt political protest.

The story of the "Black Laws" is not one of unremitting oppression, for racial progressives contested their enactment and enforcement from their earliest days. Through both individual and collective means, activists pushed against this legislation and revealed their larger human rights vision of a nation free of both slavery and discriminatory law. From the late 1830s, the movement took in diverse people from across these four states, including white and African American abolitionists, northern states' rights advocates, and African American participants in the Black Convention Movement.

The simplest form of resistance to the "Black Laws" lay in the very presence of African American communities in the Old Northwest, and their refusal to obey efforts to drive them out and uproot their settlements. While there were few incentives and many impediments to forming a large local population of African Americans in this time period, some did establish small free communities. These stalwart African American populations proved that the "Black Laws" failed to exclude them, and over time, thousands moved to the region. Whether enslaved or free, African Americans demanded admission to these young states, and defiantly lived where the "Black Laws" tried to bar them. The hard battle they fought to stay there and create northern African American communities enabled fugitives to blend in more readily. This free presence, so physically close to slavery, flouted the "Black Laws," the fugitive slave laws, and the claim that the only place for African Americans was a servile one.[75] Their local populations and the biased laws they lived under inspired Old Northwest people to help them, but some indirectly resisted these laws by thriving, in spite of the laws' punishing character.

* * *

When African Americans achieved success in the Old Northwest, they gave the lie to common antebellum ideas about their incapacity and dependency. Frank McWhorter and his family exemplify one such victory over adversity. They came to Illinois and founded New Philadelphia in Pike County in 1835. This town, along with other small African American communities in western Illinois, claimed a secure place in the state despite the Illinois "Black Laws." The McWhorters, beyond their economic achievements, also took up community building efforts to ameliorate the worst of the problems the laws caused African Americans.[76] Like this pioneering family, other African Americans and their white allies refused to bow before racism in the Old Northwest borderland, and organized "Black Law" resistance built on the foundation of such bold residency choices. These success stories proved that biased laws not only failed to keep African Americans out, but that African Americans, in fact, led communities. In their own towns and beyond, both Old Northwest African Americans and their white allies offered fugitive aid that also directly opposed race-based law.[77]

From the Old Northwest states' earliest days, activists there frequently helped fugitives and resisted their recapture. Reaching out to slaves in need closely complemented these reformers' other activities throughout the antebellum era, and this was one of the most direct ways they defied racialized law. Also, even though the Fugitive Slave Act of 1793 was legally a federal concern, activists believed that the same fears of African American mobility catalyzed it and the state-level "Black Laws." Indeed, the local laws increased the fugitive slave law's burden and inspired intense resistance.

Fugitive slave support took a number of forms, including shelter and transportation; antislavery women concretely contributed support through their hours of labor with needle and thread. They formed antislavery sewing circles that made and gave goods—especially clothing—directly to fugitives. As fugitives passed through, and stayed in Old Northwest communities temporarily, many local women became aware of their desperate need for clothing as they were fleeing. Most enslaved people were destitute, for few had accumulated possessions, and the circumstances of flight usually made it impossible to carry much.[78] Former slaves' clothing deficit, and this aid in response, continued past the Civil War.[79] They also sold such items at antislavery fairs and used the proceeds to support individuals and societies. This work was essential both to fugitives who relied on their goods and to the variety of antislavery enterprises that the fairs funded.[80] In its recognition that African Americans had rights to succor and stability, this labor affirmed antislavery women's commitment to honoring fugitives' humanity, and to meeting their immediate needs, regardless of the law's dictates. They, along with their fellows, followed the higher law doctrine, the religious conception that God's law was superior to that of men.

Underlying Old Northwest reformers' opposition to the "Black Laws" was a shared belief in Christian duty toward their fellow man, one that also contributed to their objections to fugitive slave laws. According to the opponents of the "Black Laws," these laws defied not only earthly rights but also Christian morality. In 1840, an antislavery group from Will County, Illinois, argued that the provision in the Illinois statute of 1833 that barred Illinoisans from providing aid to people in need was an effort to "nullify the law of God."[81] This law forbade concealing or caring for fugitives, the assistance that fulfilled the basic principles of Christian charity.[82] Ohio's equivalent laws also dismayed Anne Thomas of New Garden, Ohio, who in April 1839 noted that the "Black Laws" clause that outlawed granting aid to runaway slaves, under penalty of a fine, particularly disturbed her. This was, she believed, a policy of exceptional cruelty.[83] By violating activists' sense of justice, the laws incited these people's opposition. In the view of such reformers, the laws created unwarranted separations between people, which their religion would not countenance.

Religious convictions about the laws' injustice inspired many antislavery churches to also publicly work for the repeal of the "Black Laws." This included the Society of Friends, and some in their faith had already been arguing over abolition and fugitive slaves. The Indiana Yearly Meeting of Friends (which had many members who lived in Ohio and Illinois) published an address in 1843 to the Ohio citizens against their "Black Laws."[84] As did the Will County Society, they believed they had secular, "moral and religious obligations" to oppose slavery and race-based laws. Their central argument was that distinctions drawn upon lines of race displeased God and disobeyed the Golden Rule.[85] Along with their fellow anti-discrimination activists, they used religion to claim that all people were entitled to the same rights.[86] Beyond the Friends, by the mid-1840s, the Congregational Church in Illinois also opposed that state's requirement that they deny aid to slaves.[87] Their church activities aside, Old Northwest foes of the "Black Laws" shared a longstanding willingness to use state laws against anti-fugitive legislation.

The antebellum Old Northwest felt like an increasingly perilous environment for African American rights, so antislavery and egalitarian activists implemented every strategy in their repertoire to protect them, including personal liberty laws and anti-kidnapping statutes. As early as 1804, various states passed such measures. Most northern states had some version of these laws that aimed, at minimum, at protecting free African Americans. Sometimes they also extended to accused fugitive slaves. Pennsylvania had passed the first personal liberty law in 1826, inaugurating the practice of subjecting fugitive removal to a judicial review process, rather than allowing alleged slaveholders to take people to the South with no trial.[88]

Indiana and Michigan both passed early anti-kidnapping laws, if not explicit personal liberty laws. From 1816, Indiana allowed judges to call for a jury trial to determine whether claims for certificates of removal—needed for people to take alleged slaves with them out of the state—were valid.[89] Later, an 1824 law allowed fugitives trial by jury in appeals for cases where judges had ruled against them. Both of these provisions could at least slow the return of slave catchers to the South with people they claimed as fugitives. In Michigan the 1827 anti-kidnapping statutes sent a mixed message, for they were part of a body of "Black Laws" that also mandated that African Americans register and post bond upon moving to the state.[90] The following year, Michigan strengthened its anti-kidnapping laws, and from the 1840s on, it saw major public displays of aid to fugitive slaves.[91]

Abolitionist and state sovereignty arguments both increased hostility to fugitive slave capture, beginning in the 1830s. Even where personal liberty laws were not in operation, many Old Northwest residents refused to comply with fugitive slave laws, but this did not necessarily indicate that they had egalitarian views. Some Old Northwest whites merely saw anti-kidnapping laws as a means to prevent southerners from trampling on their state autonomy.[92] Over time, fears escalated that residents of the region, Black and white, might have to use force to defend their interests against southern interlopers. These concerns grew after the passage of the federal Fugitive Slave Act of 1850 and as the Kansas situation degenerated later that decade, but such defensive sentiments existed even earlier.[93] Ohio had short-lived laws in 1819 and 1831 that were intended to protect African Americans from kidnapping. The 1831 Ohio law required slaveholders to bring accused fugitives before a judge and prove ownership. Also in 1831, Indiana passed an anti-kidnapping statute, as did Michigan in 1838.[94] In Ohio in 1837, activists petitioned for jury trial for all African Americans accused of being fugitives.[95] In the latter two states, some Whigs provided personal liberty laws with essential support, proving that some joined their more radical contemporaries in the opinion that anti-fugitive laws posed grave dangers to the Old Northwest.[96]

Among the Old Northwest states, Illinois had the weakest provisions for fugitive protection. This is not surprising, for the state was also unique in the North in largely subscribing to the southern idea that African Americans were, by default, slaves, and thus lacked due process rights to protect their freedom. While in northern Illinois it became difficult to return escaped slaves to the South, this was not the case in the southern part of the state.[97] Illinois laws tended to hurt rather than help runaways, as in an 1829 law that enshrined the perception that all African Americans were runaways until they produced a certificate that proved otherwise. The only relevant law there that aided African Americans accused of being fugitives passed in 1833, and it limited slaveholder autonomy only slightly. The law provided penalties when people captured suspected slaves with the goal of removing them from Illinois without first following proper federal procedures.[98] However, the state Supreme Court was willing to convict Illinois residents for fugitive slave aid, which was also unusual for a northern state. The Illinois lawmakers had very conflicted positions through the 1840s, even as the state developed a corps of antislavery lawyers.[99] In Illinois the longstanding notions in the region about African Americans' low status had unusually strong consequences, but this was not a consistent position across the region, or even in the state.

* * *

In Old Northwest governments, fugitives met with occasional but valuable allies who worked against the fugitive slave clause of 1793. Activists as early as 1837 found opposition to fugitive persecution from the bench; lawyer Salmon P. Chase claimed that the federal fugitive slave clause was invalid since it clashed with the US Constitution and with the spirit of the Northwest Ordinance.[100] From 1839 to 1843, Ohio had a state fugitive slave law, one that also mandated proof of legitimate ownership prior to removing accused fugitives from the state. although the aggressiveness of slave catchers made it unpopular.[101] In 1843, the Ohio legislature repealed most of the pro–African American statutes of the 1831 law that had granted accused fugitive slaves some legal rights, but kept the anti-kidnapping statute.[102] The Ohio state government was thus an unreliable ally, but even Illinois was not universally hostile to African American rights.

The national fugitive slave law and the "Black Laws" could, on occasion, come into conflict with each other, with libratory consequences. In 1849, the *Illinois Supreme Court v. Thornton* represented an attempt to use the "Black Laws" to regulate fugitives; the case revealed that jurisdictional squabbling could actually benefit fugitives. In that incident, the Sangamon County constable captured Missouri fugitive Hempstead Thornton, despite his protestations of illegal restraint. In this case, the "Black Laws" overreached their bounds and thus served to Thornton's advantage. A provision in the revised Illinois statutes of 1845 aimed at aiding in the retrieval of fugitives within the state. Under this law, Illinois officials automatically presumed all African Americans who entered Illinois without free papers were fugitives, and thus subject to arrest and jailing. The county sheriff had to "advertise" the captives' presence in a newspaper for six weeks. If still unclaimed, the sheriff could sell the labor of these people for twelve months if no stated "owner" came forward.

The Supreme Court decision in the Thornton case changed this practice, as it argued that the Illinois legal system had no right to interfere in an area of federal jurisdiction. The logic followed that since fugitive regulation was an area of United States congressional purview, "the arrest of the prisoner was without authority of law, and he must be discharged from custody."[103] In this instance, while the Illinois Supreme Court claimed to uphold federal fugitive slave legislation, it simultaneously undermined pro-slavery claims by removing one of the tools for the recapture of fugitives in the state.[104] The courts and laws could thus be tools activists might use against the "Black Laws," but they pushed for the law to do much more.

* * *

Activists' direct resistance to the "Black Laws" also encompassed civil rights arguments. As many of the same reformers also did with abolition, they drew on rights language in a period when they innovated in this area.[105] Their basic principle was that discriminatory laws that made illegitimate distinctions among people had no place on the books. These laws were no instrument of order or justice, but rather a bludgeon to remind all Old Northwest people of African Americans' tenuous political and social position.

Radical activists of both sexes and across racial lines overtly resisted the "Black Laws" and drew much support from the broader Old Northwest antislavery struggle. In Michigan, the fight began with statehood, for by 1837, the antislavery society there already was contributing to the effort to oppose the "Black Laws." They and other Michigan antislavery people, including those in the Liberty Party after its foundation, fought for the African American vote.[106] In 1837 and 1838, the abolitionists asked the Michigan legislature for jury trial for all accused fugitive slaves, and to amend the state constitution to grant "the colored man" the vote.[107] The outspoken opposition of Michigan abolitionists to the "Black Laws" continued through the Civil War and after.

The many antislavery foes of the "Black Laws" saw working against such legislation as a necessary part of their broader mission. They made sweeping public claims about the laws' injustice and about the unity of all people.[108] The Ohio Anti-Slavery Society's work against the "Black Laws" dated back to its foundation in 1835.[109] They collected data about the laws and their effects, and about African Americans' lives in general.[110] Their affiliate, the Cuyahoga County Anti-Slavery Society in the Western Reserve, argued in 1838 that their legislators must do away with the "Black Laws." Austinburg, Ohio abolitionist Betsy Mix Cowles joined in, publishing papers in 1846 and 1847 that demanded the repeal of the Ohio "Black Laws." While Cowles remained a staunch immediatist, she asked abolitionists of all stripes to join her in this effort.[111] This determination to enact repeal was common, for in 1841 in Indiana, the Henry County Female Society also resolved to take direct action against prejudice and to fight racism in their communities. They deployed the frequently cited antislavery trope that all were equal and of the same ancestry, "all nations of the earth are of the same blood."[112] In Illinois in 1843, the Putnam County Female Society adopted opposition to discrimination as its objective, equal with that of fighting slavery, for equal rights convictions motivated their activism. They wrote, "the equality and brotherhood of man is the foundation of abolitionism."[113] The cross-reform ties common throughout the region demonstrate reformers' sweeping, long-term commitments to fighting racial prejudice.

No shy violets themselves, Old Northwest activists wielded other weapons in the battle for public opinion: they used the printed word to broadcast their efforts against the "Black Laws," both to register their disgust with these laws and to provide a rationale for their eradication. Across the region, they advertised their campaign against the "Black Laws" and demanded policy change. In Illinois in 1840, the Galesburg Anti-Slavery Society passed resolutions against the laws, and the Will County Anti-Slavery Society published a pamphlet entitled *The Slave Code of the State of Illinois, Being an Abstract of Those Laws Now in Force in This State, Which Affect the Rights of Colored People, as Such, Both Bond and Free.*[114] With this title the Will County Society overtly equated Illinois' unjust laws with those that governed slaves. In this pamphlet, the Illinois abolitionists excerpted and critiqued the race-based portions of the state constitution in order to prove the need for reform.

Publications like this became central tools against the "Black Laws." The Will County Society had previously resolved that they needed to publicize in northern Illinois the "Revised Laws" and their many discriminatory provisions. This inspired the pamphlet, wherein these abolitionists reproduced the legal code in lay terms to arouse their fellow citizens to act. Such analysis, they argued, would elicit among their peers "astonishment" that their government permitted what they saw as such approximations of slavery. They expected their readers to feel "disgust" at northerners' acts that rendered them mere "tools and panders of southern patriarchs." Also in 1840, the Ohio Yearly Meeting of Friends denounced what they saw as the nefarious practice of hiding the truth from the public concerning slavery's wide-ranging effects, including the "Black Laws." They argued that it was their duty to overcome these silencing efforts, and to spread the truth about slavery and these laws' oppressions to "our fellow citizens."[115] For similar reasons, the Indiana

Free Labor Advocate printed the "Black Laws" of Indiana in its pages in 1841—with a critique of them from the Henry County Society—and in 1848.[116]

As antislavery people argued against the "Black Laws," they frequently critiqued pro-slavery southerners and their laws. To draw attention to the "Black Laws" and illustrate white self-interest in opposing them, they argued that Old Northwest people were weak, and conformed to southern mores. The Will County Society promoted its underlying goal of removing biased legislation by proving that the "Black Laws" had no place in their free state. They showed how these laws violated constitutional law and egalitarian ideas, and differed little from those of slave states in phrasing and intent.[117] Similarly, in 1843 the Ohio American Society argued that the "Black Laws" proved that slavery was not a sectional institution confined to the South, for it infected the entire nation with its influence.[118]

Antislavery observers in both the Old Northwest and the East saw in the "Black Laws" complicity with slavery and a direct effort to appease neighboring slave states. In 1840, the Will County Society claimed that the ways their state laws obligated individuals and the government to aid slave catchers showed "a servility unequalled by any of her sister states."[119] A New York Whig paper, the Rochester *Democrat*, too, agreed in 1848 that these laws meant that Old Northwest states submitted to the will of the slave states, and that they preyed upon people who lacked the means to defend themselves. Citing the notorious prejudice in Illinois, they strongly argued against this inequality and for universal citizenship.[120] The "Black Laws" certainly became infamous outside the region, but most practical resistance against them arose from within. Like their eastern allies, many Old Northwest activists believed fighting the racial prejudice of the "Black Laws" was essential to achieving their antislavery goals. This was, in the words of New York editor Samuel E. Cornish, the deeper struggle, the "real battleground" they faced, since slavery's effects were wide-reaching in this hostile climate, and inspired African Americans and their white allies to fight them.[121] These effects included warping the nation's laws in directions that reformers could not justify.

The Old Northwest opponents of the "Black Laws" saw extensive proof of their unconstitutionality, and lamented this. The Will County Society claimed the "Black Laws" imposed penalties that violated the constitutional provision that the punishment should fit the crime. These laws set African Americans apart from the rest of the US population by levying excessive punishments and by treating them as criminals for acts that other people could perform with impunity, including the ability to move freely.[122] They also asserted that the laws did not meet the United States constitutional standard wherein "citizens of each state" are "guarantee[d] . . . all the privileges and immunities of the citizens in the several states."[123] Specifically, Illinois' requirement that African Americans who were citizens of other states post bond upon their entry—against becoming a public burden on society—violated this universal right.[124] In 1842, Ohio lawyer John Joliffe made a similar argument, claiming the Ohio laws also breached that same clause of the constitution. He argued that African Americans were citizens, and aimed to prove the inconsistencies of the "Black Laws": "Admit free negroes to be men, and to be born free in the United States, and it is impossible to frame even a plausible argument against their citizenship."[125] This claim would not have persuaded everyone, certainly, since many of their fellow citizens disagreed with him on even the most basic claims about African American rights.

Antislavery foes of the "Black Laws" extended their arguments about constitutionality even further. The Will County Society found the laws "violated numerous other provisions of the Illinois State Constitution. These included the right to a jury trial and protection against "unreasonable" and unfounded arrests.[126] The Indiana Friends (writing about Ohio) echoed these claims in 1848 by arguing that the discriminatory "Black Laws" contradicted the "spirit and principles" of the United States government's foundation, and violated the terms of both the Northwest Ordinance and the US Constitution. They asserted that all people were entitled to their freedom, both under the terms of the Bill of Rights and of the Ohio Constitution.[127] Activists' concerns with the laws' inequities extended into the hardships they caused African American children.

Anti-"Black Law" activists targeted the provisions that imposed school inequities on the African American population. As their numbers in the Old Northwest grew slowly, they made only minimal progress in the area of schooling. Segregation and race-based limitations on educational rights were the norm. As was the case across the North, getting even limited access required a hard fight.[128] Prior to 1829, there were no laws formally barring African Americans from Ohio's schools, but with the establishment of public schools that year, such exclusion became formalized.[129] Under the new legislation, private schools could still educate African Americans, but public schools could not. In 1849 the Ohio legislature established a formally segregated school system that allowed mixed classrooms in areas with small African American populations.[130]

African American children had gained the right to an education, but not one of equal standing or location. Illinois law also excluded African Americans from schools, even where they paid taxes equal to those that whites paid.[131] The first Michigan constitution barred African Americans from the schools, and later the degree of segregation varied by place. In some areas, it led to African American children's complete exclusion. Public sentiment in Indiana also kept them out of schools.[132] From the perspective of African Americans and their allies, this segregation substantially impeded the path to full equality of opportunity, and they fought hard against it.

Old Northwest anti-prejudice activists resisted these laws and expanded African Americans' educational rights by founding schools and teaching in them.[133] The Indiana Friends, most notably those from eastern Indiana, were major opponents of the "Black Laws" who established integrated schools and opposed the creation of segregated ones.[134] These reformers also took their grievances directly to the courts and the legislatures whenever they could.

* * *

Some opponents of the "Black Laws" worked from within the legal system, as did early Ohio state attorney and judge Francis Dunlavy. He pushed antislavery and pro–African American positions from the bench in the 1830s. In 1836 he used a legal opinion to proclaim slaves brought into Ohio—with the consent of their owners or in their company—free and secure from court prosecution. He believed that those who fled against their masters' will were not entitled to their freedom, but those whose masters brought them to the state under legitimate circumstances had the right to resist unjust capture.[135] By 1840, antislavery organizations had taken up this argument and used states' rights to claim that slaves became free when they entered Ohio. This rationale had gained traction by the 1850s when officials presumed African Americans that entered Ohio were free, unless they were fugitives.[136]

The courts helped activists in another respect when they were unwilling to enforce the "Black Laws"; reformers used this to publicize their cause. While African Americans lacked the right to testimony under the "Black Laws," the Ohio Supreme Court granted them the right to submit "affidavits," which gave them some limited say in the court.[137] In the fall of 1842 an Ohio judge spoke out against the legality of the "Black Laws," claiming the legislature lacked the power to stop African Americans from settling in the state.[138] In addition, when in 1843

William Logan of Richland County, Ohio, went on trial for providing food to a fugitive, the County Court dismissed the case. They did so on the grounds that this provision of the "Black Laws" was "unconstitutional."[139] Interestingly, the Court refused to make this judgment known openly—as the *National Anti-Slavery Standard* wrote—for they feared offending Ohioans who favored stringent punishment for this act.[140] It was up to antislavery people to bring to light such judicial opposition to the "Black Laws."[141] These legal victories notwithstanding, some Old Northwest activists directly experienced the impact of the "Black Laws" and concretely resisted them.

A wide range of Old Northwesterners—both African American and white—had to fight the effects of the "Black Laws" in the courts. Alabama-born abolitionist William T. Allan wrote in June 1846 to the *Western Citizen* about his misadventures in attempting to travel across Illinois with one of his family's former slaves, an older man named Richmond. Allan's father had freed his slaves upon his death, and they had moved to Illinois, where Allan and four of his five siblings lived. When the two men were in Peoria, Richmond was working in a stable when a man observed him and forced him to the magistrate's office, and subsequently, to the sheriff's. The man claimed Richmond was a runaway, and despite Allan's intimate knowledge of Richmond's true free status, the court refused to admit him as a witness, claiming he was a "party interested." The judge put Richmond in jail and arrested Allan for aiding a runaway. Allan was, in accordance with the "Black Laws," forced to pay $500 for this act and, as of the time of his writing, was scheduled for a trial the following October. The judiciary imposed this strict punishment for what Allan described as "the *crime* of riding in a buggy with an old friend!"[142]

While Allan had quickly obtained evidence proving the elderly man's freedom, including his father's will, the judge claimed this was insufficient. In his letter, Allan argued that this proved the "Black Laws" were unjust in violating Richmond's rights—and his own. The Illinois government, in his view, obsequiously followed the dictates of the slave states. He argued that Illinois was in fact a "mere appendage" to the states where slavery itself was legal. For him, this wrongful treatment exemplified the disgrace Illinois sustained on account of the "Black Laws."[143] In Allan's view, the court exhibited substantial bias in such cases, which influenced his determination to combat these laws in their entirety.

Beyond Allan, other Old Northwest "Black Laws" foes criticized this legislation for its effects on African Americans as both potential perpetrators and victims of crimes. The Will County activists injected a note of sly wit into their critique of the Illinois laws with a summary of section 24. This clause enabled the government to levy a fine upon people who allowed "slaves or servants of color" to gather in groups "for the purposes of reveling" in buildings or spaces they owned. The authors claimed that they could not tell if the lawmakers intended this measure to protect whites against African American uprisings, or the latter group against immorality. If virtue or fear of riot were at issue, the abolitionists argued that a better course would have been to "have prohibited intercourse with the whites."[144] They thus insinuated that the white population was the source of debauchery for African Americans. On a more serious note, they also argued that the present law insufficiently protected African Americans in Illinois from abuse. Under the revised laws of 1833, certificates of freedom were sometimes inadequate evidence against slaveholder claims, which carried more weight in the court.

These laws permitted slaveholders to fraudulently take people into slavery and even sell African Americans, or the owner of their labor could assign them to work for someone else. They supposedly had the right to refuse employment they did not desire, but in the view of the Will County authors, they would be unlikely to exercise this right, given the "arbitrary and irresponsible power" masters exerted over them.[145] This wide-ranging critique demonstrates the willingness of anti-"Black Laws" activists to draw on the evident parallels with slavery that the laws created. This also explains the inextricable nature of reformers' opposition to the "Black Laws" and slavery. They knew that the laws' effects extended well beyond formal legal discrimination, and could affect the most private aspects of African Americans' lives.

* * *

Opponents of the "Black Laws" across the Old Northwest extended their egalitarian convictions to the laws' controversial efforts to regulate interracial marriage. They opposed marriage restrictions despite the fact that unions across racial lines had been unpopular nationally since the mid-eighteenth century. Legislatures outlawed such marriages, revealing a preoccupation with interracial sex at both the state and national levels. Lawmakers barred these pairings to preserve white privilege and social stratification.[146] Indiana's long history of regulating interracial relationships dated back to 1818.[147] In Illinois, an 1829 law forbade interracial marriage outright with significant potential penalties that included fines, whipping, or imprisonment.[148] In relatively permissive Michigan, the legislature nonetheless outlawed interracial marriage in 1838, deeming such marriages invalid, and the resultant children to be without legitimacy. Initially, this law went unenforced, but the legislature subsequently stipulated a $500 fine for officiants, and fines and jail time for couples. In the late 1850s, anxieties about such marriages grew, as the press in Michigan evidenced.[149] While many of its other laws were stringent, Ohio came very late to the official banning of interracial marriage, for it only passed its first such law in 1861.[150]

"Black Laws" opponents frequently discussed interracial relationships, despite that this was a treacherous topic. Support for them potentially risked playing into the hands of proslavery people who used this contentious issue to discredit reformers by claiming they advocated it. In 1841, the *Philanthropist* railed against laws regulating marriage choice.[151] They called them "a disgrace" and an "impertinent interference with individual liberty." While the author argued that the government had no business interfering with marriage, they also implicitly denied that abolitionists and other foes of the "Black Laws" favored interracial matches, and insinuated with disdain that legislators did: "If our legislature chose to pass resolutions binding *themselves* never to marry colored women, they are at liberty to do so—probably some such pledge may be needed to restrain an erratic choice. But, the *people* require no legislative enactment to regulate *their* taste," since this was a private matter, and not one of government's "legitimate functions."[152] The author may have intended this reference to "erratic choice" to distance him or herself from association with interracial marriage, an accusation antislavery people often faced from their foes.[153] This could have been either a concession to Ohio's racist society, or another example of activists mocking the bias of others.

In the antislavery press, writers linked their opposition to marriage restrictions to the larger burden that "Black Laws" discrimination imposed. In February 1842, the *Free Labor Advocate* denounced the state legislature for forbidding interracial marriage. The editor of the *Advocate* denied that he promoted such marriages, but decried laws on this issue as beneath the "dignity" of the legislature. They were "tyrannical," and could increase the load Old Northwest African Americans shouldered—the "prejudice which is crushing to the earth the free people of color in the professedly free states." The Indiana law included draconian provisions to create a "board of inspections" to ascertain the race of people who wanted to marry.[154] Despite the shaky footing on which support for these controversial unions put them, antislavery activists engaged with the debate over racial categories and boundaries in order to advance their fight for a more equal society. While some areas in the North acted more quickly to permit interracial marriage, both the former Old Northwest and the South left most of their anti-miscegenation laws in place long after the Civil War, and indeed, these restrictions continued through the 1960s.[155]

Old Northwest activists' discussions of interracial relationships occasionally ventured beyond consensual marriage to recognizing that the "Black Laws" could contribute to whites' attacks on African American women. The Will County Society decried how the Illinois "Black Laws" facilitated white sexual license and denied African Americans legal recourse for sexual assault. With this, they tapped into a wider concern at the time about how slavery and biased laws led to the sexual exploitation of women. While the Illinois legislature had forbidden interracial marriage, it placed "illicit intercourse" under minimal sanction. Old Northwest agitators claimed that the result was white immorality and tyranny; the testimony law meant that "any pale faced scoundrel" could invade the home of "a colored man" and attack "his family" with impunity. They constructed this crime as an offense against men and the family unit, not one against the individual women or girls who would be the likely victims of such a "scoundrel."[156]

Thus while they addressed the delicate subject of interracial sexual abuse—and implicitly protected women—the Will County authors did so using language that invoked African American men's right to an intact family unit. In effect, they presented this safe family as a gender protection men deserved. A privilege of manhood was the right to have the household undisturbed by other men, and the "Black Laws" violated this by denying African American men this defensive right. These activists drew upon the rhetoric of domesticity and the sanctity of the family to enhance their anti-discrimination claims. With such arguments they would doubtless have aimed at persuading their readers to see the flaws in the legislation.

* * *

Beyond publications like the Will County pamphlet, opponents of the "Black Laws" used petitions extensively to capture their legislatures' attention and demand action. The Quakers were among the pioneers of this effort, and those in Indiana petitioned their state legislature each year calling for repeal of these laws.[157] Petitions against the Ohio "Black Laws" began in 1829.[158] The Ohio legislature greeted African Americans' petitions with a controversy in 1839 when they debated whether recognizing them would acknowledge African American citizenship.[159] In 1843, the Ohio American Society also petitioned for repeal.[160] Eventually both the Ohio general assembly and the state senate, under Liberty Party pressure, acknowledged the anti-"Black Laws" petitions by appointing a committee to review them in the 1840s, although repeal came slowly.[161]

Antislavery societies from across the region and throughout the decades often used petitions to protest against the "Black Laws," especially the women among them. The Putnam County (Illinois) Female Society resolved to send one such petition to the Illinois legislature in January 1843, along with another that was against Texas annexation. They claimed that free states must remove the local "Black Laws," all national discriminatory legislation, and provisions that forced free state citizens to prop up slavery. Their own duty, as they saw it, was to make their views known to Congress and the Illinois legislature.[162] In 1846, the Galesburg Anti-Slavery Society followed suit, and that same year in Michigan, the 46 members of the Female Benevolent and Antislavery Society of Lenawee petitioned their legislature to remove the word "white" from the state constitution's limitations on rights.[163] They asked other women throughout Michigan to join their effort, and thus exemplified the links between the work against slavery and the "Black Laws."[164] "Black Laws" opponents provided further evidence of their diverse strategies with their willingness to seek aid even in unlikely places, such as in the usually cautious political parties.

* * *

The harsh critics of the "Black Laws" were not confined to African American activists and immediate antislavery organizers, for their work was both affected by and influenced all politics in the Old Northwest. At times more radical activists collaborated with politicians from third party as well as mainstream factions. Among the political antislavery men who took on the "Black Laws" was the Whig, Benjamin Wade, who served in the Ohio Senate beginning in 1837. He rapidly took a stand against these laws, but this early effort failed. The Democrats, there—as ever—stalwart opponents of African American rights, quickly regained control of the legislature in 1838, but Wade and his law partner Joshua Giddings continued to represent African American rights in the antislavery wing of the Whig Party while it lasted.[165] In 1846, Asahel Lewis, the Whig candidate for the Ohio Senate from the Western Reserve, also made "Black Laws" repeal a priority. Democrats tried to portray this as radical abolitionism to undermine him, but Lewis ultimately won the closely contested election.[166] Outside of Ohio, some Michigan Whigs also worked to obtain the vote for African American men.[167] These men were fairly unusual in their vocal opposition to the "Black Laws," for among Whigs the willingness to work for rights, regardless of race, was rare. In the Old Northwest, they faced substantial competition, including from the antislavery third parties that influenced most of them usually to oppose African American rights.

The Liberty Party was less cautious, and repeatedly proclaimed a belief in equality, notably in the major party platform of 1844. Especially in Illinois, Ohio, and Michigan, it fought against the "Black Laws" and for Black suffrage and personal liberty laws. The Illinois Liberty Party passed resolutions against the "Black Laws" in May 1842, a position that local organizations in the state echoed.[168] This included the 1842 Bureau County Liberty Convention which resolved that such "unjust" laws delimited by skin color were "absurd, and consequently of no moral force or obligation."[169] Similar claims came from Knox County that same year.[170] Since the Liberty Party took a stronger stance for African American rights in the Old Northwest than did other parties, they gave it some support in return. African Americans were active participants in the Michigan Liberty Party, and in Ohio, biracial schoolteacher Charles Langston, among others, joined in. Langston, a Virginia-born Oberlin alumnus, was an outspoken foe of the Ohio "Black Laws" and a frequent participant in Ohio antislavery societies.[171] Across the region, African American speakers often addressed Liberty conventions, and the 1843 Black National Convention at Buffalo endorsed the Liberty Party.[172] That year, Liberty Party candidates placed "Black Laws" repeal on their platforms, including Dr. Demming of Jefferson County, Indiana, who advocated cleansing the Indiana legal code of such laws.[173]

The actions of white political antislavery activists in the Old Northwest stretch extant knowledge about this group's racial views and reform practices. Previous scholars have revealed white antislavery reformers' failure to push for sufficient social change and combat their own deeply imbedded racism. While evidence of prejudice is widespread, the claim that white activists' racial visions were inevitably limited remains open to question.[174] Race certainly affected social and political relations nationally, but in the Old Northwest it was impossible for activists to ignore its local effects on rights. White political abolitionists' actions there against the "Black Laws" belie arguments that they were largely ignorant of African American problems. Avowing rights and resisting white privilege, both in their region and nationally, they operated in a period of shifting and solidifying racial categories.[175]

In the tense racial environment of the Old Northwest, some unusually egalitarian people pushed the boundaries of the expected, even for Liberty Party adherents who were already outside of the mainstream for their time. In one such case, the views of Illinois antislavery women of the Liberty Party in the 1840s mark them as radicals for their gender and their party. Their willingness to address equal rights for African Americans counters other claims that most white antislavery women were indifferent to the post-emancipation fate of former slaves, for these Old Northwesterners actually displayed more interest in egalitarianism than historians have previously noted.[176] The views on race they articulated as they fought the "Black Laws" were so groundbreaking that they placed these reformers beyond the typical understanding of the Liberty Party platform.

While some political antislavery people's racial justice convictions were weakening by 1842, this was not universally the case. At that point the Liberty Party had begun to shift its rhetorical emphasis away from immediate emancipation and equal rights for African Americans and toward expounding fears that a southern conspiracy, the "slave power," would subvert the northern economy and its political independence.[177] Despite this trend, some Liberty men and women continued to advocate race equality in ways that resemble those usually associated with Garrisonian abolitionists, writing both anti-racist and pointedly radical public proclamations and newspaper articles.[178] Some of them, like Illinois antislavery activist Mary Brown Davis, argued that African Americans' mental and emotional capabilities justified abolishing slavery and removing laws like the "Black Laws" that impeded equal rights. In 1844, Davis explicitly disputed claims of African American mental deficiency as she wrote, "The colored race, so far from being inferior to the white, would with the same advantages, not only equal, but surpass them in intellectual acquirements." She claimed that her fellow Illinois activists needed to uncover and root out inequality and slavery.[179] The Liberty Party was decentralized enough to permit a spectrum of political activity within its boundaries. These positions on African American rights and capabilities were actually even on the fringes of immediatism for their awareness of the wide-ranging effects of discrimination, and thus also particularly unusual for the relatively more moderate Liberty Party.

While the Liberty Party typically opposed the "Black Laws," it did not support the African American vote across the board.[180] While its national strength was waning by 1848, nonetheless that year in Illinois the party still included African Americans and was going strong against the "Black Laws." It passed equal rights resolutions and rallied against the 1848 state constitution that enhanced race-based discrimination. Despite activists' concerted efforts, the new constitution passed.[181] For all of the diversity of these methods, the ever-resourceful anti-"Black Laws" activists had still more; they pushed for justice with other levers, since the local struggle for legal equity had strong connections with the Black Convention Movement.

* * *

Along with white lawyers, editors, and abolitionists, African Americans who fought the "Black Laws" interracially, alone, and through organizations proved their mettle in working for their own rights. Many, including a pioneering corps of college-educated men and tradesmen, joined a local and national movement for racial advancement.[182] From the 1830s through the 1860s, the Black Convention Movement had a broad agenda that fought numerous political and social ills, but chiefly of interest here are the ways it advanced rights by pushing to overturn the Old Northwest "Black Laws" and fugitive slave laws. It was a key method African Americans used to promote a broad human rights agenda they shared with their white allies like Benjamin Stanton.

Both the National and the State Black Convention Movements were expansive tools in the fight for the equality that Old Northwest African Americans demanded. A lull followed a brief stint of national activity in the early 1830s, and state-level meetings ensued. The first National Negro Convention met at Philadelphia in 1830, and these assemblies came together annually through 1834, before merging in 1835 with white activists to form the American Moral Reform Society, which had a broader agenda. Old Northwest African American leaders had initially only minimally participated in the national conventions. They had two delegates at the conventions from 1832 to 1834, but there is no evidence of their representation in 1831 or 1835.[183]

Later, as they founded local organizations, Old Northwest African Americans became much more active. They began to organize state meetings as early as 1835 in Ohio.[184] In 1841 they started more thoroughly publicizing their efforts, as the Ohio State Committee of Colored Men worked for "Black Laws" repeal.[185] In Cleveland, the local African American population and their white allies actively combatted against these laws; they petitioned their state legislature and hired several itinerant lecturers.[186] Another early meeting was in January of 1842, when a group of African American men in Detroit rallied to enfranchise the men of their state. They proposed a petition to their state legislature for that purpose, but despite an enthusiastic response from the state legislative committee that received the petitions, they did not achieve this goal quickly. The government's stance on the issue wavered, and they only took decisive action on this right in 1870.[187] The Convention movement fought a drawn-out battle for equality there, as elsewhere.

As the locations of these meetings indicate, some anti-"Black Laws" activism was urban in nature. In this era, the battle against the "Black Laws" in the Old Northwest's few burgeoning cities relied upon a critical mass of African American people that at times drew the ire of racist whites. Cities not only threatened oppression, however, for their larger populations enabled African Americans to develop a centralized leadership corps.[188] The majority of the population of the Old Northwest was outside of the cities, and rural regions and smaller towns also had their fiery leaders and rank-and-file activists, especially before the 1850s. The cities, nonetheless, were the logical location for such large-scale meetings.

The Black National Convention Movement revived as a separate movement in Buffalo, New York, in 1843. Leaders of the Black Convention Movement in their home states participated in these national meetings, but most men who planned the 1843 convention were easterners. Ohio was the only Old Northwest state represented in the organization process, although the attendees included representatives from Illinois, Ohio, and Michigan.[189] The adherents met irregularly, with the next national meeting following at Cleveland in 1848.[190] After the movement's national rebirth, organization of state Black conventions proceeded apace.[191]

The national conventions of the 1840s had wide-ranging agendas, but particularly focused on the "Black Laws" and the right to vote. The attendees at these meetings also worked to overturn the social and economic barriers their fellow citizens had erected, including colonization.[192] At the 1843 convention, the assembled men stated that they would fight any laws that impeded their mobility, settlement, and educational rights. They called for egalitarian rule, and "laws, just and equal for all the people."[193] In terms of methods, while the convention displayed little faith in political parties, calling them "the slaves of slavery too," the men there remained hopeful that the reform work of societies such as theirs could reveal the errors of the biased laws in the otherwise promising Old Northwest. The Old Northwesterners at the convention used this platform to publicize the problems with the "Black Laws." Their compatriots understood these challenges, but at these conventions they nevertheless created numerous arguments that this region would be an auspicious place for African Americans to relocate. While they had few illusions about the Old Northwest's flaws, the attendees argued that the region's people suffered from mere redeemable human errors, and would eventually replace these faulty laws as the people acquired "a better understanding of the great laws of humanity."[194] According to these men, their conventions' actions would be central to enacting the necessary change.

The presenters at the 1843 convention believed their course was clear, for they argued that self-organization held the key to equality. Despite the interracial, egalitarian work of white activists, the Convention movement's participants also argued they must take separate action in their own behalf. While they appreciated white abolitionists' good intentions and refrained from directly criticizing them, African American activists refused to wait and expect others to take care of their rights. They wrote that in addition to interracial activity, they must pursue the "rich boon of freedom and equal rights" for themselves.[195] From their perspective, whites' principled efforts had created insufficient change in African American people's lives, and thus interracial activism may not have been working quickly enough, by their standards.

Independent African American activism may not have grown out of a desire to supersede biracial methods, but instead found its motivation in ideas of autonomy and in the desire to continue with a multifaceted strategy. To the "Black Convention Movement" attendees, both integrated and independent activism appeared appealing and necessary. Also in 1843, the Michigan Black Convention admired their allies' persistent efforts. While whites in Michigan had fought on their behalf for "fourteen years," they remained under attack. To attain full citizenship, African Americans thus had to augment the efforts of these "warm white friends" with their own work for rights. This self-determination, as the delegates to that Michigan convention saw it in gendered terms, could demonstrate that they deserved equality, as they could prove by their "upright, correct, and manly stand in the defence of our Liberty."[196] By this logic, self-determination and manliness were linked.

Some of their peers saw disadvantages to separate activism, including Old Northwest antislavery groups like the Ohio Society that were mainly white. They opposed holding separate Black Conventions in 1850, for while they did support a convention, they thought that it should be integrated, because segregation had contributed to prejudice. They wrote, "every thing that tends to separate the colored people from the whites, aids in building up an impassible barrier to their progress." In effect, they regarded separate action as implicitly condoning segregating measures like the "Black Laws."[197] Nevertheless, their African American peers felt differently, and proceeded with their convention. Given the extent of the discrimination they faced, they required aid from all available sources.

* * *

Across the Old Northwest, the Black Conventions targeted the "Black Laws" by deploying classic antebellum universal rights arguments and tactics. The 1843 Michigan Convention used what its attendees called universal justice principles to argue against their state legislature's refusal to grant them citizenship rights, the franchise, and education, and to denounce their "taxation without representation." Using the Declaration of Independence, they claimed citizens' right to form, modify, or depose governments that violated their founding principles. To claim this right, all men should have the vote—in their terms, "a natural right belonging to man"—due to both his humanity and his ability to take responsibility for his actions. Since they claimed these rights were universal, the provisions in the second clause of the Michigan Constitution reserving the right to vote for white men conflicted with the first clause, "which expressly declares that no man or set of men are entitled to exclusive or separate privileges."[198] They called for Michigan's African Americans to petition their legislature continually until they obtained equal rights and the vote, and did so at least six times between 1843 and 1859. In addition to conventions and petitions, these men also used referenda and the legal system to fight their deprivation of rights.[199] The 1844 Ohio Convention used similar arguments concerning the "almost insurmountable barriers" to equality the "Black Laws" imposed.[200]

The Black Conventions subjected what they saw as racist whites' flawed logic to sharp scrutiny to prove the "Black Laws'" weak and unjust foundations. The men at the Michigan meeting published an address by William Lambert to publicize the cause among their fellow citizens. This address argued that African Americans' treatment ought to elicit compassion from those who blocked their progress by ascribing their low status to innate character and intellectual defects. While Lambert's critique, as a whole, encompassed a range of original arguments, one passage clearly proves that activists forged strong intellectual links between national and state Black conventions. Lambert drew directly on an 1835 national address by William Whipper, Alfred Niger, and Augustus Price for a section of his Michigan address of 1843.[201] Lambert gave no indication of the borrowed origin of these words and ideas. The speech attacked notions of African American inferiority by noting that the weight of injustice lay so heavily upon their shoulders that any of their achievements that appeared to parallel those of whites actually by far surpassed them:

> If then, amidst all of the[se] difficulties . . . we present an equal amount of intelligence with that class of our fellow citizens that have been so peculiarly favored; a very grave and dangerous question presents itself to the world, on the natural equality of man: and the best rule of logic, would place those who have oppressed us, in the scale of inferiority.[202]

This critique brought the obstacles preventing African American rights into sharp focus, and mocked their antagonists. These men, "the oppressed of this state," proclaimed their determination to work tirelessly against this discrimination, with their words and in their private and public writings, until they saw justice served.[203] They had many strong leaders in that cause.

* * *

A notable anti-racist organizer from Illinois was John Jones, a major player in the Black Convention Movement and that group's work for the repeal of the Illinois "Black Laws." His actions, and the situation in Illinois, provide a case study of the struggle for rights in the Old Northwest, and how confronting the "Black Laws" head on remained a necessity as African Americans' neighbors sought to reinforce these laws. This freeborn biracial man began his public life in 1847, two years after he and his wife Mary Jane had moved to Chicago, when that city was still in its infancy. John opened a tailoring shop on Clark Street, one of the pioneering African American–owned businesses in that city, which at the time had fewer than 300 African American residents.[204] In those early years, Jones met two white abolitionist allies, Charles V.

Dyer, a doctor, and Lemanuel Covell Paine Freer, a well-known lawyer. They maintained friendships for the rest of his life. Freer aided Jones in his correspondence and subsequently taught him to read and write.[205]

John Jones began to formally fight the "Black Laws" in 1847 by joining the debate about that year's Constitutional Convention. Many delegates there claimed that an African American influx into Illinois would imperil white labor. In response, Jones wrote a series of articles in the *Western Citizen* that argued for African American rights and legal equality. Among his chief points against the "Black Laws" were that the definition of free citizens omitted the word "white," the Enlightenment's ideals, the principles of republican government, and African Americans' patriotic efforts in the Revolutionary War.[206] Jones argued that the "Black Laws" bore primary responsibility for African Americans' poverty in Illinois, and that they restricted all aspects of their lives, from economic to civil to personal.

He knew this from his own direct experience. In accordance with these laws, both John and Mary Jane had obtained certificates of freedom from the clerk in Madison County prior to their move to Chicago. As they had traveled through Illinois, local authorities used the "Black Laws" to detain them, claiming they might be fugitives. With the good word of their stagecoach driver, the Joneses acquired their freedom once more, and continued along their way.[207]

Jones was in good company in opposing the laws: there were scores of concerned people within the Illinois antislavery movement. Many of them submitted anti-"Black Laws" petitions in 1847. The Illinois Senate responded to these petitions with claims that no laws could ever match such unequal parties, "no acts of legislation will or can ever raise the African in the country above the level in which the petitions find him."[208] This blunt refutation helps clarify why, in January of 1848, the Reverend Levi Spencer feared that the Illinois legislature would add to the "Black Laws," which they did later that year. Spencer, born in New York, moved in 1839 to Galesburg, Illinois, and thereafter to Bloomington.[209] He argued that the legislature's 1848 act proved the extent of political and moral corruption prevalent in Illinois, which "cruel prejudice" had created.[210]

Despite these vehement objections, the Illinois legislature indeed passed the anti-immigration provision, Article XIV of the 1848 Constitution. A popular vote overwhelmingly confirmed it. Jones wrote to the *Western Citizen* in July of 1848 about this measure, claiming that it deprived Americans of their rights: "I view it with regret and alarm, because it attempts to prohibit natural-born citizens of the United States from settling in this state on account of the color of their skin."[211] While this was dire news to the foes of the "Black Laws," the Constitution of 1848 did contain one measure they applauded, which was that it finally and explicitly outlawed slavery in Illinois.[212]

This overall setback failed to dissuade African American activists in Illinois, for they made increasingly outspoken protests against discrimination through formal organizations. In August 1848, African American Chicagoans met and chose John Jones and the Reverend Abraham T. Hall as the delegates to that year's Colored National Convention in Cleveland, where the main subject was repeal of the Old Northwest's discriminatory laws.[213] The fifty to seventy delegates who met there on September 6 included more westerners than attended the 1843 meeting. They elected Frederick Douglass president and Jones vice president. Among other topics, the participants discussed repeal of the "Black Laws" and how they could improve African Americans' living conditions and status.[214] Jones's solution was that they needed to replace menial labor with skilled and professional jobs. Upon his return to Chicago in September, Jones united with other local African American activists in a correspondence committee aimed at political organization, including continuing to petition the legislature for repeal of the "Black Laws."[215]

The Old Northwest saw some positive changes in the late 1840s, thanks to the Black Convention Movement's lobbying and the aid of political abolitionists. The partial repeal of Ohio's "Black Laws" in 1849 was, to a degree, an outcome of political antislavery efforts as well as negotiations among the political parties in Ohio. In addition to finally addressing the series of petitions against the "Black Laws" that began in 1829, this change also drew strength from a deal between the Democrats and the Free Soil Party in which the Free Soil legislators from the Western Reserve were instrumental. Even though the Free Soil Party had quite moderate attitudes, including containment of slavery rather than its immediate abolition, and a preference for southern African Americans staying in the South, it nonetheless fought for "Black Laws" repeal.[216] In Indiana, the Free Soil politicians also unsuccessfully opposed the provisions of their state's 1850 constitution that shored up their own racialized laws.[217] Political antislavery people, then as earlier, were unpredictable but occasionally useful allies.

Partisanship influenced the outcome of the 1849 Ohio repeal. Then the legislators abolished the registration requirement and the bond payment, testimony, and job restrictions, but the state kept its remaining "Black Laws," since the Democrats refused to support egalitarianism. Even the progress that this repeal exemplified was thus highly qualified, and the fight for the laws' full abolition continued for decades.[218] In fact, the Ohio Democrats espoused increasingly strong anti–African American views and support for the "Black Laws" as the Republican Party emerged and gained in strength.[219]

While the 1849 repeal removed some of the Ohio "Black Laws," legalized discrimination remained strong. African Americans remained disfranchised, without jury rights, subject to the poor relief law, and faced new inequities in the schools. "Black Laws" repeal consequently stayed at the top of the Ohio Convention's agenda, as well as in the other states. In 1849 and 1850, they composed and disseminated petitions against the remaining laws. The 1850 Black Convention attendees targeted both the Ohio "Black Laws" and national unequal laws, for in their resolutions, they acknowledged that they had no obligation to obey unjust legislation. This language approached nullification, the radical political strategy that nineteenth-century Americans usually associated with southern states' rights theories.[220] In 1850, the Ohio Convention reiterated the essential nature of their right to vote, but they and their compatriots in other states retained wider-ranging concerns, which in their hostile area began to more frequently include efforts to aid fugitives.[221] The longstanding connections activists drew between the "Black Laws" and federal fugitive slave legislation also eventually informed their responses to the worsening legal ambiance when the Fugitive Slave Act passed in 1850.

* * *

The racial climate of the Old Northwest, and resistance to it, set the context for struggles not only against the "Black Laws" but also against slavery there. Advocates of abolition, too, found significantly enhanced resistance in the region due to their neighbors' racial views, which made it all the more difficult to change the local social and political environment.

These struggles over the "Black Laws" prove that in the antebellum Old Northwest, people hotly contested community and ideological boundaries, and activists frequently faced both hostile words and weapons. Many of the residents of these newly settled polities were exceptionally unsympathetic to antislavery and egalitarian ideas. Their pervasive public resistance to activism—which extended well past the few previously studied incidents—demonstrates that recently founded communities sought social cohesion. In the face of this intense local opposition, Old Northwest antislavery people sought support elsewhere, uniting with national reformers and forming networks across vast western distances. While their experience as activists differed from that of their peers in northeastern states, they were unusually connected with one another over the miles. Whether mobile or stationary, they became hardened to opposition and resolute in their determination to gather publicly and shape their region's political culture.

3 / "Stand Firm on the Platform of Truth": Freedom of Assembly and Local Antislavery Organizations in the Old Northwest

As a state we influence the west, the west influences our nation, and our nation the world.

—THE ILLINOIS ANTI-SLAVERY CONVENTION OF 1838

In 1843, the McLean County Anti-Slavery Society struggled to meet in Bloomington, Illinois. As elsewhere in the Old Northwest, activists there found that securing freedom of assembly was arduous, and involved substantial risk of violence. The Reverend Levi Spencer's 1840s experiences illustrate immediate abolitionists' difficulties in organizing in the region. At the 1843 Bloomington meeting, one hundred men armed with clubs prevented fifteen abolitionists from gathering in a church; they had to relocate to a private home. The anti-abolitionists followed, and while they did not enter the house, they did damage the building.[1] With this persistent opposition, these community members openly demonstrated both their contempt for local abolitionists and their refusal to permit meetings that advocated ideas repugnant to them.

Little community consensus existed on the appropriateness of antislavery and anti-prejudice organization in Bloomington, as elsewhere in the Old Northwest. Spencer had advocated abolition there for two years, but he had made little headway. He still found the extent of opposition dangerous and distressing. In 1844 Spencer and his allies tried to publicize another upcoming gathering, but most local ministers refused to read their announcement. Still, they met, and their opponents joined them in the meeting hall.[2] The abolitionists peacefully began their meeting, but their adversaries interrupted Spencer's address, throwing bricks and making noise. Spencer finished his speech regardless, and wrote in triumph of what he saw as the downfall of his antagonists, for they had asked permission for one of their number to speak. The abolitionists had agreed, but unfortunately for their foes, the meeting had actually converted this man, Mr. Hunt, and he had embraced abolition. He stood, said so, and sat down. The gathering concluded quietly, which was one fleeting triumph for activists' freedom of assembly and the persuasiveness of their message.[3]

The Spencer family's problems nonetheless carried on for years, which indicates that abolitionists' unpopular efforts to meet could have long-term consequences. The Spencers feared for their safety, and the constant threats they faced from their fellow citizens made them miserable. This continued to be a problem, and in 1846, local residents planned a public meeting to coordinate ejecting "the abolitionists" from town.[4] As the prominent local organizer, Spencer remained a focal point for anti-abolitionist aggression. Other people in town held him accountable for disrupting their community. Among other incidents, in June 1846 a group of men he claimed were volunteers for the Mexican War attacked his house. This act of violence against the Spencer residence had its precedents in the Old Northwest, including the September 1841 raid on the house of John Rankin, antislavery minister of Ripley, Ohio.[5] Spencer's attackers threatened to burn down the building but refrained, and then tried to get him outside to tar and feather him. Upon failing to extract him, they threw eggs and bricks into the windows, inflicting substantial damage. These missiles forced Spencer's family, including his elderly mother, to flee into the corners of the house and away from the broken glass. Spencer finally managed to get help from a neighbor in the wee hours of the morning, whereupon the men departed, not wanting more witnesses to their actions.

The mob also attacked some of Spencer's abolitionist neighbors, but they directed their main assault at the Reverend. The following night the military men departed, and Spencer claimed this restored quiet to the town. He identified many of his assailants (which he saw as consequently motivating some to leave Bloomington), but he opted not to prosecute, for reasons he kept to himself. He may have chosen not to confront his attackers in court, as he knew he was unlikely to face a jury of his peers when his views were so unpopular.[6]

The town eventually became a bit more tolerant of antislavery gatherings, despite the way Spencer's neighbors made him a scapegoat for his unpopular ideas. The county antislavery society successfully held a meeting in Bloomington in April 1847. The change was minor, however, for that May the Justice of the Peace warned Spencer that he should not speak locally on abolition.[7] By October of 1848, Spencer had

had enough, and decided to move to Peoria. He thought there he could perhaps escape the strong bias he had encountered in Bloomington, for his pioneering efforts in organizing antislavery meetings.[8] As Spencer's experiences reveal, the choice to coordinate actions against slavery in the Old Northwest was not one local reformers could take lightly, and yet they nonetheless persisted with this work. The frequent violent efforts to stifle antislavery people's freedom of assembly in the region failed to drive them away. Indeed, many of them actually drew inspiration from the opposition they faced—even if, like Spencer, they had to relocate to continue expressing their opinions.

* * *

Beginning in the 1830s, antislavery and anti-prejudice activists like Spencer brought their movement to the Old Northwest to uplift what they saw as a problematic region. Antebellum reformers were an evangelical lot who widely sought converts to their cause, and they particularly targeted these young states. The same characteristics that made them appealing reform venues—debates over social structure and order, ideologically mixed and geographically diverse populations, economic growth, racist laws, politics in flux—also made them places that strongly resisted when antislavery people publicly claimed the right to organize. These were difficult locales in which to be activists, for the possibility of violent attack was real.

Old Northwest antislavery reformers stated, as they planned their meetings, that they were ready and willing to face substantial challenges. They prove that people who fought slavery and prejudice in this volatile region took on a substantial burden. They also had a keen sense of the importance of their work and the myriad trials they faced. When an abolitionist who called herself "Maria" wrote in the Chicago Liberty Party newspaper the *Western Citizen* in May 1844 that local activists' convictions meant they could "stand firm on the platform of truth" and face obstacles down, she spoke to the internal strength that motivated them as they gathered publicly.[9] Reformers like "Maria" carefully considered their choice to embrace movements for change, for they could lead to ostracism and danger within these dispersed and unwelcoming communities. In this region, local activists who met to discuss abolition catalyzed conflicts over social control. Nonetheless, they created reform cohorts that incorporated diverse antislavery views, which only added to their controversial reception as they gathered to improve their region.

Old Northwest activists believed that to promote their goals, they had to meet freely and form local societies. They spent enormous amounts of time and energy organizing, joining in, and discussing their meetings. Seth Hinshaw, an Indiana abolitionist, explained in 1842 why people needed to attend such gatherings even if they had already embraced abolition. He claimed that meetings told people how they could work to get rid of this scourge, "the serpentine imp" of slavery, and find out "what there is for you to do. . . . "[10] According to Hinshaw, these assemblies were key to their particular activist quest. While reformers were always in the minority with their unpopular positions, they nevertheless made significant progress in spreading the antislavery movement across the difficult Old Northwest terrain. To do so, they had to band together and meet.

Antislavery organizers sought freedom of assembly so that they could form an antislavery public sphere for the diffuse populations of these racially tense states. While finding public space for activists in the region was a necessary step to spreading their message, they faced many problems—including violent opposition—as they did so. In states hostile to abolition and African Americans, activists had to find ways to make their views politically and socially resonant to a scattered, sparse populace. Unlike the public sphere the foundational theorist Jurgen Habermas imagined, theirs included politics, activist networks, and religion. As abolitionists tried to secure open public discussion, their opponents responded with persistent violence.[11]

The public sphere in antebellum America was the site of significant conflict and debate. People's civic life focused and thrived on both the local and the municipal levels. By the 1830s, the public meeting had become a regular form of gathering, in theory accessible to all. The opening of this "democratic public space," along with the expanded voting population that had come to include all white men, permitted individuals of various backgrounds to partake in political debates. In practice, anti-abolitionists often challenged activists' "open access to the political sphere" in the Old Northwest—by interrupting their meetings, for example—and it thus was not always as open as in theory.[12] In the eyes of many in the region, controversial ideas with the potential to enact social and political transformation remained largely unwelcome in public.

Accessing the public sphere nonetheless remained a priority for the activists who closely guarded their freedom of assembly. They linked this goal to the broader rights struggles of the era. This meant that they had to fight not only anti-abolition mobs, but also local and national limitations as to which people could congregate to make change. Some used petitions—a virtual gathering of ideas—to evade attacks on their right to convene. Many local residents met meeting organizers' requests to assemble publicly with proprietary disdain, but the organizers persisted nonetheless.

* * *

From their earliest days of activity in the region, Old Northwest antislavery and anti-prejudice activists, male and female, faced external threats from their neighbors, who challenged their freedom of assembly. As early as 1836, the Ohio Society meeting at Granville encountered an anti-abolitionist mob armed with eggs and stones. These they soon aimed at some delegates; they also shaved the tails of many of the delegates' horses. The abolitionists stood down their opponents, and tricked them by finishing their business and dispersing one night earlier than scheduled.[13] They found a way to avoid assaults on their right to meet, while still accomplishing their goals. These challenges to abolitionists' freedom of assembly lasted for decades in the Old Northwest, and required activists to have both ingenuity and self-motivation.

Activists' personal ties and common circumstances contributed to their reform awakenings and to their ability to stay focused on acting for change. For example, Old Northwest female antislavery activists frequently shared similar religious and social roots. Many western female antislavery fighters, especially in Indiana, came from Quaker backgrounds. Like male abolitionists, there were also many Presbyterians, Baptists, and Methodists in their ranks. Whether married or single, these white women frequently had kinship or marriage ties to prominent male ministers and educators. Among the married, the majority of their husbands held strong abolitionist sentiments.

In the specific case of Illinois, many of its female antislavery activists had histories of reform work. Mary Avery Bent Blanchard of Galesburg was married to Jonathan Blanchard, who became the president of Knox College in that town in 1847. The Blanchards chose Knox, a coeducational stronghold of abolitionist sentiment, after beginning their reform careers in Ohio.[14] In Peoria, both Eliza Chappell Porter and her husband, the Reverend Jeremiah Porter, zealously supported religious and benevolent activism. Shortly after their 1835 marriage, the couple moved to Peoria, where they briefly joined a small but expanding antislavery community. Some of Porter's neighbors became enthusiastic abolitionists, and Jeremiah Porter's (and later William T. Allan's) church, the Main Street Presbyterian

Church, formed a center of their activism.[15] These examples aside, this community was far from united on slavery, even inside the marriage bond.

* * *

The divisions over slavery ran right through some activists' marriages. The controversial Peoria newspaper publishers and reformers, Mary Brown Davis and Samuel H. Davis, exemplify this ideological split within couples, for they held dissonant positions on the issue for years. Prior to marriage, Samuel had worked as a printer in the East and the upper South. The Davises had most recently published a weekly newspaper in Winchester, Virginia.[16] They and their five sons arrived in town from that state via the Illinois River in 1837, and began publishing the *Peoria Register and Northwestern Gazetteer* that April. Both spouses had direct ties to slavery, for Virginia-born Mary's family owned at least 45 slaves, while northern-born Samuel claimed until at least March 1843 to own two slaves in Virginia.[17]

Samuel H. Davis involved himself in many aspects of his new town, but avoided an abolitionist stance for years. As the editor of one of the two Peoria newspapers, he maintained a strong public voice in other arenas, including the Peoria Temperance Society, Lyceum, and Colonization Society.[18] He directly participated in politics as the Peoria County delegate to the Whig State Convention in Springfield in 1841.[19] He thus served as a pillar of the community through his activism in numerous non-abolitionist organizations, and those that resisted direct action against slavery for political or strategic reasons.

In marked contrast to her moderate husband, Mary Brown Davis campaigned against slavery as early as 1837, and organized extensively for the cause. She was a founding member of both the Illinois Female Anti-Slavery Society and the Peoria Female Anti-Slavery Society. Davis also was the most published abolitionist woman writing in Illinois in the 1840s. Her first writings appeared in the *Genius of Universal Emancipation* on June 28, 1839, and in addition to her work editing and writing for the *Register*, Davis became a regular columnist in the Chicago *Western Citizen* from 1842 to 1849. She used the newspaper as a platform to argue for racial equality and to claim that women must take direct, public action against slavery.[20] In this venture, her agenda diverged from that of her husband.

As the Davises exemplify, one partner in a couple could push a reluctant spouse toward abolitionism. Samuel Davis lacked his wife's early, candid devotion to the abolitionist cause, and continued to support the

Whig Party into the mid 1840s.[21] Mary —and circumstances in Peoria—exerted some influence on Samuel over time, and he eventually converted to increasingly vocal abolitionism. He publicly demonstrated this change when he served as president of the State Liberty Party convention in July 1846. Cholera cut his life short in 1849, and the surviving family moved to Galesburg. Mary Brown Davis remained active in journalism and social reform into her old age.[22] These personal details of abolitionists' lives and their underlying principles uncover the material soil in which their activism grew to fruition. Local and regional adversity also fertilized this blooming of reform, as Illinois conflicts including the Davises' own experiences from 1843 to 1848 illustrate. There, many antislavery people—whether male or female—found concrete proof of the necessity of their action in their neighbors' violent resistance to their initial organizational push. This opposition to activists' freedom of assembly strengthened their convictions, as became abundantly clear in Peoria's early antislavery organizing.

* * *

On February 10, 1843, the Whig newspaper the *Peoria Register and Northwestern Gazetteer* announced: "The Peoria Anti-slavery society will hold a meeting in the Main-street Presbyterian church, on Monday evening the 13th . . . for the purpose of organizing and electing officers."[23] This was the Illinois river town's first antislavery effort, and one open to both women and men.

From the outset, Peoria's anti-abolitionists publicly denounced antislavery organizing in their town, and refused to let the meeting occur. Calling themselves the "citizens of Peoria," in the Peoria *Democratic Press*, the local Democratic paper, they first held a public assembly of their own at the courthouse on February 12, 1843, to thwart the abolition society at its gathering the following day. They expressed their "entire disapprobation" of their foes' "views and principles," and argued that antislavery doctrine directly conflicted with federal and state law. These men claimed that abolitionism would create sectional and interstate animosity, "discord and disunion." They alluded to the possibility of violent reprisal, resolving to use force to suppress the society, "*when all other measures* have proved unsuccessful."[24] The anti-abolitionists publicly announced their goal of silencing their opponents by reading their resolutions aloud and printing their meeting minutes in the *Democratic Press* three days later. This was not unusual, for anti-abolitionists frequently published the records of their meetings, and broadcast their intentions to mob their opponents in advance of their attacks—or in this case, explained them in print shortly thereafter.[25] That announcement implied to the antislavery people in Peoria that violent confrontation was a real possibility if they carried out the idea of congregating publicly.

As planned, the anti-abolitionists at the courthouse attended the February 13 antislavery meeting at the Main Street Presbyterian Church to stop the Peoria Anti-Slavery Society from forming. The local abolitionists, women and men, gathered in their humble church building. When they convened, their opponents stifled the nascent society, claiming that "antislavery principles were illegal, unconstitutional, and disorganizing, and that if [the abolitionists] would not peaceably dissolve the meeting, they would do it by violence."[26] That Monday evening, the antislavery faction was vastly outnumbered, but nonetheless attempted to conduct their business, without success. In Peoria, the anti-abolitionists had overtly silenced discussion of the nationally controversial movement to eradicate slavery.

The two bitter factions published competing narratives of the meeting. John S. Zieber, the editor of the Peoria *Democratic Press* and a member of the mob, later claimed that his group had allowed the abolitionists to go about their business after voicing their objections to any local association.[27] Both sides agreed that after a prayer led by the church's Reverend William T. Allan, the abolitionists proceeded, until their adversaries interrupted with their own resolutions. William T. Allan and his wife Irene, an Oberlin alumna, shared an active interest in abolition. They had recently moved to Peoria.[28] At the meeting, Allan disputed the anti-abolitionists' points, eliciting quiet dissent from them, until he raised the issue of African American rights. The mob would not listen to this, and interrupted Allan with "loud and boisterous yells and stamping." When he attempted to read further, the crowd cut him off with more noise. The anti-abolitionist throng curtailed freedom of assembly by shouting over the speakers, making it clear that the productive portion of their gathering was over. This yelling, and what the antislavery people called an escalating "spirit of violence" in the room, led them to adjourn. They realized the futility of proceeding in the mob's presence, and feared for their safety.

The anti-abolitionists remained in the church until all of their foes had left in disgust. Their mission accomplished, they "then gave three cheers and retired in quiet." The anti-abolitionist group thought that their show of strength had banished this menace from their town, and proven the "determination of the citizens of Peoria, that its fair fame shall not be tarnished by a public organization of a nest of negro stealers."[29] They thus branded their adversaries as thieves of human property, and scofflaws, and closed the evening with one final disruption: they sent Allan's buggy careening into the nearby lake.[30]

In a letter to the *Western Citizen*, five of the abolitionists told their version of events, arguing that while they had escaped "*personal* injury," the mob had "*rudely* and *violently*" abrogated their "INALIENABLE RIGHTS."[31] They believed that their antagonists had illegitimately curtailed their freedom of assembly. Allan characterized the evening, and the public abolition effort in Peoria, as a "fiery ordeal."[32] In that *Western Citizen* letter, the antislavery authors stated that the Peoria activists had offered no physical rebuke to their foes. They wrote, "[o]ver these defenseless females, and Christians, who will not resist evil with evil ... the 'respectable citizens' secured a glorious triumph!"[33] These authors thus constructed the attack on the Peoria abolitionists as unwarranted due to their passivity, but the reality was more complicated. While the neophyte antislavery society had not met the mob with violence, their organizing efforts meant that they had in fact begun to actively oppose their community norms. Their fellow citizens would not permit them the freedom of assembly to do so openly and safely, for their ideas appeared too hazardous and disruptive.

The mob action at Peoria galvanized abolitionism among both women and men in Illinois. By confronting unresisting men and women in a church, the Peoria crowd transgressed many activists' views of the boundaries of justifiable conduct. Local antislavery agitators convened a meeting at nearby Farmington on March 9, 1843, to discuss how Peorians had suppressed the abolitionists' freedom of assembly. The attendees denounced the silencing action and praised the local activists, particularly for their refusal to retaliate when attacked. That March in the Chicago *Western Citizen*, Mary Brown Davis cited the local mob as she proclaimed that the antislavery cause continued to progress in Peoria, despite community resistance. She called local anti-abolitionists hypocrites for violently assaulting their fellow citizens, and mocked their conduct. Davis also could not resist noting that local and statewide interest in the cause had vastly increased since the attack on the meeting, as had sympathy in the surrounding area.[34] She thus claimed that the anti-abolitionists' suppression had the opposite effect to the one they intended. Davis stood down her foes and pressed on to form a local antislavery group, as did her compatriots elsewhere in the region.

The previous spring, Washington, Illinois, had faced analogous issues when activists tried to organize and convene an abolition society. A group of their fellow citizens met to oppose their impending scheduled meeting, and verbally requested that the abolitionists refrain from gathering. They threatened violence with language very similar to that of the nearby Peoria anti-abolitionists. In response, Samuel H. Davis had defended their freedom of assembly in an editorial. He affirmed abolitionists' rights in Washington and also in Peoria itself when Owen Lovejoy came to town to hold a meeting. This antislavery minister and later politician was the brother of Elijah Lovejoy, murdered in Alton in 1837.[35] Old Northwest activists' right to congregate was a hotly contested issue, and they refused to bow to their opponents' pressure.

* * *

By invading a meeting convened to organize a mixed-gender Peoria Anti-Slavery Society, the anti-abolition group clearly aimed to control the social and political culture of their town.[36] Like those in Peoria, other mobs of the era were often well-planned, and composed of men of social and economic prominence who bore "little fear of indictment or public censure." Anti-abolitionists feared that local activists would try to change their towns, and consequently attacked them.[37] In attacks on antislavery people, local residents who sought social control implemented vigilante justice, often motivated by their political and economic milieus.[38] Old Northwest anti-abolitionists frequently found their inspiration in desire for community control and the social order. Indeed, local norms could be particularly troubled in the region, and violence was a means anti-abolitionists used to enforce these boundaries, albeit one which reformers refused to sanction themselves.

Anti-abolitionist attacks in the Old Northwest add nuance to the study of antebellum mob violence. Historians have explored this phenomenon under myriad names, including mobs, riots, lynching, vigilantism, and extralegal violence. Central to all were local community control and the threat or use of physical force. Determining the boundaries of permissible conduct—and thus whether violence can be deemed "extralegal" in a particular place and time—is challenging, and such borders were particularly fuzzy in "frontier" areas like the Old Northwest, where the legal system was rudimentary, and where people disagreed about rights.[39] While the Fifth Amendment enshrined due process in law, people applied the concept unevenly in practice, and in the 1830s and 1840s due process only restrained the federal government's ability to restrict people's rights.[40] Even as reformers argued that the Constitution guaranteed them freedom of assembly, their foes mobbed them with local sanction, guided by what they perceived to be the best interest of the community.

Mob violence and threats of it were in fact frequent tools anti-abolitionists used to stifle activists' freedom of assembly. Although historians have established that extralegal violence against reformers was common enough in the antebellum period, they have tended to isolate anti-abolitionist attacks both chronologically and regionally. The Peoria incident conformed, to a degree, to patterns of anti-abolition violence historians have observed; most such episodes occurred as a response to initial organizing efforts, and declined after 1837 due to fears of loss of white liberties.[41] This was one such initial effort, but the Old Northwest in fact remained the site of vital antislavery organizing and antiracist activism throughout the 1840s and even as late as the 1860s.[42] Concurrently, crowds continued their efforts to silence activists across the region for decades. Also, while abolitionists across the Old Northwest met with mobs upon initially organizing, those in communities that already had vibrant local movements did so as well, thanks to strongly rooted local opposition.

While Old Northwest antislavery people's experiences with mobs coincided to some extent with existing scholarly notions about the causes and functions of vigilante violence, they also differed from that of the national picture and that of the other sections.[43] The antebellum North was far from unified, and analyses that only divide the North from the South omit the distinctive nature of the antislavery movement in the Old Northwest. The limitations of North versus South comparisons are evident in historian David Grimsted's claim that northern mobs focused on property while southerners attacked both people and property.[44] While slavery's opponents faced much easier circumstances in the North than in the South, they nonetheless, even there, often had to physically battle for their freedom of assembly, particularly in the Old Northwest. Their foes attacked them, not just their property. While taking action against racism and slavery was controversial throughout the nation, it was particularly explosive in the Old Northwest, as became apparent in activists' struggles in the region. In turn, this volatile environment affected the frequency and severity of local anti-abolitionist violence, as reformers sought freedom of assembly.

Places like Peoria reveal a history of the popular, extralegal violence that Old Northwest activists often faced as they challenged the burgeoning prejudice of their era and the concerns that the region's increasing economic integration aroused. In river towns in Ohio, Indiana, and Illinois, many local residents engaged in southern trade, and consequently sought to stifle abolitionist discussion. The Mississippi River Valley's expanding market system sent crops or processed commodities to market towns and then downriver to St. Louis or New Orleans.[45] Geography and crop choice pushed residents of Indiana, Illinois, and Ohio toward this economic exchange, while Michigan's location made this trade less essential to them. In the first three states, abolitionists themselves often promoted growth and increased interaction with the "market economy," so they did not resist trade in the abstract, only the ways its conflicts of interest could limit their freedom of assembly and their ability to fight slavery. While economic and personal ties to the South were less salient for Michigan than in the northeastern states, it appears that they mattered there nonetheless.[46] In all of these states, activists found people who wished to silence them with fists or bricks, rather than permit antislavery gatherings.

Across the Old Northwest, many mob members acted not only out of economic interest, but also because they feared that antislavery and anti-racist activists sought to entrench an African American presence in their towns.[47] Indeed, their worst fears—that abolitionism would bring about heterogeneity and egalitarianism, if not racial mixing—coincided with the goals of the most radical among the reformers there.[48] Many also found women's activism on behalf of African Americans especially offensive.

* * *

Some Old Northwest individuals faced more difficulty than others in securing freedom of assembly; this was usually the case for activist women in the region, although both women and men faced efforts to prevent their meetings. Women seized a public presence in the face of particularly strong attacks on their freedom of assembly. Their communities ardently resisted when such women tried to gather to reform them. Female activists participated in both separate female and mixed-gender organizations, and their actions challenged the relationship between gender and politics. In the face of even more formidable logistical and cultural obstacles than their male counterparts encountered, they carved out a space for their reform work. Though formally excluded from politics, they took partisan stances and pushed for a larger public role than their eastern contemporaries. Also, while antagonism followed antebellum women's activism across the nation, in the Old Northwest its scope and duration was unparalleled. Antislavery women there made a powerful, fervent contribution to local reform even as they faced major hostility. As female activists fought to obtain a public voice, they claimed a political place in this unsettled polity.

A cohort of female abolitionists labored to aid African Americans, both slave and free, and stretched the boundaries of political action with their publications, meetings, and petitions. Old Northwest female antislavery organizers whose work extended from the early 1830s through the Civil War wielded great power for social change, and resisted the limitations that their social norms prescribed.

In fact, women reformers took advantage of the unsettled environment of the Old Northwest to push against the boundaries of masculinity and femininity. Even as gender stereotypes hardened in the wider culture, both women and men strategically deployed ideas about their proper social roles to justify their public work for change. Old Northwest activism in the context of this politics of exclusion warrants scholarly attention for the gender diversity it reveals. The region's obvious problems with racialized legislation and women's work against it made women especially prominent in activism there. They responded to the inequities that they saw in their society and seized their chance to change them. This was difficult, however, and these gender concerns added another complication to abolitionists' Old Northwest battles for freedom of assembly.

Female antislavery societies in Illinois in the 1840s provide a case study of the challenges Old Northwest activists faced in securing the liberty to gather freely. These women's activities catalyzed debates over antislavery tactics and who had the right to gather to participate in an increasingly politicized movement. They were important activists in the region, and reveal how this reform milieu worked, what motivated people, and the obstacles they found to their efforts to create change with antislavery organizations at the local level. In Illinois and throughout the Old Northwest, women regularly participated in antislavery and Liberty Party political activity. Most of the Illinois abolitionist organizations of the 1840s—mixed, all-male, and all-female—identified with the Liberty Party, the main national antislavery third party. As a result, Illinois women's antislavery efforts not only stretched gender roles by taking public action, but also integrated them directly into partisan politics. They boldly called for abolition and African American rights, even as their identity made this particularly challenging. They defied their exclusion from politics and publicly claimed partisan identities, all in the process of fighting slavery. A focus on local-level organizers reveals the vital activist labor women performed in smaller communities across the Old Northwest.

Even with their neighbors' violent efforts to control their towns and stifle their freedom of assembly, Illinois women would not allow anyone to derail their reform mission. They began to establish separate female antislavery organizations after the February 1843 Peoria mob attack, and demanded the right for these organizations to gather publicly. These new associations were inclusive of all women, as in Putnam County, where the new female society welcomed anyone "friendly to the anti-slavery cause" to join with them in their fight. The newly organized women lost no time in setting up their infrastructure.[49] These abolitionist women's efforts to formalize their organizations prove their commitment to public action despite community displeasure with their activism.

In Peoria, women met on July 27, 1843, in the Main Street Presbyterian Church to form a Female Anti-Slavery Society. Mary Brown Davis organized the women's meeting and provided the minutes for the *Western Citizen*. Male abolitionists attended the Reverend William Allan's opening address, but they then departed and the meeting proceeded. The women chose this male Illinois Society agent to speak to their first meeting, possibly out of a desire to adhere to gender conventions about female public speech. By having a man deliver the lecture, they could have diminished controversy at their point of initial organization, even as they asserted their right to assemble.[50]

The women of Peoria immediately created an antislavery agenda for their community. They elected officers, chose Davis as secretary, and sought to delineate their role in the town at large.[51] The women agreed that they should submit antislavery petitions to the state and national legislature, and they soon did so, and also shared their views publicly in other forums.[52]

* * *

Old Northwest activists, including the Peoria women, used their contentious local climate and freedom of assembly struggles to publicize and spread the antislavery message. When she wrote in the *Western Citizen* about the Peoria Female Society's organization, Mary Brown Davis asked other women to form female antislavery societies. She entitled her article "Character of Peoria in Some Degree Retrieved," and noted with pleasure that the women's meeting had proceeded mostly undisturbed, in contrast to that of February 13. The anti-abolitionists left the women alone, but attacked Mr. Allan and his carriage yet again in retribution for his participation in the gathering. He "had the wheels taken from his carriage and thrown into the river, and was threatened with . . . 'tar and feathers.'"[53] Davis was careful to state that Allan did not plan or take an active role in the meeting, which left the agency in female hands, even though the women had granted Allan the public speaking platform. These Illinois women, as did their sisters elsewhere, took the lead in the local fight against slavery when men confronted excessive mob danger.[54]

At least in July 1843, the Peoria anti-abolitionists appeared reluctant to physically harm female activists. This is just one way activist women used gender protections to their advantage. The female society formed with more immediate success than their male counterparts, for the effort to create a mixed or male Peoria abolitionist organization faltered until 1844, in the face of mob opposition. In this town, as with other physical battles in the Old Northwest, antislavery women reversed the gender norms by leading the vanguard action that anti-abolition mobs denied to local men.

* * *

Not content with local-level organizations, on May 23, 1844, Peoria's female abolitionists united with other women as the Illinois Female Anti-Slavery Society, a state organization affiliated with the Liberty Party. Controversy plagued its meetings from the outset. On April 25, Peoria's antislavery women, including Irene B. Allan and Mary Brown Davis, had begun to publicize the first convention of the Illinois Female Society in the *Western Citizen*. They included men in this convention, inviting "all friends of the slave, whether male or female."[55] Irene B. Allan argued that a state society would provide their cause with strength in numbers and a better way to distribute their resources.[56] Allan's characterization of the new organization was benign, but not all Illinoisans agreed with her perspective.

Women who organized meetings faced significant gender-based challenges. In order to assembly publicly, female reformers had to explain to their state's skeptical population their presence in worldly affairs and their desire to meet. A key example of this was from May 1844, when Illinois antislavery women's efforts to openly gather as a state association catalyzed debate. This controversy reveals the social consequences their opponents saw in women's public action, and gender's impact on freedom of assembly. Mr. Norris, the editor of the Chicago Whig Party paper the *Daily Journal*, harshly criticized the Peoria women for their abolitionist activities. He castigated them for stepping outside of the household with this state female society, writing:

> Shut up your 'little responsibilities,' ye mothers—initiate your husbands into the mysteries of your kitchens and larders, ye wives—and hasten to Peoria to look after the concerns of the Nation. Pay no regard to your domestic duties—they are minor considerations.

Western Citizen editor Zebina Eastman quoted from the article in the *Journal*, and then printed the women's rebuttals.[57]

The activist women fought back with Norris's own words, and argued that they had an essential public role to play in abolition. This debate before the Peoria organizing convention had broad implications, for the women responded to the attack on their organizing efforts by using elements of the restrictive separate spheres ideology in a liberating way. This was just one of a number of instances where Old Northwest antislavery women's public activism contradicted domestic ideology by rejecting the separation of women's and men's worlds.[58] Mary Brown Davis claimed that women's forays into politics enhanced their ability to perform their "responsibilities." " . . . Anti-slavery women," she wrote to the *Western Citizen*, "are the best wives, the best mothers, and the most useful part of the community."[59] In her view, activism complemented women's domestic obligations. At the same time that Davis embraced these traditional duties, she argued that women's public work was morally necessary. The aforementioned "Maria" also expressed anger and frustration at Norris's mockery as she refuted him, by asserting that women must, on principle, take action against slavery.[60]

In the newspaper debate, as in their response to anti-abolition mobs, these Illinois women manipulated Norris's gendered language of sex difference, and used it to justify their antislavery meetings and actions. With their words, Illinois female abolitionists vowed a commitment to conventional domesticity, but also discursively accommodated and enabled a range of actual political activity. Some women deployed stereotypes about women's particular aptitudes to rationalize their reform work and defend their right to gather. Old Northwest antislavery women developed a unique sense of female strength, firmly rooted in their activism on behalf of others; they manipulated, challenged, and disregarded the mores of their era.

The rhetoric and political activity of Old Northwest antislavery women complicates the understanding of antebellum women's public action.

While they did not seek the vote, they behaved in ways outside the norms of female passivity and non-partisanship.[61] Their most groundbreaking actions and words troubled the relation between women and politics. Over time, these women found that their moral commitment to eradicate slavery required them to contest some gender norms. They avoided suffrage, but nonetheless spoke out in a variety of settings, confronted authority, and broke laws that they regarded as unjust, such as fugitive slave legislation. Complicating their outspokenness, their moral stance allowed them to claim their activity as appropriate for women, while nonetheless reinforcing the social expectations that placed women at the moral center of society.

Despite the ongoing controversy, numerous women nonetheless attended the 1844 Illinois Female Society convention at Peoria. This meeting coincided with that of the Illinois Society, as the two organizations deliberately scheduled separate and parallel women's and general annual meetings that year and the next. Forty-five women attended, and there read and unanimously adopted a constitution, planned business for the upcoming year, and elected a board of officers. Davis rejoiced in the *Western Citizen* that the meeting went very well and remained largely undisturbed, despite the earlier mob activity: "Truly, we may say, "*Peoria is redeemed.*"[62] This success shows that women's persistent efforts to secure freedom of assembly could prove fruitful in the end, and that they used controversies to their own purposes to spread the antislavery message. Abolitionist women—in Illinois as in the neighboring states—pushed to engage in a range of public action. Illinois was hardly alone in hosting a cohort of dedicated female abolitionists, and women's actions brought them into public life and overlapped state boundaries.[63] A main tactic used by organizers of antislavery meetings including these women was the petition; with this method, activists could continue their reforms even after their meetings had ended. In this way, they gathered together their names on paper to show their support for a cause, without necessarily putting their bodies at risk.

* * *

Like their stalwart defense of their right to activism, the petitions that grew out of antislavery meetings were another strategy Old Northwest reformers used to evade attacks on both women's and men's freedom of assembly. They were central to their antislavery efforts, and women found them especially vital since they had a small number of political options; female activists' delimited circumstances and few political rights drove them to this method of influencing their legislators. Dating back to feudal France and Russia, the petition was the traditional means for "subordinate" people to claim rights without violating the parameters of their social roles.[64] Petitions did not require public gathering, and thus could avoid some of the controversy meetings elicited, especially for women. In her study of national antislavery women's petitions, Susan Zaeske writes that by petitioning, women pushed beyond the usual boundaries of petitions as a deferential form and used them to "justify" their "collective exercise" of this political tool.[65] With this choice, they also demonstrated the local and individual initiative that characterized Old Northwest activism.

As was true in the East, petition campaigns became a common technique among Old Northwest abolitionists in the 1830s, and one that enmeshed them in a First Amendment battle. This region produced large numbers of antislavery petitions. In 1836, the volume of petitions to Congress had become so high that proslavery representatives pushed through the first "gag rule," which ordered the tabling of all petitions to the House of Representatives that addressed slavery. Congress followed this law with others, and blocked most antislavery petitions until 1844. An implicit gag rule also prevailed in the Senate from 1836 to 1850, when senators routinely tabled petitions from the North that mentioned slavery.[66] In the House, among other representatives, John Quincy Adams put up a spirited fight to obtain a hearing for both male and female petitioners.[67] Abolitionists extensively critiqued this limitation of their freedom of expression with claims that the gag rule violated their First Amendment rights.[68] The gag rule also flouted the tenet of natural law that obligated leaders to take delivery of and address petitions from their constituents.[69] Activists persisted in submitting thousands of petitions, but the actual power of this right was consequently very limited at this time.

The link between petitions and meetings existed on another level, too, for locally, Old Northwest activists used their meetings to protest against the gag rule and its infringement of their constitutional rights. As early as 1838, the Ohio Society asserted antislavery freedoms with a resolution that thanked Adams and Thomas Morris for defending the petition right.[70] This pattern persisted into the 1840s, for antislavery activists extended their appreciation to Ohio Whig representative Joshua Giddings for his opposition to the gag rule. One place where this happened was at the 1842 Bureau County Liberty Convention in Illinois, where the attendees denounced slave-owners' attacks on what they deemed "the dearest rights of freemen," including petitioning, "free debate and discussion."[71] Liberty men again cited Adams for his outspoken actions, as in the Knox Liberty Convention that April.[72] Adams and the Liberty men were not the only protestors, for women felt the gag rule's impact keenly, as they lacked the vote.[73] They, too, dissented from it and continued to petition in large numbers, and some among them broadened their efforts to include protests against the "Black Laws."

* * *

Old Northwest female abolitionist organizations' petitions stretched the limitations of their era in another sense: they used them to create pathbreaking arguments against racial prejudice. They evaded attacks on their freedom of assembly with assertions that they had a direct relation to the state and a clear right to activism. Illinois antislavery women used petitions to openly express their political opinions and views on race. In 1843, the women of the Putnam County Society rushed to sign one such petition to Congress and the Illinois State Legislature that opposed the "Black Laws." They circulated it successfully, obtaining 163 signatures, and stated that they would submit further petitions to abolish all laws that "strengthen the hands of the slaveholders."[74] The Illinois women's petition efforts did not end there, for in 1847 Davis led the Illinois Female Society in a concerted effort for a statewide women's petition to repeal their "Black Laws."[75] Their sisters in Indiana joined in similar efforts in their state by defying the restrictive racialized laws endemic there.[76] These petitions, with their emphasis on transforming local racial laws, exemplify women's more radical action that grew out of Old Northwest antislavery activism. This was a progressive local development, not, as historian Beth Salerno claims, a sign of the decentralization, even declension, of a national movement.[77] Regional activists responded to the most pressing conditions they noticed, and at times they established different priorities—in this case, the local plague of the "Black Laws" drew Old Northwest antislavery women's immediate attention.

In this region, women's antislavery and anti-prejudice activism demonstrates that antebellum non-suffrage politics, far from being stagnant and staid, could have radical potential to improve the racial order. With their struggles for access to politics and public life, these women joined the larger battle for Old Northwest freedom of expression. As such, they reveal a new perspective on these struggles, one of people ostensibly on the margins of politics who claimed, nonetheless, to wield "an almost irresistible power" for change.[78]

* * *

The moment of female societies in the Old Northwest was significant, but of short duration, as is visible in the limited tenure there of female abolitionists' separate public presence. There was a steep climb and decline of women's participation in these organizations, as seen in Illinois from 1842 to 1845. After their organizational spike in 1843, the Illinois Female Society met in 1846 and 1847, but with diminished attendance. Previous scholars have tied this shift in Illinois antislavery women's participation in the movement to the growth of the Liberty Party at the expense of immediatist organizations.[79] Since many of these women identified with the Liberty Party throughout the 1840s and found some acceptance for this (as seen with Davis's Liberty Party columns in the *Western Citizen*), depicting the party itself as the culprit is unlikely to tell the whole story.

In the latter years, between 1845 and 1847, there was a small upsurge in calls for women's participation in the Liberty movement, particularly in Michigan, where women established the greatest number of female societies. Women's involvement there in organized abolition nonetheless declined as electoral politics obtained greater sway, the antislavery press focused on men's activities, and the Liberty Party fell apart.[80] Following some sporadic activism in Indiana until 1849, the evidence of separate female antislavery societies in the Old Northwest had vanished by 1852.[81]

Contrary to historians' tendency to consider Old Northwest activists as a less advanced form of their eastern counterparts whose organizations followed in their footsteps, the increased divisiveness that supposedly pushed women out was not just a result of the region catching up with the East or finally gaining its attention.[82] This argument places no agency in the hands of Old Northwest abolitionists. In places like Illinois, activists did squabble over women's roles beginning at the time of the schism in 1840, but they had reached less consensus in their outcomes and attitudes on that issue—as was the case with others—than had the East. They diversified their efforts, but women hardly became invisible in Old Northwest antislavery and anti-prejudice activism. In small numbers with disproportionate strength, they joined forces with men and carried on their work in other forums, including newspapers and public lectures.

* * *

Abolitionists' exertions to protect their freedom of assembly in the Old Northwest prove that, despite substantial risks, a broad cohort of activists in the region organized meetings and asserted their right to public action for their cause. These local organizers—women and men—publicized and spread their movement using a range of public methods, including holding meetings and forming organizations. Old Northwest activists lobbied state and federal governments about slavery and the "Black Laws." They used petitions to shape their government, and those who could, used the vote. Freedom of assembly and public gatherings like meetings and lectures were essential to all of these activities. In their quest to express themselves publicly, reformers had to grapple with their foes' other efforts to limit their liberties. For them, freedom of the press was no easier to secure than freedom of assembly, and indeed, formed the focus of a major contest in the region.

4 / "The Palladium of Our Liberties": Freedom of the Press in the Old Northwest, 1837–1848

I have long regarded the conductors of the public press, as a class of persons who have assumed upon themselves a fearful responsibility . . . their influence is powerfully seen and felt, for weal or for woe to the human family.

—ARNOLD BUFFUM IN *THE PROTECTIONIST*, JANUARY 1, 1841

In the antebellum era, the newspaper was a central tool for transforming the nation, and freedom of the press was thus essential to activists. The members of the Ohio American Anti-Slavery Society who gathered at Cadiz in October 1842 proclaimed abolitionist periodicals a vital means to awaken others to the ills of slavery. Newspapers could publicize both slavery's true "nature and influence" and the human and material costs of its continuance.[1] These activists believed that such publications comprised an integral part of the public expression and expansion of the antislavery agenda in the Old Northwest, and their editors indeed took on a "fearful responsibility." Local reformers consequently prioritized protecting and funding antislavery newspapers in the region to help them carry on their work.[2] Abolitionists of both sexes took advantage of this burgeoning forum, and relied upon newspapers both to make converts and to justify their public action. Newspapers from both East and West were key to activists' ability to exchange information, tactics, and energy with one another. They—and the concurrent press revolution of the era—were vital tools reformers needed to cross the miles that separated them.

Antislavery publications became the locus of struggles for freedom of expression and human rights in the Old Northwest. As the battleground of ideas, the region was rife with conflict over the right to publish abolitionist arguments and advertisements in newspapers. These disputes grew out of the fact that Old Northwest antislavery activists and their foes interpreted the American Revolution's legacy in wildly diverging ways. Bitter factions disputed the founders' intentions regarding free expression, and each used them for their own purposes.

Men and women in the Old Northwest fought to protect the press, a crucial component of the antislavery publicity machine, against challenges that were unique to their tense local climate. Anti-abolitionists, often trying to defend their political parties from turmoil, suppressed freedom of the press through violence and economic pressure, while reformers expanded contemporary understandings of this as a guaranteed right. In three bustling commercial hubs in Illinois and Ohio, from 1837 through 1848, press freedom for antislavery advocates remained a hotly contested issue. Local residents fought over which ideas could enter the public sphere, one affected not only by partisanship, racism, and social stratification, but also by the growing trade systems that enmeshed the region in southern commerce. The debate over freedom of the press in these states was no abstract discussion of citizenship privileges, for it was deeply bound up with the politics of the era. Anti-abolitionists—who ranged from community leaders, to party stalwarts, to prominent tradesmen—saw that inflammatory journalism could undermine the slave system and the stability of the political parties. Both slavery and those parties needed to sweep criticism of the "peculiar institution" under the rug.

For abolitionists in this isolated region, newspapers played a principal role in transmitting a shared sense of identity, a sense of membership in a community. They facilitated commonalities and bonds among people who were often not in direct contact with one another, but who shared values.[3] As such, newspapers were important cohesive links people used to connect their networks across great distances, determine strategy, and debate underlying principles. While they faced vociferous opposition, they also received funds and support from outside sympathizers. Thus joined with one another and able to buoy one another's spirits, Old Northwest antislavery people remained committed to their mission of organization and conversion.

* * *

The press was of vital importance to antislavery advocates as it sustained their movement over large distances and gave them another public voice. They and their opponents fought hard to control publications at a time when both the press and literacy were rapidly expanding in the United States. From 1801 to 1833, the number of newspapers in the nation and its territories increased by 600 percent. In 1830, the total daily news circulation was approximately 78,000, and by 1840, it had ballooned to 300,000.[4] The numbers give only a partial picture, however, for contentious debates over press freedom dated back to the nation's youth; the founders had addressed it in the debate over the Bill of Rights in 1787.[5] Nationally, abolitionists had fought for this freedom since the early 1830s, but their struggles in the Old Northwest were unlike those of older eastern cities.[6] These growing communities had tenuous but important commercial ties with the South, and fiery local political contests shaped the character of their arguments over freedom of the press.

Technological and organizational innovations ushered along the press revolution in the Old Northwest and across the country, and these enabled abolitionists to expand their public presence. The successive developments of the iron press and the increased use of the steam-driven press made printing an easier task, as did improvements in papermaking technology. Infrastructure developments—the railroad and, after 1844, the telegraph—also accelerated the distribution of news across the nation.[7] Abolitionist editors asked itinerant lecturers and subscription agents to disperse their papers, and agents collected money and issued subscriptions for both local and national papers in the Old Northwest.[8]

By these means, the antislavery press connected local activists with their counterparts across the nation. Old Northwesterners read eastern papers and vice versa, and expanding numbers of newspapers emerged to push particular agendas. After 1830, these papers played a crucial role in the circulation and promulgation of antislavery ideology in the region. In 1842, the Chicago *Western Citizen* revealed its view of the newspaper's substantial efficacy as a propaganda device: "the thoughts that are in its columns may influence ten thousand for good, and produce effects which volumes of essays, sermons, or narratives, could not effect, and especially where they could never reach."[9] Both local newspapers like the *Citizen* and national ones soon served as tools for determining strategy and debating underlying principles. Antislavery papers gathered new support for their cause, and formed a vital component of the communication between local, state, and national reformers.[10] They were central to spreading activism across the antebellum North, and joined in fiery disputes that encompassed a range of participants.[11]

Antebellum African Americans were no mere passive objects of reform, for they also wrote and published antislavery newspapers. In addition to male editors active across the nation—including Samuel E. Cornish, Frederick Douglass, and Martin Delany—Mary Ann Shadd Cary, the peripatetic educator, lawyer, and editor of the *Provincial*

Freeman, moved in and out of Canada and the Old Northwest in the 1850s.[12] She focused her publication efforts north of the border, however. Most Old Northwest entrants into the battle for press freedom were white, as the case studies here reflect, and as was also true nationally.

The newspapers' increasing prevalence and efficiency of distribution in this era allowed people to rapidly exchange essential information that was often of a partisan or otherwise slanted nature. While antislavery newspapers attracted disproportionate wrath and violence, the overtly ideological content in their pages was common for the press of the time. Antebellum American newspapers and news editors usually adopted partisan affiliations, and papers provided the most convenient and accessible source of political information for widely dispersed populations.[13] In one such case, the Chicago *Western Citizen*, which the members of the Liberty Party in the Old Northwest read widely, made no secret of its partisan affiliation. For the election of August 1843, the paper printed a list of congressional candidates with the Liberty ticket in large type, while the Whig and Democrat candidates appeared in smaller type under the heading "Pro-Slavery Ticket."[14] Some Old Northwest editors held press freedom convictions that meant they printed antislavery perspectives even when they did not share them, but all labored in a tense, often dangerous, environment.

Partisan newspapers that spoke for the major political parties and reform publications like the antislavery newspapers differed in important ways. The former had both funding and influence over their message from advertisers and centralized party structures that resisted risking voter support by advocating unpopular perspectives. They also had much broader circulation. The latter had less consistent financial support and more specific targeted audiences, both of which left them freer to put forth controversial messages—and more endangered by community hostility.

* * *

Like their fellow activists the local organizers, antislavery publishers and journalists tenaciously fought to protect their freedom of the press, for the newspaper was indispensable to the expansion of the antislavery ranks. In this weighty battle, the very vitality of their movement and its principles were at stake. When mobs and fellow newspapers attacked antislavery papers to suppress them, they endangered not only the exchange of activist information but also the movement's nourishment and expansion. On both the local and national levels, spreading abolitionist ideas would have been impossible without the press and its capacity to organize, coordinate, and extend antislavery networks.

While antebellum people expected partisan commentary in their newspapers, many nonetheless drew the line at antislavery perspectives, as the attempts to stifle controversial voices in the Old Northwest press reveal. The human rights agenda of reformers proved unpalatable to the sensibilities of many in the region. Seen in this way, local efforts to stifle discourse about abolition in public print emerge as part of the larger national trend to silence the struggle over slavery and criticism of the major national parties. For abolitionists, freedom of the press was more than a means to convey their message. Instead it transformed into a parallel cause for which they willingly battled. While some of activists' notoriety was not of their choosing, they often consciously aroused explosive responses from their communities with their rhetoric and actions. Indeed, they took part in a highly contested effort to expand African American rights and freedom of expression for all.[15] Old Northwest abolitionists crafted innovative arguments for their right to voice unpopular sentiments, and risked their personal safety by advocating divisive positions in hostile situations. Like other advocates who stirred up rights debates beginning in the 1830s, they melded liberalism, republicanism, and evangelical religion into a larger rationale for universal rights.[16] Across organizational lines, they harnessed these ideas to overtly political arguments that claimed the common humanity of all people. Newspapers played an integral role in promulgating these rights arguments.

Old Northwest antislavery proponents intimately tied their efforts to protect the press to their increasingly expansive use of the First Amendment in self-defense. As early as 1835, the American Society asserted that freedom of the press was an inheritable right, but did not cite any legal authority; this right was a new creation. English common law had given the American colonists few protections for press freedom, and indeed, people could censor or ban works after they had been published. Even in the mid-eighteenth century, printers in the colonies used the courts to fight for the right to print controversial material. In the revolutionary era, many Americans came to value freedom of the press, and included it in nine of the eleven state constitutions they passed then, but the federal constitution lacked any specific mention of freedom of the press until the Bill of Rights.[17] In its 1835 address, the American Society claimed as "American citizens" that freedom of the press was one of the "blessings we have inherited from our fathers," which they intended to pass on.[18]

That interpretation appealed to an ever-growing constituency after the national controversy over the gag rule in the House of Representatives began in 1836. The gag rule increased antislavery people's political isolation and reinforced the opposition of the major political parties to their rights, for northern Democrats joined southern Democrats and Whigs in their support for these silencing measures.[19] Desire for press freedom expanded even more following the mobbing and killing of antislavery editor Elijah Lovejoy at Alton, Illinois in 1837.[20]

Both the gag rule and the Lovejoy incident clarified that antislavery people faced threats to their freedom of expression from proslavery southern state governments, but also from legislatures and ordinary citizens across the nation. Extralegal violence, in particular, put shadowy concerns over liberty under a glaring spotlight. As was the case with freedom of assembly, abolitionists and their allies conceived of these new rights as both federal/constitutional rights and as "basic human right[s] that state constitutions protected."[21] Activists grappled their way toward a sweeping definition of guaranteed constitutional rights.[22] When abolitionists' freedom of expression came under fire, they gained many new recruits to the cause as well as supporters for this new, broader understanding of their rights.

Antislavery people came to understand that they could use mob attacks strategically to strengthen their claims that both the institution of slavery and its constitutional protections threatened democracy. Some resorted to physical means for self-protection, while others retained nonresistant (nonviolent) methods.[23] The conflicts in Alton and Peoria (in Illinois) and Cambridge, Ohio, are provocative examples of Old Northwest antislavery persistence and self-defense. They also show that anti-abolitionists, too, saw the press as central to the expansion of antislavery sentiment, as became clear from their efforts to suppress it across the region.

* * *

The murder of editor and Presbyterian minister Elijah Parish Lovejoy constituted the final event in a chain of conflict that extended back to his early attempts to print the religious newspaper, the *Observer*, in Alton. As the escalating tension in this Mississippi River town revealed, advocacy of unpopular positions in a hostile environment could radicalize individuals. Maine-born Elijah Lovejoy was not initially an abolitionist when he moved to St. Louis and first began publishing that religious newspaper there.[24] Missouri slaveholders always saw him as an abolitionist, and over the course of 1834 and 1835 that description became increasingly accurate. Growing exposure to the realities of slavery and its effects—especially on his press freedom—changed him, and he gradually incorporated more immediate antislavery arguments into his paper.[25] Lovejoy was not alone in this trajectory of conversion, for across the North repression of abolitionists' rights, including freedom of the press, won over people who were opposed or indifferent before the crisis. In some cases, this was out of self-interest, as they believed that such silencing and gag rules threatened white people's rights.

By the summer of 1835, St. Louis's slaveholders grew intolerant of any discussion of slavery. The rising tide of anti-abolition sentiment threatened to engulf Lovejoy, and his allies counseled him to desist or depart, but even then he steadfastly defended his right to press freedom. Eventually, his opponents forced him to leave St. Louis, after he condemned a lynch mob that had burned Francis McIntosh to death. McIntosh was a free man of mixed race ancestry who had killed an officer in the process of resisting arrest. When Lovejoy denounced McIntosh's murder, local residents expelled him to Alton "under the threat of personal injury." Lovejoy moved there, across the river from St. Louis, in July 1836. His reputation preceded him, and upon his arrival, anti-abolition citizens immediately dumped his press into the river, quickly displaying their opinions on press freedom.[26] He ordered a new press, certain he should persist in printing the paper in his new town. The young minister was determined to pursue his chosen path, regardless of the consequences, and his allies supported this position.

Even in Alton, locals strongly opposed abolition, but Lovejoy refused to temper his press freedom or activist agenda. He extolled the correctness of his approach in his Alton *Observer* that September. If his foes took away the right of "FREE DISCUSSION," he explained in the language of universal rights, then "we have nothing left to struggle for."[27] His growing notoriety aided in the recruitment of other Illinois abolitionists. Having decided that Illinois needed a state organization, he issued a call in the *Observer* on July 6, 1837, for an Illinois State Anti-Slavery Society. Despite a positive reception among other abolitionists, many of his fellow residents of Alton abhorred this move. On July 11, his opponents convened a town meeting to oppose his organizing efforts, and demanded that he cease local antislavery activity.[28] Then, as later, Lovejoy refused to back down.

In August and September, Lovejoy encountered further problems in his new home. First, a mob of eight to ten "respectable" Alton men attempted to tar and feather him, and while they ultimately released him unharmed, that night they nonetheless destroyed his press for the second time. Lovejoy continued to print about abolition, and the next month, the mayor himself watched while a "quiet and gentlemanly mob" destroyed a third press. By this time Lovejoy had captured the attention of allies outside of Alton; following the destruction of the first three presses, newspapers discussed him and he received supportive letters and money from across the state.[29]

At the time, Alton had a new charter that only provided for ill-realized government and law enforcement. In areas like this that lacked formal legal institutions, citizens on occasion relied on vigilante justice.[30] Law enforcement in the era was rudimentary, but abolitionists repeatedly demanded protection for their rights. The regulatory system that did exist was often biased, for governments did not typically pay locally elected constables to stop crimes in progress or to keep the peace. Municipal authorities thus had little motivation to take such actions, especially when, as was the case with abolitionists, "the victims of crime or disorder were unpopular minorities."[31] Control over community norms thus often fell into the hands of the people themselves. In Alton, this lack of enforcement for press freedom had disastrous consequences.

* * *

Lovejoy's antislavery commitment deepened further as he and his loved ones repeatedly came into direct confrontation with anti-abolitionists. October 1837 proved an eventful month both in his life and in Alton. Early that month, while Lovejoy was visiting his wife's family in St. Charles, Missouri, 23 miles northwest of St. Louis, another mob attacked him. After he had preached twice against slavery in a local church, angry residents entered his mother-in-law's house and beat him severely, despite the efforts of his wife, mother-in-law, and sister-in-law to defend him. His wife Celia Ann "was smiting them in the face with her hands . . . and telling them that they must first take her before they should have her husband."[32] Her actions prove that protecting her spouse's safety and press freedom were inextricable. Like other women in the Old Northwest, she physically defended a man from an anti-abolitionist attack.[33] This assault also demonstrated that Lovejoy's notoriety so inflamed his foes that they would beat him even if it meant possibly injuring women in the process. Back in Alton, on October 24 a group of prominent citizens met in the Presbyterian Church to form a colonization society. This was a deliberate effort to oppose local abolition. They denounced Lovejoy as divisive, in contrast to colonization's "beneficial" uniting effects.[34] This alternative effort failed to quash the state antislavery society, because Lovejoy and his allies were determined to exercise their freedom of expression and to take action.

On October 26, the State Anti-Slavery Convention held its inaugural meeting in Alton as planned, a public display of Illinois abolitionists' solidarity with Lovejoy's ongoing efforts. The members deemed themselves the "friends of *free discussion*," and thus explicitly grounded their right to organize in the struggle for liberty of expression. Nonetheless, local anti-abolitionists repeatedly infiltrated their meetings and advanced pro-slavery resolutions. The antislavery group realized that their antagonists outnumbered them, and so decided to clandestinely reconvene their meeting at the home of the Reverend Theodore B. Hurlbut. There the new society finally managed to hold its organizing meeting in peace. They voted to support Lovejoy in the continued publication of the *Observer* in Alton. Concerned with both civil liberties and the national stain of slavery, the newly organized society combated attempts to silence abolitionism, and overtly justified forming an immediatist society by arguing that the entire country had a stake in these issues. No matter the costs of such an outspoken position, they argued against what they called "fetters" of the mind. The new Illinois Society also struggled against bias and for absolute equality of rights for all men, aiming to "remov[e] public prejudice."[35] They claimed for themselves, for the moment, the same adherence to nonviolence that they advocated for slaves. Events in Alton soon brought their commitment to those principles into question.

At the Alton meeting, it became clear that Lovejoy was not the only person whose adoption of press freedom grew out of efforts to organize against slavery. Much as Lovejoy's trials had radicalized him, his co-members claimed that they had doubted the necessity of a society until they had viewed the virulence of their opposition, and had seen "that some organized systematic effort, was absolutely necessary to save our own liberties from the ruthless hands of unprincipled men." This threat was real, for they knew that a fourth press for Lovejoy's *Observer* would soon arrive, funded by sympathetic allies in the community and abroad. They planned to store it in the warehouse of merchants Benjamin Godfrey and Winthrop S. Gilman.[36] Anticipating their future difficulties, they declared the legality of their public abolitionist actions. To them, violence seemed so likely that they wrote bluntly: "No one has any right to hinder us by law or by force."[37] This assertion would not go unchallenged.

Several days later on October 30, armed abolitionists raised local tempers as they guarded a speech Lovejoy's fellow Illinois Society organizer the Reverend Edward Beecher gave at the Alton Presbyterian Church. Born in 1803 to Lyman and Roxana Beecher, Edward was the brother of Harriet Beecher Stowe and Catharine Beecher. President of Illinois College in Jacksonville since 1832, Beecher had become an outspoken advocate of "free speech and free press," as he proved by helping to guard Lovejoy's press the night before his death.[38] Anti-abolitionists threw a stone into the meeting, but the reformers there were prepared. William Tanner called to attention the assembled members of an informal but armed abolitionist protection company who soon "flanked" the door.[39] Beecher finished his speech without further violence, one small victory for the abolitionists. This triumph granted a modicum of legitimacy to their brinksmanship by demonstrating that their threat to defend themselves was sufficient to stop an attack.

* * *

The anti-abolitionists publicly and vocally debated Lovejoy and his allies. On November 2, a large meeting at the counting room of John Hogan and Company continued to dispute local press freedom. Hogan, the vice president of the colonization society, argued against Lovejoy and his antislavery compatriots. Edward Beecher, Winthrop S. Gilman, and Lovejoy himself defended abolition and press freedom. Gilman declared that every citizen had the right to "speak, write, or print his opinions on any subject." John Hogan subsequently presented a disingenuous argument that Lovejoy had agreed to cease advocating abolition upon moving to Alton.[40] Hogan himself later admitted that Lovejoy had made no such promise, but Lovejoy's opponents repeated this assertion nonetheless. Many local residents would have preferred that this had been the case, for it allowed them to denounce him as a meddling outsider and as an unreliable man who failed to keep his word.[41] This was a specious claim, but they repeated it all the same.

At that same debate, Lovejoy eloquently defended his actions, citing universal rights and asking for protection from the community. He revealed his and his family's fears for their safety, but noted that he would not stand down even if it entailed dying for the causes of abolition and press freedom. The civil authorities present there argued that they could not stop mobs from silencing Lovejoy, and the mayor himself stated that he disapproved of the editor for bringing slavery, abolition, and press freedom into public discussion in Alton.[42] With their continual persecution of Lovejoy, Alton's anti-abolitionists denied he was entitled to print his views. In response, Lovejoy invoked "universal, abstract rights" and adhered to the religiously based higher law doctrine.[43] Anti-abolitionists vowed that they would control Alton public discourse, and they found license to attack Lovejoy in the mayor's acquiescence and willingness to blame him for local tensions.

* * *

Elijah Lovejoy's fourth printing press arrived at Alton late in the evening of November 6, 1837, on the steamer *Missouri Fulton*. The supporters of the embattled minister and printer placed the press in Godfrey and Gilman's warehouse under their own armed watch. By 10 p.m., they could no longer ignore the swelling crowd outside of the warehouse. The mass soon grew to between 150 and 200 rioters, of whom 50 to 80 were armed. From inside, merchant and warehouse owner Winthrop Gilman proclaimed that the defenders of the warehouse would stand their ground, they would "protect their property, and that serious consequences might ensue" should the mob attempt to enter the warehouse. In his post-riot letter to the Democratic Party paper, the Alton *Spectator*, Mayor John M. Krum recalled the members of the mob stating that they wanted the press, and that although they "did not wish to injure any person," they *would* destroy it.[44]

The mayor and other unnamed "civil authorities" made ineffective efforts to stop the mob. Mayor Krum, himself a Democrat, claimed that they could not separate the crowd due to the assailants' superior numbers: "No means were at my control . . . by which the mob could be dispersed and the loss of life and the shedding of blood prevented."[45] Krum and his colleagues made no other attempt to help the men under siege in the warehouse.[46]

The mob fired upon the building and attempted to force entry into it. A young carpenter in the crowd outside, Lyman Bishop, was the first to die, taking a bullet from an abolitionist in a defensive counterattack. Following Bishop's death, there was a short lull followed by the mob's renewed onslaught.[47] The anti-abolitionists then set the roof of the warehouse afire, and Lovejoy met his death from four bullets. Even after the voice of abolition had been silenced, the crowd was not satisfied, and refused to disband.

After Lovejoy died, the defenders of the warehouse fled, and the mob destroyed the press. A large crowd of men entered the building, and "threw the press upon the wharf, where it was broken in pieces and thrown into the river." Finally contented with the deed's completion, the mob left the other property in the warehouse unharmed. They then departed, not acknowledging in their actions that two men and the freedom of the press had met their demise that night.[48] Local courts never tried or convicted anyone for the deaths of Lovejoy or Bishop, although they did indict men on both sides of the conflict for the crime of rioting.[49]

* * *

After the incident at Alton, abolitionists both locally and nationally had a horrific example of where conflicts over their right to freedom of expression could lead. Many told a narrative of martyrdom and of Alton's brutality and degeneracy. Others saw a more universal story of the slave system's influence in the river town as symbolizing the institution's hold on the nation; to them, Alton meant that slavery's survival relied on the silencing of dissent.

Lovejoy's death forced many abolitionists to question their attitudes to violence. He was not the first immediate abolitionist in the region to reject the common precept of passive nonresistance. Among his predecessors were participants in an 1836 meeting of the Ohio Society at Granville, who used clubs to drive away a mob that attacked them. In effect, Old Northwest antislavery people rarely adhered in practice to absolute nonresistance, especially since their foes so frequently assaulted them. Most abolitionists were ambivalent, but respected Lovejoy's choice to arm in his own defense, even as some condemned and others lauded his actions.[50]

This incident constitutes a justifiably maligned chapter in Illinois history. Its significance is not under dispute here, but its usual interpretation is, for even recent accounts of the events at Alton privilege glorifying the individual man as martyr over exploring the reasons why a press freedom debate led to Lovejoy's death. Myths of the Lovejoy murder do little to illuminate the local political culture in which this episode of anti-abolitionist violence occurred.[51]

Omitted from virtually all readings of Lovejoy's "martyrdom," as both contemporaries and later historians called it, is any sense of Alton's particular social or political climate.[52] When contrasted with related events a mere six years later, upstate in Peoria, Alton reveals that in the Old Northwest, geography determined neither actions nor ideology. While Illinois was a northern free state, the relationship between place and political climate was complex. Support for human bondage and opposition to fighting it thrived well outside of the South. The ideological border between an antislavery North and a pro-slavery South lacked definition in the young states of the Old Northwest, and the idea of clear sectional division emerges, upon closer analysis, as both arbitrary and unsatisfactory.

Any attempt to explain conflict over abolition in antebellum Illinois requires consideration of local political operations. Alton and Peoria's prominent citizens' efforts to suppress antislavery views in the press were but two instances in a history of conflict over the right to promulgate such views in the Old Northwest. These altercations represent a pattern of local contestation over abolitionists' rights that continued through the 1840s and beyond.

Upon revisiting the 1843 anti-abolition assault in Peoria, it is evident that while in the intervening years since Lovejoy's death, antislavery people had broadened their strategies to include political abolition, this made them no more popular. Political antislavery formally organized with the Liberty Party in 1840, but had little quantitative impact in Illinois. The Democrats maintained overwhelming control of the state from the 1830s until the rise of the Republicans after 1854. Still, the Liberty Party's foray into politics, if anything, made it more dangerous to oppose slavery publicly, especially in 1843, when the next year's presidential election weighed heavily on many partisan minds. While the Liberty Party never actually posed a numerical threat, in pockets of Illinois it succeeded in disseminating its message quite effectively, to the point where, in 1844, the state hosted 8 out of the 28 counties in the country where the Liberty Party attained over 10 percent of the vote.[53] This shift was hardly welcomed by all. In the era's closely contested elections, the party's ability to siphon off even this small percentage of voters made the major parties want to shut down the Liberty Party—and silence abolitionists in general. These developments strongly informed the situation in Peoria.

In February 1843, a faction of Peoria's prominent citizens sought to stifle the local antislavery presence. This conflict subsequently exploded into another fiery press freedom battle that local partisan politics exacerbated. Peoria lacked anything approaching consensus on the contentious issues of abolition and the racial basis of civil rights, and the mainstream parties wished to suppress dissent. When the abolitionists gathered in a Peoria church, their opponents shut down their meeting in an attempt to repress local antislavery organization. A mob curtailed freedom of expression in that town without opposition from the larger community, apart from their ally in the press, Samuel H. Davis.

The debate in this Illinois River town arose out of the antagonistic cultures in the state—and in the region—in the 1830s and 1840s. As an embattled region that bordered the South and often shared in its commercial fate, the Old Northwest was at the front lines of debates over abolition and racial equality. This local battle over antislavery rights was but one flare-up in an extended Illinois controversy that dated back to Lovejoy's pioneering efforts in the state. In contrast, in Peoria, the muzzling of the press in the 1840s, while violent, never extended to mortal injury. The conflicts there prove that activists who lived in the antislavery battleground continued to fiercely resist being silenced with assertive rights arguments, and the lower degree of violence there facilitated their ongoing efforts.

In Illinois, as in other parts of the Old Northwest, people played out national fights about slavery, abolition, and party politics on the local level by arguing about freedom of expression. In Peoria, the contest over slavery molded local political agendas, and party lines mandated suppressing antislavery discussion; in fact, the national political parties' demands to stifle this divisive subject increased friction in the region. Notwithstanding prominent citizens' efforts to filter local-level discourse, evidence of contestation and dissent on the issues of race and abolition leaked through. This conflict of interests contributed to confrontation and violence. Throughout the region, concern for party messages, localism, social order, racist ideology, and the call of commercial profits created a permissive attitude toward extralegal violence, which hampered activists' abilities to avert attacks on press freedom.

* * *

When considered in the light of the better-known 1837 incident of anti-abolitionist violence at Alton, the forcible stifling of abolitionism in Peoria appears restrained because it did not involve fatalities. While the Alton incident culminated in an armed standoff and the deaths of Elijah Lovejoy and Lyman Bishop—one extreme outcome of abolitionist organizing in an adverse environment—Peoria's anti-abolitionists secured their victories largely without bloodshed. This contrast speaks to the disparate levels of antislavery assertiveness in the two towns, and to significant differences in the resulting levels of violence.

The incidents at Peoria in the 1840s belie the findings of historians who claim that gradual withdrawal of the "sanction" of public opinion for mob violence led to a drastic decrease in the violent oppression of abolitionists after 1840. Further proof of the persistence of violence is the

1847 whipping of Bloomington, Illinois, abolitionist and minister Levi Spencer.[54] In fact, such mob attacks continued in the Old Northwest for decades, as people maintained stark disagreements about the validity of antislavery perspectives throughout the antebellum era, and supported these positions with their fists. Perhaps fearing such hostility, the Peoria abolitionists waited nearly seven years after the Illinois Anti-Slavery Society's creation before attempting to organize locally, despite the fact that nineteen Peorians were founding members of the state society.[55]

A focused look at Peoria can deepen understanding of the trajectories and resolutions of violent mob action in the Old Northwest. In Peoria in 1843, as earlier in Alton, abolitionism opened up a chasm in the community, unleashing conflict over the right to print antislavery statements. Abolitionists acted as willing provocateurs in these inhospitable situations, seeking to promulgate their message despite the risks. In post-Lovejoy Illinois, abolitionists could counter such violent acts with strong arguments in favor of their own civil liberties. Press freedom for antislavery people in Peoria was a hard-fought right, one that partisan politics made even more difficult to secure.

The conflict in antebellum Peoria was a local manifestation of a contentious national political environment. The two major political parties sought to silence discussion of abolitionist opinions and squelch efforts for African American rights, and aimed to prevent either of these divisive positions from expanding or claiming their voters. Both the Democrats and the Whigs were invested in maintaining a neutral or accommodating stance on slavery. They feared sectional discord and the fracturing of their political structures, and in the early 1840s in the Old Northwest, they faced the additional electoral threat of the Liberty Party.[56] The major parties could only suppress discussion over slavery in the arenas that they controlled, however, such as the US Congress and national party platforms. Dissent and contestation in other venues—like the newspapers and local politics—proved more difficult to contain, although party men did try to do so through their participation in some anti-abolition mobs.

The Peoria fight for press freedom played out in a context of national and local partisan conflict. The local disputes not only represented battles of Whigs versus Democrats, but also the agendas of the established parties versus those of the immediate abolitionists and the Liberty Party. Returning to the publishing history and public lives of Mary Brown Davis and Samuel H. Davis provides one window into the effects of partisanship on the press and on the conflicts in Peoria in the 1830s and 1840s. Their *Peoria*

Register and Northwestern Gazetteer had a neutral political agenda from its inception in 1837 to 1840. As Samuel stated in the paper's prospectus, it was impartial; the paper aimed to give locals and easterners facts on Peoria and the surrounding area, with a focus on agriculture and business.[57] Editors wrote prospectuses to justify their papers' necessity, explain their goals, and set out their fundamental ideologies. Davis's neutral agenda contrasted sharply with that of Arnold Buffum when the latter established *The Protectionist* in New Garden, Indiana, in January 1841. Buffum aimed to reveal to his fellow northerners the influence of what he called the "slave power" on their independence and prosperity. Buffum, a Quaker of Rhode Island birth, was a founding member of the American Society who helped the Indiana Anti-Slavery Society affiliate with the American and Foreign Anti-Slavery Society in the 1840s. An interesting figure, Buffum called himself an immediatist who voted antislavery.[58] As slavery continued to encroach upon their freedoms, he declared that *The Protectionist* would be one means for them to push back.[59] Samuel Davis had no such expansive plans for his paper.

Nevertheless, Davis soon changed his mind, and began to run the *Register* as a Whig Party newspaper in 1840. The partisan switch stemmed from the founding that year of a local Democratic paper, the Peoria *Democratic Press*, with its southern-born editor, John S. Zieber.[60] Davis subsequently published advertisements for Whig party events, as well as increased partisan content.[61]

As did other editors of the time, Davis took direct political stands in his pages, but he believed in the free circulation of ideas and did not restrict his newspaper to those that he himself held. At least through 1843, Davis advocated a strong Whig agenda in his editorial commentary, claiming that he had no taste for abolition and actually found it troubling. He nonetheless granted abolitionists their say and their right to organize. Notwithstanding his dim view of abolitionists and of the Liberty Party, Samuel printed announcements of their activities.[62] His explanation was simple and universal, for despite his personal dislike of abolitionism and his belief in 1840 that the Liberty party was a diversionary device the Democrats had created to siphon off potential Whig voters, Davis steadfastly supported a free press: "Our views of the freedom of the press and the right of free discussion often compel us to publish things . . . we individually disapprove of."[63] He felt obligated as an editor to ensure the unhindered circulation of ideas. Controversy over the publication of antislavery information haunted the *Register* from its early issues, but Samuel H. Davis made press freedom a priority.

To demonstrate Davis's commitment to open public discussion, and despite his allegedly neutral stance on the issue of abolition, the *Register* occasionally published pieces that opposed slavery.[64] He printed advertisements for antislavery societies and for the Liberty Party, which caused much consternation for some anti-abolitionist readers. Interestingly, these advertisements and editorials would sometimes appear in the same issue as advertisements for runaway slaves. Davis may have done this out of the need to keep the paper afloat financially.[65]

On several occasions, he pointed out to his readers that he still owned two slaves in Virginia, as if to show his own interest in the subject, but this did not shape his stance on press freedom. In December 1837, Davis wrote of Lovejoy's death: "We may possibly be the only slave owner connected with the press in this state . . . and yet we hesitated not to lift our feeble voice against the outrages the moment we heard of them." As soon as news of the 1837 Alton riot reached Peoria, Davis supported Elijah Lovejoy, arguing that he merely acted to protect his property—his press—and to enact his right to speak his opinions. Davis was one of only three Illinois editors to rebuke the Alton attackers, and he did so despite being a slave owner. He grounded his position in the correctness of law and the protections that press freedom afforded American citizens, and refused to censor discussion of the institution, regardless of his self-interest.[66] In defiance of his stated impartiality on slavery and his claims to be a slaveholder, Samuel Davis also editorialized on June 4, 1841, that he regarded it as a "moral, social and political" evil, but that the South could control it where it already existed.[67] Later, in April 1841, Davis advocated the unqualified right of all citizens to petition Congress, a position that many opponents of abolition wanted to deny to antislavery people through the continuation of the gag rule.[68]

However, Davis also highlighted another of the lessons of Alton, for even as he affirmed abolitionists' right to free speech—as he did again in May 1842 regarding the controversial antislavery meeting in nearby Washington, Illinois—he tempered his willingness to allow them a public forum with a desire to refrain from giving them too much attention.[69] His new understanding that Lovejoy's martyrdom and "any action, even the mildest mobbing with rotten tomatoes or eggs, hatched abolitionists," proved as true in Peoria as in Alton, as he and his wife soon saw.[70]

* * *

While her views on slavery were clearer, Mary Brown Davis also pushed the boundaries of the embattled abolitionist press, and sought to shine a spotlight on antislavery activism. Female abolitionist journalists actively participated in western antislavery publications, and Mary Brown Davis represents the pinnacle of their achievements. She used newspapers, including the *Genius of Universal Emancipation* and the *Western Citizen*, to broadcast her views. Davis was the leading female abolitionist writer in the Old Northwest in the 1830s and 1840s, and her publications continued into the following decade.

Davis had important allies, including Zebina Eastman, the Vermont-born editor of the *Western Citizen* who had moved west as a young man and taken up abolition by 1837. When he came to Illinois, he worked on a series of papers, including one with pioneering antislavery editor Benjamin Lundy. After Lundy's death in 1839, Eastman took over his press, and in 1842 he brought it to Chicago as a Liberty Party paper. At the young age of twenty-seven, he began to run the new *Western Citizen*, which did not win immediate acceptance from the surrounding community. Eastman faced threats to his person and his press, but no one ever actually mobbed him.[71] In this growing city—which was developing a fervent antislavery community—anti-abolitionist ire stopped short of the heights it reached in Boston or even in Alton. The paper had many supporters, and its significant subscriber base extended beyond Illinois into northern Indiana, Wisconsin, and Iowa. It also lasted until October 1853, surviving the transition to the Free Soil Party.[72]

Eastman used his editorials to not only promote political abolition—and argue against slavery in general—but also to proclaim the doctrine that all men are created equal and should have equivalent rights, regardless of race. In his pages Eastman argued for full citizenship for African Americans, and the repeal of the Illinois "Black Laws."[73] Moving beyond rhetoric, Eastman also employed free African American H. O. Wagoner as a compositor in 1846. Wagoner was a well-traveled abolitionist, schoolteacher, and experienced newspaperman who shared Eastman's interest in the Underground Railroad.[74] Eastman's own arguments and actions for racial equality help explain his willingness to publish other authors—including women—who agreed with his stance.

In contrast to other newspaper editors of the period who attacked women for transgressing their supposed assigned sphere (and like his mentor Lundy), Eastman welcomed female journalists and granted them a free voice in the press. He expected that they would appeal to women and attract them to the abolitionist cause. Eastman wrote, "The article on our first page, headed Mary Brown Davis, 'The Cruelty of Slavery,' will be particularly interesting to our female readers."[75] Thus Eastman explicitly acknowledged that both women and men read his political abolition newspaper.

Women like Davis played a leading role in the antislavery newspaper culture of the Old Northwest, and newspapers were vital to disseminating their contributions and ideas.[76] They drew upon concepts of female gender identity to speak to and on behalf of other women and their families, and claimed the newspaper as an appropriate public forum for their antislavery propaganda. They boasted of their successes in expanding the movement, and made cutting-edge arguments for racial equality and against the sexual oppression of slave women.[77]

Davis's articles typically appeared on the first and second pages of the *Western Citizen*, and the prominence of her columns from 1842 to 1849 indicates that Eastman took her seriously as a journalist. In the four-page weekly *Citizen*, Davis's columns shared the first two pages with local, national, and international news, and her writing was equally prominent with that of male journalists.[78] In the eyes of many Old Northwesterners, the antislavery and anti-prejudice message was bad enough coming from a man, but a woman's pen was even more poisoned. Davis's articles, those of her male counterparts, and the antislavery press generally all brought activists into conflict with their many anti-abolitionist neighbors. The Old Northwest environment meant that they had to struggle to express their views.

Mary Brown Davis's physical location limited her press freedom, and her comfort level with controversial subject matter varied. While she composed outspoken antislavery and anti-racist pieces for the *Western Citizen*, published 175 miles from Peoria, she wrote most of her articles for the *Register* on more conventional antebellum women's issues. Closer to home, she focused on sentimental poetry and stories, temperance, love, the importance of being a good wife, Christianity, the nature of "woman," and motherhood.[79] When contrasted with her bold writing elsewhere, this may indicate that she found her local context threatening, for all of her organizational bravado. She may have had greater press freedom—and found it easier to make radical arguments—at a larger distance from her person, or the person of her husband. Even as Samuel was an outspoken proponent of freedom of the press, he may have limited his wife's ability to speak out.

In her early columns away from Peoria, Mary Brown Davis typically addressed her audience in a tone of supplication. As she explained her antislavery goals, she rhetorically requested a public forum from the newspaper editors and their readership. In Davis's first column in the

Genius of Universal Emancipation in 1839, she thanked the editor in language typical of the era, expressing her appreciation that he had granted her the "privilege" of "lending my feeble aid, through the columns of your paper, to the cause of the oppressed."[80] Several years later, she wrote to *Western Citizen* editor Eastman that he could use her articles if he found "them worthy a place in your paper." This tone of deference toward the reading public corresponded with the hesitation some antislavery women evinced as they formed their societies.[81]

Davis's initial caution soon yielded to assertive claims, for she declared the newspaper an appropriate venue for women's contribution to the movement, and proclaimed her expertise on slavery. In an early column, Davis wrote that she chose journalism as one forum for her activism, since publishing her firsthand accounts of the depravity of the South could "expose some of the horrors of slavery."[82] Davis also repeatedly claimed that her tales of southern decadence and horror were strictly accurate: "I will send some facts in my next article . . . they are presented just as they occurred."[83] Here she addressed the greater mandate for authenticity that critics applied to abolitionist speakers and writers.[84] She presented herself as a birthright expert with special insights on the evils of slavery, and like the famed immediate abolitionist Sarah Grimké, Davis explained that her upbringing led her to abhor the institution.[85] Davis offered cutting assessments of the need for Old Northwest women to take antislavery action. In publications outside of Peoria, she even included a call for them to exert political leverage.[86]

While they adhered to some traditional arguments concerning women's role and special virtues, Mary Brown Davis and her fellow female journalists experienced sufficient press freedom to advance a radical racial agenda in papers like the *Western Citizen*. Davis overtly declared her support for racial equality, fugitive slave rights, and abolition. She drew attention to her own direct aid to fugitive slaves and stated her support for their flight: "my gate . . . has never been closed against the poor and needy, the stranger, or the outcast."[87] Davis appealed to her readers' sense of common humanity, and conveyed the urgency of the cause of freedom. Not content to merely agitate for abolition in the abstract, she concretely argued for African American rights, and claimed former slaves would become productive members of society, "independent and good citizens," upon attaining their freedom.[88] Davis argued for African American women's and men's advancement.[89] This is but one telling example of the progressive racial vision of female abolitionist journalists, as Mary published it outside of Peoria; it also is distinct from the mildness of Samuel's arguments.

Despite her more conventional tone in the *Register* and her husband's reluctance to discuss the topic, Davis nonetheless wrote a few antislavery pieces for the Peoria paper, using freedom of the press to introduce her radicalism into the local print milieu. Shortly after moving to Peoria in 1837, she wrote an editorial describing her joy at leaving the South. She was happy to escape the "blighting, withering, desolating influence" of slavery, and offered publicly a "fervent prayer" for its destruction.[90] She told the *Register's* readers—as she called for them to sympathize with slaves—that she gloried in escaping daily contact with the institution, and sought to alleviate the suffering of people caught in its grip.[91] Davis's public efforts to do so, in combination with other like-minded souls who sought to organize locally, brought Peoria into a state of turmoil.

* * *

It was evident to both antislavery and press freedom advocates that Peoria's anti-abolitionists had tried to coerce the reformers in their community into silence. Unable to find a local Whig or Democratic paper willing to publish their account of the attack on their February 13 meeting, five Peoria abolitionists used a letter to the Chicago *Western Citizen* to articulate their frustration with the law's representatives—the sheriff, peace officers, and established citizens present at the meeting—who had refused to intervene when the anti-abolitionists had assaulted them. Three of them—Moses Pettingill, John Reynolds, and A. T. Castler—had been present at the Alton founding meeting.[92] The inaction of the officials had granted an air of legitimacy to the silencing of the Peoria antislavery group. Despite abolitionist claims that this repression conflicted with the right to free expression that they were in the process of expanding, extralegal violence found both a significant following and political sanction in this western Illinois river town.[93]

Following the riotous disturbance at the February 1843 Peoria antislavery meeting, Samuel H. Davis condemned "these outrages" against press freedom. His self-published pamphlet, "Free Discussion Suppressed in Peoria," argued against extralegal violence, served as an important piece of abolitionist propaganda in Illinois, and even reached a national audience.[94] Davis sent the pamphlet east with H. H. Kellogg, who planned to distribute it as a publicity device as he traveled to raise awareness of Illinois abolitionists' plight. It reached New York that April, and the *National Anti-Slavery Standard*, the organ of the American Anti-Slavery

Society, published excerpts from it. In May, the *Standard* revisited the Peoria conflict as a battle for "free discussion," and drew attention to "S. H. Davis" as the "one noble exception" to local acquiescence to the will of the mob. He gained adulation from the national antislavery leadership for choosing to place "himself openly in the ranks of the friends of free discussion."[95] Many locals had quite a different view of Davis than did the *Standard*.

Despite being accustomed to partisan commentary in their newspapers, most residents of Peoria placed controversial abolitionist content beyond the pale, and attempted to stifle it in their midst. Davis had sold his press to fellow Whig printers William H. Butler and Samuel G. Butler in September 1842, but continued to edit the newspaper for a time because the new owners were ill.[96] After the *Register*'s new publishers refused to condemn the anti-abolition attack of February 1843—or even allow neutral discussion of the issues—Davis severed all contact with the newspaper. The Butler brothers feared publishing Samuel H. Davis's rebuke of the mob, for their advertisers had threatened a boycott if they circulated abolitionist information. The anti-abolitionists who met at the courthouse that winter imposed direct economic pressure on the newspaper owners, forcing them to refuse publicity to abolition societies.[97] They baldly stated this intention in their resolutions: "If any of them refuse to comply with such request . . . we [will] withdraw our support and patronage from such newspaper press." John S. Zieber, editor of the town's other paper, the *Democratic Press*, presented himself as a shining example of a press uncorrupted by antislavery doctrine, noting he had "never . . . published either the proceedings of or a notice for an abolition meeting, though repeatedly requested to do so."[98] The new editor of the *Register*, the Whig lawyer Lincoln B. Knowlton, had also actively condemned the Peoria abolitionists at the "citizen" meetings, and proclaimed after taking over the paper that he could censor any subject he wished in its pages.[99]

The local gag rule that the anti-abolitionists imposed proved too much for Samuel H. Davis's moral code, and his pamphlet made a clear rebuke. He argued that a publisher ought to print notice of "all public meetings of whatever sort," and linked the struggle with the national gag-rule debate. He presented John Quincy Adams, key actor in that controversy, as a heroic "champion of the dearest right granted in the charter of our liberties." Since the "right of free discussion" was so precious, he claimed that attacks on it would have serious consequences. Davis wrote that the smothering of press freedom in other communities had inevitably led them down the path to civil and economic ruin, and directly linked "free discussion" with "prosperity."[100] He noted the stifling of Lovejoy's freedom and its impact on once-thriving Alton, which since the editor's death had shifted into a state of real estate depreciation and stagnant trade.[101] Antislavery newspapers commonly discussed Alton's economic decline.[102] As a counterexample, Davis offered Chicago, "the very hotbed of abolitionism," as the home of flourishing expansion and business opportunity.[103]

In the pamphlet, Davis based his argument on the right of all people to think for themselves and discuss whatever issues and subjects interested them. He wrote, "I never doubted the right of the anti-slavery society to meet whenever they chose, and do their business in their own way, in the same manner any other society in this free country might do." Citing the First Amendment and Illinois legal codes, he argued both that the abolitionists had every right to meet and that their antagonists had acted contrary to law. Davis quoted the Peoria abolitionists' letter that laid out the local suppression of their rights. Since the Peoria newspapers had refused to publish this letter, only the *Western Citizen* and Davis's self-published pamphlet finally granted it public circulation. In this letter, the abolitionists cited God and the "law of love" to justify their meeting. They claimed the mob's actions were inexplicable, for they had not broken any laws by assembling, and had refused to resist with violence.[104]

At the courthouse on February 14, the evening following the antislavery gathering, the anti-abolitionists had led another meeting to condemn the local reformers and to assert their need for town unity. Samuel Davis noted that there were two hundred to three hundred people present, but stated that only forty-four actively voted in the resolutions. Davis thus emphasized that the majority did not actually support mob action, but rather were "friends of law and order."[105] Refuting Davis, the anti-abolitionist voice in the press, John S. Zieber of the Peoria *Democratic Press*, argued that actually "probably over four hundred persons" were present, and that they shared great unanimity on the issue of slavery.[106]

At that meeting, a committee of prominent lawyers, merchants, and industrial entrepreneurs prepared deliberately non-partisan resolutions setting forth their positions.[107] They stated that abolition was unconstitutional and fostered sectional tensions, and then alluded to the presence of interlopers in the community with reference to "a very small minority of our citizens and others" who were attempting to organize an antislavery society in Peoria.[108] By this reference to "others," they could have intended to imply that either the female abolitionists (by some definitions, not citizens) or people they identified as outside activists in their community were acting out of place. They might have categorized as outsiders the easterners and New Englanders in their midst. They claimed in a later resolution that the Reverend William T. Allan was a foreign agitator and a "disturber of the public peace." While of southern birth and already well known as an abolitionist when he arrived in 1842, Allan actually held a legitimate position in the community of Peoria. He lived in town, was the minister of Peoria's Main Street Presbyterian Church from 1842 to 1844, and lectured for the Illinois Anti-Slavery Society from 1840 to 1846.[109]

While claiming high regard for principles of freedom, the anti-abolitionists restricted this to their own faction and to ideas that they found palatable. They directly advocated censorship of publications and meetings that opposed their ideas, and boldly silenced those who sought to introduce to their town what they regarded as destructive antislavery activity. They claimed most town citizens "opposed" abolition and found it not only unlawful but also "revolting to all those sentiments of pride and self-respect which white men ought to possess." Their resolutions from the February 14 meeting read like a laundry list of classic anti-abolition fears, including runaway slaves, "free negro loafers, practical amalgamation, treason, disunion, civil war, the destruction of all those civil rights of 'life, liberty, and property' (to which we have at least an equal claim with negroes) and other evils, necessarily resulting from the establishment of abolition principles." In this view, abolitionism would turn their ordered society upside down. They further demonstrated their scorn for African Americans and their focus on interracial sex with the statement that they did not want "the negro race . . . in our bed chambers and around our tables." State lawmakers had borne out this concern over interracial sex in an 1829 law that forbade interracial marriage, and laws against both remained on the books through the 1960s.[110] This was a blatant effort to shut down antislavery discussion by citing exaggerated potential consequences for their community.

In point of fact, there were few African Americans in Peoria at the time, and they did not participate in these debates over abolition. In the early period of Illinois abolitionist organizing under study here, free African Americans—who numbered seven in Peoria in the 1840 census—did not take an active role in the struggle.[111] Their small numbers and significant legal disabilities blocked the creation of a strong public voice. The community—like many in Illinois—saw African Americans as possessing only suspect freedom, which gave them a very small and insecure platform for activism. The demographics there later changed, for Peoria newspapers reveal significant local free African American activism beginning in the 1850s, but they did not appear to have played a direct role in the anti-abolitionist conflicts of the previous decade.[112] Formal African American political activism accelerated in Illinois after 1847, and then focused more on repealing the restrictive "Black Laws," not on abolition of southern slavery.[113] While African Americans certainly did not provoke the anti-abolitionists, nevertheless these reactionary citizens regarded the importance of maintaining social and racial stratification as self-evident. These rationalizations failed to persuade Samuel Davis, among others.

* * *

In this crisis, Samuel H. Davis balanced on the line between his political and personal principles. In his writings, he staunchly maintained his ignorance of the ongoing local abolitionist efforts, a stance surely duplicitous given his wife's prominent role in this organizing. In his pamphlet he claimed, "[o]f the proposed anti-slavery meeting also I had thought nothing and cared nothing. Of the principles, views, and objects of the anti-slavery men (and I may add women), I had never sought to inform myself, the study thereof not being in accordance with my inclination."[114] Here, Samuel slyly alluded to the presence of women organizers, while reserving comment on their identity. He thus skirted mention of Mary's abolitionist activism, despite the public evidence of her newspaper columns and prominent role in the local and state antislavery movement. Indeed, he claimed that he did not learn of the riot until the day after it occurred, which was highly unlikely for a man living in the same house as someone who attended the meeting.[115]

One reason for this deceit may have been that Samuel wanted to retain his Whig affiliation, which in that partisan environment entailed eschewing abolitionism. He defended the Whigs and contributed to Peoria's political divisions with his claim that the Democrats instigated the riot. He also argued that the Democrats had convinced some Whigs to join to take the blame for the disorderly conduct. Seeking to preserve their good name, he denied that these Whigs represented the "true" spirit of that party—the protectors of liberty of expression and action.[116] In case any question about his views remained, he also baldly stated that his objections to mob rule did not mean that he had embraced antislavery: "There are some ignoramuses in this community who think, because I condemn these disgraceful proceedings, that I am therefore an abolitionist!" His March 1843 participation in a Farmington, Illinois, convention—called to combat anti-abolition actions and the suppression of freedom of the press in Peoria—may have contributed to this impression. The Farmington attendees denounced anti-abolitionists, and argued that the Peoria abolitionists' lack of violent resistance meant that they had behaved nobly despite extensive abuse. At Farmington, Davis affirmed the importance of freedom of the press, and largely excerpted his speech from his pamphlet.[117] That convention also revealed that Peoria's struggles took on symbolic importance for Illinois abolitionists.

Soon enough, by the late 1840s Samuel had changed his tune, and he openly opposed slavery and racism. He served as the President of the State Liberty Convention in July 1846, and in 1847 he signed a petition for the repeal of the Illinois "Black Laws." Along with 38 other Peorians, including Mary Brown Davis (and four other women) and their son James Scott, he petitioned the Illinois General Assembly that February.[118] While Samuel Davis changed, fellow residents of his town failed to welcome these shifts.

* * *

In Peoria and other areas of antebellum America where new communities were taking shape, local "respectable" elements could not sanction efforts to push press freedom in radical directions, such as racial equality or abolitionism. When abolitionists and their allies made claims about universal humanity, their opponents equated activism with sectional conflict and the dissolution of the nation, including their valuable commercial ties with the South.

In both Peoria and Alton, the participants in the extralegal violent attacks on press freedom intended to silence abolitionism's problematic voice within their society and so promote social stability. Vocal activism against slavery violated the "tacit consensus" that town leaders in early Illinois believed was necessary for the populace to remain orderly.[119] The abolitionists themselves declared no wish to be a part of this consensus, aiming to question the social structures they found unjust.

Many of the active anti-abolitionists in these towns had significant local economic and political clout. Some used their influence to publicize their plan to shut down the abolitionists. The Alton anti-abolitionists represented a wide range of occupations and social strata, from prominent merchants, doctors, lawyers, and ministers, to ordinary mechanics, workmen, and laborers.[120] In Peoria, the mob drew on both major parties, and its main leaders were distinguished attorneys, including several who held political office as Whigs and Democrats.[121] A number of them were active in the local colonization movement in at least 1839 and 1840.[122] Samuel H. Davis noted the presence among their members of prominent legal men such as Norman H. Purple, then candidate for a judgeship.[123] In their number were less eminent lawyers, as well as wealthy merchants, capitalists, and more than one banker.[124]

As these notable participants demonstrate, anti-abolition mobs often feared losing their social stability, which was both precarious and predicated on racial, gender, and economic domination. Even as they were leading white men, their position nonetheless seemed to rest on shaky foundations—as their preoccupation with maintaining hierarchy reveals. In Peoria and Alton, newspaper discussions of abolition and racial equality panicked these men about the civil disruption these issues could bring to the social order of their river towns, and that of the nation as a whole.[125] A fear of sectionalism animated their arguments, and the men vehemently stated their desire to retain national unity. Local economic connections to the South added to the mandate for silence on slavery prevalent in many parts of the North, for among the Old Northwest states Illinois had the strongest southern connections.[126] Some of the anti-abolitionists had direct ties to the South. These included Andrew Gray, a merchant in partnership with a Virginian, and Henry Stillman, a steamboat owner.[127]

As their southern links indicate, attitudes toward abolition—and a willingness to silence it—were intimately connected with the changing economy. Over the course of the 1830s and 1840s, Peoria experienced rapid expansion and commercial volatility. The town settlers were a mixture of transplanted easterners and southerners, but as William T. Allan and Mary Brown Davis prove, southern nativity did not necessarily mean sympathy to slavery. Illinois joined the Union as a state in 1818, but the population remained scattered into the 1830s and 1840s, with most people living in towns along its waterways. Much of the economy relied on water transport, and Illinois had numerous options, including Lake Michigan and its tributaries on the north, the Mississippi on the west, the Ohio River on the south, and the Illinois and Kaskaskia rivers winding through the middle of the state.[128] Local economic and political struggles informed those that took place on the state, regional, and national levels. With the diffusion of transportation improvements throughout the Old Northwest, much of the economic fortune of the nation as a whole had become directly or indirectly linked to slavery.

Peoria's debate about press freedom exemplifies the effects of conditions in developing Illinois towns that increasingly depended on southbound river commerce. The town's origins were in the 1690s under French rule, and the settlers chose the site on the Illinois River for its connections with the Mississippi.[129] The chief local industries in the 1840s centered on farming, with an emphasis on wheat, corn, and hogs. Entrepreneurs processed those commodities into flour, beer, whiskey, and meat. All these benefited from and fed into the burgeoning southern trade. Peoria's steamboat traffic began in December 1829, with the ship the *Liberty*.

By 1833, as was true across the entire Ohio River valley, Peoria was already seeing significant exchange with the South, especially with St. Louis and New Orleans. Across the region's river towns, including those in southern Indiana, people divided sharply over slavery thanks to this southern trade.[130] Peoria merchants and entrepreneurs could thus argue that disruption of this traffic would have had significant economic consequences. Illinois anti-abolitionists used what they saw as the permeable boundary between North and South as but one justification for silencing press freedom. Their partisan identities, fears of social disorder, the influence of outsiders, and racial leveling all created an environment where anti-abolitionists felt comfortable using extralegal violence to stifle local activism. They sought to preserve their social order in the face of these threats. For their part, abolitionists did not lack weapons, and they deftly maneuvered anti-abolitionists' efforts to censor them into advantageous claims for freedom of the press. By defending themselves with the right to free expression, they drew on the principles underlying the American polity. The anti-abolitionists in Peoria and elsewhere thus did not vanquish the local antislavery spirit, although they tried to use force to do so throughout the decade.

* * *

Peoria's determined abolitionists faced violent opposition through the late 1840s, despite moments of relative calm, and they expressed their dismay about this in antislavery newspapers. In May 1844, the Illinois Society held a surprisingly tranquil annual meeting at Peoria, although they perhaps choose this location due to the symbolic value of its tumultuous recent history.[131] However, that lull aside, persecution of abolitionists continued there into 1846. In May, after a throng of Peorians broke up the local society's meeting at the courthouse and "unmercifully egged" several abolitionists, they had to move their gathering to Moses

Pettingill's storeroom. Pettingill, a wealthy merchant, was an avowed abolitionist despite the risks this entailed to his business and his person. He opened Peoria's first hardware store in 1834, and as a temperance man, refused to sell liquor there. He ran, unsuccessfully, as the Liberty Party candidate for the state senate in 1848.[132]

A mob also broke up the second 1846 meeting and viciously attacked some of the attendees. Local antislavery people saw this as an infringement on their right to meet, and Samuel Davis and Jonathan Blanchard, the president of Knox College in Galesburg, again resorted to the *Western Citizen* to strongly protest this incident.[133] After sustaining repeated anti-abolitionist attacks, including threats to tar and feather traveling abolitionist Ichabod Codding, they arranged for armed reinforcements and to keep Codding safe in Pettingill's house. Codding was a New York-born Congregationalist minister active as an itinerant in Illinois and across the Old Northwest from the 1840s through the Civil War.[134] The town authorities displayed a concern that had been missing from the 1843 incidents, for the mayor of Peoria came to Pettingill's house and stayed with them. This collaborative effort dissuaded their intended attackers, but they met further local challenges.[135]

Later in 1846, Samuel H. Davis himself suffered from a brutal anti-abolitionist attack intended to silence his printed words. He had remained a polarizing figure locally, and a scapegoat for anti-abolition wrath. His assailants claimed that an antislavery article in the *Western Citizen* (which they erroneously attributed to Davis) had angered them. The men attacked and beat the former editor in broad daylight on a busy Peoria street, and he sustained serious injuries, as did his son who attempted to help him. Even a magistrate could not stop the assault, but finally two private citizens intervened and took Davis home. That same day local authorities fined one of the assailants, while the other fled the vicinity. Despite the severity of his wounds, Davis had the presence of mind to use this situation to his advantage. He agreed to not press charges in exchange for a future promise of noninterference with the Liberty Party in Peoria, as well as the use of the courthouse for antislavery meetings.[136] Davis succeeded in this trade, and his commitment to freedom of the press had ultimately led him along the path to full-fledged abolition even as it placed him in the direct path of harm.

* * *

The dim regard for the antislavery press and view of its perils extended to Ohio, too, where a fellow newspaper editor faced notable community opposition. The antislavery message had become no more palatable in the Old Northwest in the late 1840s, for other editors in the region also had to fight for press freedom as the partisan climate heated up. Even then, when they published arguments against slavery, editors faced brutal personal and property attacks for speaking out. This opposition contrasts with other historians' accounts that after 1845, violence against the antislavery press largely ceased. According to these arguments, the major parties then introduced antislavery planks into their platforms, and the slave controversy became more about sectional disagreements than about splits within the North.[137] In fact, the slow introduction of a moderate antislavery agenda to mainstream politics (actually somewhat later with the Republicans in 1854) made opposition to slavery neither more appealing nor much safer to report about in the Old Northwest.

In 1848, those developments were still a few years away, and antislavery editing remained a hazardous job. Cambridge, the county seat of Guernsey County in southeastern Ohio, had an intense engagement with politics in the 1840s, including a strong Whig presence.[138] Into this environment came the brash local newspaperman Mathew R. Hull, who began publishing the *Clarion of Freedom* in 1844. Quoting from the biblical Matthew, Hull wrote, "[t]hank God we came not to Cambridge 'to send peace, but a *sword.*'"[139] Hull clearly did not dispute that he and his coeditor Joseph Wolff disturbed the town's tranquility with their paper, for he saw that as an essential part of the reform mission. Hull, an outspoken antislavery man, a Wesleyan Methodist, and a Liberty Party supporter, served on the executive committee of the 1843 meeting of the Indiana Anti-Slavery Society.[140] Hull and Wolff presented bold and outspoken arguments against slavery, racism, and both major political parties (but especially the Whigs).

In the summer of 1847, Hull faced a prolonged period of attacks on his newspaper office and on his press freedom. His problems appear to have had partisan and moral origins, as he had a knack for blunt criticism. He spoke out against the "Black Laws" and racial prejudice in the local schools, and denigrated the ongoing Mexican War as "this slaveholding Whig war."[141] He had disparaged local and national Whig politicians for their stance on slavery, and claimed that the former incited attacks on him to stifle "our liberty of thought, and the liberty of the press."[142] Hull's neighbors certainly had little interest in seeing his perspectives aired in print.

Over the course of several weeks that summer, an infuriated crowd repeatedly attacked the office that also served as Hull's family home.

Hull was ill and recovering in the building, but his weakened state did not stop his foes from egging and stoning the house and breaking the windows on July 23 and 25. The attacks continued, he claimed variously, for 17 or 18 nights, and the crowd "threatened to tear down our press—to blow up our building with powder, and to burn the house over our heads." Observers in Cambridge noted that local officials made no effort to secure Hull's property, his family's safety, or freedom of the press.[143] The editor vehemently argued that no one could silence him. His foes, he wrote, "will bite the dust before we will." He was confident that the *Clarion* had widespread support, and claimed "[t]he whole country is roused in our behalf."[144] The facts do not bear out Hull's bluster that most of his neighbors were on his side, since a number of men in his "country" freely attacked him for his views.

Despite this fact and even with their pain and trials, Hull and Wolff boasted that the throwing of rocks and eggs only increased their subscription base, and printed testimonials to demonstrate that they had numerous allies in the surrounding community. Hull did have his supporters, who held meetings in Cambridge and points north, east, and south, as far away as 177 miles, all aimed at reinforcing his right to express his views. They spoke out against the numerous violent assaults, as did a Michigan paper that reprinted an account of the attacks, claiming "we think the supply of rotten eggs will fall short before he knuckles under."[145] Hull received positive attention from other Ohio newspapers, including the *Anti-Slavery Bugle*, and published numerous letters of solidarity from the surrounding area in Ohio, and even from Pennsylvania and Washington, DC.[146] The press coverage was not universally positive, however, for the Pittsburgh *Gazette* claimed that Hull had brought the mob on himself through his slander and use of profane language, as well as physical violence, but they supplied no details of such violence. The *National Era* quickly refuted this account with an elaborate refusal to allow any justification for mob activity.[147]

The violence against Hull continued, and on its final night his opponents gathered in a crowd in the street. These evidently angry men added blackened oil to the collection of missiles they threw in the windows, which stained the interior of the house. They proclaimed they would "whip every Abolitionist in town" and "knocked down two or three with clubs, while others escaped to places more secure than the public streets." Jonathan Davis, a local butcher, beat Wolff and Hull, and they "offered no resistance." Like the Peoria abolitionists, they refused to retaliate physically when attacked. While the authorities arrested Davis, he did not serve time, and Hull claimed that local Whig politicians paid his court costs.[148] The authorities again declined to protect Hull's freedom of speech, and highlighted with their actions the legitimacy of the assaults on him.

Ultimately, the anti-abolition attacks drove Hull and his family from town in September 1847. To Hull, Davis's beating proved the true extent of the danger that local partisan politics posed for him. He thus chose to take drastic action: "we concluded to shake the dust from our feet and flee to another city." The Whigs responded to this announcement of his departure by convening a meeting both to continue to "denounce us, and in mercy to call off their dogs." There, they tried to get the Democrats to join their anti-Hull efforts, claiming their common interest in silencing the *Clarion*, but were unsuccessful.[149] Having driven the editor out of town, they wanted to get in the last word on the situation.

Hull became an itinerant for a time, and spoke strategically through his own newspaper, which Wolff continued in his absence. He remained in contact with his hometown by correspondence from a safe distance, and along with his family finally left Cambridge to find a more tranquil home in New Concord, a mere nine miles away. In a letter to Wolff published in the newspaper, Hull wrote of how he and his "almost heartbroken wife" needed to escape, as did their children, who had endured "young mobocrats" who emulated their elders and pelted them with assorted objects.[150] The challenge to press freedom was only one of several that Hull's family faced when they moved, for his reputation followed him.

* * *

Hull subsequently traveled across Ohio to New York to meet with other abolitionists and attend a Liberty Party convention, and he began publishing the *Clarion* in its new home.[151] The *National Era* of Washington, DC, wrote that the mobbing and moving had not altered Hull's energy for the cause: "Its editor has abated nothing of his spirit." Further, his paper had actually become somewhat profitable.[152] Wolff and Hull themselves claimed a substantial circulation increase as a result of the attacks.[153] Hull's persistence in speaking out thus paid dividends in both money and publicity, and in this way helped finance his extensive travels.

The paper's new home in New Concord proved more hospitable, but hardly idyllic. When they moved, Hull and Wolff reiterated their rights to press freedom, and seized the mantle of law-abiding citizenry: "we are determined . . . to be peaceable citizens, while we claim the constitutional liberty of the press, we are perfectly willing to abide the penalty, if we violate any law."[154] They persisted in shoring up these rights, and on December 24, 1847, the *Clarion* printed the minutes of a "respectable meeting" held at New Concord. This meeting's stated aim was to support press freedom and tie its protection to the laws of the nation. The attendees vowed to shut down mob violence upon its first appearance, arguing that mobs were both illegal and immoral, and in them " . . . all are left equally unprotected in person and property." Hull and Wolff claimed that few residents of New Concord supported anti-abolition violence.[155] The free expression agenda of that meeting was nonetheless unpopular with many local residents, for that August antislavery lecturers Henry C. Wright and Charles Burleigh had trouble getting a speaking venue there. They ultimately found one, after extensive work.[156] Local sentiment on abolition changed sufficiently in the ensuing months that Hull himself lectured there by May of 1848.[157] Hull thus won a partial victory for freedom of the press, for although anti-abolitionists forced him out of Cambridge, he retained his voice by moving his family and paper to a safer place, and using the national press to publicize his efforts. These challenges show the determination of Old Northwest anti-abolitionists to stifle press freedom, the influence of partisan politics on their actions, and editors' persistence in the face of this ongoing pressure.

* * *

Under close examination, early Cambridge, Peoria, and Alton appear to have teetered on the precipice of explosive violence, but only Alton went over the edge. Extralegal conflict emerged under distinct circumstances in these three towns, and brought them to significantly different end points. The towns shared a pattern of contestation over abolition, due to a confluence of racism, economics, and politics. The armed opposition that the Alton abolitionists and their allies presented to their adversaries raised the level of violence to murder. One reason historians have given for the Alton riot's escalation was the resistance with which the Lovejoy faction met their enemies.[158] In communities that generally supported abolition, such as Oberlin, Ohio, events even as provocative as the mass liberation of a fugitive slave—as occurred in the notorious Oberlin-Wellington rescue of 1858—could proceed peacefully. Violence escalated in Alton when activists armed themselves in self-defense rather than merely speaking out.[159] The anti-abolitionists also became increasingly frustrated as Lovejoy and his allies persisted in their advocacy despite the clear message that most Alton people disdained it. Lovejoy's death reminded people on all sides of the consequences of mob activity. Advocates of press freedom learned from it, and many chose to adhere ever more closely to principles of nonresistance in the face of danger. Others saw it as a sign that anti-abolitionists would stop at nothing to silence them, and increased their outspokenness accordingly.

The press freedom advocates in Peoria and Cambridge presented less provocative resistance when contrasted to those of Alton. While the abolitionists faced strong community opposition there and maintained their right to free expression, they did not take up arms in self-defense. In addition, Elijah Lovejoy insisted upon his right to publish his radical message right where he lived, as did Hull and Wolff in less inflammatory circumstances. Samuel H. Davis offered moderate and universal messages of press freedom in Peoria. Mary Brown Davis, for her part, largely confined her most radical messages to the Chicago *Western Citizen*, writing mainly conventional articles for her local newspaper. In general, the Peoria abolitionists and free press advocates more subtly dissented from the status quo, and the local presses themselves never faced physical attack, although the abolition meetings did, as did Samuel Davis as the representative of antislavery journalism in his community's eyes. This contrast should not, however, be taken too far. While Peoria's press freedom advocates did not violently resist, they did persist, and conflict continued at least until 1846. In Cambridge, Hull and Wolff's actions were closer to Lovejoy's, in that they vehemently defended their right to print antislavery perspectives, and for a time waited out persistent mob attacks on their press. The Cambridge editors' departure from community norms was more obvious than the Peorians, but they nonetheless differed from Lovejoy and his allies in that, when attacked, they refrained from physically defending themselves.

Despite their differences, violence emerged in all three communities as anti-abolitionists denied antislavery people their press freedom. Conflict arose from this denial, as debate became pushed to the margins, and advocacy of abolition became an offense punishable by forced silence, violence, or death. The boundaries of permitted publications about slavery and race hinged upon ideas about social structure, economic stability, and partisan politics. These antislavery agitators linked their defense with larger issues, including the citizens' right to freedom of expression. The adversity Old Northwest antislavery people faced brought them support from their local and national compatriots, and confirmed the importance of the region to the broader reform struggle. The anti-abolition faction, for its part, stifled these reformers with threats of extreme violence. They linked activists' aberrant behavior with social disorder, antihierarchical acts, and the destruction of the major political parties. Old Northwest activists continued their stalwart efforts against slavery and for their liberties despite these perilous clashes.

* * *

The larger significance of these debates over abolitionists' press freedom lies in their extremism, which reveals how important these controversies were for antebellum people. The Old Northwest was particularly explosive on the slavery question, an issue that studies of anti-abolitionist violence do not explain. Historians have analyzed such attacks without delving into their larger context, and thus the events at Alton appear as an incident of fanaticism, like other riots in Boston and Philadelphia. Alton, in this view, was not a locus of larger national political debates, but one city among many that represents a larger pattern.[160] While such earlier accounts have illuminated the 1837 events at Alton and the factions involved, they omit attention to the ways liberty, politics, economics, and social norms all combined to make that town's debates over press freedom and activism (and those of other Old Northwest places like Peoria and Cambridge) distinctive. Perhaps the most important lesson these towns have to teach is that abolitionists could become the targets of overt violence if they chose to persist in converting people in such problematic environs as Alton, Peoria, and Cambridge.

In addition to demonstrating the silencing effect that partisan agendas could have upon local communities, these violent clashes over press freedom in the Old Northwest also illustrate the impact of local-level events on national debates. Such abolition struggles in this region became crucial in setting the parameters for national political discussion in later decades. The Old Northwest was the home of some of the Republican Party's earliest successes as it overturned former Democratic strongholds in Illinois, Indiana (apart from in 1840), and Michigan.[161] The region came to substantially affect national antislavery debates and sectional politics by contributing a national leadership that was well aware of and influenced by Old Northwest circumstances. The cautious political culture regarding race and abolition came to shape national politics. Establishing political consensus remained elusive for Old Northwesterners over time, and this problem spread.

By the end of the 1850s, the contingent positions produced in the Old Northwest found national expression through Abraham Lincoln, whose position on slavery became increasingly critical over the course of his life.[162] Nonetheless, over time, Lincoln still remained significantly less interested in equality than were the pathbreaking antislavery journalists and editors of his region. In the Lincoln-Douglas debates of 1858, Indiana- and Illinois-bred Lincoln argued that the "divergent attitudes" of the North and the South on slavery's morality provided their "essential point of conflict."[163] Certainly for some prominent antislavery journalists, the Republican Party represented a step backward, rather than progress for the abolition cause. Zebina Eastman—himself never mobbed—wrote against the Republicans to Ichabod Codding in April 1857, to proclaim his nostalgia for the days of the Liberty Party and its stronger stance against slavery.[164] While many radical abolitionists (and even former Liberty Party men like Eastman) saw Lincoln as insufficiently stalwart, by 1860 slavery's foes had won more space to promulgate their ideas. They had found a more moderate vision of their agenda in a major national party and in Lincoln, both rooted in the Old Northwest's contentious political culture. Nonetheless, the strong political power that the anti-war and anti-Black Democrats exerted in the region, throughout the war, substantially limited the ability of more radical activists to bring about change.

* * *

These controversies over press freedom and Old Northwest political culture in the 1830s and 1840s demonstrate that slavery and institutionalized racism were woven into the fabric of the entire nation, and not merely the South. Ideas of national unity, racism, party discipline, and support for slavery all contributed to opposition to abolition and its public expression. Racism was influential across the North, but in this region it was particularly important in shaping the reform climate. When activists witnessed slavery's national reach in shutting down their press freedom, this affirmed for them the importance of converting locals to the antislavery position, and of eliminating widespread prejudice. To them, the Old Northwest held the key to improving the nation's moral landscape, and without the ability to print and express their views, this would not have been possible.

Antebellum activists proclaimed that threats to their freedom loomed all around, and they saw ample evidence of this not only in mob attacks on presses, but also on reform lectures. The traveling lecturer and the antislavery press both played vital and intersecting roles in the struggle to convert the Old Northwest. The Massachusetts Anti-Slavery Society wrote in 1846 that newspapers, with their frequent arrival at the home of the reader, could be powerful "levers . . . to detach the system of slavery from its stronghold in the indifference or selfishness of the northern hearts." Their regular appearances could "prepare the way for the lecturer[s]," and later, discuss and share ideas from their meetings.[165]

Many strong links connected newspapers and traveling lecturers. Itinerants printed lists of their scheduled meetings in local and national papers to awaken activists to their impending arrival, and to alert friends at home where they could write to them.[166] On their journeys, lecturers also increased the circulation of antislavery newspapers, as many sold subscriptions at their meetings.[167] In turn, papers spread itinerants' influence across a larger geographic area.[168] They each had an integral part to play in the Old Northwest battle. Much as local antislavery organizers and editors confronted challenges when they claimed a public place in their towns, itinerant men and women in the Old Northwest also grappled for legitimacy and freedom of speech as they spread the abolition message. Indeed, the struggles of traveling antislavery lecturers to speak freely built upon the fight for freedom of assembly and press freedom of Old Northwest antislavery activists.

5 / "An Odd Place for Navigation": Itinerant Lecturers and Freedom of Speech, 1830–1849

John O. Wattles of Ohio toured Indiana in September 1842, crossing the north-central portion of the state, seeking out compatriots, attending and holding meetings, and observing the local progress of the antislavery campaign. In Grant County, he found and worked with steadfast new allies, "firm friends of humanity." He eloquently praised the local activists he met there:

> The abolition ship has weighed anchor, spread her sails, and, borne on by the fresh breezes of heaven, her broad banners waving in the winds, and her pendant streaming from her . . . topmast; she plunges over the billows, veering her course for freedom's port. Some of our eastern friends who dwell by *the sea*, may think it an odd place for navigation, out here in the woods, but they must like to know that abolition can go across the land, as well as across the ocean.

No mere pleasure sailors, the inland antislavery mariners were prepared for a spiritual battle against what they deemed an unholy system. In this letter to the New Garden, Indiana, *Free Labor Advocate and Anti-Slavery Chronicle*, Wattles claimed "[t]he friends of freedom are mailed in the might of principle, and Jehovah backs their purpose." Grant County's activists did not have to fight slavery and prejudice alone, however, for Wattles noted that their neighbors were also "moving in the cause of the slave. The 'incendiaries' and their firebrands have set the prairies on fire."[1]

Like other participants in the western abolition struggle, Wattles recognized that the majority of the movement's membership and organizational apparatus lay in the East. Nonetheless, he informed Indianans and eastern readers who knew little of regional circumstances that Old Northwest abolitionism was both vital and arduous. Since antebellum newspapers widely quoted from each other and reprinted one another's articles, Wattles could have anticipated that his words might travel far.[2] He asserted that easterners must shift their reform focus across the miles to the West. Of Connecticut birth himself and only then a resident of the region for three years, Wattles knew well that many eastern people saw the Old Northwest as a backward, amoral woodland sparsely dotted with hamlets.[3] He nonetheless asserted that this actually was fertile terrain, strategically essential for cultivating a new vision of American racial liberation, one he had himself only recently embraced. Hardly "an odd place for navigation," he indeed foretold that Illinois, Indiana, Michigan, and Ohio would instead prove central to the fight against slavery, and for civil rights and freedom of speech.[4] As a traveling speaker, Wattles exemplified the era's and the region's most important propaganda technique.

* * *

The abolition ship did not sail across these wooded seas uninhabited, for a dedicated cohort of traveling activists like Wattles piloted it for the antislavery cause, fighting for freedom of speech as they created and expanded antislavery networks. Since the Old Northwest's population was dispersed, propagating reform there required itinerant lecturers to promote and strengthen the cause.

As advocates for the slave moved around the Old Northwest, their lecture tours demonstrate the transitory, maturing state of the region's culture and society in the 1830s and 1840s. Activist women and men faced many challenges specific to this singular environment, which included both unusually extensive violent and nonviolent efforts to silence organizing activity, as well as the fatigue of advocating abolition across a large rural region with few allies. Itinerants' provocative labor elicited community strife, and they found their surrounding milieu unusually contentious, but nonetheless vital to national reform. Anti-abolitionists sought to regulate discussion in these communities, and used threats of extreme violence to stifle unwanted voices that questioned deference toward social order, organized religion, economic stability, and partisan politics.[5] Speakers ranging from Marius R. Robinson in 1837 in Berlin, Ohio, to Lucretia Mott in 1847 in Richmond, Indiana, vehemently claimed the right to raise their voices in protest against slavery and racism.[6] This regional context complicated itinerants' mission, for widespread mobility and population expansion meant that people were often moving into Old Northwest towns at the same time as activists were passing through. Most residents had recently arrived, but many nonetheless rapidly developed a sense that they had the right to eliminate the topics of abolition and African American rights from local discussion.

While most Old Northwest people gave itinerant abolitionists a cold welcome, they were a product of their era, and thus hardly an anomaly. Under the "agency system," national and state activist organizations employed lecturers to travel and stir up reform fervor across the United States. Itinerant organizing predated the antislavery movement; numerous other causes and reforms implemented it in the Early Republic. Evangelical religious organizations pioneered the agency system that later enabled abolition lecturers and other reformers to propagandize widely. "Parent societies" sent out agents to form local auxiliary societies across their scattered communities, which reunited *en masse* in periodic conventions.[7] The numbers of itinerant lecturers, or agents, boomed from the end of the eighteenth century onward, and they used increasingly sophisticated methods over the decades.[8] This conversion-centered tactic grew out of the era's moral environment; the Second Great Awakening—which ended in the late 1830s—inspired broad-based action against social evils.[9]

Many antebellum reforms shared common methods. Their presses publicized impending events, at public meetings people subsequently composed and approved resolutions, and they then broadcast their results.[10] Abolitionist lecturers and writers seized upon this inventive blend of critical thought and evangelical outreach to disseminate antislavery arguments across the northern states, but in the Old Northwest it was particularly necessary—and particularly difficult.

From the 1830s onward, as the population in the Old Northwest expanded, traveling individuals lectured in these new settlements. As the transportation infrastructure improved over the first decades of the nineteenth century, it became easier for a range of lecturers to reach people across the newly sprawling nation. Technological advances also enabled affordable printed materials, which travelers brought with them on their tours.[11] This expansion of the agency system meant that despite the geographic and demographic challenges their communities posed, Old Northwest people commonly found sojourners in their midst. Whether they were abolitionists, evangelical preachers, or circuit court judges, a multiplicity of voices rang across the prairies.

Since antislavery organizing in the region required it, itinerant lecturing had a long and vibrant history as an organizing technique in the Old Northwest. It remained one of the most formidable weapons of the antislavery movement there from the 1830s until the advent of the Civil War, well after the point at which historians of northeastern activists claim the practice was moribund.[12] Traveling lecturers, both local and eastern-based, joined the region's antislavery struggle beginning in the early 1830s, when Theodore D. Weld traveled extensively across the area and organized numerous societies.[13] Other lecturers simultaneously moved around the region to raise funds for causes linked to antislavery activism, such as African American schools and the anti-"Black Laws" movement.[14] The actions of itinerants varied from state to state.

* * *

The patterns of itinerant antislavery activism in the Old Northwest largely corresponded to general abolition trends in each state, in that states with stronger antislavery cultures had a greater amount of itinerant activity. This varied little between 1835 and 1861. Itinerants who inventively mixed critical thought and zealous persuasion organized in Michigan and Ohio from the early 1830s, and by the middle of the decade they were in Indiana and Illinois.[15] Ohio subsequently maintained the most comprehensive itinerant coverage in the region.[16] There and in Michigan, substantially higher numbers of itinerants visited than they did in Illinois and Indiana for any five- or ten-year period between 1835 and 1861. Itinerant traffic began later with sporadic visits to Illinois in 1837, but such speeches remained rare until after 1840.[17] Indiana's antislavery lecturing began in 1839, and that state maintained the smallest itinerant presence of the four Old Northwest states.[18] This variation, and lecturers' accounts, indicate that they faced the greatest number of difficulties and had the smallest representation in Illinois and Indiana, while Michigan, the northernmost of these states, had fewer virulently anti-abolition residents than the other three. Ohio was contentious, but abolitionists faced weaker opposition there than in Illinois or Indiana, which had much more developed anti-abolition and anti–African American cultures. Nevertheless, across all of these states, when itinerant activists aimed to address their western brethren and sisters, they consistently lacked the liberty to speak.

Much as sailors battle unpredictable storms, itinerants fought their own tempests to obtain the freedom of speech needed to spread their ideas over the Old Northwest seas. Strong-minded local people repeatedly rebuffed their attempts to lecture across the region. From at least 1835, in their speeches and writings, antislavery speakers and their supporters incorporated their work into a larger effort to ensure the free public expression of all sentiments, however unpopular. This connection began as early as 1835 with James G. Birney's attempts to publish against slavery in Cincinnati, and with Theodore D. Weld's and Augustus Wattles's abolition organizing and mobbing in Ohio.[19] Activists realized that to liberate slaves, they would have to preserve their ability to be present, well advertised, and vocal in public. While women played an unusually proactive role in the rough and tumble struggle for the right to advocate abolition, and faced more extensive opposition, all activists had to fight for this public intellectual space.[20] The continual attacks on antislavery peoples' right to public speech, and the challenges of organizing the geographically and ideologically scattered population into a reform body, meant that Old Northwest activism was different, and even more difficult, than activism in the East. In consequence, abolitionists there fervently defended the liberty of expression needed to disperse their ideas. Their vocal presence conflicted with others' conceptions of government rights and protections for unpopular ideas.

Throughout the Old Northwest, anti-abolitionists constantly worked to restrict abolitionist speech and shore up white supremacy. They claimed that they must stamp out the threat open antislavery discussion posed to an orderly society, even if it required violence. To break down the abolitionists' coordinating systems, they used mob violence, personal attacks, and property destruction to silence them.[21]

In this region, abolitionists used the law to defend themselves against this vigilante violence. They crafted broad freedom of speech claims, often based on the First Amendment, to justify their public action and face down vigilantism. Beginning in the early 1830s, abolitionists invoked state law in their defense, but soon they shifted the target of their requests for help. Prior to the Civil War, the era usually understood to mark the beginning of individual claims on the national government for rights, Old Northwest abolitionists articulated an understanding of federal rights that transcended those granted on the local level.

From the 1830s on, outside of the boundaries of extant law, antislavery people pushed for an expansive definition of freedom of speech. One early example is the aftermath of the Lane Seminary debates, where the antislavery students left in 1834 to protest the seminary trustees' stifling of their lectures, immediate abolitionism, and activism in Cincinnati's

African American community. The vast majority of these men enrolled at Oberlin College after the faculty there guaranteed them freedom of speech and interracial admission to the college.[22] Such activists changed the definition of liberty of expression so that they could continue their work even while their contemporaries besieged their rights. Legal scholar Michael Kent Curtis argues that this redefinition formed the primary check on northerners' infringements on antislavery voices. Indeed, activists responded to attacks on their freedom of speech by expanding the scope of these protections, and constructing their new rights as national, federalized, universal, "basic and inherited."[23]

Old Northwest reformers played a crucial role in changing the discussion over the First Amendment from merely addressing violations of their own right to speak to instead highlighting an impending threat to all Americans' autonomy and democracy. Freedom of speech claims drew an increasingly large audience, especially following the start of the gag rule in the House of Representatives in 1836, and after the killing of Elijah Lovejoy in 1837.[24] Increasingly, antislavery people's free speech claims hinged on federal rights. By focusing in this way, abolitionists reinterpreted the First Amendment's guarantees, since its original intent was to protect the right to free speech from government interference, not from attacks by their fellow citizens. They thus pushed for a sweeping definition of rights by invoking them as though they already existed and people could enforce them.[25] At the time it was very difficult to implement First Amendment rights, for in terms of actual court action, the measure lacked regulatory muscle until the 1868 ratification of the Fourteenth Amendment, and even then, the federal government did not use it to enforce the First Amendment on the states until the 1920s.[26] Nevertheless, given the Old Northwest abolitionists' keen need for tools for self-defense, they repeatedly called upon this new conception of a federal right to freedom of expression.

Itinerant antislavery lecturers in the Old Northwest confronted physical opposition as they sought public forums, and many responded by citing citizenship claims to defend their freedom of speech. Anti-abolition violence in the region began with Weld and his early allies, who encountered mobs in 1835 and 1836 in Ohio.[27] This phenomenon continued well beyond such famed incidents, including in the 1830s. In early 1837 hostile townspeople expelled Marius R. Robinson from a church in Hartford, Ohio. This Massachusetts-born man had attended seminary in Tennessee, and had become an avowed abolitionist by the early 1830s when he moved to Ohio. He lectured for the American Society in the

West beginning in 1836, and soon married Emily Rakestraw, herself an abolitionist and women's rights activist.[28]

At Hartford, Robinson's foes interrupted his meeting, demanding that he be silent and let them speak. When he refused, they pulled him out of their church, and held him in the town square by pinioning his arms for half an hour. They thus pilloried him in a public space to silence him and show disapproval of his message. Robinson argued that as a "citizen," he had to assert his right to speak despite such challenges: as " . . . an American citizen [I] could not so far forget my duty and my rights as such as to render obedience to their direction."[29] He maintained this conviction throughout his public career, as did his determined compatriots in the region.

* * *

In their self-defense, antislavery activists in the Old Northwest also explicitly linked their freedom of speech struggles to a gendered concept of manliness that included a martial element. As passionate women and men fought for antislavery people's liberty of expression, some revealed a preoccupation with assertive masculinity, and others questioned gender roles themselves with their activist work. In 1838 in Jacksonville, Illinois, abolitionist Albert Hale wrote to his compatriot Asa Turner about Turner's fitness for the position of Illinois antislavery agent. Hale thought that they both lacked the mental fortitude to face volatile Illinois activism. This agent would confront the "thorough manly & deep discussions of . . . the freedom of speech and the press and the freedom of the slave" needed for that position.[30] Thus Hale claimed that only a man who could forcefully argue against slavery could defend freedom of expression. Since abolitionists had to fight for a public forum, Hale and others relied upon projecting masculine force against their opponents. They used then-prevalent ideas of proper manhood as independent and powerful to decide who should be their Illinois advocate.[31] Four years later in Knox, Illinois, the Liberty convention agreed, claiming that "history" had shown them that they must use a "prudent and manly regard to our own right" to face down attacks by the slave power."[32] They argued that without this vigor, antislavery activists lacked sufficient leverage to bring about slave liberation.

In fact, many abolitionists realized that in practice, literal manhood alone could not ensure free discussion or itinerant safety. Indeed, women could guard freedom of speech, as seen elsewhere in Illinois, where women protected men against anti-abolition mobs. In 1844,

Irene B. Allan of Peoria shared an anonymous letter in the Chicago *Western Citizen* that detailed an incident from the early days of Illinois antislavery organization, presumably the late 1830s. The unnamed writer defended her fellow abolitionists against unfriendly residents of her town: "I stood sentinel at the kitchen door myself, and can answer for it that none came in without a pass." She was thus instrumental in repudiating an anti-abolition mob.[33] This woman's reference to the "kitchen door" also reveals that this meeting took place in the ostensibly private space of a home, blurring the lines of public and private even as she acted outside of gender norms. Also in 1844 in western Illinois, Laura B. Coleman discussed women's defensive presence at a speech by the Reverend Ichabod Codding in McDonough County. The women refused to leave upon the request of the mob members that sought to attack the men: "We told them that we had no idea of leaving yet." Instead, Codding continued as planned and lectured for two hours.[34]

These physically assertive female bodyguards complicated discussions of manhood as needed to guard freedom of speech. This rhetoric may have fortified men's confidence, and in some cases its proponents ignored local activist women's contributions, but in reality female abolitionists frequently faced down anti-abolition challenges. At times women's defensive strategy proved quite effective, which is surprising given that elsewhere in this same era, mobs showed few scruples about targeting women. In 1838 in Philadelphia, anti-abolitionists burned Pennsylvania Hall in a violent mob attack on attendees of the second National Convention of Anti-Slavery Women—clear evidence that women were not immune to anti-abolition violence.[35]

Women's bravery extended across racial lines, too, for whether or not they embraced overt organization, African American women in the Old Northwest exhibited no hesitation about defending themselves and their families from slave catchers and others who sought to harm them.[36] This protection was far from absolute across the region, as female meeting attendees and lecturers found throughout this era when they worked to secure the right to openly advocate their views. This was an essential right in the eyes of Old Northwest activist women and men, and both actively engaged in the struggle to speak on a range of platforms.

* * *

Abolitionist navigators in the Old Northwest fought to present their views to the public. Whether they were men or women, one main arena in itinerants' local battle for antislavery expression was the fight to obtain speaking venues. Anti-abolitionists in the Old Northwest (and elsewhere) tried to silence visiting activists by refusing them space to advocate their message. Some objected to individual itinerants, others to antislavery lectures as inappropriate for the space in question, and still others opposed any sort of abolitionism in their town; all forced activists to be creative in finding speaking platforms. Local residents tried to control the flow of ideas through restrictions on abolitionists' usage of a wide variety of buildings. Many of the determined Old Northwest abolitionists maintained their right to hold local meetings, despite dire consequences, and the presence of itinerant lecturers thus elicited conflict within communities.

Marius R. Robinson's expansive 1837 tour of Ohio exemplifies this determination, for he covered a large area of the state, including numerous small towns itinerant abolitionists infrequently visited, with few like-minded residents. Robinson arrived in Berlin, Ohio, in June, and asked permission to use a building to hold a meeting. Locals refused him the use of churches, schools, and public halls, so Robinson opted to speak in a private home. In resorting to holding meetings in houses—or in ambiguously public spaces like churches—he and other abolitionists politicized spaces that prevailing ideologies defined as domestic, troubling the boundaries between public and private.[37] In Berlin, Quaker merchant Jesse Garretson and his wife offered to let Robinson use their house. On June 2, he held one quiet meeting there, and scheduled a second meeting two days later to discuss his antislavery views on the Bible. This proposed religious theme and his persistence in organizing in the community incensed some town residents. Mob rumors began to circulate, which Robinson disregarded; they later proved to be accurate.[38]

Robinson depicted his freedom of speech trials in his account of the incident, called "Free Discussion," in the New Lisbon, Ohio, *Aurora* of June 15, 1837, published near his in-laws' home where he recuperated after the attack. June 3, the night before his second meeting, Robinson sat in Garretson's store and chatted with him, his wife, and J. F. Powers. About ten o'clock at night, local anti-abolitionist Mordecai Hughes burst into the store and grabbed Robinson by the arm. He attempted to pull him out the door, claiming that he must depart since he had "' . . . disturbed the peace of our citizens long enough.'" Mrs. Garretson rose to his defense, intervening and claiming, "'If you take him, you must take me too.'" A second man pulled Robinson by his other arm, aiming to get him outside. Mrs. Garretson continued her defensive efforts, and tried to prevent the rest of the men crowded outside from coming in. The mob entered the store regardless, and pulled Robinson toward the exit, although the Garretsons delayed them.[39]

While they struggled, Hughes commanded that Mr. Garretson "dismiss" Robinson from his property. Garretson would not, and asked the crowd to "stop and reason the matter." They refused, and Robinson disparagingly noted that "brute force" ruled this encounter. He commented that the mob gave Mrs. Garretson no special handling despite her sex. They roughly pushed her over, and Robinson claimed that this attack made the crowd's savagery apparent. This incident would perhaps look different were Mrs. Garretson's perspective available, for she evidently volunteered to enter the fray in Robinson's defense. Did she look for chivalry, or just defend a friend under siege without expecting gentler treatment as a woman? To add insult to injury, Hughes then chastised and attacked her for violating propriety in defending Robinson, told her to stop, and "pushed her." Mrs. Garretson defied then-prevalent stereotypes of passive, retiring femininity, for despite the threats, wounds, and actions of her fellow town residents, she refused to abate her defense of Robinson until the crowd had bodily forced him into the street. After the men had departed, they left her bruised, with a sprained wrist and "considerable pain and soreness" in her breast.[40]

Once they had removed Robinson from the Garretsons' protection, three men forced him to walk at least a mile out of the town limits. They dragged, harassed, and jabbed Robinson along the way, until they stopped outside of town to tar, feather, insult, and threaten him. After completing their "ministrations," they held him fast and took him ten miles out of town to Canfield. There, where he knew no one, they left Robinson just before dawn.[41]

Robinson's assailants told him they aimed to prevent him from holding his Berlin meeting the following day. They thus wished both to punish this lecturer for his transgression of town norms, and to make it impossible for him to speak as planned. In Canfield, Robinson found shelter with a sympathetic family named Wetmore, who cleaned him up and tended his wounds. These included burns from the hot tar and two serious cuts, including a deep one in his hip, incurred in the store as the men pulled him into some scythes.[42] The Wetmores also lent him clothes. Robinson attended two church services in Canfield that day and gave an antislavery address in the evening. It was Sunday, and even grave insults and injuries could not keep Robinson out of church and off the lectern, although he did not succeed in speaking again in Berlin.[43]

Robinson's attackers made no effort to hide their identities, and were well known in town. He publicized their names by printing them in the extended narrative of his trials for freedom of speech.[44] The sheriff later confronted the anti-abolitionists, but pressed no charges.[45] Local authorities never prosecuted any members of the crowd, and while they indicted Robinson for "inciting a mob," they did not convict him.[46]

Robinson tied this silencing incident with a larger issue, the hold that slavery had over the nation, and its power to restrict individual freedoms. He saw the events as a "gross violation of my rights, in common with those of my fellow citizens," and as proof that the "spirit" of slavery existed in the North as well as the South. Indeed, this spirit only respected violence, not "reason truth nor right." He held few illusions about his attackers' goal: to silence him at any cost. When one of them said "'Don't you see we have the power?'" Robinson saw this as a local expression of slaveholder sentiments.[47] Thus Robinson, along with other itinerants, regarded the anti-abolitionists' effort to keep him quiet as part of a larger national system of oppression and suppression of potential controversy and of activists' rights.

In the face of this rancor, Robinson left the area and recuperated for a month at the home of his in-laws in Guilford, Ohio. He recovered sufficiently to return to lecturing in August. His health remained poor for some time, but he continued to tour through the end of 1837. He failed to recover his full strength until he took a lengthy hiatus from speaking.[48] Berlin changed over the years, and by 1849 was so altered as to host an "immense gathering," the convention of Ohio Anti-Slavery Young Men and Women, a substantial contrast to the violent community response and attack on Robinson 12 years prior.[49]

Robinson remained a lifelong combatant in the free speech fight. He became editor of the Salem, Ohio, *Anti-Slavery Bugle* in 1851, and after his break from speaking, he reemerged on the platform with an October 1853 address to the Michigan State Anti-Slavery Society in Adrian. He ascribed such great power to "free speech" and "free thought" that he claimed they were the tools needed to dismantle the slave system. In his view, slaveholders knew of this link, and thus opposed abolitionist speeches and publications.[50] Pro-slavery people had to suppress open discussion, for permitting it would be tantamount to allowing the abolitionists to make further converts. For their part, Old Northwest antislavery people overtly denounced their foes' widespread efforts to stifle their free speech.

* * *

Robinson's travails were hardly anomalous, for other Old Northwest anti-abolitionists publicly proclaimed that they would use violence to exclude the antislavery message from their buildings. Churches, as ambiguously public structures, were quite restrictive, for clergy and congregants were often reluctant to address slavery or give a platform to outsiders. There does not appear to be a correlation between any particular denomination and these negative responses. Churches were inconsistent from one denomination to another, even one parish to another, as to whether they admitted abolitionist meetings.[51]

Some church authorities—including trustees and ministers—defended abolitionists' freedom of speech. At Smithfield, Ohio, in 1841, local people refused to publicize Dr. Erasmus D. Hudson's meeting, and some locals tried to lock him and his modest audience out of the church building. Hudson did get in, however, with the aid of the trustees, and he wrote that they had a "profitable meeting." Almost as an afterthought, Hudson wrote that some anti-abolitionists also lobbed "addled eggs" at them.[52] Hudson's casual attitude toward this attack indicates a willingness to stand firm in the face of frequent challenges.

This victory aside, anti-abolitionists in Old Northwest communities frequently prohibited itinerants from using churches. Even when these lecturers were themselves ministers and behaved with caution, they still encountered silencing of their freedom of speech in these religious settings. The Reverend William T. Allan, who traveled Illinois in May 1841 as the agent of the Illinois Society, believed that Alton remained dominated by the "spirit of pro-slavery violence," even four years after the riot that had ended with Elijah Lovejoy's death. When he visited there that May, Allan successfully preached on one occasion in a local church, despite the town's history of opposing free discussion and pro-slavery sentiment. This victory was short-lived, as he saw when he tried to hold more meetings. The following day a group of local people petitioned the mayor, begging him to stop Allan from speaking again. The mayor, in turn, wrote to the trustees of the church, asking them to refuse to allow Allan access. The trustees complied, and locked Allan out. The Cincinnati *Philanthropist* reported that "a mob assembled," but they found the house closed and no abolitionists present to attack.[53] Allan conceded, since he had no other venues in this hostile town once the mayor and trustees rallied against him.[54] Local civic officials could thus assert their right to close even religious facilities, but they also fiercely protected secular spaces. Pro-slavery and antislavery factions battled over their right to speak out in both kinds of places.

Community members who controlled government buildings varied in their willingness to allow abolitionists freedom of speech. In June 1845, Giles B. Stebbins held a meeting in the courthouse at Warren, the county seat of Trumbull County, Ohio, when locals forbade him to speak in all other places.[55] He quickly found a solution for his issues in Ohio this time, but this was not always so easy. In April 1844, Illinois activist Ichabod Codding encountered larger problems in securing a venue in Springfield, Illinois.[56] He first tried churches, and then resorted to the State House. While the authorities allowed him in, community sentiment was evidently less decided. Levi Spencer, Codding's fellow New York-born Illinois antislavery minister who attended the talk, wrote in his diary that Codding was speaking when a "tremendous and hideous noise" rang out from the lower level of the hall and made it impossible for him to continue. Their opponents egged the meeting, but as Spencer noted, "not much harm [was] done." They rescheduled the meeting for the next day. Spencer was outraged that this "Capitol of a free state" could produce such injustice, for in his eyes, the seat of Illinois government should have heard the antislavery perspective. This was a view many Illinoisans failed to share, as their actions proved.[57]

Other communities in the prairie state strongly resisted itinerants' speeches in public buildings. On May 27, 1846, the sheriff of Bloomington, Illinois, refused to allow traveling lecturer Owen Lovejoy to address local abolitionists in the courthouse. Levi Spencer lived there, and he and other abolitionists had been battling to speak locally against slavery since 1843, when a throng of men with clubs had broken up their county antislavery society meeting and attacked Spencer. Two days earlier, he noted that he and his few allies faced threats if they proceeded with their meeting plan. The predicted mob materialized, and on that day in May, Spencer wrote in his diary that the "crowded streets" were full of "oaths, threats" and "eggs."[58] They could not get any public building, so they met in a "Mechanic's shop," where Owen Lovejoy finally spoke. While he lectured, they heard the rhythmic smacking of eggs hitting the walls of the house, and entering in the windows. The eggs flew in from "adjoining buildings" while the authorities passively watched.[59] The anti-abolitionists of Bloomington, like those elsewhere, continually persecuted activists as they relocated their meetings, and the government failed to stop them.

Community resistance to abolitionists' freedom of speech drove them to use unusual, less politicized, locations for their meetings, including lofts, warehouses, private homes, fields, groves, and even barns. In their diaries, memoirs, and correspondence, itinerants reported the myriad places where people had gathered to hear their words, whether with hostility or open ears. On one eight-month jaunt in 1841–42 through Ohio, Indiana, and Michigan, on behalf of the American Society, Dr. Hudson was often accompanied by Charles C. Burleigh, the well-traveled Connecticut-born editor and lecturer who edited the *National Anti-Slavery Standard* and contributed to other antislavery papers including the *Liberator* and the Salem, Ohio, *Anti-Slavery Bugle*.[60] Oliver Johnson, another agent for and founding member of the American Society, joined Hudson and Burleigh for part of the tour.[61] In a letter from October 1841, Hudson revealed that he and Burleigh had, over the course of several weeks, spoken in a courthouse, a private home, Methodist and Friends meeting houses, an Associate Reformed Church, and a public hall, and had conducted multiple outdoor meetings.[62] The outdoor grove had the advantage of admitting more people than any building's capacity in the small towns typical of the antebellum Old Northwest. Itinerants sought out various venues until they found one that would accommodate them and allow them a public voice, but neither this nor acquiring an audience was simple.[63]

Itinerant lecturers in the Old Northwest faced an additional challenge to obtaining audiences and securing freedom of speech, since they relied upon an array of imperfect publicity techniques. These included informal mentions of meetings, handbills, word of mouth, and announcements in newspapers. Anti-abolitionists deliberately obstructed these efforts, and the news of an impending lecture often did not reach the targeted community, as occurred in 1841 in the small town of Lexington, Indiana. There, Dr. Hudson was unable to issue any advance announcement of his lecture, but he nonetheless obtained decent attendance due to word of mouth.[64] Locals thus sometimes refused itinerants the publicity they needed to gather an audience.[65] Poor publicity also had benign causes at times, including human error, but itinerants' local foes more commonly controlled audience size and access to public forums through repressing the news of their events, a less obvious attack on freedom of speech.[66] Even where abolitionists did find public forums and could publicize their talks, they still faced resistance in the Old Northwest.

Anti-abolitionist pressure could be acute, as was the case in 1841 in Dayton, Ohio. There, even while the lecturer backed down, his acquiescence failed to prevent a riot. That January, Thomas Morris, the former Democratic senator and Liberty Party vice presidential candidate, arrived in town to deliver an antislavery speech. A local mob warned him that they would attack him if he gave his scheduled address, so he cancelled it out of fear for his safety. Despite his decision to keep silent, anti-abolitionists attacked his carriage and driver with a "shower of brick bats," and broke the windows of his host, local abolitionist Hibbert Jewett.[67]

Morris left town the next day, but Dayton remained heated, for a race riot began as the mob turned its attention to the local African American population. They first focused on a house (in some accounts a house of ill repute) where rumor had it that a white woman lived with "some negroes." When told that the woman in question was actually "yellow," or a fair-skinned biracial woman, the agitated men then asked whether there were any abolitionists in the house. A fight broke out, and the African Americans defended themselves. In the chaos, someone killed a white anti-abolitionist named McCreary, and injured several others. Throngs then attacked local African Americans and burned three houses. The conflict only ended when authorities jailed a man in connection with McCreary's death. The Indiana antislavery newspaper, the *Protectionist*, the following month printed an account that supported the African Americans' right to self-defense.[68] Nonetheless, the local African American community paid a high price for abolitionists' actions and attempts to speak, while Morris himself escaped harm. Following this riot, Dayton remained rife with controversy over abolitionists' freedom of speech.[69]

* * *

Itinerants' persistence in defending their freedom to speak could incite long-running disputes in communities, and these often betrayed strong concerns with limiting outsiders' ability to influence Old Northwest towns. On September 29, 1841, Hudson, Burleigh, and Johnson met for a three-headed assault on slavery in Richmond, Indiana, a town that was notorious among abolitionists throughout the decade for virulent attacks on freedom of expression. Even in 1847, local Quakers greeted Lucretia and James Mott with hostility and tried to silence them, for they regarded them as troublemakers.[70] Back in 1841, the three men could only obtain a small room, Warner's Hall. Their audience did not all fit inside the space, but they were "respectable" and "attentive." That evening they procured the Associate Reformed Church for their meeting, and Burleigh spoke there. A botched attempt to stop the meeting with a false fire alarm interrupted him, but the speakers continued.[71] The anti-abolitionists of Richmond used this subterfuge to try to break up the meeting, but failed.[72]

After the trio left Richmond, a local newspaper, the *Richmond Palladium*, railed against them as "disgraceful." Having failed to prevent the meeting, Richmond's anti-abolitionists nevertheless derided the lecturers when they were no longer present to defend themselves. Arnold Buffum, who edited the *Protectionist* of nearby New Garden, reprinted this denunciatory piece shortly thereafter, noting that the *Palladium*'s editor was clearly trying to turn his readers against the travelers by using "contemptuous language, and odious epithets."[73]

As Editor Holloway of the *Palladium* exemplified, a common technique used to silence antislavery lecturers was to claim that they were hired outsiders. Holloway deemed the speakers "imported lecturers," "missionaries hired by the anti-slavery societies in the East, to awaken us to a sense of our sins," and "itinerant demagogues."[74] He wrote "we will not . . . countenance *hirelings*, who travel from one community to another, exciting and disturbing all, without the least benefit to any."[75] Buffum responded that it was futile for the editor of the *Palladium* (or similar respectable others) to denounce anti-abolitionist attacks while they simultaneously condemned antislavery activists. He argued that community leaders were to blame for this contempt toward activists, and that they led the poorer elements, the "unprincipled and vicious," to wreak violence upon them.[76] With this letter he both appealed to prominent citizens to uphold free speech, and offered a justification to exonerate the people who actually carried out the attacks.

In contrast, Buffum argued that leaders could stop mob actions by respecting and protecting abolitionists' right to a public voice. The editor of the *Palladium* had instead increased community hostility to lecturers by calling them "hirelings."[77] Buffum met efforts to ostracize antislavery people with suggestions for a fair resolution of future conflicts, including allowing speakers a say, and thus granting them their freedom of speech.

Antislavery people across Indiana reviled this incident of silencing in Richmond. The Indiana Anti-Slavery Society and the Union County [Indiana] Anti-Slavery Society both criticized the town in November 1841. The Indiana Society noted that Burleigh's attempt to speak publicly presented such a threat to the people of Richmond that they muzzled him. In their words:

> The only means whereby they could shut out conviction from the minds of the people, and secure the favor of slaveholders, was to shut the advocate of truth from their houses; thereby inviting the mob-ocrats to drive him from his stand, by the use of their best argument, to wit: eggs.

They argued that these violent methods would ultimately fail as they only revealed the conspiracy to hush abolitionists shared by northern elites and southern owners of men. Rather than permitting open debate, these collaborators depended on "a league of power, with the vile passions of the mob, to stifle discussion and smother the truth."[78] Indiana abolitionists saw how they could use evidence of their silencing to condemn and weaken their enemies, as they also tried later in Richmond.

Shortly thereafter, Hudson again found pressure to keep silent in Indiana when he visited Pendleton and Anderson in early October, and he used his reception there to state his views on tyranny and freedom of speech.[79] In Pendleton, he addressed a gathering at the Baptist meeting-house. While he found attendance good, certain residents showed their contempt for abolition by hurling eggs, or "pro-slavery, rotton arguments," against the building, although no one was hurt.

Having connected free speech to liberty, abolitionists could link its denial to tyranny. When Hudson and local ally Dr. Edwin Fussell attempted to hold their scheduled meeting the following day at the nearby Anderson courthouse, their opponents locked them out and chased interested audience members from the area. Fussell—like his wife and first cousin, Rebecca Lewis Fussell—was from Pennsylvania, and an abolitionist since childhood. The Fussells found great resistance in Indiana to their customary outspokenness on abolition.[80] At the courthouse, when the anti-abolitionists raised the clichéd question, "What have we [the North, Indianans] to do with slavery?" Hudson presented the ready evidence of the locked courthouse door as proof that slavery, even there, restricted all people's rights.[81] He used this to illustrate repression of freedom of speech, and the very presence of a throng in the square to stifle local abolitionist organizing reinforced his point. A close examination of one itinerant tour, the "One Hundred Conventions" Tour of 1843, definitively illustrates the central role that small Old Northwest places like Pendleton and Anderson played in antislavery and anti-prejudice activists' struggle to speak freely.

* * *

On September 25, 1843, an irate throng expelled two abolitionist lecturers from their meeting in the Noblesville courthouse in central Indiana. Countenanced by the sheriff and prominent citizens, this small, vociferous mob from a nearby town quickly silenced visiting Massachusetts speakers Charles Lenox Remond and schoolteacher and future *National Anti-Slavery Standard* editor Sydney Howard Gay. While few locals supported abolition, and the lecturers faced advance threats, Noblesville's citizens had resolved to protect their gathering.[82] Before the meeting, the club-holding anti-abolitionists marched the village streets, loudly proclaiming that activists, especially African American ones like Remond, had no right to speak in their house of governance.[83]

The Noblesville mob entered the courthouse and demanded that the antislavery meeting disperse. Although the attendees initially resisted, the majority quickly lost their resolve, and left only a small group of abolitionists alone with the mob and the sheriff. They found no defense from him, for he also claimed that they should leave the building.[84] Disgusted, Remond and Gay departed under the proud eye of their opponents. Remond, a founder of the American Society who had been lecturing since 1838, railed against the local people as spineless cowards for succumbing to this censorship pressure.[85] While they suffered no injury, larger principles were at stake for Remond, as he wrote to his Rochester friends Amy and Isaac Post, a white Quaker couple with whom he and Frederick Douglass had recently stayed when the tour passed through their city. He seethed, "liberty was murdered by the cowardly surrender of unquestionable rights on the part of those in peaceable assembly."[86] Remond described this as mob tyranny, and was particularly offended by the fact that the interlopers were not even town residents, but nevertheless "drove the people of Noblesville from their own quiet meeting."[87]

* * *

Noblesville was but one stop on the grueling, five-month "One Hundred Conventions" lecture tour of 1843, and one of many places in the Old Northwest where Remond, Gay, and other lecturers battled local resistance for a hearing. This tour exemplifies the ever-increasing opposition to freedom of speech that itinerant antislavery lecturers faced in this racially antagonistic region. Setting out from Vermont in early July, they continued across New York, Ohio, Indiana, and Pennsylvania, ending in Philadelphia that December. This strenuous campaign sent these seven men across five states: African American speakers Charles Lenox Remond and Frederick Douglass; and white lecturers John A. Collins, George Bradburn, James Monroe, Jacob Ferris, and Sydney Howard Gay. These one hundred meetings, or conventions, constituted a reform endeavor of unprecedented magnitude in terms of time, number of participants, and towns reached.[88] In the minds of the tour organizers, both eastern and western, the Old Northwest represented essential yet forbidding terrain for fighting slavery, and they thus invested substantial time and money in it.

The tour arose in a context of interregional exchange and communication that blurred the distinctions between national and local activism. Three immediatist organizations—the Ohio American Society, the Massachusetts Society, and the American Society—called for and collaborated in planning the tour.[89] People from both regions shared this task, for all saw that it was imperative that they reform the Old Northwest. In 1842, the Ohio American Anti-Slavery Society had asked the national executive committee of the American Society to send them prominent speakers, and that May, the Massachusetts Society voted to sponsor the tour to exploit the "comparatively new field" of the Old Northwest, fresh ground for sowing abolitionist seeds.[90] They rapidly obtained their stable of lecturers for the tour, thus proving their enthusiasm for activism in the "Western and Middle" states.[91] Six of the participants—all but Gay—were experienced lecturing agents for the Massachusetts Society and the American Society. Vermont-born John A. Collins had recently gone west to make arrangements.[92]

That same month, at the American Society's Boston annual meeting, Old Northwest abolitionists also played a vital role in the tour preparations, for a group of them, including Indiana's Dr. Fussell, had traveled east on a commodious wagon that they called the "Liberator," lecturing along the way. Antislavery people reused this wagon for many years.[93] Throughout the tour, the activists corresponded with local and major national papers such as the *Liberator* and the *National Anti-Slavery Standard*, linking the regions.[94]

In the Old Northwest, antislavery activists had much work to do prior to the tour, for interregional collaboration was central to the tour's success. Local societies in Ohio and Indiana made preparatory arrangements including calls for publicity and hospitality in newspapers like the *National Anti-Slavery Standard* and several western antislavery papers.[95] In one such article, Edwin Fussell pled with his Old Northwest neighbors to give all possible assistance to both the itinerants and their local audiences.[96] While their hosts had diligently prepared for the lecturers' arrival, they could not shield them from the trials and dangers of securing freedom of speech in these hostile communities.

* * *

In this underserved region, the battlefield was belief, the weapon the spoken word. On the men's sojourn through Ohio and Indiana, numerous towns denied the lecturers the liberty to speak. Apart from the provocation of the "One Hundred Conventions" tour's antislavery message, the speakers' immediatist beliefs and interracial friendships gave hostile Old Northwesterners cause for complaint—and reason to mob. The lecturers and their local allies confronted a range of opponents that hindered their rights.

The tour threw its participants and their allies against substantial anti-abolitionist opposition. They faced both overt and covert efforts to suppress their right to speak, refusals of venues, fierce counterarguments, and, most notably, mobs.[97] After his return to the East, Gay summed up their ordeal:

> . . . [H]ouses have been sacked and burned, printing presses have been destroyed, rewards offered for men's heads, loss of reputation has been cheerfully met, every species of wrong and obloquy has been suffered; and through all, anti-slavery has lived, and the ears of the people now everywhere tingle to hear upon the subject.[98]

As Gay had seen, numerous communities that hosted conventions did so reluctantly, refusing to allow the lecturers to meet and speak freely.

Across the Old Northwest, local people denied the lecturers this liberty, but this opposition was generally milder in Ohio than in Indiana, where anti-abolition sentiment was stronger.[99] At Massillon, Ohio, around August 20, a lawyer and a Methodist preacher verbally rebutted them. The eastern lawyer William A. White, unruffled, remarked, "Neither of their speeches were worthy of notice, and I believe the proslavery people who made them their cats-paws were ashamed of them before they finished." White praised the local allies who sustained him and his fellow lecturers in the face of this challenge.[100] In Utica, Ohio, a Whig named General Warner denounced abolition, and claimed, as White wrote, that abolitionists were "the immediate successors of the Jacobins of the days of terror." Such inflammatory remarks did not daunt the itinerants, for White's companions—Gay and James Monroe of Connecticut, a future professor and politician—both dismissed Warner's claims.[101] Thus, while the lecturers often noted their verbal antagonists in their letters, they adapted to this frequent opposition.

* * *

Audience rejoinders could be unpleasant, but a more troubling hazard of antislavery lecturing in the Old Northwest was the ever-present threat of violent anti-abolitionist attacks inspired by racial bias, partisan politics, and the desire to preserve local rule and the social order. Community leaders often shepherded hostile crowds that threw eggs and threatened the lecturers and their audiences with violent assault.[102] In the case of the "One Hundred Conventions Tour," while these risks escalated when itinerants traveled in mixed-race groups, mobs assaulted the speakers even when they traveled in racially homogenous units. The attacks grew more frequent in Indiana, but Ohio was far from quiet.

While interracial contact provoked some mobs, other mobs threatened and attacked even all-white groups of lecturers. In Wooster, Ohio, early in the tour, a partisan mob nearly attacked White and Monroe even though Douglass and Remond were not with them. Locked out of indoor venues, they could only obtain the town square for their scheduled meeting, and there tried to speak to a hostile crowd. A Democratic congressman named Benjamin Jones shouted contradictions throughout White's speech. Jones's partisan identity could certainly have informed his anti-abolition views—and intensified local disputes. By the hour of the evening lecture, the townspeople had already begun to threaten an attack, but this proved to be a bluff, although someone egged a home during the night.[103] Bradburn encountered more animosity when he later traveled alone to Dayton, a place noted for its violent past and "infamous for its pro-slavery mobs." Dayton at the time had just over 6,000 residents.[104] Anti-abolitionists had previously attacked lectures that three other itinerants gave, most notoriously, that of Thomas Morris.

In 1843, Bradburn was thus pleasantly surprised when three of his four Dayton lectures proceeded undisturbed. Even though the final lecture met with the resistance he had anticipated, a "shower of stones and eggs," the attendees remained, which he saw as "great progress" for Dayton, with its ugly history.[105] Despite the violent and nonviolent resistance of such Ohio communities early in the tour, the "One Hundred Conventions" lecturers were still unprepared for the extensive trials they next faced in Indiana.

* * *

At Pendleton, in the center of the state, the silencing of abolitionists, extralegal violence, and miscarriage of justice melded together in a fiery confrontation that exemplifies the Old Northwest freedom of speech struggle. Between September 14 and September 16, men claiming to defend party politics, racial stratification, slavery, and republican government first attacked a meeting led by three of the convention lecturers—Frederick Douglass, George Bradburn, and William White—and then intimidated the local community. On the third month of the tour, the lecturers, particularly the famed speaker and writer Douglass, were already well seasoned when they arrived at the home of their congenial local hosts, the Fussell family. These men did not welcome their brutal treatment, but found it unsurprising in this contentious area of Indiana where most local people regarded their message as unpalatable. In the state as a whole, many residents held firm beliefs in their right to silence discussion of race or abolition.[106]

White, Douglass, and Bradburn arrived in Pendleton anticipating trouble, since local anti-abolitionists had threatened to stop them with violence. They expected that their opponents would shut the antislavery group out of the meetinghouse, for while a small group of outspoken Quaker enemies of slavery lived near Pendleton, local allies were very few and public abolition was unwelcome, especially when African Americans advocated it.[107] As the convention approached, the lecturers heard increasingly direct warnings of violence. White claimed that these antagonists lived in "Columbus, a miserable, rum-drinking place" that was approximately six miles away. Shortly after the meeting began, the hostile trustees ejected them from the Baptist Church.[108]

Refusing to be dissuaded, the abolitionists and their audience met immediately outside of the church, where their foes joined them; local resident Dr. John Cook acted as an intermediary, working to calm the crowd—which White claimed was inflamed by alcohol—that threatened them with violence.[109] While he was not an abolitionist, Cook affirmed "the right of speech." The anti-abolitionists permitted Bradburn to speak until a rain shower interrupted them, and many fled indoors. The crowd remained outside the church, and only mildly attacked the speakers: "The mobocrats retired without making any assault upon us, save tossing at us a single stone, and one or two 'evangelical eggs.'"[110] The antislavery lecturers stood strong in the face of steady local challenge.

That evening, a group of Pendleton citizens took action to protect local freedom of speech. They held a meeting in which they unanimously passed a resolution denouncing their silencing, and Bradburn and White spoke to the assembled audience.[111] White, pleased, "hoped we should have no more trouble," but they soon did.[112]

While the abolitionists and their free speech allies took these direct, formal measures to protect their rights, their adversaries nonetheless attacked the next day's meeting. Local organizer Dr. Fussell—foreseeing the likely need for a neutral meeting space—had set up an open-air facility in a grove near town, complete with seating and a platform; it resembled an outdoor revival stage.[113] The convention assembled in the woods, and White noted that eleven anti-abolitionists were present at the outset, as was a sympathetic audience of 100 men and 30 women. First White spoke, followed by Bradburn, in total for over one and one-half hours. Bradburn was absorbed in his speech when Dr. Cook suddenly interrupted him, after noticing that their opponents were drawing near.

This group of about sixty men elicited strong invective from the abolitionists they targeted. Bradburn and White noted their attackers' slovenly, ungentlemanly attire, their level of preparation for combat, and their partisan identities. The men were in their shirtsleeves, and appeared disheveled. They marched around the grove while prominently displaying their supply of "brick-bats, stones, and 'evangelical eggs.'"[114] They represented both major parties, for local people identified one leader, shoeless, in sagging clothing, to White as a Democrat, while the other leader, clad in a "coon-skin cap," was a Whig.[115] This fellow, whom Edwin's uncle and local Quaker Solomon Fussell later identified as "Devault [David] Crowl," evidently wore the cap with the tail in the front, lending what Bradburn thought was a ridiculous aspect to his proclamations and fierce utterances.[116] In their descriptions of their assailants, the abolitionists scorned their character. Bradburn referred to them in stereotypical terms, as "sundry unshaven, lantern-jawed, savage-looking loafers," who uttered "murderous threats, and blasphemous oaths, against abolitionists and 'niggers.'"[117] Even as Bradburn was likely to judge his opponents particularly harshly given that they had invaded and shut down the antislavery meeting, the interlopers' later attacks on the speakers, particularly Douglass, bear out this interpretation of their intentions as violent. The participants on both sides of the encounter used familiar language to justify protecting or opposing open activist discussion. This local-level violence thus embodied larger national disputes over reformers' freedom of speech, with the difference that the unsettled environment meant that these local tensions persisted longer, to an even more dangerous degree.

The situation at Pendleton quickly escalated into violence when the abolitionists refused their adversaries' order to "disperse," and stood their ground.[118] While much of the audience appeared inclined to flee, White asked them to keep to their seats. The women remained seated, attesting to their bravery, while some of the men departed. White claimed of the women, "throughout the whole they showed themselves the more courageous party, as they ever have done." He continued, noting that it was the refusal of the Pendleton citizens (presumably meaning the men present) to face down their aggressors that led to local mob power.[119] These women—possibly assuming that their sex would protect them and that their opponents would not harm them—kept to their seats and demonstrated remarkable collective cohesion, which their male counterparts lacked.

As the anti-abolitionists began to throw their airborne weapons, Dr. Cook and William White attempted to reason with their attackers, which angered them further. One anti-abolitionist, James Jackson, tried to seize control with a profanity-riddled speech about the abolitionists' political crimes, especially their nonvoting and immediatist views, including "'letting the niggers loose for nothing.'"[120] He made what White called a "most ridiculous spectacle," but in the end found that words could not convey his message with the efficacy of gesture and violence.[121] Falling silent, Jackson physically mimed his frustration, and Bradburn equated his convulsions with the jerks of a cadaver attached to a galvanic battery. His antics made the audience laugh aloud.[122] Jackson realized that the situation was escaping his control and stated that "'he could not talk, but he could fight.'"[123] Refusing to allow this mockery, he thus incited the crowd to break up the speaking platform and the meeting.[124]

Following the destruction of the platform, the brawl began in earnest. The anti-abolitionists attacked the audience, pressing in and throwing them to the ground. They "knocked down" and wounded Micajah White, a Quaker, along with two other men (Mr. Graham and Dr. Vaughan). Famed abolitionist Levi Coffin later wrote that White, his nephew, lost two teeth to a brick.[125] Douglass, despite identifying as a Garrisonian nonresistant at that time, entered the fray with a club to defend a man who the crowd was severely beating, and whom he thought was William White.[126] Nonresistant principles could bend under pressure, especially when the lecturers needed to protect one another.

The attack at Pendleton is but one example of the tension between violence and nonresistance that mob attacks against abolitionists in the Old Northwest elicited. Frederick Douglass was the most famous nonresistant on the tour, meaning that he embraced the Garrisonian practice of nonviolence, but Gay also avowed these principles. Bradburn praised Douglass for abandoning "his non-resistance not for himself, but for a friend," even though the man Douglass had saved was actually a stranger, not White. Douglass later claimed that the Pendleton incident had "cured" him of his nonresistance.[127] As for William White, he openly admitted to striking blows to protect Douglass.

Following Douglass's defensive action, his opponents wrested the club from his hands and attacked him with fury. They flung their various weapons at him, and Rebecca Fussell claimed to have placed her baby in the way to intercede when a man attempted to club Douglass. She wrote that Douglass managed to flee for a moment after "[m]yself and baby saved him from that blow."[128] Rebecca Fussell's move to protect Douglass has implications for the role of gender and even age in protecting certain activists from harm. In making her decision to place her baby Linnaeus between the angry men and Douglass, she assumed that they would hurt neither her nor the baby, and thus saved Douglass a clouting. In tandem with the other women at the meeting who kept to their seats when their antagonists arrived, she proves that Old Northwest women both stayed in dangerous situations to protect the right to free expression, and actively resisted anti-abolitionist silencing.

The dangerous itinerant milieu thus had an active place for women and children, as the lecturers and meeting attendees who wrote about the Old Northwest conventions observed. White wrote of the benefits and the costs of this gender and age diversity when he discussed Ohio meetings, noting that unlike in Massachusetts, "all the mothers bring their babies." In some cases, bringing the children must have been a practical choice if there was no one else to watch them at home, or if they had to nurse their babies. White found that this could prove disruptive, "when ten or a dozen set up a shout," but overall welcomed their presence, thanks to "the desire it shows in the mothers to attend."[129] This lecturer believed that this attendance boded well for action for the cause. Old Northwest women were willing to risk their safety and that of their families to take part in and protect meetings that interested them. This speaks to their desire to participate in reform politics and to their strong degree of integration into Old Northwest abolition.[130] Despite Rebecca Fussell's valiant effort, Douglass did not escape harm for long.

* * *

While all of the lecturers were injured, the anti-abolitionists' racial motivations are evident since they targeted Douglass, the lone African American lecturer present, and injured him the most severely with blows from rocks and fists. Chasing him, they shouted, "'Kill the nigger, kill the damn nigger.'" White claimed that the scene exemplified Indiana's racist character as the anti-abolitionist "hell-hounds" pursued him, "panting for his blood. It was a fearfully true picture of the flight of the fugitive slave, and it was fitting it should take place on the soil of this pro-slavery State."[131] One well-aimed stone hit Douglass on the head, knocking him down and creating a large lump. A circle of men quickly gathered around the fallen Douglass, aiming deadly blows at him, and wounding him on the hand and in the side.[132] They directed their worst violence at this man whose identity and message most strongly violated community norms.

The several accounts of the melee name different men who intervened to stop this race-based attack.[133] William White claimed to have done the rescuing himself, by flinging himself upon a man who aimed at striking Douglass a death blow. He walloped the back of White's head with a stone, but White's hat spared him the worst of the impact.[134] By intervening, White attracted the wrath of the attackers, and "was badly wounded and bruised."[135] Others also interceded, and the violence ended.[136] Once they had shut down the meeting and violently silenced the activists, the anti-abolitionists departed.

After Douglass's allies had halted his attempted murder, William Lukens placed him in his wagon with the aid of Dr. Fussell and his brother-in-law Neal Hardy.[137] They drove Douglass to Hardy's home about two miles away, unconscious all the while. Once they arrived, Fussell and the Hardys cared for him.[138] Douglass recovered swiftly, and surprised his friends by speaking the following day in the congenial setting of Friends Meeting House in nearby Fall Creek, albeit with a bandaged head.[139]

* * *

The activists' contemporaries were very interested in this overt silencing of freedom of speech in Pendleton; newspapers, both antislavery and general, took note of it and condemned it. Many journalists and citizens saw it as an outrageous, blatant miscarriage of justice. The Whig-identified *Indiana Courier* wrote shortly thereafter to denounce the attackers' violence and censorship intentions. The editor called the anti-abolitionists a "gang of lawless and uncivilized ruffins, armed and disguised" who recklessly assaulted a group "quietly and peaceably progressing with its business." In the writer's view, mobs were inexcusable expressions of low, wicked human emotions, especially when they aimed to stifle "the right of *free discussion*—a right as sacred as life itself and secured to every citizen by the law and the Constitution." In response, all needed to rally to protect citizenship rights, deny mobs their approval, and prosecute their participants.[140] This was not in fact what ensued at Pendleton, where freedom of speech continued to erode, and the local authorities proved disinterested in protecting activists' rights. The attack on the touring lecturers at Pendleton demonstrates the determination on both sides to either hear or silence controversial antislavery views. The local partisan and racially biased climate was too firmly seated for the activists to overturn it, and this incident proves that not all views could peaceably earn a hearing in the Old Northwest.

As this case demonstrates, conflicts over slavery and social control made securing reformers' freedom of speech unusually difficult in the Old Northwest, and these virulent reactions could transform activists' lives. Whereas itinerant lecturers certainly attracted their fair share of dramatic opposition, for them the experience was fleeting, and could cease as soon as they departed a problematic town. Since the Old Northwest was central to their shared reform mission, itinerants gave local societies mobile reinforcement and took direct action against slavery, and in turn, locals provided them essential support. The repeated challenges that resident abolitionists faced across the Old Northwest demonstrate that their institution-building and aid to visiting lecturers threatened their neighbors' conception of community control sufficiently to elicit repeated violence. This constant resistance to Old Northwest abolitionists' public activism plays an integral part in understanding itinerants' freedom of speech struggles. Locals brought the conflicts over race and slavery into their homes by opening them to travelers and collaborating with them. After itinerants left, people continued to debate the parameters of speech and action in Old Northwest towns. Resident activists' aid had serious consequences when they clashed with neighbors who refused to permit them to organize in their communities; indeed, their unwelcome message rendered them pariahs in their towns.

As the extreme case of Edwin and Rebecca Fussell exemplifies, these changes could happen almost overnight, even when they had already openly espoused abolition. At the same time as the bold attack at Pendleton inspired outrage across Indiana and the nation, the local freedom of speech drama unfolded further. The subsequent legal struggle had significant ramifications for both the Fussell family and the community. That family suffered wide-ranging effects for organizing the Pendleton antislavery meeting and hosting its speakers. Traveling lecturers like Gay knew well that eastern antislavery people "sacrifice[d]" far less than Old Northwest activists like the Fussells.[141] Prior to the "One Hundred Conventions" tour, the doctor had a well-established medical practice, and the family had many friends in the region. The couple not only lost most of their material possessions and their livelihood, but eventually they had to move away.[142] They paid substantial costs for their efforts to fight slavery and protect freedom of speech.

The Fussells and the itinerants ignited a struggle over local mores. Rebecca and Edwin Fussell's existing antislavery beliefs expanded in the inhospitable soil of the Old Northwest. Fussell and his allies publicized their trials in both local and national newspapers, and used their challenges to raise awareness of the dire circumstances reformers faced in Indiana—and in the region. In Madison County, the "One Hundred Conventions" tour left wounds in the community beyond the physical kind the abolitionists sustained.

The conflict at Pendleton—an overt battle over freedom of speech—spiraled out into a larger cultural and legal struggle at Anderson, the seat of Madison County, nine miles away. After the touring abolitionists had departed, their opponents continued to shut down local reform. The attackers at Pendleton and the subsequent throngs at Anderson were open about their intention to silence abolitionists, beginning with their advance notice that they would mob the Pendleton meeting.[143] In both towns, the anti-abolitionists freely opposed reformers' liberty to speak and the local judicial process.

In Pendleton and Anderson, mob violence was a form of community control that anti-abolitionists overtly used to stifle divisive antislavery views.[144] The night of the Pendleton attack, rioters rode through the village, warning that they would return with reinforcements to destroy the Fussells' home. The abolitionists' allies—including some Quakers—took up arms to respond to this threat, but it was a bluff. That these Quakers would violate nonresistance indicates the severity of the threat they felt. While the mobbing men did not return, the townspeople heard them shouting nearby.[145] The abolitionists at Pendleton knew they were not yet safe.

The itinerants had stayed at the Fussell home since their arrival in town, but as the threats mounted, they decided it was prudent to disperse in houses throughout Pendleton. Bradburn wrote of Rebecca and Edwin's flight from their home with much emotion:

> O, it was a painful sight to see, as I saw . . . the doctor's excellent wife, taking her leave of friends and relatives . . . and with an infant in her arms, accompanied by their two other little ones in his, hurrying stealthily out of their own house, in the evening's darkness, to avoid being buried beneath its ruins by an infernal mob.[146]

They fled to Dr. Madison C. Walker's house for safety.[147]

The abolitionists defended themselves in print, charging that prominent locals supported and legitimated the aggression at Pendleton and Anderson. After he left Pendleton, White claimed the anti-abolitionists were passive participants manipulated by "designing men," including religious and Democratic Party leaders. Bradburn agreed, specifying that mob members were Baptists and Methodists.[148] "F."—most likely Edwin Fussell himself since they used very similar language—concurred, claiming in a letter to the *Free Labor Advocate* that the Anderson mob varied in terms of social status, "not merely the rabble but 'men of property and standing.'" "F's" quotation marks indicate his awareness that he was using a conventional phrase to describe mob composition, one that acknowledged community leaders' investment in preserving the status quo, even if it entailed using illegal means.[149] With this, he supported the common view that prominent men led anti-abolition mobs.[150]

* * *

The courts also weighed in on the identity of the anti-abolitionists and their responsibility for community disruption. The anti-abolitionists thus had to face the judgment of the legal system, not merely that of their antislavery targets. Initially, the case appeared to favor the abolitionists, for a grand jury indicted "some twenty" of the rioters. One, Morris Runnels (called Reynolds in most newspaper accounts), volunteered to stand trial in Anderson as a test case, assuming that he would receive a minimal sentence. If this happened, the other indicted men planned to undergo trial, but they also announced that if the jury imprisoned Runnels, they would then demolish the jail. Local lawyers had offered Runnels free defense, which he had declined, assuming a sympathetic verdict. Runnels pled guilty, and said, as Fussell paraphrased, "he *had* mobbed the abolitionists, and he . . . had come *on purpose* to be imprisoned, and was going to be, and was coming out over the prostrate walls."[151] Presiding Judge Killgore defied Runnels's expectations, sentencing him to twenty days of jail time and a ten-dollar fine.[152] The throng outside of the court responded with outrage, reiterated their plan to free Runnels by force, and even vowed to attack the judge and jury.

The drama continued, for the local government summoned the militia in response to the anti-abolitionists' threats. Later that day, Thomas McAllister, the Democratic representative in the Indiana House, rode into town at the head of a throng of 200 to 300 men on horseback.[153] They demanded Runnels's release, and again intimated that they would destroy the jail with arms, which they claimed to have stockpiled nearby. They also threatened Judge Killgore, who, according to Edwin Fussell, responded by condemning the abolitionists for the events after the Pendleton meeting and absolving himself of the blame for jailing Runnels. Killgore claimed that since Runnels had pled guilty, the law forced him to convict. He begged the crowd to refrain from attack, for the militia would then have to respond. Instead, the judge recommended that they petition Governor Bigger to pardon Runnels. The crowd finally scattered once the messenger had sped off with the petition to Indianapolis, but its members went on intimidating local abolitionists and the people who participated in the trial.[154]

Addressed to the Whig Governor Samuel Bigger, the petition text identified its signers as local residents with a voice in county affairs. These "citizens of Madison County" pled that Runnels had committed a youthful indiscretion, out of his ignorance: " . . . the strong probability is that he was not conscious of having violated any law." Further, they argued that the penalty was overly harsh, given his lack of previous criminal behavior. They concluded by asking for Runnels's release and for pardon. The petition signers represented a spectrum of the community, including local Quakers, which surprised Edwin Fussell.[155] This petition had 220 signatures, many of which are illegible, and several appear to have been signed by the same hand. A range of citizens rallied in support of Runnels's freedom, and made an argument that the governor evidently found persuasive. On October 12, 1843, Bigger inscribed on the petition's reverse: "Pardoned as to the imprisonment in the county jail; Samuel Bigger."[156]

Madison County's residents anxiously awaited the petition results. Edwin Fussell, unable to exercise his freedom of speech, had gone lecturing with John O. Wattles and Valentine Nicholson. Persistent efforts to mob him made it increasingly evident that it was becoming impossible for him to live in Pendleton or maintain his medical practice.[157] When he returned two days after the trial, the messenger had not yet brought back the petition, and he suffered persistent haranguing from his local opponents who blamed him for the meeting and the ensuing conflict. He and his friends debated whether his family should depart, for rumors of assassination plots circulated and he believed that they would never again be safe in town. The doctor found that even his allies saw his continued residence in Pendleton as unwise, but he steadfastly adhered to his values in the face of massive local opposition.[158]

Meanwhile, local authorities searched for men to protect Anderson's official buildings from the anticipated riot, but they found few takers for this risky enterprise. The small number of volunteers and their antagonists poured into the Anderson town center. Fussell claimed that this third mob originated from throughout Madison County, and several nearby counties as well. As their numbers grew, the pardon arrived from Governor Bigger, Runnels went free, and the throng dispersed.[159] In the eyes of Fussell and his abolitionist allies, this definitively refuted local freedom of speech.

* * *

Since violent anti-abolition had so drastically altered the Fussell family's lives, they felt the pardon as a cruel blow. It was clear that activists could not rely on the authorities to use the law to defend their interests. "F." wrote that with this decision, the Governor gave what he termed "mobocrats" free rein. Now, "they may trample down, abuse, and murder abolitionists, whenever or wherever they please, and shall not be punished by the laws of Indiana."[160] While there was a perfunctory trial, the court took no further punitive action against the anti-abolitionists. In addition to revealing the shortcomings of the Indiana judicial system, this outcome drove the Fussell family out of the state. They permanently relocated after a period of moving around the Midwest lecturing and searching for a Fourierist utopian community in which to settle. The Fussells shared their interest in the community movement with other Old Northwest abolitionists and some of the "One Hundred Conventions" tour lecturers.[161] Unable to find a community, they ultimately instead moved to Philadelphia.[162]

Fussell later learned from his family and friends still in Indiana that the other indicted men never stood trial. The next court term was six months after the riot, and the remaining men appeared when summoned. The prosecuting attorney only called in anti-abolitionist witnesses, who claimed that they had not seen the indicted men "*do anything wrong.*" Despite the presence in the room of other witnesses able to provide damning evidence against the men on the stand, the judge did not call them, and dismissed the case for lack of proof.[163] The legal consequences of these Indiana attacks on itinerant lecturers and on the Fussells' freedom of speech thus vanished, along with the opportunity for them to raise their grievances in court.[164]

Fussell was outraged, and saw this as a transparent instance of politics and intimidation trumping the legal system. It was an election year, and the prosecuting attorney required the favor of the individuals in the mob and positive public opinion in order to win. In Fussell's view, this attorney accordingly selected his witnesses from among men who so feared the mob that they remained silent.[165] Fussell saw that securing freedom of speech was impossible in Madison County, and that his family had been correct to relocate for their safety. The anti-abolitionists regarded this as the necessary silencing of a voice that was outside of community norms, which threatened national stability and had continued to push an unpopular cause, even after the provocative itinerants from the East had left town. In Pendleton and Anderson, abolitionists elicited substantial disagreements about social control and their freedom to speak, which taught them that they could expect few guarantees of their rights in Indiana.

Fussell demonstrated the permanence of the move in March 1844 when he granted power of attorney to his brother-in-law Neal Hardy, and directed him to dispose of his assets. In Philadelphia, the Fussells still agitated against slavery, and persisted in their work for the community movement.[166] In 1848, upon his first return visit to Pendleton, Edwin wrote to Rebecca of his visit to their former home. Tangled remnants of wildly growing honeysuckle and roses filled their garden, while the house itself was decrepit: "The ruin is complete and all trampled down under the feet of the heathen."[167] Fussell thought its decayed condition reminded local residents of the repression of local abolitionism, and yet their wild yard still thrived, as did his family.[168] Central Indiana—and the region—remained charged for activism even after the Fussells departed for Pennsylvania with their lives irrevocably altered, for Pendleton was only one among many Old Northwest communities that resisted local abolitionist organizing and freedom of speech. Others across the region also sought to closely control problematic antislavery voices.

* * *

The hostile reaction most Indianans had to antislavery led to ongoing violence and freedom of speech battles as the "One Hundred Conventions" tour continued beyond Pendleton. Douglass, Bradburn, and

White encountered another mob in October at Richmond, the site of the Society of Friends' expulsion of eight members the previous year for their refusal to renounce antislavery activism. Their disruptive presence tapped into the town's and the state's continual political and religious controversies, and illustrates the pervasive, violent opposition they faced.

Despite this tense history, the "One Hundred Conventions" lecturers' first Richmond convention—on October 28, 1843—met successfully and freely, although the situation soon changed. Douglass spoke, and Bradburn explicitly refuted Henry Clay's positions on slavery, engaging in the earlier debates over the Whig politician there. On October 29, Douglass went to lecture at Goshen, nearly 200 miles away.[169] In Richmond, White and Bradburn led an effective morning meeting, but a church trustee locked the convention out of the building that afternoon. With the approval of another trustee in hand, a man crawled in the window to admit the audience. White began to speak, while outside a crowd with both antislavery and pro-slavery elements gathered.

Local lawyer James Green spoke out against the meeting in the street even though the abolitionists had invited him and his fellow anti-abolitionist, Wayne County senator Lewis Burke, inside to take part. Green attacked the speakers in language calculated to raise the ire of the audience, bluntly stating "that the Abolitionists ought all to be driven out of town."[170] Green selected his location wisely, for outside he faced no rebuttal. There he could, as eyewitness and local abolitionist Kersey Grave wrote, incite "the rabble" to attack the meeting. Shortly after his diatribe, someone flung "a dozzen or two of eggs . . . through the window in the direction of the speaker's stand." White had nearly finished speaking, and only a few of the eggs struck him, for most of them hit the wall. Burke, who Grave claimed was a slavecatcher, was in the egg-flinging crowd, and Grave used his presence to snipe at the mainstream Quakers, the "body Friends" that had expelled his brother Jacob the previous year for his antislavery affiliations:

> Is it possible that the people of Wayne county send such a vile egg-o-tist and violator of good order and decency, to the legislature to make laws for them? We shall see whether the 'body Friends' vote for him hereafter, and thus prove their opposition to slavery and their regard for law, order, and decency...[171]

Green and Burke refused to join the meeting, and following the egging, the anti-abolitionists paraded the town, seeking their foes.

A group of approximately fifty men proceeded away from the church, along the main street. They harassed and called on several townspeople, and pelted one man's house with stones and bricks, breaking windows and dishes.[172] This anti-abolition group confirmed their vitriol with further violence. As was also true previously in Pendleton, the antislavery people's accounts of their foes' views may have been biased, but it is nonetheless evident from the anti-abolitionists' actions that they wished to shut down antislavery discussion, even at the price of hurting others.

The Richmond convention catalyzed a broader freedom-of-speech controversy after the fact. The *Wayne County Record* printed a biased critique of Douglass's Richmond speech, and among other insults and inaccuracies, it claimed that the mob pursued and egged him to retaliate for the content of an alleged speech on October 29.[173] The editor called Douglass "impudent" as he ostensibly criticized the throng's actions:

> 'As the conductor of a public journal, we feel it our duty to condemn such disgraceful proceedings. We do not do this; because we feel a sympathy with the Negro abolition Lecturer. That he was impudent, and deserved all that he got, is perhaps true, but egging is not the way to meet such fanatics. Treat such persons with silent contempt.'[174]

Benjamin Stanton of the *Free Labor Advocate* denounced this "exhibition of spleen and prejudice against colored people." He claimed that such articles added to the racialized oppression of both slaves and free African Americans, and blamed abolitionists for their own mobbing. He saw the choice of the word "impudent" as blatantly biased: "No man in his senses would call a white man *impudent* for talking just as Douglas did [or would have, since he was not there that day], under precisely similar circumstances."[175] A reader who signed his letter P. Q. R. echoed Stanton's concerns in his next issue.[176]

Stanton used the errors and biases of the *Record's* account to deconstruct bigotry through mockery. Since Douglass was in Goshen during the Richmond disturbance, White was the actual victim of the violence: "And as his name is, so is he," wrote Stanton. He took his attack on skin prejudice to a personal level, noting that John B. Stitt, the editor of the *Record*, was in fact rather dark skinned. As was a common technique of antislavery activists who wished to ridicule absolute racial categories, and as he had done with his "colorometer," he wrote that "the difference in color" separating Stitt and Douglass is "not vastly greater than between him [Stitt] and Wm. A. White." With this claim, Stanton argued for equal rights by revealing "the folly of estimating men's merits by the color of the skin."[177] In his view, Stitt had unmasked his prejudice as he erroneously attributed White's speech to the allegedly "impudent" Douglass.

Stanton also had fiery words for another local editor, that of the Whig Richmond *Palladium*, who he claimed endorsed mobs and blamed abolitionists for their own mobbing. While Editor Holloway had advertised the antislavery meeting, he then supported Green. Stanton said Holloway claimed that Green tried to quell the mob with his speech in the street, but proved the opposite. Holloway quoted Green as misrepresenting abolitionists as partisan "hirelings," a label which would in fact escalate mob anger.[178] Holloway thus condemned abolitionists while claiming to support abstract liberty of speech. Stanton argued that Green's speech only angered a mob of people loyal to the Whigs and mainstream churches, and asserted that such community leaders contributed to violent repression of the freedom to speak. He claimed that Green influenced public opinion to suppress free discussion, for mobs formed when prominent figures like Green, "of reputed respectability and standing," countenanced anti-abolition attacks. Then, "the vulgar herd . . . are ready to assail them with their appropriate weapons, fists, stones, brickbats, and eggs."[179] He saw leaders as responsible for drawing others into such conflicts. These local temblors were but one form of upheaval that bore aftershocks across Old Northwest communities after itinerants' departure, but lecturers also sought to avoid confronting excessive danger by strategically choosing their speaking schedules. Touring activists used their communication networks to determine who could securely lead their meetings, and who had the physical freedom to speak.

* * *

While they confronted extralegal violence and pushed with their public lectures against racism and anti-abolitionism, itinerants compromised at times when a change of personnel would allow them still to speak, but to do so more safely. That October, Remond avoided speaking in Indianapolis as he had planned, for he had heard from his friends that this could prove fatal. He in fact refrained from exercising his own freedom of speech, staying at Westfield while, in the wee hours of September 27, Gay and Monroe rode off to a tense Indianapolis with Fussell (who had briefly joined the tour) and other local companions.[180] The abolitionists derided Indianapolis as vehemently anti-abolition, the "very fortress of pro-slavery in this State," and a "moral refrigerator."[181] Remond expected they would find trouble, for word had reached him that "two hundred" mounted men had been "drilling" for a week and proclaiming that they would "burn, kill & distroy" any local convention. He saw Jesse D. Bright, Indiana's lieutenant governor, whom he called a slaveholder, as responsible. Bright served in this role from 1843 to 1845, and did not actually own slaves, but was a close friend of Kentuckians Henry Clay and John C. Breckenridge.[182] By then well acquainted with Indiana's racial climate, the touring abolitionists had expected no support in the capitol.[183] Even in the seat of state government, public sentiment so strongly opposed abolition that authorities would not defend activists' rights, but they attempted local organization nonetheless. In Indianapolis, they found that the only check on extralegal violence was what the meeting attendees themselves imposed.

Once the men approached Indianapolis, they sent an advance guard to assess the safety of the situation.[184] Despite word of an impending ferocious mob, they found no immediate threats, but their notoriety meant that no one permitted them to use any buildings. They could only speak on the steps of the State House, but they lectured twice to increasing audiences.[185] At this, the pioneer antislavery meeting held in Indianapolis, they drew an audience of "influential" people, almost all of them men.[186] While the meeting was tense, the abolitionists spoke and obtained a hearing. Monroe credited the peace that prevailed to "respectable . . . citizens[']" calming presence.[187] One attendee even came so close to violence as to put a brick in his pocket, intending to hurl it at Monroe, but sympathetic audience members stopped him. The speakers believed the meeting a success since they faced down such substantial threats and secured freedom of speech. Fussell said of this city, "the great pro-slavery citadel of this State," that they left it "in a great ferment."[188] After their departure, Gay, Monroe, and Fussell reunited with Remond, and their lecture tour traveled on. While the others found freedom of speech in Indianapolis, Remond could not, and he thus provides further proof that African American activists in this region faced difficult choices between their safety and their freedom of speech.

This incident with Remond proves that under-recognized Old Northwest lecture campaigns like the "One Hundred Conventions Tour" are vital to understanding the impact of race in nineteenth-century America. Since African American populations in most Old Northwest places were tiny, traveling lecturers often closely collaborated and worked to protect one another regardless of race. Interracial cooperation was actually more common in this region than previously believed—albeit still controversial enough to elicit violence from Old Northwest observers.

Old Northwest abolition reveals that historians have underestimated the prevalence and longevity of grassroots interracial activism. Scholars have recently begun to uncover interracial activism in a variety of settings, but most studies of such amity characterize it as limited, and focus on eastern leaders. They find that few whites or African Americans were willing to pervade racial boundaries.[189] While the gleaming stars of social reform remain important, so too are the lesser constellations and orbits of human collaboration. The lesser-known activists of the era, who took risks and sought change without the rewards of fame, could call for reform in novel ways. The social vision and actions of antebellum activists in the Old Northwest reveal that, in reality, such progressive levels of interracial friendship and empathy were not confined to the very few.

* * *

For their part, anti-abolitionists saw activist lecturers as upsetting the delicate balance of Old Northwest communities, especially when they traveled in interracial groups. The camaraderie and antislavery message of lecturing parties like the "One Hundred Conventions Tour" provided many Old Northwesterners with cause for complaint—and impulse to mob. While abolition lecturers in the early 1840s often faced down violent mobs, the men of the "One Hundred Conventions" tour saw continuous heightened attention to the interracial nature of their project. This made securing their right to speak difficult in Ohio, and even worse in Indiana. Southern Indiana was particularly confrontational; en route to Milan, Remond faced "repeated and gross insults." Gay wrote of the ugly "fiendish spirit" behind local folks's treatment of Remond, noting that the tenor of the place was such that this freeborn man "may esteem himself fortunate if he escapes arrest on suspicion of being a slave."[190] Interracial activist partnerships elicited community strife, but in the face of such hostility, solidarity across racial boundaries proved central to the travelers' ability to pursue their goals, and strengthened their commitment to the cause.

Itinerant lecturers' tours transformed them, as occurred with the "One Hundred Conventions" tour where both the relatively seasoned lecturers (Douglass and Remond) and the near-novices (Monroe and Gay) forged a new solidarity and an expanded abolitionist consciousness that stretched from their homes in the East to the newer terrain they had just explored. It gave them new bonds of friendship, too. Monroe and Gay corresponded after the tour, and Monroe and Douglass remained in contact with one another for decades; Douglass wrote to Monroe in 1880 to praise his diplomatic work in Latin America.[191] They did not easily forget their adventures on the road. Antislavery activists made personal ties with their lifelong interracial friendships, but also made other important connections across racial lines.

By virtue of their own demographics and those of the towns they visited, activists who worked for freedom of speech found that their housing arrangements often crossed racial boundaries and brought concerns about African Americans' local status into Old Northwest households. In this contentious region, itinerant antislavery activists, whether they had traveled only locally or endured longer journeys from the East, were weary and needy sojourners. Old Northwest abolitionists provided the essential direct aid to itinerants that facilitated activism. From the mid-1830s through the Civil War, hospitality in private homes gave help to itinerants that was frequently invisible. Unlike the more densely settled East, the Old Northwest lacked a substantial infrastructure of commercial hospitality beyond the larger towns. Travelers thus drew upon local people for their vital needs of transportation, food, shelter, support, and company.[192] As they battled for the freedom to speak in this harsh environment, human comforts became all the more important, and traveling lecturers welcomed the efforts of locals to host and aid them.[193]

The Old Northwest's distinctive unity was also visible in local political abolitionists' open cooperation with traveling Garrisonian organizers, which helped them each in their activist goals. The Old Northwest Liberty Party collaborated with and enabled immediatist lecturers to hold unusually large and successful meetings, and invited them to speak at its own gatherings.[194] Among Old Northwest people who embraced abolitionism, ideology did not dictate all.

Transcending faction, antislavery people built fellowship in the Old Northwest that meant abolitionists who eschewed politics found warm collaboration and common cause even in the homes of political abolitionists. These cordial home stays included when Guy Beckley, editor of the Liberty Party newspaper, the *Signal of Liberty*, hosted immediatist Dr. Erasmus D. Hudson in Ann Arbor in October 1841.[195] As he moved on to Ohio, Hudson found similar treatment regardless of locals' abolitionist methods.[196] Two years later, Ohio Whig representative Joshua Giddings and his family opened their Jefferson, Ohio, home to the lecturers of the "One Hundred Conventions" tour, as did other Ohio and Indiana families, regardless of their ideological affinities.[197] The Giddings did this throughout the 1840s.[198] The aid that both Liberty Party and Whig antislavery people provided to immediatist itinerants in the region complicates the picture of their unambiguous rivalries that emerges from an exclusive focus on the East.

Lecturers and locals forged their alliances in conflict, and itinerancy was only possible thanks to this assistance. In 1843, the two groups of abolitionists on the "One Hundred Conventions" tour, which themselves were integrated, lodged with a range of hosts like white Quaker farmer Seth Hinshaw of Greensboro, Indiana. Douglass—and likely White and Bradburn—stayed with Hinshaw's family when they spoke there in late September. The capacity of local organizers to host them comfortably and with loving attention, even in the tense Old Northwest, particularly impressed the travelers.[199] These homeowners also at times simultaneously housed both lecturers and escaped slaves.[200] The pattern of interracial aid extended back to Remond and Douglass's visit with the Post family in Rochester, New York, in the early days of the tour.[201] The Posts and Remond, all longtime activists, remained close for years.[202] Itinerant lecturers appreciated this long-lasting community support, as seen when Frederick Douglass stayed with Betsy Cowles and her welcoming relatives in Austinburg, Ohio, in the late 1840s.[203] While they confronted mobs that forced them to make tough choices between self-defense and assertiveness, the travelers were thus not without solace, even as their wanderings took a toll on their bodies.

Local people mitigated the hazards of itinerancy with their widespread aid. Along with the mobs that their unpopular cause roused, itinerancy posed other physical risks: travel hazards, health problems, endless motion, and grueling schedules all wore the speakers down. In addition to the wounds Douglass and White sustained at Pendleton, Remond also incurred injuries when he fell from a carriage pulled by runaway horses.[204] In general, life on the road was rough, from the long exposure to poor weather—riding on horseback or in rickety carriages from place to place—to the sheer wear on their vocal cords from speaking several times daily without amplification.[205] The crowds taxed the health of the hard-traveling itinerants, and prompted local people to care for them.[206] These activists calmly faced down opposition and continued lecturing in the Old Northwest.

* * *

In Old Northwest towns where reliable allies supported their freedom of speech, itinerant lecturers held more productive conventions. When Remond, Monroe, Gay, and Fussell went to Westfield, Indiana, they found numerous collaborators including some "Anti-slavery Friends."[207]

Their second day in town, men threatened to attack their meeting, but the Westfield activists stood up for themselves, in Gay's words, "knowing that there was no law to protect men but the law in their own right arms." Gay approved of this bravery despite his nonresistant convictions, for even when they disagreed with their compatriots' violent tactics, the travelers still sometimes saw them as necessary. In any event, the itinerants and their audience in this case faced no attack, although many of the local men had brought loaded rifles for self-defense. Gay said of their associates' brinksmanship that it characterized both the pro- and anti-slavery people in this region of Indiana, which had a violent gun culture.[208] The resultant convention was, in Fussell's words, "numerously attended, interesting, and orderly," but periodically interrupted.[209] In Greenwood, Indiana, shortly thereafter, rumors of antislavery self-defense again deterred the anti-abolitionists who planned to invade the meeting. While attendance was sparse and Remond chose not to speak—revealing again the race-based limitations of freedom of speech—no violence materialized. Apart from the abolitionists' boldness, the severe rain and Remond's self-censorship—as in Indianapolis—may have also had an impact.[210]

Old Northwest abolition was not solely an uphill battle for freedom of speech against violent foes, for local reactions show that some of itinerant lecturers' successes in the region came more easily. In 1843, the verbal talents of Monroe, Douglass, and Remond attracted substantial attention, and at Salem and Newark, Ohio, local residents also praised Monroe.[211] The famed orator Douglass won his share of adulation in addition to mob opprobrium, and Old Northwest audiences' reactions to his and Remond's speeches demonstrate how expressive African American voices could affect the fraught racial environment of the region.[212] In Oakland, Ohio, their efficacy is evident in the words of one Presbyterian minister and Liberty Party man who extolled their "eloquence." He wrote:

> The being who could stand unmoved, under the bold and lofty bearing, the . . . burning indignation of Remond; or the keen, withering satire, the . . . soul-shivering sarcasms of Douglass—all poured forth, too, from the fullness of hearts overflowing with universal benevolence . . . must be less, infinitely less than man. What a loathsome, soul-sickening, ineffably contemptible thing is this American prejudice against color.[213]

In this man's view, the best way to invalidate racial bias was with African

Americans' forceful speeches and direct refutations of the errors of bigotry. The itinerants' efforts for local and national rights thus spoke to and inspired varied audiences—when they secured the freedom to speak.

Apart from contemporary commentary in newspapers and letters, lecturers' freedom of speech successes also emerge in the size and tone of their audiences. The "One Hundred Conventions" lecturers' letters frequently discussed how they ranged "from the faithful few . . . to the overwhelming and enthusiastic gathering at Oakland," where they found at least one thousand people from all across Ohio.[214] The conventions in several Ohio towns grew to such size as to exceed the capacity of any available building. At Salem, the lecturers lured enormous crowds, and those present—estimated at between six hundred and one thousand—had to move to a nearby grove of trees because they no longer fit in the meetinghouse. Gay wrote of this grove that it took an hour to fill, and " . . . It was a glorious meeting . . . and a most stirring sight that, a thousand people though they looked small and few beneath those tall trees." In mid-August in Marlborough, Ohio, people could not fit indoors by the second day of the convention.[215] These open-air meetings drew diverse audiences, "women with newborn babes, and old men with one foot in the grave," walking, riding, and driving wagons.[216] Such positive experiences affirmed for lecturers that their ventures could bear fruit even in the tense Old Northwest.

* * *

The "One Hundred Conventions" tour ended at the Decade Meeting, the ten-year anniversary of the American Society, at Philadelphia on December 4, 1843. The Massachusetts Society proclaimed the tour an unqualified success, and argued that they should "send out able men over as large a portion of the free States as is practicable, to startle the stertorous nation with their warning voices." The easterners thus vowed to do more of this local organization in small towns, which continued ongoing efforts in the Old Northwest since the early 1830s. Both eastern and local organizers optimistically declared itinerant lecturing an effective tool, despite the "hostile influences" that in most cases kept meetings small and besieged for decades.[217] They were well aware of the challenges that they faced in western turf, and this made them all the more dedicated to changing this difficult region and its culture.

The Old Northwest's adverse reform environment shaped locals' expression of antislavery and anti-prejudice principles. Itinerant lecturers and the allies who battled by their side demonstrated the radical commitment to their unpopular positions necessary for activism there, where their right to speak was highly contested. They crossed racial boundaries, and their collaborations sustained them through hardship and mob violence. Itinerants worked in symbiosis with local people, and each provided necessary services to the other. Human networks connected lecturers across the region and the nation, and highlighted regional differences. With their speeches, they provoked a wide spectrum of local reactions, and elicited both opposition and support for the cause.

Itinerant lecturers could in fact fracture Old Northwest communities that were antagonistic to antislavery organizing. Older considerations of itinerant abolition's timing and location have underestimated anti-abolition's formidable influence in the region, the longstanding and widely disputed efforts of lecturers there, and the consequent difficulties activists faced. As abolitionists there insisted on their right to a hearing, their foes denied that public discussion of their ideas was legitimate. Conflict arose from this refusal, as it pushed debate to the margins, and advocating abolition became an offense punishable by forced silence, violence, or death. Many locals believed that traveling activists escalated sectional animosity, and treated these "hirelings" and unwelcome "outsiders" with loathing and violence. While many itinerants were immediate abolitionists who held nonresistant principles, their harsh environment even occasionally pushed them to take up arms in their own defense.

As mobs roiled towns across the region in response to abolitionist action, men and women with widely variant views on slavery and race relations stepped outside of culturally sanctioned gender roles to defend their rights. Some women interceded to protect itinerant men from violence or endured it themselves while traveling, while still others were among the first to sling eggs in fury. Antislavery organizers saw this hotly contested and little known reform realm as so vital that they voluntarily confronted its myriad challenges. Still, many itinerants struggled on, and without their willingness to do so and without the support of local assistance, spreading abolition in this region would have been impossible.

Antislavery and anti-prejudice activists found the Old Northwest freedom of speech climate particularly challenging. While the 1830s and

1840s were anything but tranquil for itinerants in the region, persistent anti-abolitionist violence meant that they found the subsequent decade even more demanding. Itinerant activists and their foes heatedly debated race and rights as sectionalism escalated over the course of the antebellum period. Even through the Civil War and Reconstruction, the region's political and ideological divisions made securing African Americans' rights and lecturers' freedom of speech ever more elusive.

6 / Itinerant Lecturers in a Fracturing Nation, 1850–1861

When we in the dark take what we deem a right position, light is sure to come sometime.

—ICHABOD CODDING, LETTER TO MARIA CODDING, MARCH 11, 1855

In March 1861, Josephine S. Griffing ridiculed small-town Old Northwest people by detailing how controversy ensued when she spoke publicly in the region. In a letter to the *Liberator*, Griffing delicately poked fun at the ignorance of one woman she met in her sojourn across Indiana that year. Near the town of Warsaw, her hostess asked quietly "whether I was a *woman*. 'They say,' said she [of Griffing], 'no *woman* ever talked as she talks, and I never knew one to talk at all.'" The novel presence of a female lecturer led her to doubt Griffing's gender identity. Griffing argued that this woman was "terribly religious" and had a narrow worldview. This abolitionist equated the other woman's piety with a kind of silent, obedient womanhood that she herself eschewed.[1] While Griffing's letter made light of her own resistance to local mores and her actions' effects on recalcitrant community members, she had serious intentions. She demonstrated with her own transgressions—her own decision to take a "right position"—that there were multiple possible ways Old Northwest antislavery lecturers, including female ones, could behave. These activists faced distinctive challenges from 1850 through the first year of the Civil War. Griffing exemplified this, as one of a cohort of tenacious Old Northwest abolitionists who for three decades, in the face of conflict, had refused to allow their foes to silence them. While her Indiana hostess disapproved, Griffing knew that she and her allies nonetheless must disregard propriety and speak out, for only thus could they combat slavery and prejudice.

* * *

In these conflict-ridden years, Old Northwest itinerant antislavery lecturers soldiered on for freedom of speech in the face of substantial mob violence. Anti-abolitionists attacked activists even more frequently, and they felt even more "in the dark" than they had done at any time since the 1830s. The national tendency toward increasing sectionalism heightened tensions in this already-unsettled region, and the reformers' mission remained a difficult and unpopular one. The antislavery political parties accompanied and escalated sectional discord even as they became relatively powerful in the Old Northwest, where they actually found more support than in other regions. Both of these developments augmented anti-abolitionists' impulses to muzzle antislavery people locally, regardless of their views on politics. To face down this opposition, activists had to muster substantial inner motivation to continue their work. Their conviction that all necessary hands must take up antislavery tools overcame their qualms about the consequences they faced for their unpopular reform activities.

In this era, the lecturers who traveled the Old Northwest were an increasingly diverse lot. African American men remained rare but vocal itinerants there, and African American and white women joined them, still in small numbers, but more often in these years than previously. Their public speeches proved excessively provocative for some communities that rejected their message, even when it came from a relatively more neutral messenger—a white man. Many Old Northwesterners refused with particular vehemence to consider listening to ideas that subverted the social order—much less from people they considered so low within it.

While the personnel may have changed, the patterns of activism in the region did not alter substantially after 1850. Ohio remained the state that antislavery lecturers toured most, with Michigan, Indiana, and Illinois trailing, in that order. Two sources of Ohio and Michigan's strong itinerant presence were the Western Society and the American Society, which sent lecturing agents—men and women, African American and white—through the states at regular intervals.[2] While African American men like Frederick Douglass and C. S. Depp lectured in Illinois in the mid-1850s, lectures by female abolitionists were extremely rare—at least in part since a number of the itinerants were politically affiliated in that state.[3] Political antislavery had also become less welcoming of women than it had been earlier with the Liberty Party. Indiana, while still infrequently visited, saw a stronger showing of both African

American and white female lecturers, including Abby Kelley Foster in 1850 and Sojourner Truth in 1858 and in 1861, accompanied by Josephine Griffing.[4]

Abby Kelley Foster was a formidable lecturer who traversed the Old Northwest beginning in the 1840s. This Massachusetts-born activist was raised Quaker, and she had taken up immediate abolition, nonresistance, and racial equality in the mid-1830s. She became an American Society agent and activist in the women's movement in the following decade. Kelley gained increasing notoriety as she traveled the country, and married the forceful abolitionist orator Stephen Foster in 1845. That year and the next they also toured the Old Northwest to fortify the Ohio American Society against its Liberty challengers, and they helped start the Garrisonian newspaper the *Anti-Slavery Bugle*.[5] Kelley Foster also encouraged other women to become lecturers, including Jane Elizabeth Hitchcock Jones, Sallie Holley, and Josephine Griffing.[6] Griffing and Jones also published in the *Anti-Slavery Bugle* and held offices in the Western Society. Griffing hosted Kelley Foster at her home at Litchfield, Ohio, in 1850, and despite having a one-year-old baby, she agreed to go on the road as an antislavery lecturer.[7] Whether they lived in the region or visited from the East, lecturers in the Old Northwest found significant challenges as they continued to organize and speak there, for the region remained substantially hostile to abolition, regardless of who they were.

* * *

With the growing presence of women and African Americans of both genders in their ranks, Old Northwest itinerants found that the identity-based denial of freedom of speech that earlier lecturers had experienced remained widespread. Their cause could become even more unpopular when hostile people learned that the speakers' identities were outside the white male norm. In some cases, more was at stake in silencing lecturers than the antislavery message the itinerants wished to discuss, for gender and race could provide additional obstructions. In September 1853, lecturer Sallie Holley returned to her alma mater, Oberlin College, while touring Michigan and Ohio. She found her alumna status little help in securing freedom of speech at the college.[8] This New York-born woman had attended Oberlin beginning in 1847, and while there took a stand against her fellow students' racial prejudices. While the school was more racially progressive than most, not all students or faculty there opposed racial bias as strongly as she did. Upon graduating she became an abolitionist lecturer in response to Kelley Foster's invitation, and gained a lecturing commission from the American Society.[9] During Holley's visit in 1853, the faculty of the college refused to allow her to speak in the Oberlin chapel, claiming that "it was improper and unscriptural for a woman to address a promiscuous [mixed-sex] audience."[10] Antebellum Americans had linked freedom of speech to a woman's right to speak publicly ever since Angelina Grimké had stepped onto the platform in the early 1830s.[11] Religious venues had often used these gender boundaries to silence female speakers.

In Oberlin, Holley's supporters in the "Ladies' A. S. Society" and "The Young Ladies' Literary Societies" then requested a woman-specific lecture. The faculty initially denied permission, for they feared that doing so would give the appearance of supporting women's rights, but they finally relented. Their stalling left Holley and her friends with little time to publicize the meeting, but she spoke regardless. The college's goal of keeping the talk a single-sex affair did not hold, for ultimately some local men foiled the faculty's plan by attending the lecture. As a small parade of men then entered the audience throughout the lecture, the end result was, in fact, a "promiscuous audience!"[12] Even at this coeducational institute, lectures by women remained controversial, which made it all the more difficult for them to promote their cause.[13]

Female lecturers were not alone in facing hefty obstacles to freedom of speech, for in a different case of divisive identity, one particularly notorious abolitionist, William Lloyd Garrison, found that his reputation barred him from speaking in some places that other abolitionists could access. As a middle-class white man, he held more privileges and access to the public than many female or African American lecturers, but his religious and governmental unorthodoxy rendered him so infamous that some Old Northwest people quite simply outlawed his presence. When he visited Battle Creek, Michigan, in October 1853, local Methodists barred him from their meetinghouse, a site where Sallie Holley had recently held a successful meeting.[14] Garrison backed down, seeing no further options in this instance. The Battle Creek Methodists silenced Garrison by refusing him the right to lecture publicly. Holley, though a woman, was a less contentious choice of lecturer. Garrison's anticlerical, even seditious reputation meant that controversy followed him and likely kept him away from this religious lectern, proving that infamy—on top of their controversial message—could provide substantial barriers to lecturers' freedom of speech. In Michigan in the 1850s, even less famed speakers had trouble securing the freedom to address the public.

* * *

While Michigan frequently hosted antislavery lectures, community hostility to them remained widespread, and was especially fervent in some towns. In February 1856, following one peaceful meeting in the Pontiac Courthouse, immediatist lecturers Richard Glazier of Ann Arbor and Aaron M. Powell of New York encountered a hostile mob when they attempted to speak a second time.[15] Pontiac had a long history of contested meetings, for as early as February 1837, antislavery lecturer and Oberlin professor John P. Cowles had met a mob armed with "stones and snow balls" when he spoke in the local church. The man who led this mob was Nicholas Gantt, the editor of the local Democratic newspaper, the *Democratic Balance*. The sheriff and his posse had to calm the situation to prevent bloodshed.[16] Later, famed eastern lecturer Parker Pillsbury had also had to abandon his 1850 Pontiac meeting after failing to find a speaking venue. This religiously educated New Englander took his first agency with the American Society in 1839. He continued lecturing for decades, and after the Civil War, his was a rare voice in support of women's suffrage among male antislavery leaders.[17]

In 1856, Pontiac was still unwelcoming, and local officials locked Glazier and Powell out of the courthouse when the time for their second meeting arrived. They persevered, and relocated to another hall. While they filled it to capacity, locals hardly universally acclaimed them. Glazier, a lecturer for the Michigan State Society, found that when he spoke, loud voices interrupted him. More traumatically, a group of youths took a violent approach and flung beans and corn at the speakers, which Glazier called being "treated to a rather crude dish of *succotash*." Glazier saw partisan motivations behind the trouble they faced, for he believed that their foes supported the Democrats.[18]

A successive attack on the two visiting lecturers compelled Pontiac's antislavery women to take up stations as bodyguards, as women had done previously in the region to defend antislavery people's rights. Pontiac remained tense as the lecturers stayed in town and frustrated local efforts to silence them. When Glazier spoke the following day, this led to threats of violence against Mr. Drake, the hall's owner. Someone anonymously wrote Drake that if he permitted the abolitionists to use his hall again, he and the building might be attacked; he would risk both "the property" and "his head." Even so, the meeting proceeded without disturbance. When they left that evening, the speakers had a most interesting safeguard: a phalanx of "very kind and firm lady friends" accompanied

Glazier and Powell home. They gave the men, Glazier said, "protection from insult, perhaps injury," from agitated town residents who resented their reform efforts. Here, as elsewhere in the Old Northwest, women served as defensive corps against violence in threatening situations and when authorities failed to come to itinerants' aid.[19] This Pontiac incident was not, as Merton L. Dillon has suggested, an example of women rescuing men "ignominiously," but rather exemplifies how abolitionists of both sexes were creative in securing their rights—and strategically used their foes' unwillingness to attack women to their advantage.[20] The tumult at Pontiac in 1856 shows the extent of community resistance to activists' rights to publicly speak and share their message—and their own determination to exercise those same rights.

* * *

Antislavery itinerants in the Old Northwest attracted substantial opposition for their ideas and identities in the 1850s, but they found their antagonists also increasingly curbed activists' freedom of speech because anti-abolitionists feared lectures' effects on partisan politics. This had been the case to a degree since the 1830s, but Democrats and others more and more attacked this right as political abolition became stronger, and especially after the Republican Party formed. It organized in 1854 and began to present a viable political threat by 1856. In the Old Northwest, the introduction of the antislavery platform into mainstream politics with this new party's growth hardly stifled anti-abolitionists' impulse to egg and maim. These hostile acts even extended to abolitionists who eschewed politics.

Whether or not their own tactics were overtly political, antislavery lecturers confronted fierce partisan opposition from Old Northwest Democrats. A partisan mob attacked lecturer C. S. Depp in Monmouth, an Illinois Democratic stronghold, in 1856. When Depp had arrived that March, he found bellicose throngs who flung eggs at him to force his silence. Born a slave in Virginia, Depp obtained his freedom at the age of twenty-one, and by 1856 he was a professional lecturer with at least ten years of experience.[21] Depp spoke in the Baptist Church his first night in town without disturbance, but this peace did not last. The following night when he convened another well-attended meeting, people began to throw eggs and "other missiles" at him. One of them struck him in the mouth, wounding him severely enough to end the lecture. When the editor of the local Republican paper, C. K. Smith of the Monmouth *Atlas*, wrote of the incident, he identified Depp's assailants as "the

Pierce Party," meaning the Democrats. Some Monmouth Democrats saw Depp's antislavery lecture as an indubitably partisan gesture. They thus claimed that they had to attack his freedom of speech to defend their political interests, but whether Depp had such intentions for his speech is unclear.[22]

Depp, among other abolitionists, found that these muzzling efforts intensified with the growth of political abolitionism, for he had held a successful meeting in Monmouth the previous year. Smith saw the attack on Depp as proof that local "mobocracy" had escalated with the expansion of partisan tensions.[23] While political abolitionists had over time increased the prevalence of antislavery ideas in public discussion, this did not render abolitionists or their ideas safe, and in fact the reverse could be true.

Old Northwest allies of antislavery lecturers couched their objections to the assault on Depp in universal rights language. The *Atlas* editor bluntly contrasted these rights claims with extralegal violence: "The question now is—shall freedom of speech be tolerated in Monmouth, or shall mob law rule?" While this editor feared what he saw as escalating infringement on town freedoms, local government did enforce some consequences for the attack, as officials arrested two young men who had recently arrived in the area for mob participation. This was an unusual outcome, for anti-abolitionists rarely faced consequences for such attacks, and even less frequently for pursuing an African American. As he assessed this attack on Depp, Smith drew similar conclusions to others sympathetic to abolitionist lecturers—including that resisting the slave power was vital. He cited the need to protect "free discussion" and said that citizens of "free" states would not permit such limitations as these, so like those slave states imposed on their citizens.[24] These questions of partisanship and identity haunted other lecturers in the Old Northwest, and interfered with female abolitionists' freedoms in the Old Northwest at least as much as they did male ones'.

* * *

As Holley had seen, women who lectured against slavery faced distinctive free speech challenges that stemmed from the contemporary ideology of domesticity—including the view that they had no rightful place speaking in public. In many cases, notions of gender informed their opponents' reception of their lectures. African American women speakers, in this region with its "Black Laws" and the associated pervasive racial bias, confronted both increasing challenges and occasional opportunities to convert audiences from hostile to open viewpoints. Frances Ellen Watkins Harper, an eloquent free-born African American writer and speaker, experienced both of these extremes in the Old Northwest. She briefly resided in Ohio in the early 1850s, but soon returned east, where she became an antislavery lecturer. By 1857 she was lecturing as far west as Michigan and Ohio, where she married a local African American man, Fenton Harper, in 1861. Their marriage was brief since he only lived for four more years.[25] She remained a vibrant activist, one much-admired by her peers. Harper's fellow African American abolitionist, Mary Ann Shadd Cary, deemed her 1857 and 1858 Old Northwest tour wildly successful, arguing that both "the whites & colored people here are just going crazy with excitement about her." Cary, herself a lecturer, teacher, journalist, and lawyer, yielded the platform to what she deemed Harper's superior speaking talents, for "there would just be no chance of favorable comparison.'"[26] However, Cary herself also spoke across the Old Northwest and Upper Canada in the late 1850s. While her main focus was raising awareness of the emigrationist cause and funds for the *Provincial Freeman*, as an African American woman she, too, had to fight for a public platform. She consistently claimed a prominent role with her newspaper, activism in conventions, speaking tours, and work for women's suffrage.[27] Harper and Cary were lifelong and pioneering activists, and they shared their activist struggles in the Old Northwest with another, ever-quotable contemporary, Sojourner Truth.

In 1858, former slave and famed lecturer Truth undertook a solo tour of northern Indiana, where she met a reception tainted with partisanship, sectionalism, racism, and sexism. Truth—birth name Isabella Baumfree—was born into slavery in New York State around 1797. After her master illegally kept her in bondage beyond emancipation in 1827 in that state, she fled in 1829 to New York City and freedom. After a religious conversion, she renamed herself and became a traveling preacher across the East and the Old Northwest. She made extensive ties with other abolitionists across racial lines, and beginning in 1851, spent two years lecturing in Ohio, frequently working with Marius R. Robinson, before moving to Battle Creek, Michigan, in 1856.[28]

The reaction Truth found when she spoke in Silver Lake, Indiana, in September 1858 exemplified how identity and the political climate very much influenced attacks on abolitionists' freedom of speech. Her local foes had claimed prior to her arrival that she was actually a man in women's clothing who secretly worked for the Republican Party. They did not suggest that she might be a woman and a Republican—and she in fact was a Garrisonian who did not identify with the Republicans until 1861. The accusation of manhood is ironic when considered in the light of her famed 1851 speech at the Akron Woman's Rights Convention where Frances Dana Gage claimed ten years later that she asked rhetorically, "Ar'n't I a Woman?" Scholars agree that in that speech Truth herself troubled gender categories, but did so to promote women's rights and to question the racial and class limits of the women's movement.[29] In Silver Lake, Truth's local supporter, William Hayward, attributed this rumor about her sex to local Democrats, whom he called "the border-ruffian Democracy of Indiana." In his eyes, these southern sympathizers refused to permit antislavery discussion, and thus spread this falsehood about Truth's alleged manhood to silence her. Her sex and her race became tools for local partisans who aimed to quell her right to speak openly.

Disregarding the rumors, Truth still held her meeting in the United Brethren meetinghouse, and it was well attended by Democrats, anti-abolitionists, and Truth's allies. There, a Democrat named Dr. T. W. Strain interrupted Truth and boldly demanded that she prove she was a woman by showing her breast to the ladies present.[30] Despite the uproar that ensued, Truth complied. She dramatically bared her breast to all, boasting to her detractors that her body had nourished numerous white babies whose "manhood" now exceeded that of her hecklers.[31] With her adroit word choice and actions, Truth directly questioned her critics' masculinity, and denigrated them.

With her deft reply, Truth refused to permit her foes to shame or silence her. Historian Nell Irvin Painter links the Indianans' refusal to accept Truth's sex to a common discrediting tactic of denying the womanhood of other African American speakers, including Harper. This was not just about gender, for Truth's antagonists claimed she lacked "authenticity," as critics had claimed of other African American public figures, including men like Frederick Douglass on his early speaking tours."[32] As they tried to paint her as unnatural, Truth's detractors claimed she represented improper womanhood. This assertion could be both related to her unusual height and stature, and to her choice to speak publicly. Silver Lake's anti-abolitionists thus critiqued how activists inverted the social order by placing women and African Americans on the rostrum.

This fantastical incident of the audience demanding that a woman publicly expose her body with intention to discredit and humiliate is closely tied to Truth's identity as a formerly enslaved African American woman. Even her advanced age did not protect her from this attempt to mortify her. Truth had bared her arm to reveal her musculature during her 1851 Akron speech, but Strain nonetheless made what was a shocking demand of a public speaker (much less a female one) in the antebellum era.[33] In this strife-filled region, Truth's opponents attempted to derail her abolitionist lecture by focusing on her alleged partisan masquerade, and on her physical body. This taboo act reveals anti-abolitionists' ability to dominate public speech in the Old Northwest—and the lack of respect African Americans encountered there. Both were entangled with the region's extensive racial bias and sexist treatment of female speakers, as the individuals' behavior showed.

While this attack on Truth's freedom of speech became quite notorious, her compatriots among African American itinerant women also fought their own skirmishes to secure the verbal freedom needed to fight slavery publicly. In the face of these challenges, their steadfastness—based on message, race, and gender—was itself of great propaganda value. Frances Harper exemplified this with her series of lectures around Sandusky, Ohio, in February 1860. There, "thronged audiences" generally received her very well, but she did find a poor reception in one place, which her fan T. R. Davis blamed on use of alcohol and "contemptible ignorance." Davis wrote in a review of her speeches that they would both positively affect the political atmosphere and help eradicate racial prejudice, "this unreasonable prejudice against the colored people of the country."[34] This would have been powerful motivation for an African American woman lecturer to take public action, despite the obvious dangers of doing so.

The publicity potential of this opposition remained on Harper's mind later in the year, for that September, she lectured in Green Plain, Ohio. She wrote that her race prevented her from peacefully traveling on the "Cincinnati and Zanesville road" to the Western Society's 1860 annual meeting. There, she encountered hostile people who "insulted" her. Her experience shows that African Americans who lived and lectured in the Old Northwest hardly needed reminding of the problems that slavery and the "Black Laws" created. Nonetheless, touring speakers—including Harper—addressed these problems. She saw lecturing to African Americans as part of an uplifting enterprise, for in her view "elevating them" by instructing them on "build[ing] up a character" was part of the antislavery mission. She claimed so-called African American "inferiority" was at the root of discrimination, "social ostracisms and political proscription." Thus as a middle-class woman, she wanted to mold Old Northwest African American communities in her own image, to help demonstrate their capabilities.[35] In her view, whites like Jane Elizabeth Jones shared this responsibility, so she asked Jones and her fellow lecturers—Pillsbury and Abby Kelley Foster—to go visit Ohio African American towns and engage with their communities. African Americans in Ohio and Indiana had established several dozen independent agricultural communities as early as 1808, and this continued throughout the antebellum era. By the 1840s, they were pockets of self-sufficient prosperity.[36] Still, Harper showed some class bias in her belief that these towns' residents could be improved further, as she sought to have lecturers exert a positive effect on African Americans by being with them and uplifting them. To her, such an outcome would have made the risks of the road worthwhile.

* * *

Beyond the longstanding danger and violence that Harper and her compatriots risked encountering, by 1860 the larger partisan climate also created even more freedom-of-speech problems for antislavery itinerants. Even as political antislavery peoples' stars had risen in the 1850s, their tactic was not the only option in the Old Northwest. Indeed, immediate abolitionists—including Truth, Marius R. Robinson, and Griffing—had maintained separate lecture circuits throughout the decade and beyond.[37]

The Western and American Societies sent lecturers to the Old Northwest even after the Civil War began. Before then, itinerant agents of the "radical abolitionist" Western Society, including Benjamin S. Jones and Charles and Josephine S. Griffing, continued to lecture in Michigan throughout the early 1850s.[38] In 1856 the American Society attempted to replicate its 1843 "One Hundred Conventions" tour across the East and Old Northwest. The lecturers who took part included both easterners like Stephen S. Foster and Aaron Powell and locals like Michigan's experienced Massachusetts-born lecturer Giles Stebbins and Ohio's Marius Robinson.[39] In 1857, Jane Elizabeth and Benjamin Jones joined in, along with Abraham Brooke.[40] Even in 1858, famed eastern lecturers like Parker Pillsbury, Abby Kelley Foster, Foster, William Lloyd Garrison, and Charles C. Burleigh came to Ohio to lecture for the Western Society, and Kelley Foster and Pillsbury returned in 1860 and 1861.[41]

These immediatist lecturers saw their work as unfinished, and even believed that political antislavery, as Robinson wrote of the Republicans in February 1860, might interfere with their work for the cause. In that year's election, Lincoln had his successful presidential candidacy, and thus an antislavery party rose to national office. The Republican Party's success failed to convince immediatists that their work was superfluous, for they saw the party's moderate policies as too gradualist to aid slaves.[42] They thus lectured and publicized their agenda repeatedly in the Old Northwest, and witnessed persistent challenges to public organizing as they wrestled with local people for their freedom of speech in a tense sectional and partisan climate.

* * *

The connection between antislavery free speech and partisan politics arose in 1861 during two particularly tumultuous days of abolitionist meetings at Ann Arbor, Michigan. From the beginning of that fractious year, abolitionists faced massive opposition as advocates of their unpopular yet increasingly inescapable cause. Despite the tension, Josephine Griffing, Parker Pillsbury, and Giles Stebbins spoke at the annual convention of the Michigan State Anti-Slavery Society on January 27 and 28. This incident, along with others in the region in 1861, reveals that anti-abolitionist mobbing cannot have been a mere product of initial organizing efforts in the 1830s, for people met the antislavery message with violence even after decades of public agitation, and even when the fight against slavery had moved from the fringes to the center of politics.[43]

Overt threats circulated throughout the growing college town in the days leading up to the meeting. These drove away allies, and the lecturers had to search extensively for a meeting hall before they found one. This was in keeping with Ann Arbor's mixed history of allowing abolitionists meeting space.[44] Mr. Rogers, owner of the hall where they had planned to convene, learned of these risks in advance, but waited until the day of the meeting to revoke their permission to use his space. He said he favored "free discussion," but feared that the city authorities would afford him no "protection" from damage to his property. After Mayor Barry also refused the use of the courthouse, the abolitionist group turned to the Free Church of the Friends of Human Progress, a radical Friends organization that advocated nonresistance, women's suffrage, and abolition.[45] Some of their local members, including Catherine A. F. Stebbins, took part in and wrote about the gatherings.[46]

On the first evening of scheduled meetings, the lecturers' freedom of speech battle began. A throng of "drunken 'roughs'" filled the church and kept up a steady partisan roar as the itinerants attempted to speak.[47] Griffing persevered, as her touring companion and Catherine's husband Giles remembered in his 1890 memoir: "I can see her on that plain, low platform, with only a little space around her vacant, and she, fearless, erect, radiant, speaking clear tones that conquered wrath and even won a hearing part of the time."[48] In her speech, Griffing used the strongest possible terms to defend abolitionists' right to appear and speak. She cited the "necessity of our guarding free speech and our own personal rights here at the North."[49] With this call for fortitude, Griffing demanded that they face the immediate turmoil of their Ann Arbor meeting by confronting their opponents head-on.

The meeting's leaders and attendees soon found local resistance insurmountable and dangerous, for the crowd's deeds did not end with noise. This mob, "one of the fiercest" that ever confronted the much-mobbed Pillsbury, assaulted the abolitionists and their assembled audience. Pillsbury's florid language vividly depicts this attack by a "most ferocious and savage throng, composed of collegians, clerks, drunken Irish boys, lawyers, and plug-uglies . . . all mingled in a disgusting, irresponsible mass, sweeping all before it." As they escalated from words to violence, the anti-abolitionists damaged the hall severely, tearing up the benches as they vented their fury. Local activist Richard Glazier suffered kicks and blows to the face, as did other attendees.[50] The meeting organizers saw the danger they faced, and declared the assembly over. After they departed, the anti-abolitionists destroyed the windows, tore up the desk, and pulled the stovepipe out of the wall.[51] These speakers and listeners represented many of the most radical views of their era—and their communities refused to allow them to freely voice these views. While the violent attack on Pillsbury may have influenced his account of these riot, the assailants' violent determination and actions do indicate that they were angry, in all probability due to both the tense political times and the activists themselves.

The abolitionists could not rely on local law enforcement to protect them, for the "city authorities" took little action on their behalf. Pillsbury deemed the attack "worthy of Boston"—a city rife with anti-abolition violence since 1834—in its ferocity.[52] While Mayor Barry had promised "protection" to locals Giles Stebbins and Glazier, he was conspicuously absent from the meeting, having excused himself to attend a concert. Other officers did come but offered the abolitionists no help.[53]

The anti-abolitionist attack did not extinguish local reform fire, for the trio of itinerant lecturers and the local activists continued their efforts. The following day, they made rudimentary repairs to the hall, enough to permit them to hold their second day of scheduled meetings. They cleaned up, swept away the broken pieces of wood and glass, and reassembled the stove. The hall again became "well filled" with antislavery people.[54] They proceeded with the annual meeting's business, including choosing their officers. While they endured continual interruptions, Pillsbury, Griffing, and Giles Stebbins all obtained a hearing.[55]

As Griffing had the previous day, the attendees directly linked the attack to the rights to freedom of speech that they claimed, and to partisan politics. Catherine Stebbins declared that they found common ground in the face of these trials: "We were all united in one thing, at least—viz., free expression of opinion."[56] As a longtime reformer who had signed the Seneca Falls Declaration of Sentiments in 1848, Stebbins had a history of interest in broad social change. She had a clear commitment to outspoken activism, and to the liberty of expression necessary to do it.[57] When Giles Stebbins spoke, he blamed the local Democratic newspaper, the *Michigan Argus*, for inciting community hostility. He, too, argued that the mob represented "determination to crush free speech." Several other Michigan abolitionists, including Richard Glazier, also spoke at the meeting. Glazier asserted that the mayor and other prominent citizens should have stopped the mob and protected their rights.[58]

In the resolutions the Michigan State Society offered that day, they wholeheartedly presented the attack on the meeting as a free speech issue. Indeed, they saw this as a critical moment, an "hour of peril to the cause of free institutions in this young and hitherto promising nation." Their urgent task was to protect and use their "divinely given and most inalienable rights," regardless of the risk to their "reputation, property, or life." Only thus could they ensure individual and collective liberty. At this meeting, as did people elsewhere in the region, the Michigan Society drew upon language that linked their struggle to larger battles the nation faced. Rather than citing existing legal precedent, these abolitionists, as did those Michael Kent Curtis observed in his study of free speech, instead used as their resource and justification a broader claim to universal, natural rights, the "God-given rights that state and federal constitutions secured but did not create."[59] The people of the Michigan Society claimed their right to free expression in the face of continual community resistance, and in the process expanded the conversation about this protection—and their willingness to take risks to secure it.

Indeed, the anti-abolitionists remained an outspoken presence at the meeting, and they focused their greatest hostility on Pillsbury. When he spoke for a second time that afternoon he faced "noisy demonstrations," but he persevered. In his speech, he invoked the sacred nature of freedom of expression, which he argued lay at "the very foundation of free institutions," and claimed in gendered terms they must defend it. Pillsbury cited both mobs in the ancient world and contemporary ones to demonstrate that activists must "resist manfully" when attacked, to prevent their enemies from dominating them.[60] In a letter he wrote five days later, Pillsbury slyly mocked the mob's inability to stop their assembling, alluding to the abolitionists' strength by comparing their Michigan trials to well-known experiences in the East: "An occasional riot, like that at Ann Arbor, [can] relieve the monotony, clear the atmosphere, and remind us of New York State and Boston."[61] With his tone, Pillsbury depicted their opponents' impact as minimal. As he discussed mobs as a familiar, even a comforting presence, he deflated their capacity to undermine the antislavery mission, and affirmed for others the potential power of reform. Pillsbury thus inferred that he and his allies were in the right in standing up for themselves.

* * *

The fracas at Ann Arbor shows how community views on activists grew even more divided, as did their nation. Eight days after the itinerants had left town, Catherine Stebbins assessed the conflict and placed it in the town's larger context. In a letter to the *Liberator*, she voiced her surprise that such depravity could be found in Ann Arbor, given that the college was the "educational center of Michigan." Contradictorily, she also admitted that local activists had expected trouble. Prior to the arrival of the travelers, people ranging from northern and southern university students to local "merchants and business men" had issued warnings that "the meeting ought not to be held." They claimed that the Mayor should intervene and stop it since at that moment, the nation faced "such an hour of peril and excitement." This presumably alluded to the tense partisan moment and the very real threat of impending war.[62] Stirring up sectional issues was a risk some town residents were unwilling to take. The flare-up at Ann Arbor exemplified the larger disputes in the region over the wisdom of discussing abolition and race, issues likely to incite substantial debate. As the sectional conflict deepened, the heated Old Northwest abolition fights gained increasing relevance to national politics, and an ever more divisive tone.

The strain on Ann Arbor's abolitionists carried on after the itinerants departed. When Catherine and Giles Stebbins attended a concert the weekend following the contentious meetings, their antagonists recognized them and greeted their arrival with "a shower of hisses." When the mayor subsequently entered, the same men had nothing but cheers and jubilation for him. Catherine Stebbins insinuated that, in her view, Mayor Barry drew his popularity from the low sort of people rather than respectable ones, thus providing further evidence of his culpability, even his complicity, with the previous week's mob.[63] If nothing else, this account shows that the Stebbins's neighbors saw them as responsible for inciting the riotous events by supporting and participating in the antislavery meeting and affiliating with radical causes. As the Fussells and others had found in previous decades, local activists absorbed the ongoing community shocks after itinerants had continued on their way. The travelers' path, too, remained rough, because others in the state shared Ann Arborites' frosty welcome for antislavery lecturers.

Michigan tested the mettle of the recently mobbed trio of speakers, for anti-abolitionism followed them elsewhere. From Ann Arbor, Griffing, Pillsbury, and Giles Stebbins traveled on to Detroit, and then to Northville. In both places they faced mob threats, but remained resilient and agitated for "freedom of speech" and against slavery.[64] At their Farmington, Michigan, meeting shortly thereafter, an anonymous enemy lit a match wrapped in cayenne pepper and other noxious substances in an attempt to prevent their assembly. Even this did not drive them out of their meeting, for Griffing noted that they held their ground with resolve; they opened the windows and coughed their way through the proceedings. This was the end of their tour as a group: Pillsbury did one last lecture in Plymouth, Michigan, before returning east; Stebbins traveled home; and Griffing journeyed on. These lecturers kept to their planned series of speeches, indicating that they refused to allow community opposition to quell their fervor for reform.

As Griffing prepared for the next phase in her tour, she reflected on the rapid escalation of both mobbing and muzzling of abolitionists in Michigan. She saw this as proof that the nation's regions all shared in the era's rising political tension. At that moment of transition, when war appeared ever more likely, Griffing wrote from Plymouth to the *Liberator* that over the previous two weeks, she and her fellow lecturers had faced increasing physical danger, thanks to their foes and their powerful allies. She saw "the mob" as determined to overthrow orderly society and place slaveholder's priorities at the pinnacle of government. She found that abolition's opponents surrounded them, and whether North or South, all were deeply enmeshed with the "corrupt" political and religious structures.[65] Over the ensuing four months, Griffing faced further evidence of this broad-based anti-abolition challenge to lecturers' freedom of speech in the Old Northwest.

* * *

As the war began in 1861, silencing discussion of antislavery issues and politics proved increasingly difficult, but people still tried. The political and reform climate of the Old Northwest grew ever more polarized, as it did with the rest of the nation, following South Carolina's secession in December 1860. In 1861, to take one example, many ministers still discouraged mention of it from their pulpits, but congregations in places like Bourbon, Indiana, nonetheless pushed the issue. There, at least one church voted to amend the constitution to abolish slavery. The controversy raged on, as Josephine Griffing soon found in churches and on secular lecture platforms.

When Griffing toured northern Indiana in February and March of 1861, churches in Plymouth and Franklin denied her permission to speak. Prior to Griffing's arrival in Plymouth, the Methodist church had already hosted a partisan dispute when the minister had requested a prayer for President Lincoln. In response, the Democrats in the congregation had threatened to leave the church *en masse*. Having quelled that uprising, the minister told Griffing he was reluctant to court further "disturbance" and partisan splits with a speech like hers. The Franklin minister not only denied Griffing access to his church, but aired his own racial beliefs as he claimed he "would take up arms sooner than abolish slavery, and allow the '*niggers*' to come to Indiana." He thus linked her antislavery message with his greatest fear that abolition would lead to an African American invasion of Indiana. In Franklin, Griffing instead obtained a large schoolhouse for a speaking location, and filled it with an attentive audience.[66] She saw that these tensions had only worsened with the beginning of the war.

In June 1861, Griffing and Sojourner Truth lectured across northern Indiana, and the turmoil that they left in their wake exposed the links among racial prejudice, the Indiana "Black Laws," free speech, partisan politics, and mob action. While Truth had faced disruptions and interruptions to her 1858 Indiana meetings, she had toured in the Old Northwest for 25 years without encountering the extreme degree of persecution that she found in 1861 in Angola. This town, the capital of Steuben County, lies in the northeast corner of Indiana, the area where Griffing then lived. At this time a resident of Battle Creek, Michigan, Truth had visited and spoken in Steuben County four years previously "without opposition." Times had changed, for the Civil War had begun in April, and this only amplified the political disputes in Angola, a "Copperhead" stronghold with a large resident population of those Democrats who opposed the war and African American rights, and blamed abolitionists for the conflict with the South. Truth's subsequent attempt to travel and speak with Griffing reveals how anti-abolition Indianans used any means they could, including the "Black Laws" that restricted movement of African Americans into their state, to silence itinerants who advocated controversial positions in their divided region.

While on tour in Indiana, Truth publicly supported the Union war effort in her lectures, which was risky given the anti-war Democrats' strength there. Truth, as a Garrisonian, had eschewed politics until the Civil War, when she became a Union advocate—and thus an implicit supporter of the Republican Party—and argued for African American men's right to take up arms.[67] After hearing of her support, the Home Guard, a local pro-Union group, invited Truth to address a meeting at the Angola courthouse. Truth's friends in the area, the Unionist "ladies," had dressed her up in the colors and patterns of the stars and stripes. This martial style made Truth nervous; it frightened her to appear as if she were "going into battle." She rode to the courthouse in a carriage full of the men of the Home Guard, armed to protect her from arrest under the "Black Laws."[68] She knew well that speaking for the Union in Angola was a hazardous act—especially for an African American woman.

Truth was unable to deliver her speech in peace. She was in the very act of proclaiming her enthusiasm for the Union cause and demanding a military role for African American men when a loud, angry throng rushed into the building and drowned out her voice. These men menaced her with various assaults, which Griffing enumerated as "tar and feathers, eggs, rails, shooting, and a general blowing up," and closed down the meeting. This decisive push to silence her sent a clear message that Angola neither welcomed Truth nor her views.

Beyond the physical threats aimed at forcing Truth to leave Indiana, Angola's anti-abolitionists applied government pressure. The courthouse walls rang with legal actions against Truth for ten days. First they arrested her for being African American; then charged her with being a "mulatto"; and finally arrested her for coming to, then tarrying in, the state. Intending to silence her abolition and pro-Union views, the anti-abolitionists charged Truth with violating the "Black Laws" statute that stated, "No negro or mulatto shall come into, or settle in, or become an inhabitant of the State." Local anti-abolitionists also invoked the Dred Scott decision as they prosecuted eminent residents for hosting Truth in their homes. Griffing argued that this proved local residents' outrage at these leading citizens for granting Truth any of "the rights of a human being," in defiance of the majority position in the Scott decision.[69] She saw their adversaries as determined to use all available methods to close off her and Truth's attempts to speak, writing, "No dog ever hung to a bone as have these hungry hounds to Sojourner, under the cover of law." Local anti-abolitionists gave clear evidence of their commitment to silencing abhorrent views in their community.

Angola's anti-abolitionists unrelentingly pursued Truth, with tactics ranging from the legal to the violent. They even served papers to the Steuben County sheriff for allowing Truth to speak in the Angola courthouse, directly attacking the local government representative for granting this unwelcome person access to a public platform. Truth, Griffing, and their allies faced and vanquished all of these attempts.[70] After her ten days of persecution, Truth departed Angola without legal consequences. The anti-abolitionists' claims did not stand up in court, indicating that conviction of a visiting lecturer under the "Black Laws" was not as easy as it was to threaten her, interrupt her speech, delay her in her travels, and harass her for her views and her race. Town residents informed Truth and Griffing that a pile of guns lay in the back of a grocery store, and that a secret league of men planned to use these arms against them. While the anti-abolitionists themselves faced no legal consequences for violating Griffing's and Truth's right to speak, in the end the court failed to endorse their charges and Truth was free to depart, but she could not secure free speech in Angola.

This was not an isolated incident, and these events had deep roots in their turbulent context. Griffing tied all of these aggressive acts against Truth to partisanship, race, and temperance. As a resident of the region, she found it evident that the "secessionists"—as she termed them, the "Copperhead" Democrats—created this county's flaws and Truth's persecution, and were also deeply involved in what she decried as the region's extensive (and in her words "accursed") liquor trade. The conflict was wrapped up with broader debates over reforms that even went beyond politics and antislavery. She referred to all of their opponents as "the old line pro-slavery Democrats," and blamed what she saw as their disloyalty to the Union for their devotion to the "Black Laws" and their opposition to abolition and its proponents' free expression.

Freedom of speech and its government protections were at the center of this controversy. Griffing called Truth's persecutors hypocrites for using legal language and yet not permitting either woman to exercise the verbal liberty that they believed the US Constitution and Indiana state law guaranteed. She wrote that the anti-abolitionists couched their opposition to Truth in terms of "devotion" to these documents, while at the same time flouting their "highest requirements and provisions." Here, as she and others had done previously, Griffing drew upon the implicit understanding that the First Amendment guaranteed free speech. As she responded to the attack, Griffing linked her and Truth's struggle to larger national battles and to ideas of universal, natural rights that she believed the authorities should explicitly safeguard. With these words, she participated in a larger conversation about abolitionists' freedom of speech that had been ongoing in the region since the 1830s.

Griffing and Truth tapped into ideas in their reform culture that Americans' rights included freedom of speech regardless of race. Rights, race, and politics were all thus inextricable in Angola, as elsewhere in the Old Northwest. Truth, with her usual verbal dexterity, would not allow the cold racism of her foes to pass without comment. She said in the courthouse to her mobbing audience that her presence brought community tensions to the surface, "'it seems that it takes *my* black face to bring out *your* black hearts; so it's well I came.'"[71] Truth's comment about "black hearts" shows that her antagonists in Angola unveiled their deepest beliefs and prejudices when her presence provoked them. Painter writes that Griffing depicted this conflict as an issue of politics. Juxtaposing Griffing's commentary with Truth's retort about their "black hearts," Painter argues that unlike Truth, Griffing missed the racial dimensions of the situation: "Where Griffing saw politics, Truth saw race."[72] However, Griffing's response to the attacks on Truth actually shows that while she demonstrably saw politics as relevant to the situation, she presented Truth's travails in Steuben County as a race-based issue—and thus was well aware of her context. When Griffing argued that the anti-abolitionists' unwillingness to acknowledge Truth's humanity both motivated and justified their use of the "Black Laws," she claimed that the effort to silence this African American woman indeed stemmed from her race. Here, Griffing and Truth revealed their nuanced views of the ideas of race and its significance that were prevalent in Indiana and the nation, a perspective that shows why it is important to consider the Old Northwest and its singular reform climate to understand how people thought about race and rights in 1861.

Comprehension of these events in Angola also requires examining the community factors that enabled the violence. In denouncing the incidents at Steuben and discussing how to resist them, Griffing herself saw flawed manhood as key. She wrote that this county, while "intelligent and loyal," and thus not wholly anti-Union, nonetheless lacked the "proper authority" to stifle such attempts at oppression. Griffing placed the blame for this lack of backbone on her assessment that for thirty years, mobs had ruled and "thoroughly subjugated" northern men, so that they had "almost lost the identity of manhood," and they were largely afraid to obtain the "authority" required to face down a mob. They needed to do so to protect citizens' rights.

Gender mattered to activists like Griffing, for she argued that in the face of these crowds and the repression they instigated, antislavery people—as advocates of freedom, regardless of gender—must exercise masculine strength to redeem the nation. Whether the struggle would take place in military channels or in battles over freedom of speech in a small town, Griffing argued that the conflict was then inevitable. She wrote: "When manhood shall assert itself, as it must and will do, whether on marshalled or unmarshalled battlefields, by President Lincoln or Sojourner Truth, the line will be drawn, speedily and unmistakably, between Liberty and Slavery, Victory and Defeat."[73] Thus Griffing claimed that Truth could also deploy manhood, which complicates abolitionists' other usages of the term as needed to protect their rights. What were the ingredients of manhood if Truth could exert it too? With these words calling on Truth's manhood, Griffing betrayed a flexible conception of the gender identities of female abolitionists, including herself. As fighters for racial justice and freedom of speech, Truth and others could enact the masculine power that Griffing demanded. The contemporary reform vocabulary may have lacked a term for the female equivalent of the force the term "manhood" implied, the dominance that Old Northwest abolitionists knew was vital to their freedom of expression.

The courtroom battles themselves represented the struggle between silence and liberty of expression. The right to speak, with freedom on its side, confronted ruling slavery, which, Griffing wrote, "made a conquest in this country by the suppression of free speech." Presenting the conflict, "the battle of Sojourner," in these lofty terms allowed these two determined lecturers to reap the publicity benefits of notoriety, despite the fact that they ultimately failed to secure free speech in Angola. The previous fall, antislavery organizers could not safely hold a meeting in the Steuben county seat, but Griffing claimed the uproar over Truth's mobbing had roused "a hundred" local men who would act in their defense. She noted the "most influential and noble-hearted women" whose attendance in the courtroom showed Truth and Griffing the strength of local support for their freedom of speech. She called this valiance "manhood," and credited her and Truth's "persistent agitation" of what she termed the "negro" question with inspiring it. In the previous two weeks, they had aroused a new and spirited fighting force, one willing to defend physically the right of all people to speak freely.

As a result, in Angola, Indiana, and the surrounding area, Griffing proclaimed that this conflict had brought her and Truth great results for their past month of work. While "very small majorities" closed nearby churches to them in the ensuing weeks, nevertheless the two women had held successful meetings outside. Under these tense circumstances, their gatherings drew masses of brave young men and a diverse array of other people, from ancient military veterans to nursing mothers. Their message appealed to many in this moment as the war began, when the nation's future was far from evident. Griffing saw this town and this region as vital spaces to work toward freedom of expression and to open all places to "discussion."[74]

While this Indiana conflict was short-lived, nonetheless Griffing saw ahead for herself a continued life of activist conflict. She linked her and Truth's efforts to broader struggles, for still to come was the remainder of "this war of the negro," to be followed by a fight for the "rights of woman." In this incident of Indiana race and speech oppression, Griffing connected the local battles—to win herself and her friend the right to speak—to the larger Civil War, and to the future struggles for complete freedom for African Americans and all women. Griffing declared that only following these victories and only upon her death, would she cease her activism and be still, only when she reached "the quiet of the grave."[75] These freedom-of-speech skirmishes were part and parcel of the struggle to reform the Old Northwest. They reveal that there, activists found freedom of expression an essential component of their local fight—and that both they and their opponents knew that organizing in the region depended on it. Out of this understanding reformers developed legal and extralegal, formal and informal methods to push their agendas.

* * *

As they worked to gather allies through touring and lecturing, itinerants unified antislavery people from across the spectrum of beliefs, and they reached audiences that ranged from inspired to infuriated. Traveling lecturers created a unique local reform culture by traversing the Old Northwest, and the immense effort that they put into transforming the parameters of public speech in the region affirms the great importance contemporaries ascribed to this place. Itinerant speakers faced down substantial risks, and their public activism spread the antislavery and anti-prejudice message across the Old Northwest.

As Sojourner Truth saw and personally experienced, activists in the region found for decades that their struggle to secure public speech in the face of violence was closely tied to the fight against the "Black Laws." This legislation impeded both their activism and African American rights. Old Northwest reformers' battles to meet and freely express their views were but part of their overall activist agenda. Indeed, they simultaneously also actively opposed racial prejudice through organizing against it, and thus aimed to create their ideal America. Their antislavery beliefs required direct action, and they came with the conviction that reformers had to eradicate the ills they saw around them.[76] As Old Northwest activists fought racially biased laws, they sought to realize their human rights vision. Their labor against the "Black Laws" reveals how they implemented their practical commitment to changing their society. With their rhetoric and strategies, Old Northwest activists thus overtly dissented from their racist culture, despite intense opposition. In the heartland of northern anti-abolition and racism, their claim for equal rights for African Americans directly attacked the support structures of slavery and prejudice.

7 / The Potential for Radical Change: The Turbulent 1850s, the Civil War, and Resilient Racism

The universe possesses no power that can elevate error into the dignity of right.

—THE ILLINOIS STATE CONVENTION OF COLORED MEN, GALESBURG, OCTOBER 1866

The Old Northwest's racialized laws were the "error[s]" the Illinois Convention noted, which remained unresolved when they met, and indeed continued beyond 1870. Much as this history opened with an examination of the context of race and law in the Old Northwest, so in closing it explores how these same problems remained formidable from the 1850s through 1870, while slavery disintegrated. From the 1850s on, Old Northwest activists combated the "Black Laws" and other racially biased laws with an expanded set of tools, including fugitive slave aid, vigilance committees, and personal liberty laws. They also carried on using the pen, the press, petitions, lobbying, court cases, and the Black Convention Movement as they sought to create a more egalitarian world. The latter movement had its own limitations, however, as African American women found when they joined it.

While anti-prejudice activism had been continual since the 1830s, the changes in the nation and the region presented reformers with new challenges. Partisan politics held the key to many of these shifts. Although plenty of people had opposed African American rights (much as they objected to abolition) for partisan reasons since at least the 1830s, over time these pressures had grown. The country's increasing threat to fracture along sectional lines held the key for many who sought to maintain the Old Northwest's racial status quo. The pressure to contain political change and shifts in rights was substantial, especially as the debate over slavery's expansion heated up in the mid-1850s, and afterward. Even following the passage of the Fifteenth Amendment in 1870, Old Northwest activists faced down persistent legal bias against African Americans in the region.

Across numerous northern communities, abolition and racial equality were unpopular ideas, to be sure, but the racial attitudes toward African Americans and the legal obstacles to their rights in the Old Northwest made activism all the more difficult there. The actions that framed reform activities in the Old Northwest—the "Black Laws," the constraints they imposed, and action against them—reveal how and why people so strongly resisted change in this region.

While race relations in the Old Northwest—and their interactions with partisan politics—have generally not received as much attention as other areas, when they have been studied the historical pendulum has swung widely. Recent efforts to refute the region's racism, which historians had established in older works, go too far. Specifically, while Ohio repealed some of its "Black Laws" in the 1840s and some Republican politicians may have gained ground in the 1850s, the changes were largely superficial, and conditions were at least as inequitable for African Americans later. Thus the claim that the region was "against slavery" in a way that entailed reduced hostility to African Americans falls apart under closer investigation. Republican politicians—among whom there were few race radicals in the Old Northwest—did not represent the tenor of opinion on race in Ohio or the region. While such politicians occasionally took progressive racial positions, they were but a small subset of the region's population, and one with only a tenuous hold on political power.[1] The Old Northwest may have become the birthplace of many a subsequent president and of a number of important Republican politicians, but the majority of white residents of these four states continued their strong commitment to racial distinctions through Reconstruction and even after.[2]

In fact, more continuity characterizes the situation of race and rights in Ohio and in the region as a whole. Activists actually only somewhat eroded the "Black Laws" in wartime. Even as the Civil War's inception helped Old Northwest African Americans make some slow progress, they seldom found welcome, and had to persevere in the fight for the basic rights that the federal government had newly guaranteed them. Reformers faced the increasing threats of the 1860s with an accelerating tone of militancy among both African American and whites.[3] During the war and after, they expanded their efforts to repeal northern "Black Laws" and improve their status, even as most of the citizens of the Old Northwest held tight to racial stratification.

* * *

Anti-"Black Law" activism continued to rely on a range of local citizens to fight for the cause. The biracial but African American–identifying Langston brothers of Ohio exemplify connections reformers drew as they combated slavery and the "Black Laws." Schoolteacher and activist Charles Langston saw the Black Convention Movement as an essential tool to use against the Ohio "Black Laws," for at their meetings, he and his compatriots continually attacked such legislation. His younger brother John Mercer Langston became a famed lawyer with a long political career, including being the first African American man elected to office as the clerk of Brownhelm Township in 1855. He was eligible to run because he could be called white under one reading of the Ohio "Black Laws," although he consistently self-identified as African American. He took advantage of the laws to claim a right he thought all men deserved. As the younger Langston wrote to Frederick Douglass in 1855, he believed that protecting African American interests required both African American and white "Anti-Slavery persons" to do more to get them the vote. He pushed for greater change throughout his life, and was one of the most outspoken foes of the "Black Laws." In the 1880s he became the first African American to represent Virginia in Congress.[4] The Langstons illustrate how African Americans took an ongoing, active role in fighting for racial justice by the 1850s, but they did not do this alone.

The activists who campaigned against the "Black Laws" in the 1850s and after remained a diverse group with a large-scale vision of the need to change their society. While African Americans were the most vocal opponents of this legislation, white northern reformers had not—as previous scholars argued—abandoned the broader struggle for racial justice by the 1850s to focus only on the distant issue of slavery. This contention does not fit Old Northwest activists' perspective, nor does it reflect the conditions in which they labored. It did apply to moderate political abolitionists like the Free Soil partisans of the 1850s, but local radical activists maintained a broader agenda through the Reconstruction era.[5] While many bold African Americans like the Langstons confronted white racism, even within reform movements, they did not fight this battle on their own. Unlike the majority of their contemporaries, their white allies in the Old Northwest controverted the conventional wisdom of African American inferiority and necessary segregation. All foes of the "Black Laws" did their best to turn the legal system to their advantage, but this proved difficult as other Old Northwest people used the courts to uphold racialized laws.

* * *

The "Black Laws" and fugitive slave legislation infringed on African American rights in overlapping ways, and this relationship was evident in Old Northwest activists' efforts to remove both kinds of problematic laws. Fugitives had many foes, including in the Illinois state government. In 1851, Governor Augustus C. French proclaimed to Illinois' General Assembly that the state would enforce the Fugitive Slave Act. He deemed adherence to it a necessary component of national unity, and called it "the only means of restoring and preserving harmony."[6] French's views reflected the increasing concerns at the time with preserving sectional concord, if not an element of outright hostility to African Americans.

This pressure to hold the nation together contributed to state laws that dealt harshly with fugitives, and thus compounded the legal disabilities the federal fugitive slave law imposed. Activists in Illinois also fought against another way in which the "Black Laws" entrapped African Americans in slavery: the 1845 provision that permitted the sale of people who could not prove their freedom.[7] Antislavery editor and "Black Laws" opponent Zebina Eastman recalled one such slave sale in Chicago in 1852, which abolitionists thwarted. Officials had originally brought Edwin Heathcock to court for refusing to heed the orders of a white man who had not hired his labor—someone whom he had no obligation to obey, but they still prosecuted him under the "Black Laws" for lacking proof of his freedom. While the court scheduled Heathcock to be auctioned as a slave for lacking such proof, the Chicago antislavery population took action, publicizing the auction and ultimately controlling the bidding so that the sheriff could only command a price of twenty-five cents in the sale. Heathcock's new owner let him go free on the spot. The Chicago abolitionists thus outwitted the system.[8]

Where African Americans lacked the support Heathcock found, these sales could ensnare them in long-term servitude. In January 1854 the Galesburg *Free Democrat* reprinted an account of an African American man whom the local sheriff sold at auction in Quincy, Illinois. The author voiced his outrage that slave sales could happen in Illinois, arguing that the winning bidder clearly intended to take the captive man south and permanently enslave him. The victor offered to pay $600. This high sum indicated that he would likely seek some profit from the transaction, one unlikely in the mere month of service to which the auction entitled him.

The extant law did not obligate sheriffs to inquire about buyers' future plans for their "purchase," which left African Americans open to the abuse of already biased laws.[9] In cases where Old Northwest residents cooperated or turned a blind eye, this provision of the "Black Laws" could mire African Americans in dire circumstances well into the 1850s.

Much as they countered sales under the "Black Laws," African Americans and their allies across the Old Northwest carried on their related battle against the federal Fugitive Slave Act of 1850. Some chose public organization as their strategy. Fugitive slave laws placed all northern African Americans in danger of kidnapping. They also rendered activism against them in the region inextricable from work against the "Black Laws" and the Black Convention Movement. John and Mary Jane Jones, who extensively aided fugitives, regarded the new law as both unconstitutional and discriminatory, as did their fellow Chicago activists. On September 30, 1850, over 300 African American Chicagoans met at the African Methodist Church on Wells Street to determine their course of action. They argued that the Fugitive Slave Act violated both the Constitution and the Bible. Their protests continued, for John Jones wrote to the *Western Citizen* that December that it was "inconsistent with the view that all men are created equal." He saw it as purely illegal pandering to southern interests.[10]

The Fugitive Slave Act had sweeping effects, and even economic prosperity could not protect against the coercive power of the newly strengthened law. This was evident in 1853 in Indianapolis, where the courts used the law to charge a very well-to-do African American man named John Freeman as a slave. He ultimately won affirmation of his freedom, but it was obvious to his peers that only his money and network of friends had guaranteed his liberty. He decided Indiana offered him insufficient protection, and departed for Canada soon thereafter.[11] Despite their tenuous position, many other Old Northwest African Americans opted to stay in the region.

The question of their local safety and slavery's reach into the Old Northwest came directly to activists with the notorious Supreme Court decision of *Dred Scott v. Sanford* in 1857, which struck a crushing blow to African American rights all across the North. Abolitionist Marius Robinson, for one, decried the Scott decision's broad impact on the region. He saw it, as did many of his compatriots, as a clear sign that slavery was a national menace and that the government intended to use the courts to oppose African American rights. He believed it dismantled the separation of powers necessary for "liberty," and that it made "the Constitution an absurd and miserably conflicting document."[12] While northern courts and legislatures remained generally unsympathetic to pleas for equity, some did counter the Scott decision with their local rulings.[13]

Indeed, the courts could prove valuable allies to African Americans, as in Illinois in the early 1850s, where some treated fugitives as if they were free once they were in Illinois.[14] The judiciary then was increasingly willing to protect African American rights, at least those of fugitive slaves.[15] Much as some Illinois courts shifted to becoming allies for fugitives, so did some in Ohio.

Even before the courts determined Dred Scott's fate, the Ohio Supreme Court had taken a different approach to similar issues in *Anderson v. Poindexter* in 1856. The trial courts led Ohio in the direction of refusing to protect slaves as property on state soil. In 1857 Marius Robinson wrote of the Ohio court case that it considered whether a slave taken by a slaveholder into Ohio (or "going there with his consent") became free once there. The court ruled that slaves were "automatically free" when they entered the state with their owners' permission. Writing after the Scott decision, Robinson saw in this case a "clear departure" from the federal Supreme Court's view, but believed that this precedent was still insecure. Indeed, he saw the Ohio case as but a mere stopgap measure, since in his regard, the federal court could still interfere.[16]

Old Northwest activists' direct action against the Fugitive Slave Act and its increase in threats to African American freedom in the 1850s also took the form of vigilance committees, citizen police forces to stop slave catchers and protect accused fugitive slaves. At their September 1850 meeting, the Chicagoans planned strong resistance to the law, including shielding African Americans from capture into slavery. They claimed they would take direct action regardless of the consequences: "[w]e are determined to defend ourselves at all hazards, even if it should be to the shedding of human blood."[17] The vigilance committee they created to enforce this conviction joined in African Americans' long tradition of self-defense.[18] While historians often consider such committees to be African American dominated, whites also took part in protecting universal rights.[19] The Chicago men obtained the support of the Chicago Common Council—the city council—that publicly countenanced their resolutions. The next month, the council went further when nine of its ten members voted to "nullify" the Fugitive Slave Act.[20]

Beyond vigilance committees, Old Northwest activists aimed to use new laws to formally protect fugitives in the 1850s. Ohio African Americans had tried for years to obtain a personal liberty law after losing such protections in 1843. As early as 1851, the Ohio legislature passed resolutions that deemed the Fugitive Slave Act unconstitutional and called for states to continue to allow writs of habeas corpus for runaways.[21] They finally obtained an enforceable measure in 1857 when the Republicans gained control of the assembly. Antislavery politician and former "One Hundred Conventions" lecturer James Monroe of Oberlin was a key player in the passage of this short-lived Ohio personal liberty law. He had long labored against slavery and the "Black Laws" from within the Free Soil and Republican Parties. While in the state legislature from 1855 to 1862, he campaigned to persuade his fellow legislators that African Americans deserved equal rights.[22] When the Democrats regained power in 1858 they repealed the personal liberty law's most sweeping provisions and tried to pass a statute mandating enforcement of the Fugitive Slave Act.[23] Party rivalries, too, could substantially influence fugitive rights in Old Northwest states.

Ohio was not alone, for Michigan, too, had a late but strong personal liberty law in 1855 that constrained the legal process for fugitive recovery. It imposed provisions that slave catchers had to take African Americans and biracial people before a judge and accuse them of being slaves before they could be detained.[24] These legal efforts were part of the larger, ongoing strategy to overturn the region's discriminatory laws.

* * *

In the increasingly strained Old Northwest and in the nation in the early 1850s, African Americans persisted in their organized work to secure full citizenship. John Jones and his allies circulated another petition to the Illinois state legislature for "Black Laws" repeal in December 1850.[25] Elsewhere, in Indiana, the Black State Convention met in 1851 to resist the new discriminatory constitution of that year. In July 1853, after a few quiet years, the Black National Convention Movement revived with a meeting at Rochester, New York. Jones and Frederick Douglass both participated as vice-presidents, and 140 delegates from nine states met there.[26] This convention aimed at justice for African Americans and presented a comprehensive agenda, including work against the colonization movement.

The national convention technique of a broad, rights-based strategy came to the Prairie State that October, for the first Illinois Black State Convention met then in Chicago. This meeting's main focus was repeal of the "Black Laws," although the participants also discussed other issues, including education and colonization. The members elected Jones president and chair of the anticolonization committee. Delegates argued that colonization led to proslavery sentiment and depressed the morale of the African American population. In their view, the "Black Laws" were against the state and national constitutions, unjust, unequal, and even "repugnant to the principles of humanity." These laws impeded both the "moral and the mental development" of Illinois' African Americans, and they were determined to push against them. They formed a state repeal association for this purpose.[27] Despite such efforts, African Americans in the Old Northwest still lacked equal rights and opportunities, especially the women among them.

For all of these conventions' talk of equality and demand for parity of opportunity, this did not readily extend to women; the Black conventions were a male-dominated space. In keeping with the domestic ideology prevalent at the time, state and national Black conventions frequently resisted women's efforts to join their ranks, although women won this right on a handful of occasions.[28] The reception that met these women varied. Some men treated their female compatriots as mere tokens or as fulfilling a more decorative than substantive role in these conventions. At the 1857 Ohio Convention, the minutes noted of them, the "ladies, God bless them! cheered us with their smiles, and wishes, and approbation."[29] This vague praise leaves unanswered the question of what role the women took at that convention, but it was not limited to window dressing elsewhere.

African American women made their first formal request for inclusion in the 1848 national convention at Cleveland. This move, which historian Shirley Yee links in timing to the Seneca Falls Convention of that year, met with debate, but the business committee ultimately opted to redefine voters as "persons," rather than men, allowing women the right to vote there.[30] After adopting this definition, the assembled people gave "three cheers for women's rights." They also passed another resolution noting that they "fully believe in the equality of the sexes," and that women should join their future meetings. Despite this victory, a year later, at the state convention at Cleveland, the men again excluded women from participation. In response, they vowed to boycott. Mrs. Jane P. Merritt argued that it was "wrong and shameful" for the men of the meeting to invite women to attend, only to refuse them permission to speak. They won this right.[31] At the first Illinois Black Convention in October of 1853, while it was a male-only meeting, the attendees also asked for equal opportunities. They included women in their reform strategy, albeit in a limited way as the "God-given helpmeet of man." Even as women gained a role there, they did so in a very moderate way—at least in the words of their male contemporaries.

While women's participation in conventions was at times controversial, their male allies were more receptive to accepting them as witnesses to the conventions and as financial benefactors. At the 1850 Ohio convention, the women in the audience offered to fund the costs of the hall rental. Their fellow attendees gratefully accepted, as they did the following year when the women pledged to pay for the Ohio convention's publication of their proceedings in 1851.[32] Women were there, even if they did not always take an active role.

African American female leaders also joined in the conventions, with mixed results. In the 1855 national convention at Philadelphia, three women delegates attempted to join the proceedings. One was Mary Ann Shadd Cary, who represented Canada there. Her admission was very controversial, and her residence outside of the United States likely did not help. Nonetheless, the convention eventually voted to admit her as a delegate.[33] In 1858 in Ohio, Frances Ellen Watkins Harper attended the national convention, which openly "requested" that she "take part." She eventually served on the fundraising committee, and the other attendees embraced her with less controversy than Shadd had found earlier.[34] In the 1860s, the conventions became slightly more willing to recognize women, although still in very small numbers. At the 1864 national convention in Syracuse, Miss Edmonia Highgate of Syracuse spoke, as did Harper.[35] Cary also remained interested in the Black conventions, for she attended the Michigan state convention in 1865.[36]

Despite these qualified and small triumphs, women had a long fight for equality among African American activists. Much as it did in other antebellum reform struggles, conflict arose from prioritizing race over gender equality. As was the case elsewhere, the male leaders of the Black Convention Movement used gendered language of natural rights and human rights to deny women parity.[37] Even if they were not always unified, African Americans in the Old Northwest persisted in their wide-ranging campaign for rights.

* * *

In terms of results, in the 1850s the governments of these four states clearly dismissed the egalitarian claims of their African American residents. In an 1850 referendum, Michigan citizens again strongly rejected African American suffrage.[38] A common fear among whites there was that allowing them the vote would make the state attractive to Black migrants.[39] In two discouraging cases, Ohio's 1851 constitution affirmed the restriction of the right to vote to whites, and in February 1853 the Illinois legislature enacted another anti-immigration article that forbade African American or biracial people from settling there, under threat of fines. This created another form of virtual enslavement in Illinois, for local sheriffs could sell individuals who could not pay such fees to cover court costs.[40] With this decision, the Illinois legislature sought to promote harmony with nearby slave states, and keep African American populations small.

Indiana also maintained its exclusionary provisions, much to the dismay of the Indiana Friends, who vehemently protested against the "Black Laws." In 1850, Elijah Coffin wrote in his journal about his fellow Friends' efforts to use their Meeting for Sufferings to oppose that year's anti-immigration amendment to the state constitution. Since the Friends "felt low" about the positive reception that this race-based legislation had obtained at the constitutional convention, they assembled a committee and wrote a memorial to present there.[41] While ineffective in this instance—the measure passed—this direct action indicates Old Northwest reformers' capacity to rally in defense of their human rights principles in crisis situations.

Throughout the 1850s, African Americans and their allies tried to repeal these racialized laws and found occasional signs that their activism had paid off. While their efforts generally failed, activists still steadily organized against the "Black Laws," and especially for entitlement to public education, the vote, and legal rights.[42] They had some small victories to tide them over, including in 1853 when Ohio ruled that its counties must give African Americans public education, but this was usually still segregated. There was substantial variation within the state concerning education; some areas integrated by choice before the law required it, while others were recalcitrant to educate African Americans even after they had to do so.[43] In Michigan, after 1855 they won the right to vote in most school district elections.[44] Their obstacles remained formidable nonetheless.

The Black Convention Movement and other public activist measures raised the profile of the debate over Old Northwest race and rights and the "Black Laws" in national African American leadership circles. Old Northwest activists sought attention across the country for their struggles, and the fiery speech delivered at the 1854 August 1 celebration in Columbus, Ohio, and reprinted in *Frederick Douglass' Paper* aided with this publicity. There, the speaker called the United States "this seemingly

Godforsaken country," and declared no interest in celebrating the Fourth of July until the nation had been cleansed of its substantial sins: "When it shall be resurrected from the hell of infamy into which it has been plunged by the damnable degeneracy of the sons of the Pilgrims, we shall celebrate it with heartfelt hallelujahs; until then we shall trample it underfoot as an unholy thing." This vehement language, continuing in the tradition of Frederick Douglass's fiery speech from July 5, 1852, accompanied an otherwise tranquil celebration for all ages, with food, music, and a partial recitation of the Declaration of Independence by Charles Langston.[45]

As this newspaper coverage implies, national African American leaders derided the Old Northwest for its "Black Laws." This derision was not confined to Ohio, for by 1855 Illinois' dire reputation on racial issues had reached the ears of famed African American activist James McCune Smith of New York City. In a speech that he delivered at the First Colored Presbyterian Church in that city, he claimed that Illinois had "hitherto [been] covered with deeper infamy in caste than any other state." The serious legal obstacles African Americans faced in Illinois were evident to this eastern leader. Nevertheless, he saw some indications that efforts for equality there had been showing results.[46] The local fighters, too, knew that the battle was not yet won, and carried on with their organizing efforts.

For the remainder of the decade, the Ohio Black Conventions joined others in the region in making powerful arguments against their governments' "Black Laws." For them, there was no justification for disparities in rights.[47] Also in 1854, John Mercer Langston wrote a memorial to the Ohio General Assembly to counter race-based discrimination, with a particular focus on African American disfranchisement. He argued that they had more than earned the right to vote, and used as evidence their common humanity, natural rights, nativity, patriotism (including extensive evidence of military valor), tax paying, intelligence, and virtue.[48] Again in 1856, the Ohio Convention addressed their senate and house about the "Black Laws," and disseminated petitions to submit to that body in their meeting's minutes.[49]

* * *

Despite these persistent efforts, African American citizenship was far from assured in the late 1850s across the region, as the ongoing enforcement of exclusionary laws demonstrates. In 1856, the Indiana Supreme Court demonstrated its commitment to race-based exclusion with a court decision that deemed Arthur Berkshire guilty of bringing Elizabeth Keith into Indiana from Ohio. Both were African American, and they wished to marry. The court charged him as an offender against the state's anti-immigration provisions, and nullified their marriage.[50] With this decision, Indiana continued in its longstanding pattern of "exceptionally punitive" marriage prohibitions.[51]

Regardless of such blatant limitations on their rights, African Americans and their allies tenaciously fought the Old Northwest "Black Laws" at mid-decade. The 1856 Illinois State Black Convention at Alton demanded equality and took more decisive action against these laws. It aimed to recruit more members among Illinois African Americans. Their chief complaint about the laws' injustice remained their denial of the right to vote. At this convention, the attendees extensively debated whether they should assert themselves by using strong, demanding language as they called for removing their legal disabilities, "neither asking nor giving quarter, spurning all compromises." Some said they should behave thus, while others argued for a more moderate approach. They put it to a vote and retained the forthright language, but the vote was very close.[52] Even as the "Black Laws" inspired substantial anger, activists differed in their views on how best to express their frustration with the injustice they witnessed, and to push for change.

In Ohio, efforts against the "Black Laws" proceeded through the end of the decade and beyond, and shared the outspoken tactics of that Illinois faction. In 1858, the state convention demanded repeal of the "Black Laws" and resolved to send petitions and memorials to the legislature until they got it. That year, the threats African American Ohioans experienced seemed so dire that they also formed a new association, the Ohio State Anti-Slavery Society. It was open to women and men, and worked against the "Black Laws" and slavery through the Civil War.[53] This new society showed that Ohio African Americans were intensifying their efforts, even as they faced many barriers.

Obtaining rights remained an uphill battle in the Old Northwest, and a discouraging one at times. In 1858, the Indiana Black State Convention petitioned the legislature to lift the limits on their testimony. This fell on deaf ears, for that same year, the Indiana General Assembly proposed resolutions that supported the "Black Laws" and claimed that "inferior" African Americans had no right to "freedom and equality." While the resolutions failed, since the General Assembly had seriously considered them, the proposals nonetheless show the ominous tone of Indiana race relations at that time. As motions that the Democratic Party sponsored, they were also highly partisan.[54] That same year, the Michigan Supreme Court deemed discrimination and segregated accommodations legal, affirming that African Americans could be "excluded from ordinary social and familiar intercourse with white persons." African American activists were strapped for funds, and their liberties stagnated as racial violence intensified. These setbacks radicalized many, and some increased their fugitive aid, while others debated emigration to Canada.[55] Still, the convention movement persuaded many people to oppose colonization ventures, and African Americans' articulate presence belied claims of their inferiority.

While a range of activists fought on against racial distinctions, the 1850s closed on a low note. Support for the "Black Laws" remained extensive in Ohio, where in 1859 the Supreme Court again strengthened them. They disfranchised biracial people, and argued that election judges still must reject voters with a "visible admixture" of African American ancestry. The battle there carried on, with African American activist John Mercer Langston and the Ohio Anti-Slavery Society leading the way with speeches and petition campaigns that also called for the passage of "personal liberty laws" and the repeal of the Fugitive Slave Law and the "Black Laws."[56] Some, their patience wearing thin, took more direct action and seized their rights.

* * *

On April 4, 1859, a 25–year-old man who lived in Charleston Township, Ohio, went to the polls to defy and test the "Black Laws." He saw that he met the citizenship, residency, and age requirements for voting, but the men in charge of the polls disagreed, and refused to let him vote. Why? He was African American, and according to the Ohio "Black Laws," thus disfranchised. This young man, William J. Whipper, claimed the right to vote nonetheless. Whipper, a Charleston resident, wrote to Salem, Ohio, abolitionist Benjamin S. Jones that he thought himself entitled to the franchise, "notwithstanding my dark complexion," so he attempted to vote. He fought his subsequent rejection and inspired a fiery local debate. Whipper argued that the statute did not explicitly exclude him, for he quoted it as saying "that all white male citizens over the age of twenty-one *may* vote, but does not say that colored ones may not." This persuaded the election judge, Mr. Loomis, who let him vote. A local man, Dr. Heath, then sued Loomis for allowing this "illegal vote." Two local townships refused to try Loomis, which proves some Ohioans' indifference to the "Black Laws." Paris Township agreed to do so.

The judge arraigned Loomis for $300, and told Whipper to keep quiet and stay out of the legal battle. As a second-generation abolitionist, the Pennsylvania-born son of abolitionist William Whipper would not be swayed, for he saw the law on his side and "established custom" as clearly in the wrong. He wrote defiantly, "so come on with your forces, for being quiet is no part of my mission." Whipper argued that rights did not depend on race, and he was glad to see the bias of men like Dr. Heath brought to public attention. The county court acquitted Loomis the next month, vindicating Whipper, although some Ohio "Black Laws" remained in force until the 1880s, as did many in other states in the region.[57] Whipper remained an active opponent of slavery and the "Black Laws," both in the Old Northwest and nationally. He moved to Detroit during the Civil War, and later became a prominent Republican lawyer and politician in South Carolina.[58] Before he did that, he and his compatriots fought ongoing rights debates that the increasing instability in the Old Northwest accelerated.

* * *

Apart from the continual voting rights issues, as the decade drew to a close the battle for protections for fugitives raged on. Michigan weighed in on the side of fugitives, strengthening its anti-kidnapping protections in 1859, as did Ohio.[59] In 1859 and 1860 both Ohio Governor Salmon P. Chase and the state Supreme Court adhered to a strong pro–habeas corpus position, as the Oberlin-Wellington rescue case exemplified, where the state only reluctantly prosecuted fugitive slave rescuers.[60] Old Northwest people's efforts to use local laws to defeat national ones they perceived as unjust indicate that grassroots activists had a comprehensive vision for transforming race and rights in the region, and had won important allies by then.

Nevertheless, the position of fugitives was very insecure. For example, in Ohio opponents of African American rights tried to repeal the remaining anti-kidnapping provision from 1857, but were unsuccessful. This effort to take away protections demonstrates ongoing hostility to African Americans, despite scholars' claims that Ohioans were becoming more welcoming to them.[61]

Partisan politics, African American rights, and fugitive rights had a tense relationship in the Old Northwest. The political parties frequently tried to avoid becoming enmeshed in these debates. Republican Party supporters were often reluctant to ally themselves with either the antislavery movement or northern egalitarianism. In 1859 and 1860, the

Republicans—a northern sectional party—refused to take a strong stance against the pervasive racism of the "Black Laws."[62] In places such as Ohio, Republicans did decry the Fugitive Slave Act and its infringements on runaways' rights and those of their helpers.[63] Nevertheless, the expansion of the antislavery agenda to include the Republican Party was costly for the anti-prejudice movement's larger goals. Their lack of commitment to fighting racism is evident in the Indiana Republicans' attempts to appear as the "true 'white man's party,'" including their willingness to engage in race-baiting, as they did in 1860 when they denounced Democrats as proponents of interracial sex.[64] Over time, the dominance of that moderate strain of opposition to slavery led to a less firm stance against it and racism, for the Republicans largely abandoned the egalitarian principles found earlier in Old Northwest political abolition.

Among those who retained interest in African American rights, some former Illinois Liberty Party activists later supported the Radical Republican position over Lincoln's more moderate stance.[65] Racial prejudice still exerted significant sway over many northerners, and many politicians tried to reassure their constituents with public, gradualist proclamations that the end of slavery would not affect the stratified structure of their local society.[66] These moderate positions were unsatisfactory to reformers who sought more comprehensive change in Old Northwest race and rights.

By 1860 over thirty years of slow-paced progress had stretched thin the patience of many Old Northwest activists. That September, Illinois abolitionist H. Ford Douglas offered a strong critique of the progress of racial equality in the region and the nation. Douglas was born into slavery in Virginia, but escaped in 1846 and lived in Cleveland before moving to Chicago in 1856. He began lecturing for the Massachusetts Society in 1860. At the meeting of the Western Anti-Slavery Society in Salem, Ohio, that year, Douglas made a fiery and memorable speech, rife with the language of immediatism and opposition to the Constitution. He denounced the government, the major political parties, and the antislavery politicians, for he saw them all as tainted by servitude's influence. Scolding his mostly white audience for upholding these institutions, Douglas claimed that the political parties, beholden as they both were to slavery, would persist in refusing African Americans their due. They were too willing to compromise to secure election results, he thundered, but "to elevate men to office is not an object for which a man should barter away his manhood." In his view, all had the "right of self-defence," and should protect their "liberty" even at the expense of the political parties and the government, if necessary.

Douglas continued his critique of the state and the nation, arguing that governments impeded African Americans' full citizenship by acknowledging only white men's rights. Douglas maintained that the United States truly needed to honor universal human rights. Indeed, activists must teach all to "recognize the white man, the black man, the red man, *all* men, to all the rights of manhood." Thus he, as an African American, was not asking for "any special favor" but that he receive his "manhood . . . before the law," which was only his due. This required the repeal of the "Black Laws." Even as he demanded equality, Douglas's words reveal how the language of political rights in his era split along gendered lines. The phrasing of his desired goal as "the rights of manhood" conflated citizenship and gender.[67] As Douglas used these words, he likely aimed at the political principles of the enfranchised portion of his Ohio audience, the white men, to show them the rights African American men lacked but nonetheless claimed. The former, of course, held the power to vote and change the region's governments. To them and the disfranchised in the audience, Douglas proclaimed that the equation of whiteness, manhood, and citizenship could no longer suffice, and that Old Northwest African Americans and their allies in the human rights cause would continue to fight until they had achieved their objective. He exemplifies the passionate Old Northwest arguments and actions that persisted in that new decade.

* * *

In the 1860s, Old Northwest human rights activists retained the fire Douglas displayed, and when the Civil War arrived it brought some of them a new optimism. This conflict followed a turbulent and disappointing decade, for many northern African Americans had become disheartened by the stagnation of their rights in the 1850s and the intensification of violence over slavery, sectionalism, and discrimination. They had come to view achieving full citizenship as a remote possibility, and in consequence many had considered emigration and colonization potential solutions to intractable American racism. The immediate abolitionists continued their lecturing and writing for the cause, but some of the antislavery forces had dispersed into compromised forms of political abolition by the 1860s. For the small, beleaguered African American population and its white allies, the Civil War and the constitutional change that followed presented new possibilities for overcoming southern slavery and the racialized laws of the Old Northwest. Quite a few of them became more sanguine about the potential for change.

Nonetheless, they still faced extensive obstacles to their full citizenship, including the limitations of partisan politics, but even more painfully and directly, the "Black Laws" that remained in force in wartime and after.[68] In the Old Northwest they soon found their circumstances remained disadvantaged in most respects, and that the rights they had gained in law were often quite different from those that they could actually exercise in daily life.[69]

As the Civil War began in distant South Carolina, the "Black Laws" and Old Northwest racism both remained strong. When formal hostilities commenced in 1861 after years of brinksmanship, most white Americans believed in their own superiority and African American inferiority. They hardly intended the war as a stab against white domination, particularly in the Old Northwest, the region—aside from the South—with the deepest investment in racial hierarchy. These white Americans did not see the war as aiming to help African Americans, especially in its early years.[70] Indeed, those northerners who feared increased immigration by former slaves tried to put up new impediments to African American mobility. They called for strengthened exclusionary provisions once they realized the war was undermining slavery. In one such instance in Michigan, many whites proclaimed that emancipation would result in African Americans flooding the state. They even petitioned to have the personal liberty laws then in place repealed, although this petition failed. Michigan and other Old Northwest states reinforced their "Black Laws" during the war with the aim of keeping their African American populations small.[71]

These restrictive efforts aside, the Civil War and its aftermath had telling consequences for trends in Old Northwest populations: all four states saw higher rates of growth in their African American populations from 1860 to 1870 than in their overall populations in that decade. Even using the best demographic source available, the admittedly limited decadal census, makes it challenging to chart precisely when in the decade this increase occurred, but the upward movement is clear. Nevertheless, African Americans' absolute numbers in the region remained small. In Illinois, the total population grew by 48 percent, while the African American population skyrocketed by 277 percent in that same decade. In Indiana, the overall population growth rate slowed in those years to 58 percent, but that of African Americans substantially increased—by 115 percent—in that same era. In Michigan, the overall population grew by 58 percent, while that of African Americans grew faster, by 78 percent. In Ohio in the 1860s, the overall growth rate further slowed to 14 percent, while African Americans' rate leapt to 72 percent. Over time, more and more African Americans lived in the Old Northwest, and even while by 1870 they remained a small minority relative to the overall population, their growth rate was nonetheless higher. This demonstrates their refusal to permit restrictive legislation to exclude them, and their persistence in claiming a place in the Old Northwest.

This migration to the region was but one direct way that the stalwart fighters for African American equality in the Old Northwest kept to their agenda, even as the beginning of the war ushered in shifting priorities. Some activists saw that the war might fail to secure racial justice, which remained a very important priority for them. "A western abolitionist" wrote to the American Anti-Slavery Society in 1861 calling on them to constantly work against the Old Northwest "Black Law[s]." He argued that the American Society should continue to address these laws, and to aim for substantive legal changes. Presciently, he saw that despite the war's likely impact on slavery, it might be insufficient to bring about "Legislation of a just character" for the Old Northwest. He declared bluntly, "It will not answer to trust these reforms to this war."[72] While the conflict presented unparalleled opportunities for change, the sheer magnitude of the obstacles egalitarian activists faced was evident even in the first year of the war.

* * *

Throughout the Civil War, Old Northwest African Americans and their allies maintained steady pressure on their states and the nation for equal rights, but garnered minimal results in the face of substantial resistance. Despite such efforts as the 1861 Michigan Black Convention that argued for parity of rights and for suffrage, the region remained deeply racialized in law and in action.[73] This belies other historian's claims that local citizens' racial views had mellowed by this time.[74] During the war, Old Northwest citizens and legislatures struck repeated blows to the cause of equal treatment, encompassing exclusion, marriage laws, the franchise, and schooling.

African Americans faced revitalized obstacles, as in Ohio, where the General Assembly passed new "Black Laws," demonstrating that bias actually increased during the war. It was in part responding to having been inundated in late 1861 and early 1862 with petitions from more than thirty thousand constituents asking for an exclusionary amendment.[75] The next year these residents continued to petition the Ohio legislature to remove African Americans from their terrain, but the state

Supreme Court denied the constitutionality of such petitions.[76] While Ohio residents tried to limit or expel them, the number of local African Americans continued to increase regardless. The racialized nature of rights in Ohio was evident in other ways as well. During the war, the General Assembly debated the entitlement of men of mixed race descent to the vote, from which they and African American men remained excluded across the region, along with most militias until the war's midpoint. These new difficulties also extended into the personal lives of Old Northwest individuals, as laws related to marriage clearly indicate.

The Old Northwest's marriage laws exemplified the retention and expansion of strong racialized laws in the region in wartime. The Ohio legislature declared its ongoing opposition to interracial relationships with a new antimiscegenation law in 1861, the first statute of its kind in Ohio. It criminalized both interracial sex and marriage and kept in place the visual standard to determine racial boundaries.[77] This evinces an increase in race-based limitations on rights in the region. In wartime, the other three states, too, implemented or retained laws barring interracial marriage.

* * *

This growth in rights limitations was only the beginning, for the Old Northwest also remained the scene of substantial anti–African American incidents throughout 1862 and 1863. These conflicts ranged from disturbing rumors to outright attacks, and were common especially in Indiana and Illinois, but also present in Michigan and Ohio. In areas of the former states, citizens more stringently enforced the anti-immigration laws and the fugitive slave laws than before the war. During and after the Civil War, Indiana remained a dangerous place to advocate racial egalitarianism, but the effort nonetheless continued in both political and activist circles.

Government policies during the war altered Old Northwest populations in ways that both hurt and aided African Americans. At Ohio, Indiana, and Illinois border and river crossings, and even at a distance from the state lines, local authorities appointed guards to stop fugitive traffic from the South.[78] African Americans' presence thus became hotly contested. Despite lacking direct southern borders, Michigan also had its share of anti–African American violence, including a devastating riot in Detroit in 1863. Even as the states tried to impede migration, the Union Army transported many slaves—formerly owned by Confederate supporters—to the Old Northwest, including large numbers to Illinois via Cairo.[79]

Nevertheless, in wartime many of these state governments actually expended minimal effort in enforcing the "Black Laws." In some cases this inaction also extended to the citizenry, for in 1864 the Chicago *Tribune* reported that across most Illinois counties, people were ignoring the 1853 statute forbidding immigration. While these *de facto* changes slightly improved African Americans' ability to live in the Old Northwest, they still faced formidable legal and partisan obstacles. Even as they found ways to help themselves and others, activists saw that much work remained since race still strongly affected people's status in the region.[80]

* * *

The war only augmented partisan disagreements over slavery and the racial basis of rights. In particular, white supremacy also served as the bond holding together the various factions of the Democratic Party through the Reconstruction era and beyond.[81] Most opponents of the war and the draft were Democrats, as were many of the most outspoken foes of African American rights. Ohio was polarized during the Civil War, and had a strong "peace Democrat" or "Copperhead" faction. Clement L. Vallandigham led this group from his position in the US House until 1862. In wartime Indiana and Ohio, the federal government prosecuted and convicted men for anti-government organizing, including Vallandigham for his support of the Confederacy.[82]

"Peace Democrats" held power in the largest numbers in the Old Northwest relative to the rest of the nation, a fact that contributed to discrimination against African Americans during the war. Illinois was a major stronghold of theirs, for they held significant sway over the Constitutional Convention of 1862, and also at the 1864 Democratic National Convention.[83] In Indiana, the legislature abolished none of the "Black Laws" in the war years, despite the fact that African Americans' sometime allies, the Republicans, dominated the body and activists persisted in their repeal efforts. In 1864, the Indiana Democrats used race-baiting in their campaign, and asked for even greater enforcement of the exclusion law. This proved too much for some Indiana African Americans on top of their ongoing concerns, so they chose to leave for Canada. These Democrats fought against emancipation and against allowing African Americans to become soldiers.[84] Antiwar northerners were also often involved in attacks on African Americans during the war.

Nonetheless, over the course of the 1860s, Old Northwest activists found limited and shifting support for African American suffrage and political equality in mainstream politics. On the national political scene, Republicans' extreme moderation on African American rights made for a conservative agenda. Some party men remained strong proponents of colonization in April 1862, and many moderate Republicans feared endorsing African American suffrage or other rights, even in the North, for they believed this would entail loss of political support there.[85]

In the 1862 election, it became clear in the Old Northwest that while partisan arguments that slavery was immoral could elicit support for the war, and even persuade Congress and the President to accept abolition as a general rule, these claims had failed to alter many people's views on egalitarianism or ending slavery.[86] In electoral terms, such lobbying by progressive newspapers, churches, and Black State Conventions eventually drove the Radical Republicans toward advocating African American civil rights.[87] While the Republican politicians of the Old Northwest had done little to advance the cause of equality since the beginning of the war, some, including Radicals from the Western Reserve, gave their votes to congressional efforts aimed against discrimination.[88]

A complicating factor that limited politicians' willingness to address the "Black Laws" was that in wartime, the Republican Party sustained substantial electoral losses in the Old Northwest. In the 1863 midterm election, they lost control of the Indiana and Illinois state legislatures and the Ohio congressional delegation.[89] Nevertheless, by the fall of 1863, some congressional Republicans began to work in earnest to improve the nation's race issues. For most Republicans in the Old Northwest, this was a change in policy, for they had not previously been committed to measures that would drastically alter the racial structure at home, other than some acceptance of antislavery measures.[90] While this was a moderate shift in direction, much local resistance remained. The egalitarian activists of the region remained determined to pursue more sweeping reforms.

* * *

Partisan machinations aside, African Americans saw actual combat in the war as one potential solution for their lack of status in the Old Northwest. They fought for and eventually won the right to join the war effort. From the start of the conflict, many northerners opposed allowing African American men to become Union soldiers, since this implied acknowledging their equal standing as men. Many of the opponents of their enlistment were also threatened by the notion of arming African American men. The activists in the Old Northwest who sought the right to fight agreed with them about the implications military service could have for African Americans' roles in society, and this contributed to their demands.[91] The Union Army eventually was willing to exploit the militia experience of men from the self-defense organizations African Americans had founded in response to the Fugitive Slave Act, but would not permit them to lend their manpower at the beginning of the war. In 1861 activists made passionate arguments to join in the fight in Michigan and Ohio, but the Union command refused at that time.[92]

When some Old Northwest citizens and leaders balked at their admission locally, African American men from the region enlisted in units from other states. From spring 1863 on, the War Department recruited across the North for the 54th Massachusetts Colored Infantry. They hired African American leaders—including Old Northwest activists John Jones and John Mercer Langston—as agents for that regiment and those of Rhode Island and Connecticut. Northern African American men clamored for the right to fight, and by 1863 the governors of these four Old Northwest states had asked the federal government to allow induction of these residents as soldiers. Richard Yates of Illinois led the way with a vehement letter in July 1862, claiming that the crisis required "greater efforts and sterner measures," including the dire need to "accept the services of all loyal men."[93] The War Department advanced this agenda in May 1863 with General Order 143, which created the United States Colored Troops.[94] For the remainder of 1863 and into 1864, African American men, including many former slaves recently arrived in the North, entered the new Black Union Army regiments in Illinois, Indiana, Michigan, and Ohio.[95]

Soldiers were not the only Old Northwest African Americans to join the war effort in order to improve their rights. In September 1863, African American women in Chicago formed the Colored Ladies Freedmen's Aid Society that sent supplies to freed people in the camps to the south and west. Mary Jane Jones and Sattira Douglas, married to H. Ford Douglas, were among their leaders, and they also employed Mary Ann Shadd Cary to travel and raise money.[96] This activity was widespread among African American female leaders in wartime; in Cleveland, the Colored Ladies Auxiliary of the Soldiers' Aid Society of Northern Ohio prepared supplies, engaged in fundraising, and visited the wounded. They obtained much assistance from Cleveland's African American population.[97] Later, some African American leaders in the region also went south to provide aid during Reconstruction, and became politicians there.[98] African Americans seized the opportunities the war provided to advance their rights cause.

Activists across the region saw that discrimination against African Americans persisted into the war years, and continued to present arguments against the "Black Laws." John Jones of Illinois was central to this fight, for on November 4, 1864 he published a pamphlet, "The Black Laws of Illinois and a Few Reasons Why They Should Be Repealed." Addressing his fellow Illinoisans and their legislators, his wide-ranging argument encompassed "moral, economic, legal, and constitutional principles." He believed that African Americans had already proven their worth, and pointed out that they could and should claim United States citizenship on the basis of their Revolutionary and now Civil War military experience. In his view, whites could also use "self-interest" as a motive to repeal the "Black Laws" as they interfered with interracial business transactions, and they needed African Americans to be able to testify to protect their property in court cases. Jones and his allies pushed on against the "Black Laws" with petitions, correspondence committees, and repeal associations.[99] The activism of like-minded people during the war continued the pressure that created incremental change in the Old Northwest racial milieu.

In the war's final months and later, the Black Conventions remained a valuable weapon in the human rights fight. In January 1865, the Ohio Black Convention attacked the "Black Laws" with new vigor, and began to shift to an equal rights league, with a wider agenda that included education and soldiers' rights. They hired a man to "labor with the General Assembly" and lobby it for their rights. Even the privileges that they had already gained—especially those of education—were little known among the general population, so they vowed to write a "circular" to publicize them. Finally, they also used the meetings to express concern with the large numbers of African American soldiers who faced unequal treatment by both the Union command and the enemy.[100] They rallied substantial support for their goals, for one thousand of their members petitioned their legislature against the "Black Laws" that same month.[101] Their concerns with equity continued even as the war ended in April 1865, and Lincoln's assassination soon followed.

Later that year, the National Black Convention Movement began to transform into the National Equal Rights League, which held its first meeting in Cleveland that October. The new name reflected the goals of these meetings of maintaining the quest for full citizenship, and to eradicate all racialized laws and residue of slavery. Illinois, Michigan, and Ohio sent representatives. They argued that nowhere in the United States were legal limitations "on account of race or color" welcome, and indeed, such laws were "void." The Illinois representative, D. B. F. Price from Cairo, noted that his state's racial climate remained oppressive. He spoke of how he and his neighbors suffered greatly from racialized violence. In his southern Illinois town, the "rebel sympathizers" had an overpowering presence, and their attacks had left him physically scarred. At this first meeting of the new association the attendees had trouble agreeing on many issues, including their funding structure, who should be recognized as a member, and other minor governance concerns. This organization nonetheless became a major national proponent of African American legal protections at least through the end of Reconstruction.[102] Perhaps the most long-lasting effect of the convention movement was that it developed both local and national leaders that served the African American community for decades.

* * *

Reconstruction inaugurated a new phase in the ongoing struggle for racial equality. Old Northwest activists could not merely look back on their past greatness, glory, and success in implementing egalitarian values against an oppositional culture, for much work remained. The end of slavery wrought transformations that in turn altered radical arguments, fundamentally reconfiguring them and destabilizing the justification that the institution of bondage had provided for racial stratification. While thorny problems of race and rights remained, and worsened in some areas, the terms of debate in the region had indeed changed.

While the abolition of slavery pleased activists, their larger human rights task was incomplete. They thus continued to push for African American legal equity, which was far from a foregone conclusion in 1865, or in 1870. These reformers had longstanding disagreements about whether the Thirteenth Amendment and abolition were sufficient to improve African Americans' status in the nation. Some sought further steps toward more general equality.[103] Then and thereafter, Old Northwest activists struggled for "Black Laws" repeal and to put Reconstruction-era legislation to their own uses. This illustrates two facts about the Old Northwest: first, that its culture remained deeply racist, as the longevity of the "Black Laws" shows; and second, that activists there were unusually persistent in their quest to acquire equal rights, despite overwhelming odds.

* * *

After the smoke had settled, fighters for equality in the Old Northwest found that their major battle for African American rights remained. After emancipation, arguments for African American subordination could no longer rest on claims of their natural servility, which had relied on the fiction of the compliant slave, a myth no longer plausible when so many former slaves had quickly seized their freedom. This strengthened the case for equality. Nevertheless, the problem of racial prejudice remained, and in fact grew more complex and required new oppositional strategies.[104] While the federal government had shunted aside the overt obstacle of legal servitude, white supremacy remained entrenched in the developing postwar culture of the Old Northwest. Across the region, efforts to maintain stratification and racial bias in the law constrained African Americans' lives even as the law offered some new protections for them.

In the early years of Reconstruction in the Old Northwest, African American rights were an open question. In this region, these discussions drew particular complexity from their dual nature, for the states' residents debated race's role in both local and national laws. States amended their existing "Black Laws" (or refused to do so) even as the federal government also asserted new concepts of national citizenship and voting rights for all men regardless of race. From 1865 to 1870, legislating race and rights thus proceeded on two tracks that occasionally intersected. The people and these states' legislatures and supreme courts all tried to say their piece.

In the era when people were rebuilding the nation, African Americans reaped some results for their ongoing activism. They won some small victories over racialized laws both in the Old Northwest and across the country. These included the integration of streetcars in Cincinnati and Cleveland.[105] More overtly, in 1865 Indiana repealed its testimony law and Illinois its anti-immigration provisions.[106] In January 1865, Richard Yates, the outgoing Republican governor of Illinois, responded to relentless activist pressure and strongly encouraged his legislators to remove these laws. Inspired by Yates and by large numbers of petitions from their constituents that flooded in from all parts of the state, the Illinois lawmakers laid the groundwork for repeal. The federal government sent the Thirteenth Amendment to the states for ratification on February 1, 1865, and Illinois was the first to do so in combination with its repeal of the anti-immigration statute. Springfield African Americans commemorated the occasion by firing a sixty-two-gun salute, one for each legislator who had voted for the bill. They chose John Jones to light the cannon fuse, the symbolic end of the "Black Laws."[107] This was only a qualified victory, however, for discrimination remained widespread there and across the Old Northwest.

Testimony as to the resiliency of anti-Black sentiment existed even at the moment of that 1865 partial repeal in Illinois. Then, Governor Yates affirmed that his focus was on Illinois' "free, white citizens," even as he simultaneously felt concern for African Americans. He deemed them "that unfortunate class of our fellow beings whom Providence, in its wise and inscrutable plans, has placed in our care."[108] This was hardly a resounding egalitarian argument, and this attitude helps explain the many inequities that remained in the Old Northwest even as the laws began to change.

Despite the limited nature of these victories, Old Northwest activists possessed some new federal legal tools to advance their arguments. They put Reconstruction-era legislation to their own uses, and tried to apply the Civil Rights Act of 1866, as well as the Fourteenth and Fifteenth Amendments, to invalidate laws that had formerly limited African Americans' legal status and rights of mobility. This proved to be a substantial challenge, for while in many Old Northwest communities African Americans rallied for suffrage in public meetings and faced down widespread opposition to their rights, these amendments were not universally acclaimed. The amendments did receive sufficient approval to pass, for the states ratified the Fourteenth Amendment in 1868, and the Fifteenth in 1870. Nonetheless, despite the Radical Republicans' efforts and some small victories, Old Northwest society was hardly transformed. Even as the laws began to shift in less biased directions, both partisan tendencies and cultural beliefs remained formidable obstacles there.

The Republican and Democratic parties continued to influence the Old Northwest states through their recalcitrance in adopting African American rights and the vote at the beginning of Reconstruction. As had been true since the 1830s, the political parties restricted the extent of change to civil liberties that Old Northwest people considered. Many local politicians retained contempt for African American rights. These limitations were most overt in reference to suffrage, but also held true for a number of other elements of the "Black Laws."

In 1865 and 1866, political leaders across the four states remained opposed to African American suffrage at the state level, and prevented the people of their states from voting on it. Many Republican leaders and northern voters who supported Black suffrage in the South opposed it in the North in these years, for they favored the rights of distant people over those of local African Americans with whom they shared space. Ohio's senators had resisted the national civil rights provisions because they saw this as a way to keep southern African Americans out of the state.[109] Democrats refuted these egalitarian ideas even more strongly, as the Ohioans of that party proved with their race-baiting in the 1865 state election. White Ohioans continued to resist the African American vote into 1866.[110]

This political push against African American rights met its countervailing force from ongoing collective activism in the Old Northwest. In Illinois, the third State Convention of Colored Men met at Galesburg in October 1866 to fight the remaining "Black Laws." After the partial repeal in 1865, the African American population of Illinois had increased rapidly, allowing some progressive change. By 1870 their numbers there exceeded 28,000. The 1866 meeting convened in Edward Beecher's church, and its attendees claimed equal citizenship on the basis of their labor and birthright. African Americans in Illinois still faced significant restrictions: taxation without representation, exclusion from juries, disfranchisement, and being barred from holding political office as well as from the "free public schools." These men intended to address those grievances, affirming that their children deserved better. "We appeal to you," they wrote, "in behalf of eight thousand colored boys and girls, with expansive minds, ready and willing to drink from the fountain of literature and learning." To work toward removing their remaining legal obstacles, they hired a general agent to travel the state rallying support for their rights.[111] Lecture tours still were a viable reform method in the Old Northwest, even after the war.

Indiana's African Americans and their allies also contended for their full rights against substantial odds. In 1865 the Indiana State Convention of Colored People convened for this purpose at Indianapolis. Convention attendees acknowledged the problems with their current condition, and asserted that they would work tenaciously to improve it. They demanded abolition of the state's "Black Laws," including its limitations on schooling and testifying in court. They obtained the right of testimony in 1865, and in 1866, the Indiana Supreme Court invalidated but did not remove the exclusion clause of the 1851 Indiana Constitution.[112] The vote, for the moment, was out of reach.

The franchise also remained elusive for Michigan's African Americans after the war. That state continued to use the "visible admixture" rule. After an 1866 state Supreme Court case, William Dean, a biracial man from Nankin Township near Detroit, won the right to vote in Michigan on the basis of partial white descent, "less than one fourth" African ancestry. The court claimed since he appeared more white than African, he could exercise the franchise.[113] In his majority opinion Justice James V. Campbell argued that pigment was useless in determining race since people varied, and so he used "ancestry" as the benchmark. In this case, men with less than that fraction of African ancestry could vote. Partisanship was also a key factor in this case, for the Democrats were instrumental in Dean's prosecution for illegal voting. The Dean case did not definitively settle the issue, however, for local officials still drew the color line arbitrarily, and excluded people who had no white ancestors. Even under this decision, the law denied the vote to men with more than that fraction, and they had to sue to secure this right.[114]

Even when the Republicans lent them some assistance, Michigan's African Americans found that acquiring the right to vote remained difficult. While Republicans called for universal manhood suffrage at the 1867 Michigan Constitutional Convention, they had a hard battle to fight.[115] This issue elicited strong debate, but the convention ultimately rejected it. In 1868 the state's voters also refused to approve a new constitution that granted African American men the vote.[116] This mixed picture is reflected across the region, even though it was the home of one of the most important legislative changes to federal rights.

* * *

While the US Representative from Ohio, John Bingham, authored the Fourteenth Amendment, the Old Northwest states treated it with relative reluctance, and they took some time to ratify it after the first northeastern states did so in the latter half of 1866. They all did ratify it early in 1867. The cautious Ohio Republicans appreciated its moderation, particularly the fact that it stopped short of guaranteeing the African American vote. During the decline of Presidential Reconstruction and as the Radical Republicans gathered steam in 1867, more Republicans became willing to accept African American suffrage. The national Republican Party then became more receptive to African American rights, but this did not always translate to the local level. Some white Ohio Republicans did support the African American vote that year, but when it went to a popular referendum they failed to persuade their fellow Ohioans to follow their lead, and they voted it down.[117] The Republicans were not operating from a position of strength, for the Democrats won more seats in that election.[118] In January 1868 these Ohio Democrats used their new domination of the state legislature to rescind their state's ratification of the Fourteenth Amendment. The Republicans objected, and much disputation ensued. Despite Ohio having withdrawn its endorsement, that July the US Congress nonetheless counted the state as a party to the Fourteenth Amendment's ratification.[119]

The ongoing rights struggles Old Northwest people faced were evident to activists across the nation. As had been the case with earlier National Black Conventions, some distant allies knew of their problems, as the Colored Men's Border State Convention made clear in 1868 with a plea on behalf of men in all of the many states who still then lacked the vote. They called for Congress to implement the provision of the Fourteenth Amendment that mandated reducing the representation of discriminating states proportional to the numbers of men to whom they denied the franchise. They also saw that they needed another law, declaring "[i]f nothing better give us a Constitutional Amendment to secure the right of suffrage--and give it to us now."[120] Reconstructing the North and guaranteeing rights were thus vital issues for African Americans in this era of civil liberties disputes; the Old Northwest conflicts were closely linked with the national racial problems of their era.

While regional differences and disparities within regions still mattered in 1870, nonetheless it is evident that these Old Northwest states, the mid-Atlantic, and the upper South then shared strong commitments to unequal, racialized rights. In contrast, the New England states (apart from Connecticut), were relatively accepting, and had been the first to embrace the African American vote, even before the Fifteenth Amendment.[121] In 1870, they were solidly Republican and many of their schools were integrated. These states were the most open to African American rights, but they only appear so in contrast to the other regions of the country.[122] They, too, were hardly egalitarian.

While, broadly speaking, discrimination and segregation tied to partisan politics existed elsewhere in the North and in the upper South, these biases emerged differently in these various regions. In the Old Northwest, even where Republicans held power, African American rights remained divisive in 1870. This shows the true caution of Old Northwest Republicans, which they exhibited with their unwillingness to grant African Americans their rights even when the law had already guaranteed them. By 1870, the Democrats had made some inroads, mostly in Ohio and to a degree also in Illinois and Indiana. This corresponded with a weak commitment to African American rights.

Continual efforts to subordinate African Americans after the Fifteenth Amendment extended out of the Old Northwest, including to the mid-Atlantic states and the upper South. In the mid-Atlantic region, citizens' attempts to suppress African American voting and keep schools segregated indicate that the national culture of racism had spread to an area formerly more hospitable to African Americans than the antebellum Old Northwest had been. The political precariousness also contributed to this hostility, particularly in the Democrats' northern stronghold of New Jersey, but also in New York and to a degree in Pennsylvania. African Americans encountered more substantial problems in the upper South, where even as by 1870 some among them held political offices as Republicans, the Democrats had begun to retake power and to introduce extensive anti–African American policies, including segregation and evasions of the Fifteenth Amendment.[123] In the upper South, this transition in rights was thus closely tied to the Democrats' resurgence, as was also true in nearby Ohio to a lesser extent.

African American's status in Ohio remained much debated even after the Fourteenth Amendment controversy, for the Democrats soon tried to erect further obstacles to their voting rights. The Democrats led opposition to ratifying the Fifteenth Amendment, and spearheaded the state legislature's re-imposition of the "visible admixture" rule as grounds for denying the right to vote there in 1867. Later that year in the case of *Monroe v. Collins* the Ohio Supreme Court nullified it, deemed it unconstitutional, and acknowledged its arbitrary nature and the difficulties in enforcing it.[124] The court's wording still denied the franchise to men with over half African American ancestry, for it protected the right to vote of men "in whom the white blood predominates" by deeming them "white male citizens within the meaning of the Ohio constitution." The court did not deny that some men nonetheless lacked these rights because of their race. Ohio African Americans also lost some allies, for the state's Republicans abandoned their support of the vote for all men.[125] It took the federal government to overrule these state measures, using the Fifteenth Amendment once it had become law, but even then the process was hardly simple, there as across the region.

Despite these problems, Ohio did ratify the Fifteenth Amendment in 1870, but it faced ongoing challenges. These are clear from a court case in southern Ohio where a judge convicted a man of intimidating Stuart and Jupiter Wilson, two African American men who by then were legally entitled to vote. The remaining Ohio "Black Laws" stayed on the books until 1886, and the word "white" persisted in the state constitution as the definition of a voter until 1923.[126] Even as so many states revised their constitutions in more inclusive directions in the Reconstruction era, Ohio would not.[127] It is surprising that postwar Ohio proved to be more hostile to African American rights than did Illinois and Indiana, the Old Northwest states that formerly appeared to be harsher in this respect.

The picture was moderately less bleak in Illinois, where African Americans first voted in 1870, but only after ratification of the Fifteenth Amendment. Opportunities continued to expand there, including in 1869 when African Americans gained the right to serve in political office. John Jones took advantage of this and served as the first man of his race in two public offices in Illinois. He became a notary public in 1869 with the Governor's appointment, and in 1871 the Republicans elected him to the Cook County Board of Commissioners. He followed the egalitarian demands of his early public career with a new commitment to working within party structures, which meant that he rejected radical solutions to racial and class problems. Jones's moderate course was not the only option, for among his contemporaries, some still retained the desire for more militant transformation in the face of ongoing legal bias.[128]

Under the law, African American men could also vote in Indiana beginning in 1870, but some vestiges of discrimination remained on the books for over a decade there. Indiana Democrats returned to dominance in the 1870s, ahead of most northern states, which led to deterioration in local African American power. The Democrats pushed for white supremacy with weakening resistance from Republicans during the Jim Crow era. The state kept its race-based laws regarding the vote in its constitution until 1881, but some African Americans were nonetheless voting by then.[129]

Even in Michigan, the voters only barely ratified the Fifteenth Amendment in 1869 since the Democrats strongly opposed it. In other respects, that same year Michigan became more egalitarian, for it amended its constitution to delete the need to be "white" from the franchise, office, jury, and militia requirements.[130] These were important victories over the "Black Laws." In November 1870, a strong push from within the African American community finally reinforced universal male suffrage in Michigan with a state constitutional amendment. Although this was after the Fifteenth Amendment had been ratified, which in theory had guaranteed that right to all men nationally, it was still a close contest, and the small margin of victory demonstrates the extensive racial bias at the time, even in that most moderate of these four states.[131]

This prejudice emerged undiluted in the ongoing efforts to bar interracial marriages in the Old Northwest states during Reconstruction. Indiana led the way, and the other states also subsequently adopted bans on these marriages. Indiana upheld its marriage restrictions even after the Fourteenth Amendment and the 1866 Civil Rights Act, and used the logic that the federal government had no right to regulate marriage in the state to justify doing so.[132] As late as 1871, in *State v. Gibson* the Indiana Supreme Court voided a marriage between a biracial man and a white woman, and maintained the ban through 1965.[133] Interracial marriage remained illegal in Michigan for decades, and only in the 1880s did the state ultimately repeal this ban and overturn segregation.[134] The General Assembly of Ohio revisited the issue of interracial marriage in 1877, reinforced the prohibitions on it, and retained the fine.[135] The extant laws remained in force in Illinois then, too.[136] All four of these states shared a commitment to racial disparities in marriage rights, because most of their residents continued to believe that the races ought to remain separate, in the household and in public life. This view also contributed to obstacles to the ability of future generations to thrive in the region, including laws that directly infringed on children's opportunities.

* * *

It was obvious to many old Northwest African Americans that their children required equal access to education in order to attain parity of status in society. This necessitated ongoing activism during Reconstruction, and educational equity regardless of race remained elusive for years, since segregated schools were widespread across the region. Illinois provided African American children with no guarantee of education at all, and segregation remained common in public schools there well into the 1870s.[137]

For their part, Indiana, Ohio, and Michigan had segregated schools in most places, and the problem of educational inequity for African American children worsened in this era. It, too, remained severe well after Reconstruction. In 1869, the Indiana General Assembly required separate schools in communities with "sufficient numbers" of African American children, but in 1877, the Indiana Supreme Court integrated schools in cases where school districts would not create such segregated schools. Neither circumstance was ideal for the children attempting to obtain an education. Regulations in that state kept African American children out of the public schools and in segregated schools well into the twentieth century.[138] Ohio's schools clearly demonstrated the disjuncture between the law and reality; the state's General Assembly outlawed segregated schools in 1888, but practical implementation was halting in places until after *Brown v. Board of Education* in 1954.[139]

Michigan's progress on educational discrimination remained slow, although relatively more rapid than in the other states. The Black State Convention and other African American activists fought an extended battle against segregated schools, and in 1867 the legislature finally recognized their complaints by outlawing school segregation. Mary Ann Shadd Cary found this discrimination still persisted beyond that point when she attempted to teach in Detroit. It took a state Supreme Court decision to bring the Detroit schools in line.[140] Well into the 1870s and beyond, many white people in the Old Northwest felt they could still deny this fundamental right of citizenship—the right to acquire an education—to African Americans.

* * *

Even with the Union victory in the Civil War and some limited signs of local progress, the recognition of African American equality in the North was hardly a foregone conclusion. The war had brought immense economic prosperity to the region, and the entire nation had seen its effects and those of the ensuing Reconstruction. The destruction of slavery and its tumultuous aftermath intensified Old Northwest African Americans' demands for improved status. They saw their region thrive in this era, and yet they shared in few of the benefits. Despite their diligent efforts, African Americans reaped minimal results, for even small steps to improve their station elicited substantial reactions from white supremacists.

Old Northwest activists possessed some limited leverage from the 1850s through 1870 to push for shifts in race and rights in the region. A split arose, nonetheless, between those reformers who deemed emancipation and voting rights satisfactory measures of a transformed racial order, and those who found these wanting. The disjuncture between legal rights and actual practice was substantial, for the national voting right for all men—among other rights—had only been partially implemented, and much segregation remained there, too. The reformers who saw their work as incomplete retained an agenda of political and social change oriented around principle and moral right, but found that the biases deeply entrenched in the culture of the Old Northwest endured as substantial obstacles to equality. The legacy of the "Black Laws" in the region, and the aggressive resistance to abolition that activists had faced since the 1830s, remained strong, even as the law offered them some new protections.

Conclusion

Old Northwest activists grappled with the immense challenge of securing rights regardless of race in their reluctant region. While the battles over slavery and the "Black Laws" were inescapable for residents there, they were not merely of local concern. The Old Northwest was vital to the larger antislavery and anti-prejudice campaigns of its era. As activists fought the clutches of the slave system at home, they debated the broader national questions of all Americans' freedoms and African Americans' status. Old Northwest reformers defended their values in the face of constant attacks—both ideological and physical—from supporters of the slave system and from people who feared African American proximity. The "peculiar institution" obeyed no state boundaries, and Old Northwest activists formed a distinctive movement in response to the singular challenge of living as literal and cultural neighbors to slavery. There, often-isolated individuals encountered both enthusiastic supporters and enraged mobbers. Few people maintained neutrality, and their ideological differences often emerged in legal and physical battles. Discussions of race and slavery ignited this region in a particularly explosive fashion, affected organizational efforts, gender roles and expectations, and generated new ideas about rights, especially the right of freedom of expression.

While modern observers can see that these Old Northwest activists' vision of equality took decades of effort to realize, these reformers lived and fought in a moment of possibility. Their hopes and convictions that they would attain their goals carried them forward, even if they did not reach their destinations rapidly, or at all. Their aims of racial egalitarianism—forged in this arena of pro- and antislavery clashes—deserve a place on the social reform spectrum of this period. Taken on their own terms, they made extraordinary efforts against slavery and prejudice in the combat zone of the Old Northwest.

The Old Northwest activist culture was an inextricable and vital component of the national movement to improve African Americans' lives. In contrast to reformers elsewhere, organizers in the Old Northwest had more direct encounters with anti-abolitionists, set distinctive factional boundaries, and had a diverse membership that was active in the most dangerous aspects of their work for change. This region of open spaces and wide rivers, like no other, called to a stalwart cohort of reformers there to work against slavery and prejudice. Its local organizers altered their reform landscape, and an examination of their labors proves the importance of investigating how race relations differed from region to region in the nineteenth century.

The tiny African American populations and their white allies across the Old Northwest had ample weapons to fight for equality, and made their mark locally with interracial activism against prejudice. Their work against the "Black Laws" concretely manifested their desire to revolutionize race relations in their communities, a project they saw as continuous with the abolition struggle. Activists who lived under such legislation had to resist not only abstract mores and distant institutions, but also concrete laws.

* * *

These reformers crafted substantial challenges to the racial culture of the Old Northwest. While they were very much products of their place and time, the people who sought to transform the bias endemic in their society nonetheless refused to allow the exclusionary ideas of their fellow citizens to limit them. Indeed, they turned the hatred and scorn for African Americans and activists' rights into assets for building a more just society, even if this was only in its infancy in 1870. Historians have firmly established that Reconstruction's goals were only partially fulfilled in the South, but the northern postwar experience also left egalitarians there wanting more, including full citizenship for African Americans.

Local people wedded to racist principles proved willing and able to stymie federal legal guarantees, but the activists who challenged Old Northwest biases had nevertheless achieved some gains by 1870. In the process, they shifted grassroots understanding of how to use the law to defend groups that local regulations and social practice singled out for opprobrium. There is more than ample evidence of pervasive limitations on African Americans' rights in the Old Northwest. That is not the entire story, however, as proved by the ongoing crusade from 1830 to 1870 to improve African Americans' circumstances, whether they were distant slaves or local farmers. Both the struggles Old Northwest activists confronted and the arguments they made transformed the conception of rights in the nineteenth century. For reformers, even though this place frequently refused to embrace them, it nonetheless was so central and so vital to their slow trudge toward a more just society that they refused to relinquish their ground.

Prejudice in the region died hard, and by 1870 most African Americans retained a precarious economic status and lived in inferior housing, while *de facto* discrimination remained, if not *de jure*.[1] Throughout the region, even as the letter of the law (especially in the Fourteenth Amendment) stipulated that government could not discriminate, others still could, and did.[2] Prescriptive laws also lingered, and anti-African American sentiment and action prevailed for many years in the Old Northwest. The years from the antebellum period through Reconstruction established the basis for later racism, and planted seeds for the region's notorious white supremacy in the late nineteenth and much of the twentieth century. Their descendants were visible in these states' sundown towns, housing discrimination, Ku Klux Klan chapters, and lynchings. As early as 1868, the Ku Klux Klan had already established a small presence in Michigan.[3]

Despite this ugly past and the future obstacles to African American rights in the region, the claims and actions of the singular agitators of the Old Northwest uniquely contributed to American activist history. Whether they were itinerant lecturers, local organizers, news editors, or participants in the Black Convention Movement, these steadfast activists challenged the restrictions of their racist environment and gave wholeheartedly to the struggle to reform the Old Northwest. Even as their small numbers limited their influence in the region, they fought on. While they could not escape anti-abolition influences and racial bias, they developed ingenious forms of activism adapted to their local circumstances and trials that changed the shape and substance of American reform.

Appendix: Old Northwest Population Statistics, 1800–1870

Illinois

Status	1800	1810	1820	1830	1840	1850	1860	1870
Aggregate population	—	12,282	55,211	157,445	476,183	851,470	1,711,951	2,539,891
Free Blacks	—	613	457	1,637	3,598	5,436	7,628	28,762
Slaves	—	168	917	747	331	0	0	0

Indiana

Status	1800	1810	1820	1830	1840	1850	1860	1870
Aggregate population	5,641	24,520	147,178	343,031	685,866	988,416	1,350,428	1,680,637
Free Blacks	163	393	1,230	3,629	7,165	11,262	11,428	24,560
Slaves	135	237	190	3	3	0	0	0

Michigan

Status	1800	1810	1820	1830	1840	1850	1860	1870
Aggregate population	—	4,762	8,896	31,629	212,267	397,654	749,113	1,184,059
Free Blacks	—	120	174	261	717	2,583	6,799	11,849
Slaves	—	24	0	32	0	0	0	0

Ohio

Status	1800	1810	1820	1830	1840	1850	1860	1870
Aggregate population	45,365	230,760	581,434	937,903	1,519,467	1,980,329	2,339,511	2,665,260
Free Blacks	337	1,899	7,723	9,568	17,342	25,279	36,673	63,213
Slaves	0	0	0	6	3	0	0	0

Source: Data from United States Bureau of the Census, *Population Schedule of the Ninth Census of the United States* (Department of Commerce Bureau of the Census: Washington, DC, 1870), and Clayton E. Cramer, *Black Demographic Data, 1790–1860: A Sourcebook* (Westport, CT: Greenwood Press, 1997), 110–13.

Notes

Introduction

1. Stephen Middleton, *The Black Laws: Race and the Legal Process in Early Ohio* (Athens: Ohio University Press, 2005), 9.

2. Nathan Dane to Rufus King, 16 July 1787, in *The Letters of Members of the Continental Congress*, ed. Edmund Burnett, vol. 8 (Washington, DC: Carnegie Institute of Washington, 1936), 621–22.

3. Ibid., 11, 17.

4. Robert R. Dykstra, *Bright Radical Star: Black Freedom and White Supremacy on the Hawkeye Frontier* (Cambridge: Harvard University Press, 1993); James Edward Davis, *Frontier Illinois*, A History of the Trans-Appalachian Frontier (Bloomington: Indiana University Press, 1998), 280. The Old Northwest is a fascinating place to pursue the puzzle of antebellum ideas about race, as these recent studies have shown: Middleton, *The Black Laws: Ohio;* H. Robert Baker, *The Rescue of Joshua Glover: A Fugitive Slave, the Constitution, and the Coming of the Civil War*, Ohio University Press Series on Law, Society, and Politics in the Midwest (Athens: Ohio University Press, 2006); Stacey Robertson, *Hearts Beating for Liberty: Women Abolitionists in the Old Northwest* (Chapel Hill: University of North Carolina Press, 2010). While this volume shares a number of common intellectual interests with those books, it is based on my own reading and interpretations of the original sources. See also Dana Elizabeth Weiner, "Racial Radicals: The Antislavery Movement in the Old Northwest, 1830–1861" (PhD diss., Northwestern University, 2007). Regions within the Old Northwest have become the subject of renewed interest, as Leslie Schwalm exemplifies for the upper Midwest and Stanley Harrold does for the lower North. Leslie A. Schwalm, *Emancipation's Diaspora: Race and Reconstruction in the Upper Midwest*, John Hope Franklin Series in African American History and Culture (Chapel Hill: University of North Carolina Press, 2009); Stanley Harrold, *Border War: Fighting over Slavery before the Civil War*, Civil War America (Chapel Hill: University of North Carolina Press, 2010). For

an older perspective on the Old Northwest antislavery movement, see Gilbert Hobbs Barnes, *The Antislavery Impulse, 1830–1844* (New York: Harcourt, 1964).

5. This approach draws on Barbara Fields, David Roediger, Joanne Pope Melish, and Leslie Schwalm, among other historians. Barbara Fields, "Slavery, Race, and Ideology in the United States of America," *New Left Review* 181 (1990); David R. Roediger, *The Wages of Whiteness: Race and the Making of the American Working Class*, rev. ed. (New York: Verso, 1999); Joanne Pope Melish, *Disowning Slavery: Gradual Emancipation and "Race" in New England, 1780–1860* (Ithaca: Cornell University Press, 1998); Joanne Pope Melish, "The 'Condition' Debate and Racial Discourse in the Antebellum North," *Journal of the Early Republic* 19, no. 4 (1999); Schwalm, *Emancipation's Diaspora*, 3.

6. Peggy Pascoe, *What Comes Naturally: Miscegenation Law and the Making of Race in America* (Oxford: Oxford University Press, 2009), 12.

7. James Brewer Stewart, *Abolitionist Politics and the Coming of the Civil War* (Amherst: University of Massachusetts Press, 2008), xi.

8. Thomas F. Gossett, *Race: The History of an Idea in America*, New ed., Race and American Culture (New York: Oxford University Press, 1997); Schwalm, *Emancipation's Diaspora*, 3, 15.

9. *Free Labor Advocate*, February 4, 1843; June 30, 1848; October 6, 1843; October 13, 1843; Arthur Raymond Kooker, "The Anti-Slavery Movement in Michigan, 1796–1840: A Study in Humanitarianism" (PhD diss., University of Michigan, 1941), 106, 108.

10. Following Roy Finkenbine's definition, the "Black Laws" are "the body of scattered state statutes and constitutional provisions that discriminated against Blacks." Ray E. Finkenbine, "A Beacon of Liberty on the Great Lakes: Race, Slavery, and the Law in Antebellum Michigan," in *The History of Michigan Law*, ed. Paul Finkelman and Martin J. Hershock (Athens: Ohio University Press, 2006), 104.

11. Eugene H. Berwanger, *The Frontier against Slavery: Western Anti-Negro Prejudice and the Slavery Extension Controversy* (Urbana: University of Illinois Press, 1967), 1, 4.

12. Pauline Maier, *American Scripture: Making the Declaration of Independence*, (New York: Knopf, 1997), 206–7.

13. Daniel T. Rodgers, "Rights Consciousness in American History," in *The Bill of Rights in Modern America after 200 Years*, ed. David J. Bodenhamer and James W. Ely (Bloomington: Indiana University Press, 1993), 16, 8–9.

14. For related views on Iowa, see Dykstra, *Bright Radical Star*, viii.

15. John W. Quist, *Restless Visionaries: The Social Roots of Antebellum Reform in Alabama and Michigan* (Baton Rouge: Louisiana State University Press, 1998), 4. Cincinnati, for example, while a place with substantial racial tension and activism, was nonetheless an anomalously large and established city that stood apart from the region as a whole: Nikki Marie Taylor, *Frontiers of Freedom: Cincinnati's Black Community, 1802–1868*, Ohio University Press Series on Law, Society, and Politics in the Midwest (Athens: Ohio University Press, 2005).

16. Robertson, *Hearts Beating for Liberty*, 157.

17. Richard Franklin Nation, *At Home in the Hoosier Hills: Agriculture, Politics, and Religion in Southern Indiana, 1810–1870*, Midwestern History and Culture Series. (Bloomington: Indiana University Press, 2005), 3; Jacquelyn S. Nelson, *Indiana*

Quakers Confront the Civil War (Indianapolis: Indiana Historical Society, 1991), 4–5; Ruth Ketring Nuermberger, *The Free Produce Movement: A Quaker Protest against Slavery*, Historical Papers of the Trinity College Historical Society. Series 25 (Durham: Duke University Press, 1942), 33–34.

18. Stanley Harrold developed a related framework in his 2003 book about border regions—particularly the area around Washington, DC—that fostered direct action against slavery. While the Old Northwest was quite different, it was similarly unstable. Stanley Harrold, "John Brown's Forerunners: Slave Rescue Attempts and the Abolitionists, 1841–51," *Radical History Review* 55 (1992): 94; Stanley Harrold, *The Rise of Aggressive Abolitionism: Addresses to the Slaves* (Lexington: University Press of Kentucky, 2004), 115; Stanley Harrold, *Subversives: Antislavery Community in Washington, D.C., 1828–1865*, Antislavery, Abolition, and the Atlantic World (Baton Rouge: Louisiana State University Press, 2003), 37–38, 12; Harrold, *Border War*; Mary P. Ryan, "Civil Society as Democratic Practice: North American Cities During the Nineteenth Century," in *Patterns of Social Capital: Stability and Change in Historical Perspective*, ed. Robert I. Rotberg (New York: Cambridge University Press, 2001), 234; Craig J. Calhoun, *Habermas and the Public Sphere*, Studies in Contemporary German Social Thought (Cambridge, Massachusetts: MIT Press, 1992).

19. Leonard L. Richards, *"Gentlemen of Property and Standing"; Anti-Abolition Mobs in Jacksonian America* (New York: Oxford University Press, 1970), 3, 76–77, 15; Russel Blaine Nye, *Fettered Freedom: Civil Liberties and the Slavery Controversy, 1830–1860* (East Lansing: Michigan State University Press, 1964), 175.

1 / Activist Taproots: Place, Reform, and the Quest for Unity

1. Erasmus Hudson, "From Sherman, St. Joseph's County, Michigan," *National Anti-Slavery Standard*, November 25, 1841.

2. One source of such ideas was Lyman Beecher's *A Plea for the West*. While his chief agenda with that book was to shore up the evangelical Protestants' foothold on the new states of the Old Northwest [over the Catholics], Beecher's ideas of the region's importance nonetheless had a larger impact. Lyman Beecher, *A Plea for the West* (Cincinnati: Truman and Smith, 1835), 11–12; Bryan Le Beau, "1990 MAASA Presidential Address: 'Saving the West from the Pope': Anti-Catholic Propaganda and the Settlement of the Mississippi River Valley," *American Studies* 31, no. 1 (1991): 106–7.

3. Sidney Howard Gay, *National Anti-Slavery Standard*, March 7, 1844.

4. Josiah H. Blackmore II, "Not from Zeus's Head Full-Blown: The Story of Civil Procedure in Ohio," in *The History of Ohio Law*, ed. Michael Les Benedict and John F. Winkler (Athens: Ohio University Press, 2004), 445.

5. Mary Van Vleck Garman, "'Altered Tone of Expression': The Anti-Slavery Rhetoric of Illinois Women, 1837–1847" (PhD diss., Northwestern University, 1989), 63, 67; Matthew Mason, *Slavery and Politics in the Early American Republic* (Chapel Hill: University of North Carolina Press, 2006), 151; Stephen Middleton, *The Black Laws in the Old Northwest: A Documentary History*, Contributions in Afro-American and African Studies (Westport, CT: Greenwood Press, 1993), 346.

6. Finkenbine, "A Beacon of Liberty on the Great Lakes," 84.

7. Maria W. Stewart, *Maria W. Stewart, America's First Black Political Writer, Essays and Speeches*, ed. Marilyn Richardson (Bloomington: Indiana University Press, 1987); David Walker, *Appeal to the Coloured Citizens of the World*, ed. Sean Wilentz (1829;

reprint, New York: Hill and Wang, 1995); National Convention of Colored Citizens, *Minutes of the National Convention of Colored Citizens: Held at Buffalo, on the 15th, 16th, 17th, 18th, and 19th of August 1843* (New York: Piercy and Reed, 1843).

8. A wealth of historical scholarship lays out African American pioneers' essential role in the birth of the organized antislavery movement. Timothy Patrick McCarthy and John Stauffer, "Introduction," in *Prophets of Protest: Reconsidering the History of American Abolitionism*, ed. Timothy Patrick McCarthy and John Stauffer (New York: New Press, 2006), xviii; Benjamin Quarles, *Black Abolitionists* (New York: Oxford University Press, 1969); Richard S. Newman, *The Transformation of American Abolitionism: Fighting Slavery in the Early Republic* (Chapel Hill: University of North Carolina Press, 2002), 86; James Oliver Horton and Lois E. Horton, *In Hope of Liberty: Culture, Community, and Protest among Northern Free Blacks, 1700–1860* (New York: Oxford University Press, 1997); Herbert Aptheker, *Abolitionism: A Revolutionary Movement*, Social Movements Past and Present (Boston: Twayne Publishers, 1989); Paul Goodman, *Of One Blood: Abolitionism and the Origins of Racial Equality* (Berkeley: University of California Press, 1998).

9. Massachusetts Anti-Slavery Society, *Fourteenth Annual Report Presented to the Massachusetts Anti-Slavery Society, by Its Board of Managers* (1846; reprint, Westport, CT: Negro Universities Press, 1970), 55; Aileen S. Kraditor, *Means and Ends in American Abolitionism: Garrison and His Critics on Strategy and Tactics, 1834–1850* (New York: Pantheon Books, 1969), 17–18.

10. Ronald G. Walters, "The Boundaries of Abolitionism," in *Antislavery Reconsidered: New Perspectives on the Abolitionists*, ed. Louis Perry and Michael Fellman (Baton Rouge: Louisiana State University Press, 1979), 13–14; Blanche Glassman Hersh, "'Am I Not a Woman and a Sister?' Abolitionist Beginnings of Nineteenth Century Feminism," in *Antislavery Reconsidered*, 272, 274; Blanche Glassman Hersh, *The Slavery of Sex: Feminist-Abolitionists in America* (Urbana: University of Illinois Press, 1978), 10, 26.

11. Julie Roy Jeffrey, *The Great Silent Army of Abolitionism: Ordinary Women in the Antislavery Movement* (Chapel Hill: University of North Carolina Press, 1998), 135; Vernon L. Volpe, *Forlorn Hope of Freedom: The Liberty Party in the Old Northwest, 1838–1848* (Kent, OH: Kent State University Press, 1990), viii.

12. Volpe, *Forlorn Hope of Freedom*, 138.

13. Timothy Patrick McCarthy and John Stauffer have observed this for the political/immediatist division. McCarthy and Stauffer, "Introduction," xix, xx.

14. James Brewer Stewart, *Holy Warriors: The Abolitionists and American Slavery* (New York: Hill and Wang, 1976), 103–4, 110.

15. Examples of this in the Old Northwest include *Western Citizen*, June 20, 1844; August 8, 1844; April 6, 1843; January 25, 1844; Reinhard O. Johnson, *The Liberty Party, 1840–1848: Antislavery Third-Party Politics in the United States*, Antislavery, Abolition, and the Atlantic World (Baton Rouge: Louisiana State University Press, 2009), 252, 254; C. Peter Ripley, ed. *The Black Abolitionist Papers: The United States, 1859–1865*, vol. 5 (Chapel Hill: University of North Carolina Press,1985), 214.

16. Volpe, *Forlorn Hope of Freedom*, 81–82.

17. Michael F. Holt, *Political Parties and American Political Development: From the Age of Jackson to the Age of Lincoln* (Baton Rouge: Louisiana State University Press, 1992), 30, 27–28; Jeffrey L. Pasley, *"The Tyranny of Printers": Newspaper Politics in*

the Early American Republic (Charlottesville: University Press of Virginia, 2001), 10; Charles Sellers, *The Market Revolution: Jacksonian America, 1815–1846* (New York: Oxford University Press, 1991), 388.

18. Sean Wilentz, *The Rise of American Democracy: Jefferson to Lincoln*, (New York: Norton, 2005), 513.

19. Holt, *Political Parties and American Political Development*, 57–58, 87; Merton Lynn Dillon, *The Abolitionists: The Growth of a Dissenting Minority*, Minorities in American History (DeKalb: Northern Illinois University Press, 1975), 24–25.

20. Sellers, *The Market Revolution*, 388; John Ashworth, *'Agrarians' and 'Aristocrats': Party Political Ideology in the United States, 1837–1846* (New Jersey: Humanities Press Inc., 1983), 222.

21. William Lee Miller, *Arguing About Slavery: The Great Battle in the United States Congress*, (New York: A. A. Knopf, 1996); Richards, *"Gentlemen of Property and Standing."*

22. Quist, *Restless Visionaries*, 11.

23. Johnson, *The Liberty Party, 1840–1848*, 192.

24. Donald Richard Deskins, Hanes Walton, and Sherman C. Puckett, *Presidential Elections, 1789–2008: County, State, and National Mapping of Election Data* (Ann Arbor: University of Michigan Press, 2010), 90–91, 159, 164, 178; Tony L. Hill, "Illinois," in *Encyclopedia of U.S. Campaigns, Elections, and Electoral Behavior*, ed. Kenneth F. Warren (Thousand Oaks: Sage, 2008), 312; Justin Corfield, "Indiana," in *Encyclopedia of U.S. Campaigns*, 322; Corfield, "Ohio," in *Encyclopedia of U.S. Campaigns*, 470–71; Corfield, "Michigan," in *Encyclopedia of U.S. Campaigns*, 407–8.

25. Johnson, *The Liberty Party, 1840–1848*, 214.

26. Wilentz, *The Rise of American Democracy*, 919.

27. Ibid., 919, 636.

28. Holt, *Political Parties*, 244; Wilentz, *The Rise of American Democracy*, 791.

29. Stewart, *Abolitionist Politics and the Coming of the Civil War*, 27.

30. Eric Foner, *Free Soil, Free Labor, Free Men: The Ideology of the Republican Party before the Civil War* (New York: Oxford University Press, 1994), 194; Frederick J. Blue, *No Taint of Compromise: Crusaders in Antislavery Politics* (Baton Rouge: Louisiana State University Press, 2005), 101, 103, 111.

31. Thomas G. Mitchell, *Anti-Slavery Politics in Antebellum and Civil War America* (Westport, CT: Praeger Publishers, 2007), 79, 106.

32. Foner, *Free Soil, Free Labor, Free Men*, 10, 14, 16, 56.

33. Mitchell, *Anti-Slavery Politics in Antebellum and Civil War America*, 79, 106.

34. Foner, *Free Soil, Free Labor, Free Men*, 309–10.

35. Newman, *The Transformation of American Abolitionism*, 8–9.

36. Volpe, *Forlorn Hope of Freedom*, 5, 12, 13, 70; Quist, *Restless Visionaries*, 435, 438, 442.

37. James Brewer Stewart notes that these included the Western Reserve and Forelands of Ohio, Indiana's eastern "Burnt District," and "Lower Michigan's southeastern and central counties." Stewart, *Abolitionist Politics and the Coming of the Civil War*, 214.

38. Hicksites adhered to an offshoot branch of the Society of Friends. Under the leadership of Elias Hicks, they split off from what were then called the Orthodox Friends over both theological and lifestyle differences. Gerda Lerner, *The Grimké*

Sisters from South Carolina: Pioneers for Women's Rights and Abolition (New York: Oxford University Press, 1998), 91, 130, 47.

39. Thomas D. Hamm, *God's Government Begun: The Society for Universal Inquiry and Reform, 1842–1846*, Religion in North America Series (Bloomington: Indiana University Press, 1995), 50–51, 30.

40. "Mr. Clay and the Abolitionists," *Peoria Register*, November 4, 1842; Jacob P. Dunn, "The Visit of Henry Clay to Richmond, Ind.," Jacob P. Dunn Papers, Manuscript Collection, Indiana State Library, Indianapolis, Indiana.

41. Edwin Fussell, "Progress in Indiana," *National Anti-Slavery Standard*, September 7, 1843; "Thirteen Other Anti-Slavery Conventions," *Free Labor Advocate and Anti-Slavery Chronicle*, September 8, 1843; Dunn, "The Visit of Henry Clay to Richmond, Ind.," 5.

42. Dunn, "The Visit of Henry Clay to Richmond, Ind.," 1, 5; Thomas D. Hamm, David Dittmer, Chedna Fruchter, Ann Giordano, Janice Mathews, and Ellen Swain, "Moral Choices: Two Indiana Quaker Communities and the Abolitionist Movement," *Indiana Magazine of History* 87 (June 1991), 146–47; Anna Davis Hallowell, ed. *James and Lucretia Mott: Life and Letters* (New York: Houghton Mifflin, 1884), 292; Lucretia Mott to Nathaniel and Elisa Barney, 30 and 31 October, 1847, in *Selected Letters of Lucretia Coffin Mott*, ed. Lucretia Mott et al., Women in American History (Urbana: University of Illinois Press, 2002), 156–58.

43. Arnold Buffum, *The Protectionist*, October 1, 1841; Hallowell, ed. *James and Lucretia Mott: Life and Letters*, 292; William Lloyd Garrison, "To the *Liberator*. Richfield, Ohio, 25 August, 1847," in *The Letters of William Lloyd Garrison*, ed. Walter McIntosh Merrill (Cambridge: Belknap Press of Harvard University Press, 1971), 518–21; William Lloyd Garrison and Louis Ruchames, *The Letters of William Lloyd Garrison*, vol. 4 (Cambridge: Belknap Press of Harvard University Press, 1971), xxv-xxvi.

44. C. Peter Ripley, ed. *The Black Abolitionist Papers: The United States, 1830–1846*, vol. 3 (Chapel Hill: University of North Carolina Press, 1985), 423; Nelson, *Indiana Quakers Confront the Civil War*, 4–5.

45. *Western Citizen*, November 2, 1843.

46. Matthew Spinka, "Organization of the General Association and After, 1844–1865," in *A History of Illinois Congregational and Christian Churches*, ed. Matthew Spinka (Chicago: The Congregational and Christian Conference of Illinois, 1944), 94.

47. George Bradburn, "Letter from George Bradburn," *National Anti-Slavery Standard*, September 18, 1843; Sarah Galbreath to Cousin, 3 July, 1838, Nathan M. Thomas papers, Manuscript Collection, Bentley Historical Library, University of Michigan, Ann Arbor, Michigan (hereafter cited as Thomas Papers).

48. William Sullivan to Thomas Chandler, 24 December 1839, Elizabeth M. Chandler Papers, Manuscript Collection, Bentley Historical Library, University of Michigan, Ann Arbor, Michigan; Kooker, "The Anti-Slavery Movement in Michigan," 148, 199–200, 283; Merton Lynn Dillon, "Elizabeth Chandler and the Spread of Anti-Slavery Sentiment to Michigan," *Michigan History* 39, no. 4 (1955): 494; Charles N. Lindquist, *The Antislavery-Underground Railroad Movement in Lenawee County, Michigan, 1830–1860* (Adrian, MI: Lenawee County Historical Society, 1999), x.

49. Quist, *Restless Visionaries*, 435, 438, 442.

50. Johnson, *The Liberty Party*, 224.

51. *Free Labor Advocate*, January 8, 1842.

52. *Free Labor Advocate*, February 16, 1842, Records of the Henry County Female Anti-Slavery Society, County Manuscripts Collection, Indiana State Library, Indianapolis, Indiana (hereafter cited as Records of the Henry County Female Anti-Slavery Society); Minute Book of Neel's [Neils'] Creek Anti-Slavery Society, Indiana State Library Manuscript Collection, Indianapolis, Indiana; Lydia S. Lewis, *Western Citizen*, April 6, 1843; *The Protectionist*, December 4, 1841, 363; George Washington Julian, *The Rank of Charles Osborn as an Anti-Slavery Pioneer*, Indiana Historical Society. Publications. Vol. 2, No. 6 (Indianapolis: The Bowen-Merrill Company, 1891), 256; Charles Osborn, *Journal of That Faithful Servant of Christ, Charles Osborn, Containing an Account of Many of His Travels and Labors in the Work of the Ministry, and His Trials and Exercises in the Service of the Lord, and in Defense of the Truth, as It Is in Jesus* (Cincinnati: Achilles Pugh, 1854), xiii; Beth A. Salerno, *Sister Societies: Women's Antislavery Organizations in Antebellum America* (DeKalb: Northern Illinois University Press, 2005), 18; Nuermberger, *The Free Produce Movement*, 19, 48, 56; Deer Creek Monthly Meeting of Anti-Slavery Women Friends, Society of Friends Collection, Manuscript Collection, Indiana Historical Society, Indianapolis, Indiana. For more on the free produce movement, see Weiner, "Racial Radicals."

53. *Free Labor Advocate*, March 18, 1843, Thomas Bender et al., *The Antislavery Debate: Capitalism and Abolitionism as a Problem in Historical Interpretation* (Berkeley: University of California Press, 1992).

54. Lawrence B. Glickman, "'Buy for the Sake of the Slave': Abolitionism and the Origins of American Consumer Activism," *American Quarterly* 56, no. 4: 908.

55. Dillon, *The Abolitionists*, 127; Kooker, "The Anti-Slavery Movement in Michigan," 318; Michigan Anti-Slavery Society Daybook, vol. 4, Harriet deGarmo Fuller Collection, Clements Library, Ann Arbor, Michigan.

56. Johnson, *The Liberty Party, 1840–1848*, 7, 11, 18, 22, 51, 294.

57. Salerno, *Sister Societies*, 147.

58. Ibid., 22, 23; Kooker, "The Anti-Slavery Movement in Michigan," 97; Dillon, "Elizabeth Chandler and the Spread of Anti-Slavery Sentiment to Michigan," 484–85, 488.

59. George Evans to Friends, November 21, 1839, George Evans Letters, Manuscript Collection, Indiana State Library, Indianapolis, Indiana; Kooker, "The Anti-Slavery Movement in Michigan," 97; Dillon, "Elizabeth Chandler and the Spread of Anti-Slavery Sentiment to Michigan," 488, 489, 482.

60. Kooker, "The Anti-Slavery Movement in Michigan," 97. Beth Salerno omits this society from her history of female antislavery societies. She claims the first female society in the Old Northwest was the Economy Society of Indiana since she places Ohio in the East. Salerno, *Sister Societies*, 9, 21–22, 120, 143, 175; Dillon, "Elizabeth Chandler and the Spread of Anti-Slavery Sentiment to Michigan," 487.

61. Kraditor, *Means and Ends in American Abolitionism,1834–1850*, 5.

62. Kooker, "The Anti-Slavery Movement in Michigan," 97.

63. Salerno, *Sister Societies*, 3.

64. Kooker, "The Anti-Slavery Movement in Michigan," 137, 167, 318; Dillon, "Elizabeth Chandler and the Spread of Anti-Slavery Sentiment to Michigan," 492; Michigan State Anti-Slavery Society, *Proceedings of the Second Anniversary of the Michigan State Anti-Slavery Society, Held at Ann Arbor, June 7, 1838* (Detroit: Harsha and Bates, Printers, 1838), 6.

65. Johnson, *The Liberty Party, 1840–1848*, 177; Ohio Anti-Slavery Society, *Report of the Second Anniversary of the Ohio Anti-Slavery Society Held in Mount Pleasant, Jefferson County, Ohio, on the Twenty-Seventh of April, 1837* (Cincinnati: The [Ohio] Anti-Slavery Society, 1837), 12, 13.

66. Ohio Anti-Slavery Society, *Report of the Second Anniversary*, 12, 13.

67. In Ohio: December 1835: Oberlin Female and Young Ladies Societies; 1835: Middlebury; March 1836: Canton; 1836: Elyria; Geneva; Madison; Portage; St. Albans; Wayne; Abbeyville; Elyria Juvenile; before 1837: Cadiz; July 1837: Bloomingburg; February 1838: Cincinnati and Unionville. Marius R. Robinson to Emily Robinson, 7 February 1837, Marius R. Robinson Papers, Manuscript Collection, Western Reserve Historical Society, Cleveland, Ohio (hereafter cited as Robinson Papers); Ardath Hagaman, "Women of the Old Northwest in the Antislavery Movement" (Unpublished paper, University of Michigan Department of History Student Papers, Manuscript Collection, Bentley Historical Library, University of Michigan, Ann Arbor, Michigan, 1941), 15–16.

68. Osborn, *Journal of That Faithful Servant of Christ, Charles Osborn*; Levi Coffin, *Reminiscences of Levi Coffin, the Reputed President of the Underground Railroad* (1876; reprint, New York: Arno Press, 1968).

69. Johnson, *The Liberty Party, 1840–1848*, 214.

70. Illinois Anti-Slavery Convention, *Proceedings of the Illinois Anti-Slavery Convention: Held at Upper Alton on the Twenty-Sixth, Twenty-Seventh, and Twenty-Eighth October 1837* (Alton: Parks and Breath, 1838), 6.

71. Norman Dwight Harris, *The History of Negro Servitude in Illinois and of the Slavery Agitation in That State, 1719–1864* (1904; reprint: Ann Arbor: University Microfilms, 1968), 125, 129.

72. Hagaman, "Women of the Old Northwest in the Antislavery Movement", 7.

73. *Genius of Universal Emancipation*, February 26, 1839.

74. Ibid., June 28, 1839.

75. The Economy (Wayne Co.) Anti-Slavery Society, "The Economy (Wayne Co.) Anti-Slavery Society, Auxiliary to the Indiana State Anti-Slavery Society. Organized First Month 27th 1840. Minute Book," Manuscript Collection, Indiana Historical Society, Indianapolis, Indiana.

76. *National Anti-Slavery Standard*, June 17, 1841.

77. The *Protectionist*, March 1, 1841; Theodore C. Smith, *Liberty and Free Soil Parties in the Northwest* (New York: Longmans, Green, and Co., 1897), 51.

78. The *Protectionist*, December 4, 1841.

79. *Genius of Universal Emancipation*, June 28, 1839; *Western Citizen*, October 26, 1843; May 2, 1844. For example, in 1842 the Ohio American Society elected women as officers (two of the four vice presidents, but none of the higher level officers). *National Anti-Slavery Standard*, February 16, 1843.

80. Ohio Anti-Slavery Society, *Report of the Second Anniversary of the Ohio Anti-Slavery Society*, 7–8, 9, 11.

81. *Western Citizen*, July 26, 1842; August 26, 1842; January 6, 1843; February 9, 1843; March 16, 1843; April 20, 1843; July 6, 13, 20, 27, 1843; September 14, 1843; March 21, 1844; *The Liberty Tree*, vol. 3, no. 9 (July 1, 1846), 135–36.

82. The Jerseyville Female Anti-Slavery Society organized on April 20, 1843, followed by similar organizations women founded in Peoria and Princeton in July 1843.

Galesburg organized a Female Society on September 1, 1843, and lastly, Elk Grove organized in May of 1845. *Western Citizen*, May 16, 1844; January 30, 1845; October 23, 1845. Salerno also documented a Bureau County Female Society, founded in 1842 or 1843. Salerno, *Sister Societies*, 175.

83. Examples of this tendency are found in Horton and Horton, *In Hope of Liberty*; Ronald G. Walters, *The Antislavery Appeal: American Abolitionism after 1830* (Baltimore: Johns Hopkins University Press, 1976); Foner, *Free Soil, Free Labor, Free Men*; Kraditor, *Means and Ends in American Abolitionism*. More recent integrated studies of reform are Goodman, *Of One Blood*, and John Stauffer, *The Black Hearts of Men: The Radical Abolitionists and the Transformation of Race* (Cambridge: Harvard University Press, 2002).

84. A case in point is Frederick Douglass: David W. Blight, *Frederick Douglass' Civil War: Keeping Faith in Jubilee* (Baton Rouge: Louisiana State University Press, 1989), 26.

85. John O. Wattles, "Letter from John O. Wattles," *National Anti-Slavery Standard*, October 6, 1842. Walters gives some acknowledgement of this fluidity as he notes that this was true of "Ohio and several other states." Walters, "The Boundaries of Abolitionism," 14–15.

86. Douglas A. Gamble, "Garrisonian Abolitionists in the West: Some Suggestions for Study," *Civil War History* 23, no. 1 (1977): 60.

87. Johnson, *The Liberty Party*, 166, 389, n. 12.

88. Ripley, *Black Abolitionist Papers*, vol. 3, 422; Hamm, *God's Government Begun*, 40–42, 44.

89. A. Brooke, *National Anti-Slavery Standard*, October 8, 1840; *National Anti-Slavery Standard*, October 1, 1840.

90. *National Anti-Slavery Standard*, July 7, 1842.

91. Walters, "The Boundaries of Abolitionism," 15; Hermann R. Muelder, *Fighters for Freedom: The History of Anti-Slavery Activities of Men and Women Associated with Knox College* (New York: Columbia University Press, 1959), 158–59; Blue, *No Taint of Compromise*, 97.

92. Johnson, *The Liberty Party, 1840–1848*, 214.

93. Smith, *Liberty and Free Soil Parties in the Northwest*, 30, 43–44; *Proceedings of the Indiana Convention Assembled to Organize a State Anti-Slavery Society, Held in Milton, Wayne Co., September 12, 1838* (Cincinnati: Samuel A. Alley, Printer, 1838).

94. John W. Lyda, *The Negro in the History of Indiana* (Terre Haute, Indiana, 1953), 48.

95. In Indiana: Economy Female Anti-Slavery Society (before November 1840); Salem Female Anti-Slavery Society (after January 1, 1841); Henry County Female Anti-Slavery Society (April 1841); Newport (February 1842). See The *Protectionist*, January 16, 1841; The Economy Anti Slavery Society, Minute Book; Records of the Henry County Female Anti-Slavery Society.

96. John O. Wattles, "Letter from John O. Wattles;" Benjamin Stanton, "Report of the Executive Committee to the Fourth Anniversary of the Indiana State Anti-Slavery Society," *Free Labor Advocate and Anti-Slavery Chronicle*, September 17, 1842; Johnson, *The Liberty Party*, 214.

97. *National Anti-Slavery Standard*, June 30, 1842.

98. Gamble, "Garrisonian Abolitionists in the West," 53–56. *National Anti-Slavery Standard*, February 16, 1843.

99. Dr. Brooke, *National Anti-Slavery Standard*, October 6, 1842.

100. *National Anti-Slavery Standard*, December 1, 1842; *Letters of Theodore Dwight Weld, Angelina Grimké Weld, and Sarah Grimké, 1822–1844*, ed. Gilbert Hobbs Barnes and Dwight L. Dumond, vol. 1 (1934; reprint, Gloucester, MA: Peter Smith,1965), 286.

101. Johnson, *The Liberty Party, 1840–1848*, 294, 296.

102. Gamble, "Garrisonian Abolitionists in the West," 62.

103. Muelder, *Fighters for Freedom*, 158–59; Blue, *No Taint of Compromise*, 97.

104. *National Anti-Slavery Standard*, August 5, 1841. William T. Allen, "From a 'Son of a Slaveholder'," *Liberator*, August 25, 1843. Contemporaries variously spelled his name Allan and Allen, but there was only one Reverend William T. Allan/Allen born in Alabama who served as the agent of the Illinois Anti-Slavery Society in the 1840s. See also Allan, "LETTER FROM ILLINOIS," *National Anti-Slavery Standard*, June 29, 1843.

105. Zebina Eastman, "History of the Antislavery Agitation, and the Growth of the Liberty and Republican Parties in the State of Illinois," in *Discovery and Conquests of the Northwest*, ed. Rufus Blanchard (Wheaton: 1879), 672; Smith, *Liberty and Free Soil Parties in the Northwest*, 5; Gamble, "Garrisonian Abolitionists in the West"; Douglas A. Gamble, "Moral Suasion in the West: Garrisonian Abolitionism, 1831–1861" (PhD diss., Ohio State University, 1974).

106. *Western Citizen*, May 16, 1844; Johnson, *The Liberty Party, 1840–1848*, 191.

107. Johnson, *The Liberty Party, 1840–1848*, 199, 201.

108. Ibid., 165; Quist, *Restless Visionaries*, 376, 375, 383.

109. Lindquist, *The Antislavery-Underground Railroad Movement in Lenawee County, Michigan, 1830–1860*, 25–26.

110. Beth Salerno omits the Logan Society but lists the following as Michigan Female Societies as of 1846: Highland Township Female Anti-Slavery and Benevolent Society; Lenawee County Female Anti-Slavery Society; Van Buren County Female Anti-Slavery Society; Salem Township Female Anti-Slavery and Benevolent Society. Salerno, *Sister Societies*, 180.

111. Michigan Anti-Slavery Society Daybook, vol. 1, Harriet deGarmo Fuller Collection, Clements Library, Ann Arbor, Michigan; Michigan Anti-Slavery Society Daybook, vol. 4; Gamble, "Garrisonian Abolitionists in the West," 64.

112. Quist, *Restless Visionaries*, 375.

113. Ibid., 403; Lindquist, *The Antislavery-Underground Railroad Movement in Lenawee County, Michigan, 1830–1860*, 46.

114. Dorothy Sterling, *Ahead of Her Time: Abby Kelley and the Politics of Anti-Slavery* (New York: W.W. Norton, 1991), 287–88; Michigan Anti-Slavery Society Daybook, vol. 4.

115. Michigan Anti-Slavery Society Daybook, vol. 4, 50, 71, 72; C. A. F. S., "Pro-Slavery Mob at Ann Arbor," *Liberator*, March 1, 1861.

116. Gamble, "Garrisonian Abolitionists in the West," 66–67.

2 / Scrubbing at the "Bloody Stain of Oppression": A Human Rights Movement against Unjust Laws, 1830–1849

1. Ripley, *Black Abolitionist Papers*, vol. 3, 424. This is not the same Benjamin Stanton who resided for a long period in Salem, Ohio, and was uncle of Edwin Masters Stanton. William Henry Stanton, *Our Ancestors the Stantons* (Philadelphia: Innes and

Sons, 1922), 4, 125; Nuermberger, *The Free Produce Movement*, 104; Barbara A. Terzian, "Ohio's Constitutional Conventions and Constitutions," in *The History of Ohio Law*, 48.

2. Free Labor Advocate, *February 4, 1843*.

3. *Williams v. School District* (1834); *Polly Gray v. Ohio*, (1831), mentioned in *Reports of Cases Argued and Determined in the Supreme Court of Ohio, Printed by Authority of the General Assembly*, vol. 11 (Cincinnati: Robert Clarke and Company, 1873), 376, 377, 375, 378, 379.

4. *Reports of Cases Argued and Determined in the Supreme Court of Ohio*, 376, 381, 382, 384–85, 386. During his brief but colorful tenure on the Ohio Supreme Court, Reed (also spelled Read) made his views on African American rights clear: they should be limited, according to the laws of Ohio. He saw the solution to slavery as colonization, not abolition, and opposed efforts to remove the institution or limit its effects via broad interpretations of the law. Charles Theodore Greve, *Centennial History of Cincinnati and Representative Citizens* (Chicago: Biographical Publishing Company, 1904), 750, 753.

5. *Free Labor Advocate*, June 30, 1848.

6. Paul Finkelman, "Race, Slavery, and the Law in Antebellum Ohio," in *The History of Ohio Law*, 753.

7. Ibid., 751, 774–75. Finkelman claims that in Ohio, the trajectory of rights was in a positive direction, a perspective that focuses only on Republican politicians (who were actually rather moderate on racial issues) and omits such evidence of ongoing problems as the fact that the state imposed its first interracial marriage ban in 1861. For the 1861 law, see Middleton, *The Black Laws: Ohio*, 247, 251.

8. Sandra Anne Baumgartner, "The Legal Status of the Negro in Illinois as Determined by State Legislation and State Supreme Court Decisions, 1818–1853" (master's thesis, Southern Illinois University, 1966), 21–22, 37.

9. United States Bureau of the Census, *Historical Statistics of the United States, Colonial Times to 1870, Part 1*, Bicentennial ed. (Washington, DC: Government Printing Office, 1975).

10. *National Anti-Slavery Standard*, November 11, 1841.

11. Middleton, *The Black Laws: Ohio*, 9, 15, 17; Paul Finkelman, "Slavery and the Northwest Ordinance: A Study in Ambiguity," *Journal of the Early Republic* 6, no. 4 (1986): 357, 369.

12. *National Anti-Slavery Standard*, November 11, 1841; Middleton, *The Black Laws: Ohio*, 7; Finkelman, "Slavery and the Northwest Ordinance," 344, 357.

13. Clayton E. Cramer, *Black Demographic Data, 1790–1860: A Sourcebook*. (Westport, CT: Greenwood Press, 1997), 110–13.

14. Tho. W. Taylor to Pascal P. Enos, 26 April 1830, Enos Family Papers, Manuscript Collection, Abraham Lincoln Presidential Library, Springfield, Illinois; Middleton, *The Black Laws: Ohio*, 59, 73; Berwanger, *The Frontier against Slavery*, 7.

15. Andrew R. L. Cayton, "Law and Authority in the Northwest Territory," in *The History of Ohio Law*, 27.

16. Terzian, "Ohio's Constitutional Conventions and Constitutions," 48.

17. See Appendix.

18. Middleton, *The Black Laws in the Old Northwest*, 160; James H. Madison, "Race, Law, and the Burdens of Indiana History," in *The History of Indiana Law*, ed. David

J. Bodenhamer and Randall T. Shepard (Athens: Ohio University Press, 2006), 38, 41, 37, 39.

19. See Appendix; Madison, "Race, Law," 42.

20. Diane Mutti Burke, *On Slavery's Border: Missouri's Small-Slaveholding Households, 1815–1865*, Early American Places (Athens: University of Georgia Press, 2010), 20.

21. Middleton, *The Black Laws in the Old Northwest*, 167, 259, 271, 272.

22. *History of Madison County, Illinois. Illustrated. With Biographical Sketches of Many Prominent Men and Pioneers* (Edwardsville, IL: W. R. Brink and Co, 1882), 33–34.

23. John D. Barnhart, "The Southern Influence in the Formation of Illinois," *Journal of the Illinois State Historical Society* 32 (1939): 373; Baumgartner, "The Legal Status of the Negro in Illinois as Determined by State Legislation and State Supreme Court Decisions, 1818–1853," 16.

24. See Appendix; Bureau of the Census 1975; Harris, *The History of Negro Servitude in Illinois*, 105, 53.

25. Middleton, *The Black Laws in the Old Northwest*, 375; David G. Chardavoyne, "The Northwest Ordinance and Michigan's Territorial Heritage," in *The History of Michigan Law*, 20, 21.

26. Middleton, *The Black Laws in the Old Northwest*, 273, 349, 347; Finkenbine, "A Beacon of Liberty on the Great Lakes," 92.

27. Rowland Berthoff, "Conventional Mentality: Free Blacks, Women, and Business Corporations as Unequal Persons, 1820–1870," *Journal of American History* 76, no. 3 (1989): 754.

28. Ibid., 756, 757, 753, 755, 759.

29. *Ibid.*, 783, 761, 758–60.

30. This amorphous definition was in line with the situation in the antebellum South, where the boundaries of race as a socially constructed category ranged widely. Jane Elizabeth Dailey, *Before Jim Crow: The Politics of Race in Postemancipation Virginia*, Gender and American Culture (Chapel Hill: University of North Carolina Press, 2000), 132, 134. Racial "science" at the time was no more definitive. Gossett, *Race: The History of an Idea in America.*

31. An Act to Prohibit the Amalgamation of Whites and Blacks, Approved February 24, 1840, *General Laws of Indiana* in Middleton, *The Black Laws in the Old Northwest*, 207; Madison, "Race, Law," 43.

32. C. Peter Ripley, ed. *The Black Abolitionist Papers: The United States, 1847–1858*, vol. 4 (University of North Carolina Press, 1985), 224.

33. *Free Labor Advocate*, February 4, 1843; Middleton, *The Black Laws: Ohio*, 131, 155.

34. Finkenbine, "A Beacon of Liberty on the Great Lakes," 94.

35. Middleton, *The Black Laws in the Old Northwest*, 375, 374.

36. Middleton, *The Black Laws: Ohio*, 59, 85.

37. Leon F. Litwack, *North of Slavery: The Negro in the Free States, 1790–1860* (Chicago: University of Chicago Press, 1961), 66.

38. Middleton, *The Black Laws: Ohio*, 66, 43; Litwack, *North of Slavery*, 66; Leonard P. Curry, *The Free Black in Urban America, 1800–1850: The Shadow of the Dream* (Chicago: University of Chicago Press, 1981), 90.

39. Baumgartner, "The Legal Status of the Negro in Illinois," 21–22, 37; Berwanger, *The Frontier against Slavery*, 1, 4, 32.

40. Middleton, *The Black Laws: Ohio*, 3, 39, 49.

41. Finkelman, "Race, Slavery, and the Law in Antebellum Ohio," 757.

42. An Act to Prevent the Migration of Free Negroes and Mulattoes into This Territory and for Other Purposes, §1–5, Approved December 8, 1813, *Laws of Illinois*, in Middleton, *The Black Laws in the Old Northwest*, 291; Negroes and Mullatoes, §5, Approved February 19, 1841, *Laws of Illinois*, in Middleton, *The Black Laws in the Old Northwest*, 295; Will Co. Illinois Anti-Slavery Society, *Slave Code of the State of Illinois, Being an Abstract of Those Laws Now in Force in This State, Which Affect the Rights of Colored People, as Such, Both Bond and Free. With Notes* (Juliet: Published by the Will Co. Anti-Slavery Society, 1840), 10–11.

43. Middleton, *The Black Laws: Ohio*, 59; Litwack, *North of Slavery*, 70.

44. Middleton, *The Black Laws: Ohio*, 5; Emma Lou Thornbrough, *The Negro in Indiana: A Study of a Minority*, vol. 37, Indiana Historical Collections (Indianapolis Indiana Historical Bureau, 1957), 58, 59.

45. Thornbrough, *The Negro in Indiana*, 68; Berwanger, *The Frontier against Slavery*, 45.

46. Rebecca S. Shoemaker, "The Indiana Bill of Rights: Two Hundred Years of Civil Liberties History," in *The History of Indiana Law*, 196.

47. Madison, "Race, Law," 45.

48. Finkenbine, "A Beacon of Liberty on the Great Lakes," 86, 92, 100; Kooker, "The Anti-Slavery Movement in Michigan," 59.

49. United States Bureau of the Census, *Population Schedule of the Ninth Census of the United States, 1870* (Washington, DC: Department of Commerce Bureau of the Census); Middleton, *The Black Laws: Ohio*, 59; Thornbrough, *The Negro in Indiana*, 44; Cramer, *Black Demographic Data*, 74; Xenia E. Cord, "Black Rural Settlements in Indiana before 1860," in *Indiana's African-American Heritage: Essays from Black History News & Notes*, ed. Wilma L. Gibbs (Indianapolis: Indiana Historical Society, 1993), 99, 100, 102; Earline Ray Ferguson, "In Pursuit of Full Enjoyment of Liberty and Happiness: Blacks in Antebellum Indianapolis, 1820–1860," in *Indiana's African-American Heritage*, 132. For complete population statistics across the region see Appendix.

50. Middleton, *The Black Laws: Ohio*, 60, 70; Finkelman, "Race, Slavery, and the Law in Antebellum Ohio," 774.

51. Laura B. Gans, "Hudson Finding Aid: Hudson Family Papers, 1807–1963," http://asteria.fivecolleges.edu/findaids/sophiasmith/mnsss341_bioghist.html.

52. E. D. Hudson, "From Delaware, Ohio," *National Anti-Slavery Standard*, February 17, 1842.

53. *National Anti-Slavery Standard*, February 16, 1843.

54. Finkenbine, "A Beacon of Liberty on the Great Lakes," 86, 92, 100; Kooker, "The Anti-Slavery Movement in Michigan," 59.

55. Litwack, *North of Slavery*, 92; Carol Pirtle *Escape Betwixt Two Suns: A True Tale of the Underground Railroad in Illinois* (Carbondale: Southern Illinois University Press, 2000), 10; Berwanger, *The Frontier against Slavery*, 36; Baumgartner, "The Legal Status of the Negro in Illinois," 32; H. L. Ellsworth, *Illinois in 1837; a Sketch Descriptive of the Situation, Boundaries, Face of the Country, Prominent Districts, Prairies, Rivers, Minerals, Animal, Agricultural Productions, Public Lands, Plans of Internal Improvement,*

Manufactures, &C. Of the State of Illinois: Also, Suggestions to Emigrants, Sketches of the Counties, Cities, and Principal Towns in the State: Together with a Letter on the Cultivation of the Prairies, by the Hon. H. L. Ellsworth. To Which Are Annexed the Letters from a Rambler in the West (Philadelphia: S. Augustus Mitchell, 1837), 50.

56. Middleton, *The Black Laws: Ohio*, 23, 38, 59; Will Co. Illinois Anti-Slavery Society, *Slave Code*, 10–11.

57. Kooker, "The Anti-Slavery Movement in Michigan," 106, 108, 110, 113; David M. Katzman, *Before the Ghetto: Black Detroit in the Nineteenth Century*, Blacks in the New World (Urbana: University of Illinois Press, 1973).

58. Middleton, *The Black Laws: Ohio*, 59; Paul Finkelman and Martin J. Hershock, "Introduction," in *The History of Michigan Law*, 3.

59. Litwack, *North of Slavery*, 91.

60. Middleton, *The Black Laws: Ohio*, 53; Randolph County, State of Illinois, "To the People of the State of Illinois," 16 May 1836, Manuscript Collection, Abraham Lincoln Presidential Library, Springfield, Illinois.

61. This may have been a local law, or just an effort to enforce the state laws. Earnest E. East, "History of Peoria," c. 1950–1965, Peoria Public Library Collection, Peoria, Illinois, S1, P5. See also *National Anti-Slavery Standard*, March 25, 1841.

62. Middleton, *The Black Laws: Ohio*, 70, 73; Thornbrough, *The Negro in Indiana*, 70; Finkelman, "Race, Slavery, and the Law in Antebellum Ohio," 774.

63. Litwack, *North of Slavery*, 71–72.

64. Middleton, *The Black Laws: Ohio*, 110, 117.

65. Ibid., 2, 39, 49, 59; Will Co. Illinois Anti-Slavery Society, *Slave Code*, 10–11; Finkelman and Hershock, "Introduction," 3.

66. Ferguson, "In Pursuit of Full Enjoyment of Liberty and Happiness," 124–25.

67. Will Co. Illinois Anti-Slavery Society, *Slave Code*, 5.

68. Ibid., 10; Middleton, *The Black Laws: Ohio*, 5.

69. John Michael Vlach, "Above Ground on the Underground Railroad: Places of Flight and Refuge," in *Passages to Freedom: The Underground Railroad in History and Memory*, ed. David W. Blight (Washington: Smithsonian Books in Association with the National Underground Railroad Freedom Center, 2004), 115.

70. Middleton, *The Black Laws: Ohio*, 47; Juliet E. K. Walker, *Free Frank: A Black Pioneer on the Antebellum Frontier* (Lexington: University Press of Kentucky, 1983), 3, 91. While fugitive slave aid itself was an important corollary action for many of these activists, it has been ably explored elsewhere, so is not a major focus here. On militant resistance and the Underground Railroad, see Horton and Horton, *In Hope of Liberty*, 257; Charles A. Gliozzo, "John Jones: A Study of a Black Chicagoan," *Illinois Historical Journal* 80 (1987): 183; Dillon, *The Abolitionists*, 184–87; Pirtle, *Escape Betwixt Two Suns*; Vlach, "Above Ground on the Underground Railroad," 115; Keith P. Griffler, *Front Line of Freedom: African Americans and the Forging of the Underground Railroad in the Ohio Valley* (Lexington: University of Kentucky Press, 2004), 6–7.

71. Will Co. Illinois Anti-Slavery Society, *Slave Code*, 7.

72. See *Peoria Register and Northwestern Gazetteer*: April 21, 1838; July 14, 21, 28, 1838; August 4, 11, 1838; September 8, 15, 1838; August 24, 31, 1839; September 7, 14, 21, 28, 1839; November 2, 1839; July 30, 1841.

73. Middleton, *The Black Laws: Ohio*, 47.

74. Finkelman, "Slavery and the Northwest Ordinance: A Study in Ambiguity," 348, 356, 357.

75. Griffler, *Front Line of Freedom*, 6–7.

76. Walker, *Free Frank: A Black Pioneer on the Antebellum Frontier*, 112, 116–17, 164.

77. Griffler, *Front Line of Freedom*, 133.

78. Emma Hough to Oliver Huff, 8 August 1905, Huff–Nixon Papers, Friends Manuscript Collection, Earlham College, Richmond, Indiana; Betsy M. Cowles and Martha [Cowles] to Cornelia [Cowles], February 3, 1846, Betsy Mix Cowles, Papers, Special Collections, Kent State University, Kent, Ohio (hereafter cited as Cowles Papers); Records of the Henry County Female Anti-Slavery Society; Coffin, *Reminiscences of Levi Coffin*, 113, 301; Constitution of the West Grove Sewing Circle, Dugdale Papers, Friends Historical Library, Swarthmore College, Swarthmore, Pennsylvania.

79. James M. McPherson, *The Struggle for Equality: Abolitionists and the Negro in the Civil War and Reconstruction* (Princeton: Princeton University Press, 1964), 188.

80. These activities are explained in more detail in Weiner, "Racial Radicals"; Robertson, *Hearts Beating for Liberty;* Salerno, *Sister Societies*, 8, 38–39, 120.

81. Will Co. Illinois Anti-Slavery Society, *Slave Code*, 7.

82. Ibid., 9.

83. Anne Thomas to Nathan M. Thomas, 2 April 1839, Thomas Papers.

84. Nelson, *Indiana Quakers Confront the Civil War*, 5.

85. Indiana Yearly Meeting of Friends, *Address to the Citizens of the State of Ohio Concerning What Are Called the Black Laws, Issued in Behalf of the Society of Friends of Indiana Yearly Meeting, by Their Meeting for Sufferings, Representing the Said Yearly Meeting in its Recess [a Large Portion of the Members Reside in the State of Ohio]* (Cincinnati: A. Pugh, 1848), 4.

86. Ibid., 10, 15.

87. Spinka, "Organization of the General Association and After, 1844–1865," 94.

88. Thomas D. Morris, *Free Men All: The Personal Liberty Laws of the North, 1780–1861* (Baltimore: The Johns Hopkins University Press, 1974), 222, 52–53.

89. An Act to Prevent Manstealing, §3, *Laws of Indiana*, 1816 in Middleton, *The Black Laws in the Old Northwest*, 228–29.

90. Middleton, *The Black Laws in the Old Northwest*, 353; Finkenbine, "A Beacon of Liberty on the Great Lakes," 84, 85.

91. Finkenbine, "A Beacon of Liberty on the Great Lakes," 89–90.

92. Morris, *Free Men All*, 52–53; Gliozzo, "John Jones," 181–82; Richard Junger, "'God and Man Helped Those Who Helped Themselves': John and Mary Jones and the Culture of African American Self-Sufficiency in Mid-Nineteenth Century Chicago," *Journal of Illinois History* 11 (Summer 2008): 118.

93. Dillon, *The Abolitionists*, 225.

94. Offenses against Lives: Kidnapping and Selling as Slaves, §17–18, Approved July 15, 1838, [Michigan] *Revised Statutes*, in Middleton, *The Black Laws in the Old Northwest*, 356–57; An Act to Prevent Kidnapping, Approved February 15, 1831, *Laws of Ohio* in Middleton, *The Black Laws in the Old Northwest*, 27; *Revised Laws of Indiana in Which Are Comprised All Such Acts of a General Nature as Are in Force in Said State; Adopted and Enacted by the General Assembly at Their Fifteenth Session. To Which Are Prefixed the Declaration of Independence, the Constitution*

of the U. S., the Constitution of the State of Indiana, and Sundry Other Documents, Connected with the Political History of the Territory and State of Indiana. Arranged and Published by Authority of the General Assembly (Indianapolis: Douglass and Maguire, 1831), 183.

95. Morris, *Free Men All*, 88.

96. Stewart, *Abolitionist Politics and the Coming of the Civil War*, 216.

97. Paul Finkelman, "Slavery, the 'More Perfect Union,' and the Prairie State," *Illinois Historical Journal* 80, no. 4 (Winter 1987): 268.

98. Ibid., 263; Morris, *Free Men All*, xii, xi.

99. Finkelman, "Slavery, the 'More Perfect Union,' and the Prairie State," 266.

100. Morris, *Free Men All*, 89.

101. Middleton, *The Black Laws: Ohio*, 93, 159.

102. An Act to Repeal the Act Entitled "An Act Relating to Fugitives from Labor and Service from Other States, Passed February 26, 1839," §1–2, Approved January 19, 1843, *Laws of Ohio* in Middleton, *The Black Laws in the Old Northwest*, 129; Morris, *Free Men All*, 124.

103. Illinois Supreme Court, *Decision of the Supreme Court of Illinois in Relation to Arrest of Slaves. Ex Parte Thornton. The Process by Virtue of Which the Prisoner Was Arrested, and Is Now Detained, Was Issued under the Provisions of the Fifth Section of the Seventy-Fourth Chapter of the Revised Statues*, 1850.

104. Elmer Gertz, "The Black Laws of Illinois," *Journal of the Illinois State Historical Society* 61, no. 3 (1963): 469.

105. Rodgers, "Rights Consciousness in American History," 9.

106. Katzman, *Before the Ghetto*, 33.

107. Michigan State Anti-Slavery Society, *Report of the Meeting of the Michigan State Anti-Slavery Society, June 28, 1837, Being the First Annual Meeting, Adjourned from June 1st, 1837* (Detroit: George L. Whitney, 1837), 20; Michigan State Anti-Slavery Society, *Proceedings of the Second Anniversary of the Michigan State Anti-Slavery Society*, 5, 6, 8.

108. Middleton, *The Black Laws: Ohio*, 97.

109. Kenneth L. Kusmer, *A Ghetto Takes Shape: Black Cleveland, 1870–1930*, Blacks in the New World (Urbana: University of Illinois Press, 1978), 7; Michael Mangin, "Freemen in Theory: Race, Society, and Politics in Ross County, Ohio, 1796–1850" (PhD diss., University of California at San Diego, 2002), 281.

110. Ohio Anti-Slavery Society, *Report of the Second Anniversary of the Ohio Anti-Slavery Society*, 12, 13.

111. Oberlin College Archives, "Betsy Mix Cowles," "Papers of Other Individuals (Group 30)," accessed 20 May 2011, http://www.oberlin.edu/archive/resources/women/group30.html; Betsy M. Cowles and Martha [Cowles] to Cornelia [Cowles], February 3, 1846; Linda L. Geary, *Balanced in the Wind: A Biography of Betsey Mix Cowles* (Lewisburg: Bucknell University Press, 1989), 13, 16, 58–59, 69, 95; Donna M. DeBlasio, "'The Greatest Woman in the Reserve': Betsy Mix Cowles, Feminist, Abolitionist, Educator," *The Old Northwest* 13 (1987): 227.

112. Records of the Henry County Female Anti-Slavery Society, April 4, 1841, and June 6, 1841: 2–3, 5–6, 8–9.

113. Lydia S. Lewis, *Western Citizen*, April 6, 1843.

114. Matthew Norman, "From an 'Abolition City' to the Color Line: Galesburg,

Knox College, and the Legacy of Antislavery Activism," *Journal of Illinois History* 10, no. 1 (Spring 2007): 5.

115. *National Anti-Slavery Standard*, November 19, 1840.

116. *Free Labor Advocate*, July 8, 1841; March 25, 1848.

117. Will Co. Illinois Anti-Slavery Society, *Slave Code*, 10–11.

118. *National Anti-Slavery Standard*, February 16, 1843.

119. Will Co. Illinois Anti-Slavery Society, *Slave Code*, 8. See also *Western Citizen*, in *Free Labor Advocate*, April 15, 1848.

120. Rochester *Democrat* in *Free Labor Advocate*, June 16, 1848.

121. Samuel E. Cornish, "Our Brethren in Philadelphia," *Colored American* (New York, NY), 15 March 1838, in Ripley, *Black Abolitionist Papers*, Vol. 3, 263–64; Robert Purvis et al., *Appeal of Forty Thousand Citizens, Threatened with Disfranchisement, to the People of Pennsylvania* (Philadelphia: Merrihew and Gunn, 1838); Samuel E. Cornish, "Hints About Prejudice," *Colored American*, 9 June 1838, in Ripley, *Black Abolitionist Papers*, Vol. 3, 265–66.

122. Will Co. Illinois Anti-Slavery Society, *Slave Code*, 10–11.

123. U.S. Constitution, Article IV, § 2.

124. Will Co. Illinois Anti-Slavery Society, *Slave Code*, 6.

125. John Joliffe, *Philanthropist*, quoted in *National Anti-Slavery Standard*, August 11, 1842; Middleton, *The Black Laws: Ohio*, 199.

126. Will Co. Illinois Anti-Slavery Society, *Slave Code*, 6.

127. Indiana Yearly Meeting of Friends, *Address to the Citizens of the State of Ohio*, 4–5, 9, 7.

128. Litwack, *North of Slavery*, 113.

129. Middleton, *The Black Laws: Ohio*, 15.

130. Ibid., 55, 84.

131. Will Co. Illinois Anti-Slavery Society, *Slave Code*, 10–11.

132. Middleton, *The Black Laws: Ohio*, 59; Finkenbine, "A Beacon of Liberty on the Great Lakes," 94.

133. Horatio C. Ford, 8, 9 February 1848, Horatio C. Ford Diaries, the White-Ford Family Papers, Manuscript Collection, Western Reserve Historical Society, Cleveland, Ohio.

134. Nelson, *Indiana Quakers Confront the Civil War*, 5; James Eastman to Daniel Holt, 31 March 1849, Manuscript Collection, Indiana Historical Society.

135. Francis Dunlavy, Legal Opinion, 17 October 1836, James G. Birney Papers, Clements Library, Ann Arbor, Michigan.

136. Middleton, *The Black Laws: Ohio*, 119.

137. Michael Les Benedict, "Civil Liberty in Ohio," in *The History of Ohio Law*, 689.

138. Sandusky *Clarion* in *Free Labor Advocate*, September 17, 1842.

139. *National Anti-Slavery Standard*, February 16, 1843.

140. *National Anti-Slavery Standard*, June 1, 1843.

141. Finkelman, "Race, Slavery, and the Law in Antebellum Ohio," 764–65.

142. William T. Allan, "Letter from William T. Allan," *National Anti-Slavery Standard*, August 13, 1846. [Italics in original].

143. Ibid. [Italics in original].

144. Will Co. Illinois Anti-Slavery Society, *Slave Code*, 6.

145. Ibid., 4.

146. Barbara C. Cruz and Michael Berson, "The American Melting Pot? Miscegenation Laws in the United States," *OAH Magazine of History* 15, no. 4 (2001): 80.

147. An Act to Prohibit the Amalgamation of Whites and Blacks, Approved February 24, 1840, *General Laws of Indiana* in Middleton, *The Black Laws in the Old Northwest*, 207.

148. Berwanger, *The Frontier against Slavery*, 36; Baumgartner, "The Legal Status of the Negro in Illinois," 32.

149. Finkenbine, "A Beacon of Liberty on the Great Lakes," 96, 97.

150. Middleton, *The Black Laws: Ohio*, 250–51.

151. Madison, "Race, Law," 43; Thornbrough, *The Negro in Indiana*, 125, 126–27; Lori B. Jacobi, "More Than a Church: The Educational Role of the African Methodist Episcopal Church in Indiana, 1844–1861," in *Indiana's African-American Heritage: Essays from Black History News & Notes*, ed. Wilma L. Gibbs (Indianapolis: Indiana Historical Society, 1993), 5.

152. *Philanthropist*, in *National Anti-Slavery Standard*, April 15, 1841. [Italics in original].

153. L. M. Harris, "From Abolitionist Amalgamators to 'Rulers of the Five Points': The Discourse of Interracial Sex and Reform in Antebellum New York City," in *Sex, Love, Race: Crossing Boundaries in North American History*, ed. Martha Hodes (New York: New York University Press, 1999), 199–200.

154. *Free Labor Advocate*, February 16, 1842.

155. The impetus for the final repeal was *Loving v. Virginia*, the 1967 Supreme Court ruling that these laws were unconstitutional. Peggy Pascoe, "Miscegenation Law, Court Cases, and Ideologies Of 'Race' In Twentieth-Century America," *Journal of American History* 83, no. 1 (1996); Peggy Pascoe, "Race, Gender, and Intercultural Relations: The Case of Interracial Marriage," *Frontiers: A Journal of Women Studies* 12, no. 1 (1991): 6.

156. Will Co. Illinois Anti-Slavery Society, *Slave Code*, 8.

157. Thornbrough, *The Negro in Indiana*, 122.

158. Middleton, *The Black Laws: Ohio*, 98.

159. Ibid., 100. This is the only instance of Old Northwest resistance to African American petitions that I have found.

160. *National Anti-Slavery Standard*, February 16, 1843.

161. Middleton, *The Black Laws: Ohio*, 103.

162. Lewis, *Western Citizen*, April 6, 1843.

163. Norman, "From an 'Abolition City' to the Color Line," 5.

164. Hagaman, "Women of the Old Northwest in the Antislavery Movement," 42.

165. Middleton, *The Black Laws: Ohio*, 126–27; Frederick J. Blue, *No Taint of Compromise*, 216, 217.

166. Robert Meredith Watson, "The Anatomy of a Crusade: A Western Reserve Township and the War against the Slaveholders, 1831–1865" (PhD diss., Memphis State University, 1978), 320; Volpe, *Forlorn Hope of Freedom*, 103, 105.

167. Stewart, *Abolitionist Politics and the Coming of the Civil War*, 216.

168. Johnson, *The Liberty Party, 1840–1848*, 252, 254, 192.

169. "Abolition Movements: Bureau Liberty Convention," *Peoria Register*, May 20, 1842.

170. "Proceedings of the Liberty Convention in Knox County, ILL," *Peoria Register*, June 17, 1842.

171. Ripley, *Black Abolitionist Papers*, vol. 5, 214.

172. Johnson, *The Liberty Party, 1840–1848*, 244, 246, 250, 255; Wilentz, *The Rise of American Democracy*, 552, 553.

173. *Free Labor Advocate*, December 21, 1842.

174. Chris Dixon, *Perfecting the Family: Antislavery Marriages in Nineteenth Century America* (Amherst: University of Massachusetts Press, 1997), 129, 7, 34–35, 130; Merton Lynn Dillon, *Slavery Attacked: Southern Slaves and Their Allies, 1619–1865* (Baton Rouge: Louisiana State University Press, 1990), 174–75; Jane H. Pease and William H. Pease, "Antislavery Ambivalence: Immediatism, Expediency, Race," *American Quarterly* 17, no. 4 (1965): 693, 695; Stanley Harrold, *Subversives: Antislavery Community in Washington, D.C., 1828–1865*, 263.

175. On white privilege, see Roediger, *The Wages of Whiteness*. On contemporary shifts in racial thinking, see Melish, *Disowning Slavery*, 192; Melish, "The 'Condition' Debate and Racial Discourse in the Antebellum North," 657–58; James Brewer Stewart, et al, "The Emergence of Racial Modernity and the Rise of the White North, 1790–1840," *Journal of the Early Republic* 18 (1998): 197, 236; James Brewer Stewart, "Modernizing 'Difference': The Political Meanings of Color in the Free States, 1776–1840," *Journal of the Early Republic* 19, no. 4 (1999).

176. Jeffrey, *The Great Silent Army of Abolitionism*, 4, 36.

177. Stewart, *Holy Warriors*, 103–4, 110; Johnson, *The Liberty Party, 1840–184*, 227.

178. *Western Citizen*, September 2, 16, 1842; April 6, 1843; January 25, 1844; June 20, 1844; August 8, 1844.

179. *Western Citizen*, January 6, 1843; June 6, 1844; October 14, 1842; January 25, 1844; July 25, 1844; December 30, 1842; August 17, 1843; August 12, 1842; May 16, 1844; *Genius of Universal Emancipation*, July 26, 1839; June 28, 1839; Mary Brown Davis, *Scenes of Oppression in the Refined Circles of the South; Addressed to the Women of Illinois by Mrs. M. B. Davis* (Peoria County Anti-Slavery Society, 1846), 5–6, 8.

180. Volpe, *Forlorn Hope of Freedom*, 104.

181. Johnson, *The Liberty Party, 1840–1848*, 199, 202.

182. Middleton, *The Black Laws: Ohio*, 84, 85; Ripley, *Black Abolitionist Papers*, vol. 4, 67, 70.

183. Middleton, *The Black Laws: Ohio*, 144–45; Howard Holman Bell, *Minutes of the Proceedings of the National Negro Conventions, 1830–1864*, The American Negro: His History and Literature (New York: Arno Press, 1969); Carleton Mabee, *Black Freedom: The Nonviolent Abolitionists from 1830 through the Civil War* (New York: Macmillan, 1970), 59.

184. Taylor, *Frontiers of Freedom*, 108.

185. Middleton, *The Black Laws: Ohio*, 125.

186. John Malvin, *North into Freedom: The Autobiography of John Malvin, Free Negro, 1795–1880*, ed. Allan Peskin (1879; reprint, Kent, OH: Kent State University Press, 1988), 17, 66; Russell H. Davis, *Black Americans in Cleveland from George Peake to Carl B. Stokes, 1796–1969* (Washington: Associated Publishers, 1972), 47.

187. *National Anti-Slavery Standard*, April 13, 1843; Katherine DuPre Lumpkin, "'The General Plan Was Freedom': A Negro Secret Order on the Underground Railroad," *Phylon* 28, no. 1 (1967): 66; Katzman, *Before the Ghetto*, 34, 37.

188. Curry, *The Free Black in Urban America, 1800–1850*, vii–viii, 110, 104–5, 240.

189. National Convention of Colored Citizens, *Minutes 1843*, 8, 40.

190. Middleton, *The Black Laws: Ohio*, 145.

191. *Minutes of the State Convention of the Colored Citizens of Michigan, Held in the City of Detroit on the 26th and 27th of October, 1843, for the Purpose of Considering Their Moral and Political Condition as Citizens of the State* (Detroit: Printed by William Harsha, 1843), 6.

192. National Convention of Colored Citizens, *Minutes 1843*, 3; Ripley, *Black Abolitionist Papers*, vol. 3, 42, 403.

193. National Convention of Colored Citizens, *Minutes 1843*, 4–5.

194. Ibid., 7, 35.

195. Ibid., 6–7; Horton and Horton, *In Hope of Liberty*, 246, 236, 257.

196. *Minutes of the State Convention of the Colored Citizens of Michigan, 1843*, 13, 15, 6.

197. "Anniversary of the Ohio Anti-Slavery Society in Massillon, Stark County, May 27, 1850," *National Anti-Slavery Standard*, June 18, 1850.

198. *Minutes of the State Convention of the Colored Citizens of Michigan, 1843*, 10–11.

199. Ibid., 23; Katzman, *Before the Ghetto: Black Detroit in the Nineteenth Century*, 33, 34.

200. "Address of the State Convention," *Palladium of Liberty*, November 13, 1844.

201. The relevant portion of the 1835 address read, "If amidst all the difficulties with which we have been surrounded and the privations which we have suffered, we presented an equal amount of intelligence with that class of Americans that have been so peculiarly favoured, a very grave and dangerous question would present itself to the world, on the natural equality of man, and the best rule of logic would place those who have oppressed us, in the scale of inferiority." *Minutes of the Fifth Annual Convention for the Improvement of the Free People of Colour in the United States, Held by Adjournment, in the Wesley Church, Philadephia, from the First to the Fifth of June, Inclusive, 1835* (Philadelphia: William P. Gibbons, 1835), 25–26. This address was also reprinted in the 1837 minutes of the American Moral Reform Society, see *The Minutes and Proceedings of the First Annual Meeting of the American Moral Reform Society, Held at Philadelphia, in the Presbyterian Church in Seventh Street, Below Shippen, from the 14th to the 19th of August, 1837* (Philadelphia: Printed by Merrihew and Gunn, No. 7 Carter's Alley, 1837), 9–11.

202. *Minutes of the State Convention of the Colored Citizens of Michigan, 1843*, 20, 21.

203. Ibid., 12, 23.

204. Gliozzo, "John Jones," 178–79; Lerone Bennett, *Forced into Glory: Abraham Lincoln's White Dream* (Chicago: Johnson Publishing Company, 2000), 190.

205. Gliozzo, "John Jones," 177, 178, 179.

206. Ibid., 179, 180.

207. Ibid., 179, 180.

208. Illinois Senate Report of the Judiciary Committee Relative to Negroes, 1847, in Middleton, *The Black Laws in the Old Northwest*, 298–99.

209. Jonathan Blanchard, *Memoir of Rev. Levi Spencer: Successively Pastor of the Congregational Church at Canton, Bloomington, and Peoria, Illinois* (Cincinnati: American Reform Tract and Book Society, 1856), 16–18, 35–36.

210. Levi Spencer, 29 January 1848, Levi Spencer Diaries, Manuscript Collection, Abraham Lincoln Presidential Library, Springfield, Illinois (hereafter cited as Spencer Diaries).

211. Gliozzo, "John Jones," 180.

212. Finkelman, "Slavery, the 'More Perfect Union,' and the Prairie State," 266.

213. Middleton, *The Black Laws: Ohio*, 145.

214. Gliozzo, "John Jones," 180; *Report of the Proceedings of the Colored National Convention, Held at Cleveland, Ohio, on Wednesday, September 6, 1848* (Rochester: Printed by John Dick, at the North Star Office, 1848), 16.

215. Gliozzo, "John Jones," 183.

216. Middleton, *The Black Laws: Ohio*, 128, 143, 144, 153; Kusmer, *A Ghetto Takes Shape*, 7; Smith, *Liberty and Free Soil Parties in the Northwest*, 2; Quist, *Restless Visionaries*, 409; Richard H. Sewell, *Ballots for Freedom: Antislavery Politics in the United States, 1837–1860* (New York: Oxford University Press, 1976), 155–56, 170, 180–83, 187.

217. Sewell, *Ballots for Freedom*, 182.

218. Middleton, *The Black Laws: Ohio*, 157.

219. Paul Finkelman, "The Historical Context of the Fourteenth Amendment," *Temple Political and Civil Rights Law Review* 13, no. 2 (2004): 398.

220. Nullification in fact was soon also a strategy that some Republicans proposed to resist the 1850 Fugitive Slave Law. Eric Foner, *Free Soil, Free Labor, Free Men*, 134, 181.

221. *Minutes of the State Convention, of the Colored Citizens of Ohio, Convened at Columbus, January 9th, 10th, 11th, and 12th, 1850*, in *Proceedings of the Black State Conventions, 1840–1865*, ed. Philip Sheldon Foner and George E. Walker, vol. 1 (Philadelphia: Temple University Press, 1986), 252.

3 / "Stand Firm on the Platform of Truth": Freedom of Assembly and Local Antislavery Organizations in the Old Northwest

1. Spencer Diaries, 13 December 1843.

2. Blanchard, *Memoir of Rev. Levi Spencer*, 97.

3. Spencer Diaries, 13 February 1844.

4. Ibid., 23 June 1846; 2 July 1846.

5. The group of men who crossed the Ohio River for this attack claimed that Rankin's notorious aid to fugitive slaves provoked them. When they attempted to set the barn and house on fire, one of Rankin's sons and his nephew defended the home with pistols, and gave chase to their assailants. John Rankin, *National Anti-Slavery Standard*, December 9, 1841.

6. Spencer Diaries, 12, 13 June 1846.

7. Ibid., 7 April 1847; 31 May 1847.

8. Ibid., 21 October 1848. His reason for thinking this is unclear, given Peoria's own violent anti-abolition history.

9. *Western Citizen*, May 30, 1844.

10. Seth Hinshaw, *Free Labor Advocate and Anti-Slavery Chronicle*, August 3, 1842.

11. Ryan, "Civil Society as Democratic Practice," 234; Calhoun, *Habermas and the Public Sphere*.

12. Mary P. Ryan, "Gender and Public Access: Women's Politics in Nineteenth-Century America," in *Feminism, the Public and the Private*, ed. Joan B. Landes, *Oxford Readings in Feminism* (New York: Oxford University Press, 1998), 199, 203, 217–18.

13. Julia Prat to Susan Smythe, 30 April 1836, Wright–Smythe–Condon–Hosack Family Collection, Manuscript Collection, Ohio Historical Society, Columbus, Ohio;

Barnes and Dumond, *Letters of Theodore Dwight Weld, Angelina Grimké Weld, and Sarah Grimké*, vol. 1, 298–302.

14. The coeducational policy of this college was unusual but not unprecedented, for Oberlin, founded in 1837, was both coeducational and interracial. *Genius of Liberty*, July 24, 1841; *Western Citizen*, September 2, 1842; Muelder, *Fighters for Freedom*, 1; Julia Blanchard, *Blessed Memories: The Life of Mrs. Mary A. Blanchard, by Her Daughter Julia*. (Wheaton: 1890), 58.

15. Muelder, *Fighters for Freedom*, 130, 173; Blanchard, *Blessed Memories*, 35, 44; Mary H. Porter, *Eliza Chappell Porter, a Memoir* (Chicago: F.H. Revell Company, 1892), 100–101, 119–21, 162, 170.

16. Untitled essay on Samuel H. Davis, Samuel H. Davis File, Peoria Public Library Collection, Peoria, Illinois, Peoria, Illinois; Muelder, *Fighters for Freedom*, 174, 175; Samuel H. Davis File, Peoria Public Library, Peoria, Illinois.

17. Ernest E. East, Essay on Samuel H. Davis.

18. *Peoria Register and Northwestern Gazetteer*, March 10, 1838; December 8, 1838; January 28, 1842.

19. *Peoria Register and Northwestern Gazetteer*, November 12, 1841; December 24, 1841; April 22, 1842.

20. *Western Citizen*, September 16, 1842; May 23, 1844; Davis, *Scenes of Oppression in the Refined Circles of the South*, 5–6, 8.

21. *Western Citizen*, July 4, 1844; July 11, 1844.

22. Muelder, *Fighters for Freedom*, 187, 188.

23. *Peoria Register and Northwestern Gazetteer*, Feb. 10, 1843.

24. Peoria *Democratic Press*, February 15, 1843 [Emphasis added].

25. Richards, *"Gentlemen of Property and Standing,"* 5.

26. James Taylor, Moses Pettengill, John Reynolds, A. T. Castle, and Theodore Adams, "Freedom of Speech Suppressed," reprinted in Samuel H. Davis, *Free Discussion Suppressed in Peoria* (Peoria, IL: Samuel H. Davis, 1843), 3–4.

27. Peoria *Democratic Press*, February 15, 1843.

28. Muelder, *Fighters for Freedom*, 146–47, 181.

29. Peoria *Democratic Press*, February 15, 1843.

30. Charles Ballance, *History of Peoria, Illinois* (Peoria: N. C. Nason, 1870), 110.

31. Taylor et al, "Freedom of Speech Suppressed," in Davis, *Free Discussion Suppressed in Peoria*, 3–4 [Italics in original].

32. William T. Allan, "Letter from Illinois," *National Anti-Slavery Standard,* June 29, 1843.

33. *Western Citizen*, February 23, 1843.

34. *Western Citizen*, March 23, 1843. [Italics in original].

35. *Peoria Register*, May 13, 1842.

36. *Western Citizen*, February 23, 1843.

37. Richards,*"Gentlemen of Property and Standing,"* 5.

38. Christopher Waldrep, *The Many Faces of Judge Lynch: Extralegal Violence and Punishment in America* (New York: Palgrave, 2002), 12; Paul A. Gilje, *Rioting in America* (Bloomington: Indiana University Press, 1996), 80–81.

39. Gilje, *Rioting in America*, 1, 4; David Grimsted, *American Mobbing, 1828–1861: Toward Civil War* (New York: Oxford University Press, 1998), xii.

40. Christopher Waldrep, *Lynching in America: A History in Documents* (New York: New York University Press, 2006), xvi.

41. Richards, *"Gentlemen of Property and Standing,"* 3, 76–77, 15. See also Russel B. Nye, who erroneously argues that violent oppression of abolitionists largely ended after 1840. Russel Blaine Nye, *Fettered Freedom*, 175.

42. C. A. F. S., "Pro-Slavery Mob at Ann Arbor," *Liberator* March 1, 1861.

43. I have encountered no study that captures the singular patterns of violence in the Old Northwest.

44. Grimsted, *American Mobbing, 1828–1861: Toward Civil War*, 13–14, 34, 82.

45. Susan Sessions Rugh, *Our Common Country: Family Farming, Culture, and Community in the Nineteenth-Century Midwest*, Midwestern History and Culture (Bloomington: Indiana University Press, 2001), 21; Davis, *Frontier Illinois*, 17, 170.

46. Quist, *Restless Visionaries*, 454.

47. Melish, *Disowning Slavery*, 201.

48. Nation, *At Home in the Hoosier Hills*, 2.

49. *Western Citizen*, April 6, 1843.

50. *Western Citizen*, August 17, 1843. For other such incidents see the *Western Citizen*, February 22, 1844; Muelder, *Fighters for Freedom*, 146–47, 181.

51. *Western Citizen*, August 17, 1843.

52. *Western Citizen*, August 17, 1843. [Italics in original.]

53. *Western Citizen*, August 17, 1843.

54. See chapters 4, 5, and 6 of this book. For examples of this elsewhere in the nation, see Jeffrey, *The Great Silent Army of Abolitionism*, 51.

55. See also Irene B. Allan. *Western Citizen*, April 25, 1844; May 2, 1844.

56. *Western Citizen*, August 15, 1844.

57. *Western Citizen*, May 2, 1844. See also *Western Citizen*, August 8, 1844.

58. Laura Edwards, *Gendered Strife and Confusion: The Political Culture of Reconstruction*. (Chicago: The University of Illinois Press, 1997), 3, 10; Lori D. Ginzberg, *Women and the Work of Benevolence: Morality, Politics, and Class in the Nineteenth-Century United States* (New Haven: Yale University Press, 1990), 1, 9, 69, 79, 97; Linda K. Kerber, "Separate Spheres, Female Worlds, Woman's Place: The Rhetoric of Women's History," *Journal of American History* 75 (1988); Linda K. Kerber, *No Constitutional Right to Be Ladies: Women and the Obligations of Citizenship* (New York: Hill and Wang, 1998), 15; Linda K. Kerber, *Women of the Republic: Intellect and Ideology in Revolutionary America* (Chapel Hill: Published for the Institute of Early American History and Culture by the University of North Carolina Press, 1980), 252. A key text in understanding the development of domestic ideology is Nancy Cott's classic book, *The Bonds of Womanhood: "Woman's Sphere" in New England, 1780–1835* (New Haven: Yale University Press, 1977), 8.

59. *Western Citizen*, May 23, 1844.

60. It is also possible that "Maria" was Davis writing under a pseudonym. *Western Citizen*, May 30, 1844; Michigan Anti-Slavery Society Daybook, vol. 4.

61. Nancy A. Hewitt, "On Their Own Terms: A Historiographical Essay," in *The Abolitionist Sisterhood: Women's Political Culture in Antebellum America*, ed. Jean Fagan Yellin and John C. Van Horne (Ithaca: Cornell University Press, 1994), 24–25; Nancy A. Hewitt, "The Social Origins of Antislavery Politics in Western New York,"

in *Crusaders and Compromisers: Essays on the Relationship of the Antislavery Struggle to the Antebellum Party System*, ed. Alan M. Kraut (Westport, CT: Greenwood Press, 1983), 205–6, 227; Jeffrey, *The Great Silent Army of Abolitionism*, 25–26, 54–55.

62. *Western Citizen*, June 6, 1844; June 20, 1844; August 8, 1844; April 24, 1845; Zebina Eastman, "History of the Antislavery Agitation," 660.

63. Lewis, "Address to Females," April 6, 1843.

64. James C. Scott, *Domination and the Arts of Resistance: Hidden Transcripts* (New Haven: Yale University Press, 1990), 63; Susan Zaeske, *Signatures of Citizenship: Petitioning, Antislavery, and Women's Political Identity* (Chapel Hill: University of North Carolina Press, 2003), 3; Gerda Lerner, *The Majority Finds Its Past: Placing Women in History* (New York: Oxford University Press, 1979), 114, 117, 123–25, 127; Deborah Bingham Van Broekhoven, "'Let Your Names Be Enrolled': Method and Ideology in Women's Antislavery Petitioning," in *The Abolitionist Sisterhood*, 184–87.

65. Zaeske, *Signatures of Citizenship*, 2, 6, 48, 50–51. For further discussion of the importance of antislavery petitioning, see also Jeffrey, *The Great Silent Army of Abolitionism*, 5; Nancy Isenberg, *Sex and Citizenship in Antebellum America* (Chapel Hill: University of North Carolina Press, 1998), 65–66; Ginzberg, *Women and the Work of Benevolence*, 18, 82.

66. Daniel Wirls, "'The Only Mode of Avoiding Everlasting Debate': The Overlooked Senate Gag Rule for Antislavery Petitions," *Journal of the Early Republic* 27, no. 1 (2007): 116, 133.

67. Salerno, *Sister Societies*, 64–65.

68. Alisse Portnoy, *Their Right to Speak: Women's Activism in the Indian and Slave Debates* (Cambridge: Harvard University Press, 2005), 186.

69. Zaeske, *Signatures of Citizenship*, 3.

70. Ohio Anti-Slavery Society, *Report of the Second Anniversary*, 13, 15.

71. "Abolition Movements: Bureau Liberty Convention," *Peoria Register*, May 20, 1842.

72. "Proceedings of the Liberty Convention in Knox County, ILL," *Peoria Register*, June 17, 1842.

73. Portnoy, *Their Right to Speak*, 82. For more on this, see Weiner, "Racial Radicals."

74. *Western Citizen*, October 15, 1843; April 6, 1843.

75. Muelder, *Fighters for Freedom*, 182–83.

76. Records of the Henry County Female Anti-Slavery Society.

77. Salerno, *Sister Societies*, 127.

78. Lydia S. Lewis, "Address to Females," *Western Citizen*, April 6, 1843.

79. Garman, "'Altered Tone of Expression,'" 142, 150–51, 153.

80. Quist, *Restless Visionaries*, 423–25; Salerno, *Sister Societies*, 180.

81. Salerno, *Sister Societies*, 147–49.

82. Ibid., 146–47.

4 / "The Palladium of Our Liberties": Freedom of the Press in the Old Northwest, 1837–1848

1. *National Anti-Slavery Standard*, December 1, 1842.

2. *National Anti-Slavery Standard*, December 30, 1841.

3. Benedict R. O'G. Anderson, *Imagined Communities: Reflections on the Origin and Spread of Nationalism* (London: Verso, 1983); Pasley, *"The Tyranny of Printers,"* 11.

4. Michael Schudson, *Discovering the News: A Social History of American Newspapers* (New York: Basic Books, 1978), 4, 13; McCarthy and Stauffer, "Introduction," in *Prophets of Protest*, xxi. Among the papers consulted for this book were the *Salem (Ohio) Anti-Slavery Bugle*, the *Cambridge* and *New Concord (Ohio) Clarion of Freedom*, the *New Garden (Indiana) Free Labor Advocate* and *Protectionist*, the *Galesburg (Illinois) Free Democrat*, the *Boston Liberator*, the *New York National Anti-Slavery Standard*, the *Peoria Register and Northwestern Gazetteer*, the *Richmond (Indiana) Palladium*, and the *Chicago Western Citizen*.

5. Carol Sue Humphrey, *The Press of the Young Republic, 1783–1833*, The History of American Journalism (Westport, CT: Greenwood Press, 1996), 27.

6. William Lloyd Garrison, "My Second Baltimore Trial," *The Liberator*, January 1, 1831; John C. Nerone, *Violence against the Press: Policing the Public Sphere in U.S. History* (New York: Oxford University Press, 1994), 224–25.

7. Schudson, *Discovering the News*, 43.

8. Ibid., 16; Kooker, "The Anti-Slavery Movement in Michigan," 200; Sallie Holley and John White Chadwick, *A Life for Liberty: Anti-Slavery and Other Letters of Sallie Holley* (New York: G. P. Putnam's Sons, 1899), 94; Benjamin Stanton, "Editor's Excursion," *Free Labor Advocate and Anti-Slavery Chronicle*, February 23, 1842; Erasmus Hudson, "From Sherman, St. Joseph's County, Michigan," *National Anti-Slavery Standard*, November 25, 1841; E. D. Hudson, "From Delaware, Ohio," *National Anti-Slavery Standard*, February 17, 1842.

9. *Western Citizen*, September 16, 1842.

10. Nye, *Fettered Freedom*, 94.

11. Nicholas Marshall, "The Rural Newspaper and the Circulation of Information and Culture in New York and the Antebellum North," *New York History* (Spring 2007): 133.

12. Jane Rhodes, *Mary Ann Shadd Cary: The Black Press and Protest in the Nineteenth Century* (Bloomington: Indiana University Press, 1998), 131, 220–21.

13. Pasley, *"The Tyranny of Printers,"* 3–4; William E. Gienapp, "'Politics Seem to Enter into Everything': Political Culture in the North, 1840–1860," in *Essays on American Antebellum Politics, 1840–1860*, ed. Stephen E. Maizlish and John J. Kushma (Arlington: University of Texas at Arlington Press, 1982), 41–42.

14. *Western Citizen*, July 27, 1843.

15. Rodgers, "Rights Consciousness in American History," 3–4.

16. James T. Kloppenberg, *The Virtues of Liberalism* (New York: Oxford University Press, 1998), 15.

17. Lyrissa Barnett Lidsky and R. George Wright, *Freedom of the Press: A Reference Guide to the United States Constitution* (Westport, CT: Praeger, 2004), 5.

18. Arthur Tappan et al., *Address to the Public, Issued by the Executive Committee of the American Antislavery Society, September 3, 1835* (New York).

19. Wilentz, *The Rise of American Democracy*, 452; Miller, *Arguing About Slavery*.

20. Michael Kent Curtis, *Free Speech, "The People's Darling Privilege:" Struggles for Freedom of Expression in American History* (Durham: Duke University Press, 2000), 4, 250–51; Portnoy, *Their Right to Speak*, 186; Zaeske, *Signatures of Citizenship*, 3. The attacks on James G. Birney's Cincinnati *Philanthropist* in 1836 have been explored in detail elsewhere, and both Cincinnati's large size and its established African American community place it outside of the scope of this study. In 1840, Alton had 2,340 residents, while Cincinnati had 46,338. Peoria had 1,467 in 1840 and 5,562 ten years

later, while Cambridge had 1,845 in 1840 and 2,488 in 1850. *Niles' National Register*, October 23, 1841, vol. 61, 113; Thomas Baldwin and J. Thomas, *New And Complete Gazetteer of the United States* (Philadelphia: Lippincott, Grambo, and Co., 1854), 181; *An Accompaniment to Mitchell's Reference and Distance Map of the United States* (Philadelphia: S. Augustus Mitchell, 1845), 102; Taylor, *Frontiers of Freedom*, 110–12; Nye, *Fettered Freedom*, 106–7.

21. Curtis, *Free Speech*, 217, 228, 232, 251.

22. Ibid., 5–6, 117, 164–65, 171, 176. Freedom of the press was of course also a highly volatile subject in the Old South.

23. Nye, *Fettered Freedom*, 155; Waldrep, *The Many Faces of Judge Lynch*, 45.

24. Elijah Parish Lovejoy to Elizabeth Lovejoy, 14 February 1834, Elijah Parish Lovejoy Papers, Southwest Collection, Texas Tech University (hereafter cited as Lovejoy Papers).

25. Nye, *Fettered Freedom*, 115–16.

26. Ibid., 115–16; Henry Tanner, *The Martyrdom of Lovejoy, an Account of the Life, Trials, and Perils of Rev. Elijah P. Lovejoy, Who Was Killed by a Pro-Slavery Mob at Alton, Illinois, the Night of November 7, 1837. By an Eye-Witness [Henry Tanner]* (1881; reprint, New York: Augustus M. Kelley, 1971), 40, 51–52.

27. Alton *Observer*, September 27, 1837.

28. Tanner, *The Martyrdom of Lovejoy*, 108, 110, 117–18.

29. Ibid., 71–72, 128–29; William L. Stewart to Elijah Parish Lovejoy, 20 July 1836, Lovejoy Papers; Romulus Barnes to Elijah Parish Lovejoy, 11 September 1837, Lovejoy Papers; Isaac Gallard to Elijah Parish Lovejoy, 5 October 1837, Lovejoy Papers; *Peoria Register and Northwestern Gazetteer*, January 27, 1838.

30. Mark Allen Cyr, "'I Would Not Be a Master': Democracy and the Political Culture of Mastery in Illinois, 1837–1858" (PhD diss., Washington University, 2003), 21; Waldrep, *The Many Faces of Judge Lynch*, 47, 50.

31. Michael Feldberg, *The Turbulent Era: Riot and Disorder in Jacksonian America* (New York: Oxford University Press, 1980), 110–11.

32. Cyrall Cady to Julius A. Willard, 15 November 1837, Samuel Willard Papers, Manuscript Collection, Abraham Lincoln Presidential Library, Springfield, Illinois (hereafter cited as Willard Papers); Elijah Lovejoy quoted in Tanner, *The Martyrdom of Lovejoy*, 130–32.

33. See also William A. White, *Liberator*, October 13, 1843; *Western Citizen*, August 17, 1843; August 8, 1844.

34. *Human Rights*, December 1837, vol. 3, no. 6.

35. Illinois Anti-Slavery Convention, *Proceedings of the Illinois Anti-Slavery Convention: Held at Upper Alton on the Twenty-Sixth, Twenty-Seventh, and Twenty-Eighth October 1837* (Alton: Parks and Breath, 1838), 6, 3, 10, 20, 14, 22. [Italics in original]

36. Ibid., 10, 9; Tanner, *The Martyrdom of Lovejoy*, 135.

37. Illinois Anti-Slavery Convention, *Proceedings*, 22, 28–29, 31, 34.

38. Kathryn Kish Sklar, *Catharine Beecher: A Study in American Domesticity* (New York: Norton, 1976), 300 n. 7; *Proceedings of the Illinois State Convention of Colored Men, Assembled at Galesburg, October 16th, 17th, and 18th. Containing the State and National Addresses Promulgated by It, with a List of the Delegates Composing It, October 1866. Published by Order of the Convention*, in *Proceedings of the Black National and State Conventions*, vol. 1, 275.

39. Tanner, *The Martyrdom of Lovejoy*, 136–37.

40. Ibid., 138–39.

41. *Human Rights*, December 1837, vol. 3, no. 6.

42. Tanner, *The Martyrdom of Lovejoy*, 146–47, 138–39.

43. Cyr, "'I Would Not Be a Master,'" 67.

44. John M. Krum, letter to Alton *Spectator*, November 8, 1837, reprinted *Human Rights*, December 1837, vol. 3, no. 6; *Peoria Register and Northwestern Gazetteer*, December 16, 1837; Samuel Willard, "The Riot in Alton, Ill. Nov. 7. 1837," December 25, 1879, Manuscript Collection, Chicago History Museum, Chicago, Illinois.

45. Krum, letter to Alton *Spectator*.

46. Tanner, *The Martyrdom of Lovejoy*, 155–56.

47. Ibid., 149–50, 155, 156.

48. Krum, letter to Alton *Spectator*.

49. William Sever Lincoln, *Alton Trials of Winthrop S. Gilman, Who Was Indicted with Enoch Long, Amos B. Roff, George H. Walworth, George H. Whitney, William Harned, John S. Noble, James Morss, Jr., Henry Tanner, Royal Weller, Reuben Gerry, and Theodore B. Hurlbut; for the Crime of Riot, Committed on the Night of the 7th of November, 1837, While Engaged in Defending a Printing Press, from an Attack Made on It at That Time, by an Armed Mob. Written out from Notes of the Trial, Taken at the Time, by a Member of the Bar of the Alton Municipal Court. Also, the Trial of John Solomon, Levi Palmer, Horace Beall, Josiah Nutter, Jacob Smith, David Butler, William Carr, and James M. Rock, Indicted with James Jennings, Solomon Morgan, and Frederick Bruchy; for a Riot Committed in Alton, on the Night of the 7th of November, 1837, in Unlawfully and Forcibly Entering the Warehouse of Godfrey, Gilman, and Co., and Breaking up and Destroying a Printing Press. Written out from Notes Taken at the Time of Trial, by William S. Lincoln, a Member of the Bar of the Alton Municipal Court* (New York: J. F. Trow, 1838); Tanner, *The Martyrdom of Lovejoy*, 231.

50. Lawrence J. Friedman, "Antebellum American Abolitionism and the Problem of Violent Means," *Psychohistory Review* 9 (1980): 29, 31, 32.

51. Richards, *"Gentlemen of Property and Standing,"* Blue, *No Taint of Compromise*, 93; William W. Freehling, *The Road to Disunion Volume Two, Secessionists Triumphant: 1854–1861* (New York: Oxford University Press, 2007), 288–89; Wilentz, *The Rise of American Democracy*, 467.

52. In an 1838 memoir written by his brothers, they refer to Elijah Lovejoy as "The first American Martyr to THE FREEDOM OF THE PRESS, AND THE FREEDOM OF THE SLAVE." Joseph C. Lovejoy and Owen Lovejoy, *Memoir of the Rev. Elijah P. Lovejoy; Who Was Murdered in Defence of the Liberty of the Press, at Alton, Illinois, November 7, 1837* (1838; reprint, Freeport, New York: Books for Libraries Press, 1970), 12. For later examples of this argument, see Paul Simon, *Freedom's Champion: Elijah Lovejoy* (Carbondale and Edwardsville, Illinois: Southern Illinois University Press, 1994); John Gill, *Tide without Turning: Elijah P. Lovejoy and Freedom of the Press* (Boston: Starr King Press, 1958). Contemporaries wrote of him in these terms in antislavery newspapers, and ordinary people in the region also extensively chronicled the events at Alton in their private correspondence. Cady to Willard, 15 November 1837, Willard Papers; E. Russell to Mr. John Bachelder, 19 January 1838, Manuscript Collection, Abraham Lincoln Presidential Library, Springfield, Illinois.

53. Johnson, *The Liberty Party*, 201–2, 190, 92.

54. Spencer Diaries, 25 February 1847; Blanchard, *Memoir of Rev. Levi Spencer*, 116–17; Nye, *Fettered Freedom*, 175; Feldberg, *The Turbulent Era*, 52.

55. Taylor et al., "Freedom of Speech Suppressed," 4–5.

56. Sellers, *The Market Revolution*, 388.

57. *Peoria Register and Northwestern Gazetteer*, May 13, 1837.

58. Arnold Buffum, The *Protectionist*, August 7, 1841. Benjamin Stanton took over the *Free Labor Advocate* after one year. Hamm, *God's Government Begun*, 53; Oliver N. Huff, "Old Newport: A Paper Read by Dr. O. N. Huff. Before the Wayne County Historical Society," Manuscript Collection, Indiana Historical Society, Indianapolis, Indiana.

59. *The Protectionist*, January 1, 1841.

60. Muelder, *Fighters for Freedom*, 176.

61. *Peoria Register and Northwestern Gazetteer*, May 13, 1837; July 14, 1840; April 21, 1838; August 14, 1840.

62. *Peoria Register and Northwestern Gazetteer*, July 17, 1840; April 22, 1842; July 29, 1842; June 17, 1842.

63. *Peoria Register and Northwestern Gazetteer*, July 29, 1842.

64. *Peoria Register and Northwestern Gazetteer*, July 14, 1838; September 11, 1838; October 6, 1838; January 19, 1839; February 29, 1839; July 20, 1839; June 12, 1840; January 22, 1841; January 29, 1841; February 5, 1841; October 14, 1841; May 14, 1841; June 9, 1841; July 17, 1841; February 12, 1842; June 17, 1842.

65. See *Peoria Register and Northwestern Gazetteer*, December 14, 1839; February 1, 1840; February 18, 1843; March 4, 1842; "Abolition Movements," May 13, 1842; "Abolition Movements," May 20, 1842; July 15, 1842; August 5, 1842. Davis also published advertisements for liquor, despite being a strong advocate of temperance: *Peoria Register and Northwestern Gazetteer*, April 21, 1838; July 14, 21, 28, 1838; August 4, 11, 1838; September 8, 15, 1838; August 24, 31, 1839; September 7, 14, 21, 28, 1839; November 2, 1839; July 30, 1841.

66. *Peoria Register and Northwestern Gazetteer*, September 27, 1837; December 2, 1837; December 9, 1837; December 16, 1837; January 27, 1838; August 31, 1839; October 14, 1837; September 8, 1838; Muelder, *Fighters for Freedom*, 175–76.

67. *Peoria Register and Northwestern Gazetteer*, June 4, 1841. See also *Peoria Register and Northwestern Gazetteer*, February 1, 1840.

68. Among other issues, during the furor over the *Amistad* case from 1839 to 1841, Samuel H. Davis also reprinted material supporting the former slaves and their right to free themselves. *Peoria Register and Northwestern Gazetteer*, December 16, 1837; November 27, 1840; April 2, 1841. Unsurprisingly, Mary Brown Davis also wrote articles supporting the crew. *Peoria Register and Northwestern Gazetteer*, March 19, 1839; September 21, 1839; November 2, 1839; November 25, 1840.

69. "Abolition Movements," *Peoria Register and Northwestern Gazetteer*, May 13, 1842; "Abolition Movements—Again," *Peoria Register and Northwestern Gazetteer*, June 10, 1846.

70. Davis, *Free Discussion Suppressed in Peoria*, 2; Grimsted, *American Mobbing, 1828–1861: Toward Civil War*, 38.

71. Paula Glasman, "Zebina Eastman, Chicago Abolitionist" (master's thesis, University of Chicago, 1968), 10, 12, 19.

72. Ibid., 20, 65.

73. Ibid., 36–37; Bennett, *Forced into Glory*, 320–23.

74. H. O. Wagoner to Hon. S. H. Kerfoot, 27 September 1884, Manuscript Collection, Chicago History Museum, Chicago, Illinois; Zebina Eastman to Ichabod Codding, 22 April 1857, Ichabod Codding Family Papers, Manuscript Collection, Abraham Lincoln Presidential Library, Springfield, Illinois; Glasman, "Zebina Eastman," 51–52; William J. Simmons, *Men of Mark: Eminent, Progressive and Rising* (Cleveland: Geo. M. Rewell and Co., 1887), 680, 681–82.

75. *Genius of Universal Emancipation*, July 26, 1839; Hersh, *The Slavery of Sex*, 62; Salerno, *Sister Societies*, 21.

76. Elizabeth R. Varon, *We Mean to Be Counted: White Women and Politics in Antebellum Virginia*, Gender and American Culture (Chapel Hill: University of North Carolina Press, 1998), 6.

77. *Western Citizen*, September 2, 1842; Davis, *Scenes of Oppression in the Refined Circles of the South*, 1, 5–6, 8.

78. Garman, "'Altered Tone of Expression,'" 104; Schudson, *Discovering the News*, 14–15.

79. *Peoria Register and Northwestern Gazetteer*, December 9, 1837; May 13, 1837; May 5, 1838; June 7, 1838; July 7, 1838; August 4, 1838; October 20, 1838; April 20, 1839; May 25, 1839; May 1, 1840; June 16, 1841; October 16, 1841; November 19, 1841; January 14, 1842; April 15, 1842; March 15, March 25, 1842; September 2, 1842; October 7, 1842; February 10, 1843; February 25, 1843.

80. *Genius of Universal Emancipation*, July 26, 1839.

81. *Western Citizen*, August 12, 1842; April 6, 1843.

82. *Genius of Universal Emancipation*, June 28, 1839.

83. *Western Citizen*, September 16, 1842.

84. Nell Irvin Painter, *Sojourner Truth: A Life, a Symbol* (New York: W.W. Norton, 1996), 139.

85. *Western Citizen*, August 12, 1842; September 2, 1842; *Genius of Universal Emancipation*, June 28, 1839; Ruth Bogin and Jean Fagan Yellin, "Introduction," in *The Abolitionist Sisterhood*, 9.

86. *Western Citizen*, September 2, 1842; Davis, *Scenes of Oppression in the Refined Circles of the South*, 1, 5–6, 8.

87. *Western Citizen*, January 4, 1844; February 8, 1844.

88. *Western Citizen*, January 25, 1844.

89. *Western Citizen*, August 17, 1843; September 16, 1842; January 6, 1843; April 6, 1843; June 6, 1844; June 20, 1844; August 8, 1844.

90. *Peoria Register and Northwestern Gazetteer*, July 1, 1837; April 14, 1838.

91. *Peoria Register and Northwestern Gazetteer*, August 19, 1842.

92. Taylor et al., "Freedom of Speech Suppressed," 4.

93. Curtis, *Free Speech*, 250–51.

94. *National Anti-Slavery Standard*, April 13, 1843; Julius A. Willard to William T. Allan, 10 March 1843, Willard Papers; Muelder, *Fighters for Freedom*, 180.

95. *National Anti-Slavery Standard*, May 11, 1843.

96. *Peoria Register and Northwestern Gazetteer*, September 23, 1842; Davis, *Free Discussion Suppressed in Peoria*, 2.

97. Davis, *Free Discussion Suppressed in Peoria*, 4; *Peoria Register and Northwestern Gazetteer*, February 17, 1843.

98. Peoria *Democratic Press*, February 15, 1843.

99. *Peoria Register and Northwestern Gazetteer*, March 13, 1843; February 17, 1843; March 3, 1843.

100. Davis, *Free Discussion Suppressed in Peoria*, 6.

101. Tanner, *The Martyrdom of Lovejoy*, 231–32; *History of Madison County, Illinois*, 389.

102. *National Anti-Slavery Standard*, March 25, 1841; June 1, 1843; May 11, 1843.

103. Davis, *Free Discussion Suppressed in Peoria*, 6.

104. Ibid., 2–3; *Western Citizen*, February 23, 1843.

105. Davis, *Free Discussion Suppressed in Peoria*, 5.

106. *Peoria Democratic Press*, February 15, 1843.

107. The occupations of the leaders of this meeting are as follows: W. F. Bryan [attorney and investor in early banks]; Andrew Gray, Esq. [attorney and merchant]; William R. Hopkins [early industrialist, metal castings]; E. N. Powell [attorney]; N. H. Purple [attorney and judge]; John Rankin [owner, flour mills]. Simeon De Witt Drown, *Drown's Record and Historical View of Peoria from the Discovery by the French Jesuit Missionaries, in the Seventeenth Century, to the Present Time. Also, an Almanac for 1851, Calculated for the Latitude and Longitude of Peoria, Illinois* (Peoria: E. O. Woodcock, 1851), 160–62; *Peoria Register and Northwestern Gazetteer*, April 7, 1837; Ballance, *History of Peoria, Illinois*, 119, 129–30.

108. Peoria *Democratic Press*, February 15, 1843.

109. "Putnam County," *Western Citizen*, February 22, 1844; Samuel Willard to Almyra Willard, 12 March 1846, Willard Papers; Cyr, "'I Would Not Be a Master,'" 7, 21, 37; Drown, *Drown's Record and Historical View of Peoria*, 149; Muelder, *Fighters for Freedom*, 53, 91, 93–94, 96, 149, 178.

110. Peoria *Democratic Press*, February 15, 1843; Berwanger, *The Frontier against Slavery*, 36; Cruz and Berson, "The American Melting Pot."

111. Census results as reported in *Peoria Register*, December 11, 1840.

112. Between August 4, 1859, and August 4, 1864, the *Peoria Democratic Transcript* published at least eleven articles related to local African American rights and discrimination. Adade Mitchell Wheeler, *The Roads They Made: Women in Illinois History* (Chicago: Charles H. Kerr Publishing Company, 1977), 24; Harris, *The History of Negro Servitude in Illinois*, 226–27.

113. National Convention of Colored Citizens, *Minutes 1843*; Jane H. Pease and William H. Pease, *They Who Would Be Free: Blacks' Search for Freedom, 1830–1861*, Blacks in the New World (Urbana and Chicago: University of Illinois Press, 1990), 156.

114. Davis, *Free Discussion Suppressed in Peoria*, 2.

115. Ibid., 4.

116. Ibid., 7, 8.

117. Ibid., 7; *Western Citizen*, March 16, 1843; July 13, 1843; August 3, 1843; *Peoria Register and Northwestern Gazetteer*, March 3, 1843.

118. "To Honorable Senate and House of Representatives of the State of Illinois," February, 1847, Samuel H. Davis File, Peoria Public Library, Peoria, Illinois.

119. Grimsted, *American Mobbing, 1828–1861: Toward Civil War*, xii; Davis, *Frontier Illinois*, 287.

120. Tanner, *The Martyrdom of Lovejoy*, 138–39.

121. Norman H. Purple was a prominent lawyer at the local and state levels.

He served as a State Supreme Court Judge and Circuit Judge from 1844 to 1848. William L. May was an attorney who served one term in the Illinois legislature and two terms in the House of Representatives as a Democrat prior to coming to Peoria. Francis Voris was a pioneer merchant of Peoria who was elected to the Illinois House of Representatives in 1836 as a Democrat. Lincoln Brown Knowlton was a Whig who ran for local office in 1847, against Moses Pettingill [the Liberty candidate]. *Biographical Encyclopaedia of Illinois of the Nineteenth Century* (Philadelphia: Galaxy Publishing Company, 1875), 354–55; James M. Rice, *Peoria City and County Illinois, a Record of Settlement, Organization, Progress, and Achievement, Illustrated* (Chicago: The S. J. Clarke Publishing Company, 1912), 367–68, 372–75; David McCulloch, ed. *History of Peoria County* (Chicago and Peoria: Munsell Publishing Company,1901), 134; Ballance, *History of Peoria, Illinois*, 210–11.

122. Samuel H. Davis had formerly worked with mob members William F. Bryan and E. N. Powell in the Peoria Colonization Society. *Peoria Register and Northwestern Gazetteer*, August 31, 1839; July 10, 1840.

123. Davis, *Free Discussion Suppressed in Peoria*, 2.

124. *History of Peoria County Illinois* (Chicago: Johnson and Company, 1880), 527; Drown, *Drown's Record and Historical View of Peoria*, 160–62. Other attorneys included George Metcalfe, Elihu N. Powell, and William F. Bryan. *Peoria Register and Northwestern Gazetteer*, August 31, 1839; July 10, 1840.

125. Feldberg, *The Turbulent Era*, 34.

126. Dillon, *The Abolitionists*, 26–27; Davis, *Frontier Illinois*, xviii.

127. Another merchant was Francis Voris, mentioned above; Lewis Howell was a banker, and William F. Bryan also invested in banks; Isaac Underhill was a "capitalist" who invested in the pork industry, internal improvements, and hotels. *Peoria Register and Northwestern Gazetteer*, April 7, 1837; *History of Peoria County Illinois*, 527; *Biographical Encyclopaedia of Illinois of the Nineteenth Century*, 189; Ballance, *History of Peoria, Illinois*, 119, 129–30.

128. Earnest E. East, "History of Peoria," 1946, Manuscript Collection, Abraham Lincoln Presidential Library, Springfield, Illinois, 4; H. L. Ellsworth, *Illinois in 1837*, 28, 49, 31.

129. Ellsworth, *Illinois in 1837*, 31; East, "History of Peoria," 4.

130. *Peoria Register and Northwestern Gazetteer*, December 11, 1840; East, "History of Peoria" (c. 1950), GG1–3, KK1, DDD2; Ellsworth, *Illinois in 1837*, 34; Drown, *Drown's Record and Historical View of Peoria*, 107; William T. [Allan?] Allen, "From a 'Son of a Slaveholder,'" *Liberator*, August 25, 1843; Nation, *At Home in the Hoosier Hills*, 80; Paul Salstrom, *From Pioneering to Perservering: Family Farming in Indiana to 1880* (West Lafayette: Purdue University Press, 2007), 45–46.

131. *Western Citizen*, June 20, 1844.

132. *Missouri Republican*, May 11, 1846, reprinted in East, "History of Peoria" (c. 1950), S1 5, NN1; East, "History of Peoria" (1946), 7.

133. *Western Citizen*, May 20, 1846; June 3, 1846.

134. Johnson, *The Liberty Party, 1840–1848*, 333.

135. Spencer Diaries, 6, 7, 20 May 1846.

136. *Western Citizen*, July 7, 1846.

137. Nerone, *Violence against the Press*, 94. Erastus Hussey's press in Battle Creek

may have also suffered a similar attack in 1849. See Finkenbine, "A Beacon of Liberty on the Great Lakes," 89.

138. Cyrus Parkinson Beatty Sarchet, *History of Guernsey County, Ohio*, vol. 1 (Indianapolis: B.F. Bowen & Company, 1911), 28, 40, 257, 267–68.

139. M. R. Hull, "Cambridge Mob Meeting," *Clarion of Freedom*, September 17, 1847. [Emphasis in original.]

140. *Clarion of Freedom*, September 3, 1847; Volpe, *Forlorn Hope of Freedom*, 74.

141. "Prejudice against Color, or Caste," *Clarion of Freedom*, May 31, 1847; *Clarion of Freedom*, September 3, 1847.

142. *Clarion of Freedom*, June 14, 1847; M. R. Hull, *Clarion of Freedom*, October 1, 1847; *Clarion of Freedom*, September 10, 1847; M. R. Hull, "Cambridge Mob Meeting," *Clarion of Freedom*, September 17, 1847.

143. M. R. Hull, *Clarion of Freedom*, October 1, 1847; Isaac Oldham and Isaac Walker, *Clarion of Freedom*, September 17, 1847; J. W[olff], "Eggs-actly," *Clarion of Freedom*, July 30, 1847; J. W[olff], "Too Hard," *Clarion of Freedom*, August 13, 1847.

144. *Clarion of Freedom*, September 10, 1847; M. R. Hull, "Cambridge Mob Meeting," *Clarion of Freedom*, September 17, 1847.

145. [Boston?] *Chronotype* quoted in Michigan *Journal and Washingtonian Advocate*, December 15, 1847.

146. These meetings were at Summerfield, Stafford, Adams, Knox, Monroe, Highland, and Liberty Townships, and New Concord, Ohio. *Clarion of Freedom*, September 10, 1847; September 17, 1847; C. Sullivan, *Clarion of Freedom*, September 17, 1847; Isaac Oldham and Isaac Walker, *Clarion of Freedom*, September 17, 1847; James Black and John Monroe, "Public Meeting," *Clarion of Freedom*, September 24, 1847; A. N. Milligan and John C. Walker, "Public Meeting," *Clarion of Freedom*, October 15, 1847; W. H. Berry and W. F. George, *Clarion of Freedom*, December 24, 1847; M. R. Hull, "Cambridge Mob Meeting," *Clarion of Freedom*, September 17, 1847; M. R. Hull, *Clarion of Freedom*, October 1, 1847; "Liberty Meeting," *Clarion of Freedom*, October 15, 1847.

147. Robert Hanna, *Clarion of Freedom*, September 17, 1847; *Clarion of Freedom*, October 22, 1847; Amicus, "Franklin College," *National Era*, October 28, 1847; "Mobbing in Ohio," *Clarion of Freedom*, October 8, 1847; "Liberty of the Press in Ohio," *National Era*, October 14, 1847.

148. M. R. Hull, *Clarion of Freedom*, October 1, 1847.

149. M. R. Hull, "Cambridge Mob," *Clarion of Freedom*, October 8, 1847; M. R. Hull, "Editorial Correspondence," *Clarion of Freedom*, September 24, 1847; "The Anniversary," *Free Labor Advocate and Anti-Slavery Chronicle*, November 1, 1843.

150. Hull, "Editorial Correspondence."

151. "Liberty Meeting," *Clarion of Freedom*, October 15, 1847; M. R. Hull, "Correspondence of the Editor," *Clarion of Freedom*, October 22, 1847; M. R. Hull, "Correspondence of the Editor: Proceedings of the National Convention," *Clarion of Freedom*, November 5, 1847.

152. "Newspaper Changes, Etc.," *National Era*, December 2, 1847.

153. *Clarion of Freedom*, September 10, 1847.

154. "To the Patrons of the Clarion," *Clarion of Freedom*, October 15, 1847.

155. W. H. Berry and W. F. George, *Clarion of Freedom*, December 24, 1847.

156. "It's All Over," *Clarion of Freedom*, August 11, 1848; M. R. Hull, "Mobocracy," *Clarion of Freedom*, September 29, 1848.

157. "Agitation," *Clarion of Freedom*, May 19, 1848.

158. Richards, *"Gentlemen of Property and Standing,"* 111; Feldberg, *The Turbulent Era*, 49.

159. Roland M. Baumann, *The 1858 Oberlin-Wellington Rescue: A Reappraisal* (Oberlin, Ohio: Oberlin College, 2003), 27–28.

160. Richards, *"Gentlemen of Property and Standing,"* 110–11.

161. Johnson, *The Liberty Party, 1840–1848*, 164, 211.

162. Dillon, *Slavery Attacked*, 270.

163. Foner, *Free Soil, Free Labor, Free Men*, 215.

164. Eastman to Codding, 22 April 1857, Codding Family Papers.

165. Massachusetts Anti-Slavery Society, *Fourteenth Annual Report*, 57–58.

166. E. D. Hudson, "Letter from Richmond, Wayne County, Indiana," *National Anti-Slavery Standard*, October 21, 1841; Abby Kelley Foster to Lucy Stone, 15 August [1845–46?] in Robert S. Fletcher Papers, Manuscript Collection, Oberlin College Library, Oberlin, Ohio (hereafter cited as Fletcher Papers); William Wells Brown to Amy Post, 3 September 1844, in *Black Abolitionist Papers* Microfilm 04:0910; *The Protectionist*, July 1, 1841; "'Sifting In,'" *Liberator*, September 1, 1843; Edwin Fussell, *National Anti-Slavery Standard*, November 2, 1843.

167. Newman, *The Transformation of American Abolitionism*, 163.

168. Massachusetts Anti-Slavery Society, *Fourteenth Annual Report*, 57–58.

5 / "An Odd Place for Navigation": Itinerant Lecturers and Freedom of Speech, 1830–1849

1. John O. Wattles, *Free Labor Advocate and Anti-Slavery Chronicle*, October 15, 1842.

2. Pasley, *"The Tyranny of Printers,"* 8–9, 173.

3. Hamm, *God's Government Begun*, 4, 7–8, 221, 223.

4. See also John O. Wattles, "Letter from John O. Wattles," *National Anti-Slavery Standard*, October 6, 1842. For similar pleas for eastern attention, "Letter from Dr. Brooke, of Ohio," *Liberator*, March 24, 1843; Erasmus D. Hudson, "From Sherman, St. Joseph's County, Michigan."

5. Rugh, *Our Common Country*, 21; Davis, *Frontier Illinois*, 17, 170; Nation, *At Home in the Hoosier Hills*, 2; Gilje, *Rioting in America*, 80–81.

6. Lucretia Mott to Nathaniel and Elisa Barney, 30 and 31 October, 1847, in Mott, *Selected Letters*, 156–58; Hallowell, *James and Lucretia Mott: Life and Letters*, 292; Lucretia Mott to Edward N. Hallowell, 1 February 1870, in Mott, *Selected Letters*, 432.

7. Ronald G. Walters, *American Reformers, 1815–1860*, American Century Series (New York: Hill and Wang, 1978), 32–33.

8. Donald M. Scott, "Print and the Public Lecture System, 1840–1860," in *Printing and Society in Early America*, ed. William L. Joyce, et al. (Worcester: American Antiquarian Society, 1983), 281.

9. Walters, *American Reformers*, 23–24, 37.

10. Ryan, "Civil Society as Democratic Practice," 237; Lewis Perry, *Boats against the Current: American Culture between Revolution and Modernity, 1820–1860* (New York: Oxford University Press, 1993), 177–79.

11. Walters, *American Reformers*, 6; Newman, *The Transformation of American Abolitionism*, 157.

12. Walters, *American Reformers*, 81.

13. Vernon L. Volpe, "Theodore Dwight Weld's Antislavery Mission in Ohio," *Ohio History* 100 (1991).

14. Records of the Young Men's Antislavery Society, Recognized Sept. 14th, 1851, Oberlin, Ohio, Fletcher Papers; M. M. Clark to Prof. H[enry] Cowles, 9 January 1837, Fletcher Papers; *National Anti-Slavery Standard*, October 22, 1840; James O. Bond, *Chickamauga and the Underground Railroad: A Tale of Two Grandfathers* (Baltimore: Gateway Press, 1993), 58–62; Malvin, *North into Freedom*, 66–67.

15. Volpe, "Theodore Dwight Weld's Antislavery Mission in Ohio"; Dillon, "Elizabeth Chandler and the Spread of Anti-Slavery Sentiment to Michigan," 481, 483, 490–91; Kooker, "The Anti-Slavery Movement in Michigan," 93; Davis, *Black Americans in Cleveland*, 12; Barnes and Dumond, eds., *Letters of Theodore Dwight Weld, Angelina Grimké Weld, and Sarah Grimké*, vol. 1, 260–61. For the "agency system" outside of the Old Northwest see Newman, *The Transformation of American Abolitionism*, 163, 152–53.

16. O. E. Morse, "Sketch of the Life and Work of Augustus Wattles," *Collections of the Kansas State Historical Society* 17 (1928): 292–93; Clayton Sumner Ellsworth, "Oberlin and the Anti-Slavery Movement up to the Civil War" (PhD diss., Cornell University, 1930), 36.

17. Albert Hale to Asa Turner, 26 January 1838, Manuscript Collection, Abraham Lincoln Presidential Library, Springfield, Illinois.

18. Hamm et al., "Moral Choices: Two Indiana Quaker Communities and the Abolitionist Movement," 119–20.

19. John L. Myers, "American Antislavery Society Agents and the Free Negro, 1833–1838," *Journal of Negro History* 52, no. 3 (1967): 211; Morse, "Sketch of the Life and Work of Augustus Wattles," 292–93.

20. Newman, *The Transformation of American Abolitionism*, 8, 11, 104.

21. Gilje, *Rioting in America*, 81; Feldberg, *The Turbulent Era*, 44.

22. Curtis, *Free Speech*, 4–5; Nye, *Fettered Freedom*, 88–90; Lawrence Thomas Lesick, *The Lane Rebels: Evangelicalism and Antislavery in Antebellum America*, Studies in Evangelicalism No. 2 (Metuchen, NJ: Scarecrow Press, 1980).

23. Curtis, *Free Speech*, 12–13.

24. Ibid., 144, 231, 4, 250–51; Portnoy, *Their Right to Speak*, 186; Zaeske, *Signatures of Citizenship*, 3.

25. Curtis, *Free Speech*, 250–51.

26. Lidsky and Wright, *Freedom of the Press*, 5.

27. Barnes and Dumond, eds., *Letters of Theodore Dwight Weld, Angelina Grimké Weld, and Sarah Grimké*, vol. 1, 205–7, 237–39, 260–61.

28. Charles Robert Donaldson, "The Antislavery Career of Marius Robinson, 1834–1861" (master's thesis, The Ohio State University, 1970), 27, 32–33, 48, 95; Arthur D. Lersch, "Marius Racine Robinson: The Life and Beliefs of a Radical Abolitionist" (master's thesis, Kent State University, 1988), 59.

29. Marius R. Robinson to Emily Robinson, 25 January 1837, Robinson Papers.

30. Hale to Turner.

31. E. Anthony Rotundo, *American Manhood: Transformations in Masculinity from the Revolution to the Modern Era* (New York: BasicBooks, 1993).

32. "Proceedings of the Liberty Convention, Knox County, ILL," *Peoria Register*, June 13, 1842.

33. *Western Citizen*, August 8, 1844.

34. Ibid.

35. Richards, *"Gentlemen of Property and Standing,"* 3.

36. Joan E. Cashin, "Black Families in the Old Northwest," *Journal of the Early Republic* 15, no. 3 (1995): 472.

37. Linda K. Kerber, "Separate Spheres, Female Worlds, Woman's Place."

38. Marius R. Robinson, "Free Discussion," June 15, 1837, Robinson Papers.

39. Ibid.

40. Ibid.

41. Charles Galbreath, "Anti-Slavery Movement in Columbiana County," *Ohio Archaeological and Historical Quarterly* 30, no. 4 (1921): 366.

42. Ibid., 367.

43. Robinson, "Free Discussion."

44. Ibid.

45. Donaldson, "The Antislavery Career of Marius Robinson, 1834–1861," 43.

46. Marius R. Robinson to Emily Robinson, 29 January 1837, Robinson Papers; Galbreath, "Anti-Slavery Movement in Columbiana County," 368–69.

47. Robinson, "Free Discussion."

48. Donaldson, "The Antislavery Career of Marius Robinson, 1834–1861," 46.

49. Massachusetts Anti-Slavery Society, *Eighteenth Annual Report, Presented to the Massachusetts Anti-Slavery Society, by Its Board of Managers* (1850; reprint, Westport, CT: Negro Universities Press, 1970), 69.

50. Donaldson, "The Antislavery Career of Marius Robinson, 1834–1861," 27, 32–33, 48, 95; Lersch, "Marius Racine Robinson: The Life and Beliefs of a Radical Abolitionist," 59; Michigan Anti-Slavery Society Daybook, vol. 4.

51. See also Hudson, "Letter from Richmond, Wayne County, Indiana,"

52. E. D. Hudson, "From Mt. Pleasant, Ohio," *National Anti-Slavery Standard*, September 23, 1841.

53. *National Anti-Slavery Standard*, May 27, 1841.

54. Burleigh and Hudson found similar issues in Columbus, Ohio, later in 1841: E. D. Hudson, "Letter from Richmond, Wayne County, Indiana," *National Anti-Slavery Standard*, October 21, 1841.

55. G. B. Stebbins, "Our Cause in Ohio," *Liberator*, July 25, 1845.

56. Harris, *The History of Negro Servitude in Illinois*, 151.

57. Spencer Diaries, 13 April 1844.

58. Ibid., 13 December 1843.

59. Ibid., 25, 27, 30 May 1846.

60. Ripley, *Black Abolitionist Papers*, vol. 3, 224; *The Protectionist*, October 1, 1841.

61. Garrison and Ruchames, *The Letters of William Lloyd Garrison*, vol 4, xxv–xxvi.

62. Hudson, "Letter from Richmond, Wayne County, Indiana." See also Charles V. Dyer to Mr. Gillet, 22 May 1847, Correspondence, Treasurer, Oberlin College Archives, Oberlin College, Oberlin, Ohio; Gwendolyn J. Crenshaw and Indiana Historical Bureau, *"Bury Me in a Free Land": The Abolitionist Movement in Indiana, 1816–1865: The Catalog* (Indianapolis: Indiana Historical Bureau, 1986), 38; Massachusetts Anti-Slavery Society, *Eighteenth Annual Report*; Charles Grandison Finney, *The Original Memoirs of Charles Grandison Finney* (Grand Rapids: Zondervan, 1989),

284–85; "Abolition Convention of the Northwest," *Philanthropist,* July 16, 1846; "The Celebration of the Passage of the Ordinance of 1787," *National Era,* July 26, 1849; A Stranger, "University of Michigan," *New York Evangelist,* September 10, 1846; Garrison and Merrill, *The Letters of William Lloyd Garrison*, vol. 3, 519.

63. Hudson, "From Delaware, Ohio"; Kooker, "The Anti-Slavery Movement in Michigan," 285–86.

64. E. D. Hudson, "Letter from Oberlin, Ohio," *National Anti-Slavery Standard,* December 23, 1841. See also Thomas E. Thomas and Alfred A. Thomas, *Correspondence of Thomas Ebenezer Thomas, Mainly Relating to the Anti-Slavery Conflict in Ohio, Especially in the Presbyterian Church* (Dayton, Ohio: 1909), 27; Galbreath, "Anti-Slavery Movement in Columbiana County," 366.

65. Hudson, "From Mt. Pleasant, Ohio"; Hudson, "Letter from Oberlin, Ohio."

66. Hudson, "Letter from Richmond, Wayne County, Indiana"; Hudson, "From Sherman, St. Joseph's County, Michigan"; Hudson, "From Delaware, Ohio"; Hudson, "Letter from Oberlin, Ohio."

67. *National Anti-Slavery Standard,* February 4, 1841.

68. *National Anti-Slavery Standard,* February 4, 1841; *The Protectionist,* February 16, 1841; Thomas, *Correspondence,* 27–28, 73.

69. *National Anti-Slavery Standard,* July 8, 1841; Thomas, *Correspondence,* 29–30.

70. Hallowell, ed. *James and Lucretia Mott: Life and Letters,* 292.

71. Hudson, "Letter from Richmond, Wayne County, Indiana."

72. See also "Society of Friends in Indiana," *National Anti-Slavery Standard,* March 23, 1843; *National Anti-Slavery Standard,* December 30, 1841.

73. Arnold Buffum, The *Protectionist,* August 7, 1841.

74. Holloway, "Abolition Lecturers—Disgraceful Conduct &C," *Richmond Palladium,* October 9, 1841; *National Anti-Slavery Standard,* November 11, 1841; "Abolition-Palladium," Richmond *Palladium,* March 6, 1841.

75. Holloway, "Abolition Lecturers—Disgraceful Conduct &C"; Buffum, The *Protectionist,* August 7, 1841, 237.

76. *National Anti-Slavery Standard,* November 11, 1841. See also Catherine Stebbins in 1861: C. A. F. S., "Pro-Slavery Mob at Ann Arbor," *Liberator,* March 1, 1861.

77. *National Anti-Slavery Standard,* November 11, 1841.

78. *National Anti-Slavery Standard,* December 30, 1841; *The Protectionist,* November 16, 1841.

79. Hudson, "From Sherman, St. Joseph's County, Michigan."

80. Rebecca Lewis Fussell in Graceanna Lewis, "Anti-Slavery Reminiscences: The Mobbing of Frederick Douglass in 1843," *Friends' Intelligencer,* June 20, 1896, 398; Edwin Fussell to Rebecca Fussell, 14 April 1843, Lewis–Fussell Papers, Friends Historical Library, Swarthmore College, Swarthmore, Pennsylvania (hereafter cited as Lewis–Fussell Papers); Agnes Longstreth Taylor, *The Longstreth Family Records, Revised and Enlarged by Agnes Longstreth Taylor* (Philadelphia: Press of Ferris & Leach, 1909), 112–13.

81. Hudson, "From Sherman, St. Joseph's County, Michigan."

82. Sydney H. Gay, *Liberator,* October 20, 1843; James Monroe, *Free Labor Advocate,* October 29, 1843; Ripley, *Black Abolitionist Papers,* vol. 3, 318–19; Raimund Erhard Goerler, "Family, Self, and Anti-Slavery: Sydney Howard Gay and the Abolitionist Commitment" (PhD diss., Case Western University, 1975).

83. Gay, *Liberator,* October 20, 1843; Monroe, *Free Labor Advocate,* October 29, 1843; Edwin Fussell, *National Anti-Slavery Standard,* November 2, 1843.

84. Sydney H. Gay, *Liberator,* October 20, 1843; Monroe, *Free Labor Advocate,* October 29, 1843.

85. Edwin Fussell, *National Anti-Slavery Standard,* November 2, 1843; Sydney H. Gay, *Liberator,* October 20, 1843.

86. Charles L. Remond to Isaac and Amy Post, 27 September 1843 in Ripley, *Black Abolitionist Papers,* vol. 3, 318–19, 417.

87. Remond to Post, 417.

88. "John A. Collins and Co," *Free Labor Advocate and Anti-Slavery Chronicle,* July 4, 1843; Ripley, *Black Abolitionist Papers,* vol. 3, 422.

89. Gamble, "Garrisonian Abolitionists in the West," 57; Kraditor, *Means and Ends in American Abolitionism.*

90. Massachusetts Anti-Slavery Society, *Twelfth Annual Report, Presented to the Massachusetts Anti-Slavery Society, by Its Board of Managers* (1844; reprint, Westport, CT: Negro Universities Press, 1970), 33.

91. "Address of the Board of Managers of the Massachusetts Anti-Slavery Society, to the Abolitionists of the Western and Middle States," *National Anti-Slavery Standard,* June 22, 1843; Ibid., 33, 34.

92. John A. Collins, born 1810 in Vermont, was the general agent for the Massachusetts Society. Ripley, *Black Abolitionist Papers,* vol. 3, 88, 314, 422; Massachusetts Anti-Slavery Society, *Eleventh Annual Report, Presented to the Massachusetts Anti-Slavery Society, by Its Board of Managers* (1843; reprint, Westport, CT: Negro Universities Press, 1970), 45, 56.

93. Fussell in Lewis, "Anti-Slavery Reminiscences," 399; Edwin Fussell to Rebecca Fussell, 17 June 1843, Lewis–Fussell Papers; Edwin Fussell to Rebecca Fussell, 14 April 1843; Taylor, *The Longstreth Family Records,* 112–13.

94. Maria Weston Chapman, "One Hundred Conventions," *Liberator,* August 25, 1843; Maria Weston Chapman, "The One Hundred Conventions," *Liberator,* September 22, 1843; Sydney Howard Gay, "The Conventions. Letter from Sydney Howard Gay," *Liberator,* August 17, 1843; Sydney Howard Gay, "The Conventions. Letter from Sydney Howard Gay," *Liberator,* August 13, 1843; William A. White, *Liberator,* July 20, 1843; Maria Weston Chapman, "One Hundred Conventions," *Liberator,* July 14, 1843.

95. Abraham Brooke, *National Anti-Slavery Standard,* August 10, 1843; Edwin Fussell, "Progress in Indiana," *National Anti-Slavery Standard,* September 7, 1843; John A. Collins, "Grand Anti-Slavery Movement: *To the Abolitionists of New-York, Ohio, Indiana, and Pennsylvania,*" in "Address of the Board of Managers of the Massachusetts Anti-Slavery Society, to the Abolitionists of the Western and Middle States," *National Anti-Slavery Standard,* June 22, 1843.

96. Fussell, *National Anti-Slavery Standard,* September 7, 1843.

97. Massachusetts Anti-Slavery Society, *Twelfth Annual Report,* 35.

98. Sydney Howard Gay, *National Anti-Slavery Standard,* March 7, 1844.

99. Thornbrough, *The Negro in Indiana,* 64.

100. William A. White, *Liberator,* September 6, 1843; William A. White, "Letter from Ohio," *National Anti-Slavery Standard,* August 31, 1843.

101. White, *National Anti-Slavery Standard,* August 31, 1843; Sydney Howard Gay,

National Anti-Slavery Standard, September 19, 1843; Ripley, *Black Abolitionist Papers,* vol. 3, 422–23; Thomas A. Hendrickson, "Sheltering a Famous Fugitive Slave, Part I," *Black History News and Notes* (2001): 4; William Still, *The Underground Railroad,* The American Negro, His History and Literature (1842; reprint, New York: Arno Press, 1968), 111, 303, 748–750.

102. Massachusetts Anti-Slavery Society, *Twelfth Annual Report,* 35.

103. White, *Liberator,* September 6, 1843.

104. Campbell Gibson, "Population of the 100 Largest Cities and Other Urban Places in the United States: 1790 to 1990," (Washington, DC: U.S. Bureau of the Census, 1998), Table 7.

105. Bradburn, *National Anti-Slavery Standard,* September 18, 1843. The three men mobbed earlier were James G. Birney, John Rankin, and Thomas Morris.

106. Thornbrough, *The Negro in Indiana,* 130; Ferguson, "In Pursuit of Full Enjoyment of Liberty and Happiness," 124.

107. *Free Labor Advocate and Anti-Slavery Chronicle,* September 8, 1843; Graceanna Lewis, "Anti-Slavery Reminiscences;" Bradburn, *National Anti-Slavery Standard,* September 18, 1843; John L. Forkner and Byron H. Dyson, *Historical Sketches and Reminiscences of Madison County, Indiana: A Detailed History of the Early Events of the Pioneer Settlement of the County, and Many Happenings of Recent Years, as Well as a Complete History of Each Township, to Which Is Added Numerous Incidents of a Pleasant Nature, in the Way of Reminiscences and Laughable Occurences* (Anderson, IN: J. L. Forkner, 1897), 750.

108. White, *Liberator,* October 13, 1843.

109. Ibid.

110. Bradburn, *National Anti-Slavery Standard,* September 18, 1843.

111. Ibid.

112. White, *Liberator,* October 13, 1843.

113. Lewis, "Anti-Slavery Reminiscences."

114. Bradburn, *National Anti-Slavery Standard,* September 18, 1843.

115. White, *Liberator,* October 13, 1843.

116. Bradburn, *National Anti-Slavery Standard,* September 18, 1843; Solomon Fussell, to "Nephue," 1 November 1843, Manuscript Collection, Indiana Historical Society, Indianapolis, Indiana.

117. Bradburn, *National Anti-Slavery Standard,* September 18, 1843; White, *Liberator,* October 13, 1843.

118. Bradburn, *National Anti-Slavery Standard,* September 18, 1843.

119. White, *Liberator,* October 13, 1843. For a similar action by women in Knoxville, Illinois, in 1839, see Owen W. Muelder, *The Underground Railroad in Western Illinois* (Jefferson, NC: McFarland & Co., 2008), 22.

120. Bradburn, *National Anti-Slavery Standard,* September 18, 1843.

121. White, *Liberator,* October 13, 1843.

122. Bradburn, *National Anti-Slavery Standard,* September 18, 1843. See also Gay, *National Anti-Slavery Standard,* September 19, 1843.

123. White, *Liberator,* October 13, 1843

124. Bradburn, *National Anti-Slavery Standard,* September 18, 1843.

125. White, *Liberator,* October 13, 1843; David Heighway, "Micajah C. White: A

Forgotten Victim of the Assault on Frederick Douglass," *Preserving Indiana* (2001): 5; Coffin, *Reminiscences of Levi Coffin*, 229.

126. White, *Liberator,* October 13, 1843; Lewis, "Anti-Slavery Reminiscences"; Bradburn, *National Anti-Slavery Standard,* September 18, 1843.

127. Bradburn, *National Anti-Slavery Standard,* September 18, 1843; James H. Cook, "Fighting with Breath, Not Blows: Frederick Douglass and Antislavery Violence," in *Antislavery Violence: Sectional, Racial, and Cultural Conflict in Antebellum America*, ed. John R. McKivigan and Stanley Harrold (Knoxville: University of Tennessee Press, 1999), 132.

128. Fussell in Lewis, "Anti-Slavery Reminiscences."

129. White, *Liberator,* September 6, 1843.

130. Jeffrey, *The Great Silent Army of Abolitionism*, 50–51.

131. White, *Liberator,* October 13, 1843.

132. Bradburn, *National Anti-Slavery Standard,* September 18, 1843.

133. Lewis, "Anti-Slavery Reminiscences"; Forkner and Dyson, *Historical Sketches and Reminiscences of Madison County, Indiana*, 751.

134. White, *Liberator,* October 13, 1843; Bradburn, *National Anti-Slavery Standard,* September 18, 1843.

135. F., "Mobs in Madison County," *Free Labor Advocate and Anti-Slavery Chronicle,* November 1, 1843.

136. White, *Liberator,* October 13, 1843; Bradburn, *National Anti-Slavery Standard,* September 18, 1843.

137. Hendrickson, "Sheltering a Famous Fugitive Slave, Part I," 3–4.

138. Fussell in Lewis, "Anti-Slavery Reminiscences."

139. *Friends' Intelligencer,* June 20, 1896.

140. *Indiana Courier,* quoted in "The Mob," *Free Labor Advocate and Anti-Slavery Chronicle,* October 13, 1843; "Mob at Pendleton," *Free Labor Advocate and Anti-Slavery Chronicle,* October 6, 1843.

141. Bradburn, *National Anti-Slavery Standard,* September 18, 1843; White, *Liberator,* October 13, 1843.

142. Fussell in Lewis, "Anti-Slavery Reminiscences," 398–99.

143. Bradburn, *National Anti-Slavery Standard,* September 18, 1843.

144. Gilje, *Rioting in America*, 80–81.

145. Bradburn, September 18, 1843; Fussell in Lewis, "Anti-Slavery Reminiscences," 399; Solomon Fussell to "Nephue," 1 November 1843.

146. Bradburn, September 18, 1843.

147. Fussell in Lewis, "Anti-Slavery Reminiscences," 399.

148. Bradburn, September 18, 1843; William A. White, *Liberator,* October 13, 1843; Edwin Fussell, *National Anti-Slavery Standard,* November 2, 1843; Sarah Galbreath to Cousin, July 3, 1838, Thomas Papers.

149. F., "Mobs in Madison County," *Free Labor Advocate and Anti-Slavery Chronicle,* November 1, 1843.

150. Richards, *"Gentlemen of Property and Standing,"* 5, 16, 77, 158–59.

151. Edwin Fussell, November 2, 1843.

152. F., November 1, 1843; To His Excellency Samuel Bigger Governor of the State of Indiana, Secretary of State Early Petitions, Indiana State Archives, Indianapolis,

Indiana. F.'s account claimed the fine was twenty dollars, but the pardon petition text is a more reliable source.

153. "The Andertown Mob," *Liberator*, December 15, 1843. For McAllister's terms of service in the 1840s and 1850s, see Dorothy Riker and Gayle Thornbrough, *Indiana Election Returns, 1816–1851*, Indiana Historical Collections (Indianapolis: Indiana Historical Bureau, 1960), 275, 282, 358

154. Edwin Fussell, November 2, 1843.

155. Ibid.

156. To His Excellency Samuel Bigger Governor of the State of Indiana.

157. Ibid.; Edwin Fussell, *National Anti-Slavery Standard*, February 15, 1844; Edwin Fussell, November 2, 1843.

158. Edwin Fussell, February 15, 1844; Edwin Fussell, November 2, 1843.

159. Edwin Fussell, November 2, 1843.

160. F., November 1, 1843.

161. Fussell, *National Anti-Slavery Standard*, September 7, 1843; Edwin Fussell to Rebecca Lewis Fussell, 17 June 1843, Lewis–Fussell Papers; "Notice," *Free Labor Advocate and Anti-Slavery Chronicle*, January 1, 1844; Hamm, *God's Government Begun*, 91; V[alentine]. Nicholson, *Free Labor Advocate and Anti-Slavery Chronicle*, December 29, 1843; Massachusetts Anti-Slavery Society, *Twelfth Annual Report*, 34; Martha Hampton to John Mott, 18 December 1843, John Mott Papers, Manuscript Collection, Bentley Historical Library, University of Michigan, Ann Arbor, Michigan; Frederic May Holland, *Frederick Douglass: The Colored Orator*, ed. Carlos Martyn, American Reformers (New York: Funk and Wagnalls, 1895), 89, 90.

162. Solomon Fussell to "Nephue," 1 November 1843; Hamm, *God's Government Begun*, 99; Edwin Fussell, Edwin Coats, and John Thomas, "Chester County Conventions," *National Anti-Slavery Standard*, March 28, 1844; Edwin Fussell, "Extract from a Letter from Edwin Fussell," *National Anti-Slavery Standard*, October 3, 1844.

163. Edwin Fussell, "Extract from a Letter from Edwin Fussell;" Edwin Fussell, November 2, 1843. [Italics in original.]

164. "Triumph of Mob Law—A Governor Intimidated," *Liberator*, November 17, 1843.

165. Edwin Fussell, October 3, 1844. Anderson remained resistant to racial progressivism even into the next century. A case in point was the fact that his race prevented the famed African American leader Booker T. Washington from obtaining a hotel room in town in 1900. Madison, "Race, Law," 49.

166. Edwin Fussell, 18 March 1844.

167. Edwin Fussell to Rebecca Fussell, 15 May, 1848, Lewis–Fussell Papers. [Italics in original.]

168. Ibid.

169. Ibid.

170. Kersey Grave, *Free Labor Advocate*, October 4, 1843.

171. Ibid.; Lerner, *The Grimké Sisters from South Carolina*, 91, 130.

172. "A Mob in Richmond," *Free Labor Advocate and Anti-Slavery Chronicle*, October 6, 1843; Grave, *Free Labor Advocate*, October 4, 1843.

173. *Wayne County Record*, quoted in *Free Labor Advocate and Anti-Slavery Chronicle*, October 6, 1843.

174. Ibid.

175. "A Mob in Richmond," *Free Labor Advocate and Anti-Slavery Chronicle*, October 6, 1843.

176. P. Q. R., "To John B. Still, Esq," *Free Labor Advocate and Anti-Slavery Chronicle*, October 13, 1843.

177. Ibid.; *Free Labor Advocate and Anti-Slavery Chronicle*, October 6, 1843. For the "colorometer," see also *Free Labor Advocate*, February 4, 1843; June 30, 1848.

178. "The Mob," *Free Labor Advocate and Anti-Slavery Chronicle*, October 13, 1843; Benjamin Stanton, "The Palladium—The Record," *Free Labor Advocate and Anti-Slavery Chronicle*, November 8, 1843; *Richmond Palladium*, September 2, 1843; October 7, 1843.

179. Stanton, *Free Labor Advocate and Anti-Slavery Chronicle*, November 8, 1843; *Richmond Palladium*, October 28, 1843. Leonard Richards echoed this point in his 1970 study. Richards, *"Gentlemen of Property and Standing,"* 5, 132.

180. Gay, *Liberator*, October 20, 1843; Monroe, *Free Labor Advocate*, October 29, 1843.

181. *Free Labor Advocate and Anti-Slavery Chronicle*, September 8, 1843.

182. Remond to Post, 417, 423; Fussell, *National Anti-Slavery Standard*, November 2, 1843.

183. *Free Labor Advocate and Anti-Slavery Chronicle*, September 8, 1843.

184. Gay, *Liberator*, October 20, 1843.

185. Fussell, *National Anti-Slavery Standard*, November 2, 1843; Gay, *Liberator*, October 20, 1843; Ibid. See also *Free Labor Advocate and Anti-Slavery Chronicle*, September 8, 1843; Fussell, *National Anti-Slavery Standard*, September 7, 1843.

186. Monroe, *Free Labor Advocate*, October 29, 1843; Fussell, *National Anti-Slavery Standard*, November 2, 1843.

187. Gay, *Liberator*, October 20, 1843; Monroe, *Free Labor Advocate*, October 29, 1843.

188. Monroe, *Free Labor Advocate*, October 29, 1843; Fussell, *National Anti-Slavery Standard*, November 2, 1843.

189. McCarthy and Stauffer, *Prophets of Protest*; Stauffer, *The Black Hearts of Men*, 1; Goodman, *Of One Blood*, xvi, 45.

190. Gay, *Liberator*, October 20, 1843.

191. Sydney Howard Gay to James Monroe, 5 September [1844?], Monroe Papers; Frederick Douglass to James Monroe, 17 April, 1880, Monroe Papers.

192. Benjamin Stanton, "Editor's Excursion," *Free Labor Advocate and Anti-Slavery Chronicle*, February 23, 1842; Gay, "The Conventions," *Liberator*, August 17, 1843; White, *National Anti-Slavery Standard*, August 31, 1843; Coates," *National Anti-Slavery Standard*, September 28, 1843; White, *Liberator*, September 6, 1843; White, *National Anti-Slavery Standard*, August 31, 1843; Gay, *National Anti-Slavery Standard*, September 19, 1843; Perry, *Boats against the Current*, 178; Massachusetts Anti-Slavery Society, *Twelfth Annual Report*, 35–36.

193. Massachusetts Anti-Slavery Society, *Twelfth Annual Report*, 35.

194. *The Protectionist*, October 1, 1841; E. Q. [Edmund Quincy?], "The Hundred Conventions," *Liberator*, September 29, 1843; Sidney Howard Gay, "The Conventions," *Liberator*, August 17, 1843; Bradburn, *National Anti-Slavery Standard*, September 18, 1843.

195. E. D. Hudson, "Letter from Oberlin, Ohio."

196. Hudson, "To The Editor," September 16, 1841; E. D. Hudson, "From Mt. Pleasant, Ohio," *National Anti-Slavery Standard,* September 23, 1841; Hudson, "Letter from Richmond, Wayne County, Indiana."

197. Massachusetts Anti-Slavery Society, *Twelfth Annual Report,* 35–36. See also Gay, "The Conventions," *Liberator,* August 13, 1843; Gay, "The Conventions. Letter from Sydney Howard Gay," *Liberator,* August 17, 1843; Gay, *Liberator,* October 20, 1843.

198. G. B. Stebbins, "Our Cause in Ohio," *Liberator,* July 25, 1845; Abby K.[elly] F.[oster], 8 November 1846; Giles Badger Stebbins, *Upward Steps of Seventy Years. Autobiographic, Biographic, Historic* (New York: United States Book Company, 1890), 89. Local activists also at times crossed partisan lines as they accompanied the itinerants and spoke along with them. Gay, "The Conventions," *Liberator,* August 17, 1843; White, *National Anti-Slavery Standard,* August 31, 1843; Coates, *National Anti-Slavery Standard,* September 28, 1843; Fussell, *National Anti-Slavery Standard,* November 2, 1843.

199. Gay, *National Anti-Slavery Standard,* September 19, 1843. For other accounts of Old Northwest hospitality, see E. D. Hudson, "Letter from Richmond, Wayne County, Indiana"; James Monroe, *Free Labor Advocate,* October 29, 1843; Gay, *Liberator,* October 20, 1843; Coffin, *Reminiscences of Levi Coffin,* 228.

200. Gay, *National Anti-Slavery Standard,* September 19, 1843; Thomas D. Hamm, *The Anti-Slavery Movement in Henry County, Indiana: A Study of the Local Abolitionists* (Henry County Historical Society Inc., 1975), 2.

201. Remond to Post, 416, 417, 420; Massachusetts Anti-Slavery Society, *Twelfth Annual Report,* 35–36.

202. Charles Lenox Remond to Susan B. Anthony, 26 November 1857, in Elizabeth Cady Stanton, Susan B. Anthony, and Ann D. Gordon, *The Selected Papers of Elizabeth Cady Stanton and Susan B. Anthony* (New Brunswick, N.J.: Rutgers University Press, 1997), 359.

203. DeBlasio, "'The Greatest Woman in the Reserve,'" 231.

204. Gay, *Liberator,* October 20, 1843; Remond to Post, 416–17, 419–20.

205. Donaldson, "The Antislavery Career of Marius Robinson, 1834–1861," 37.

206. Maria Weston Chapman, "The One Hundred Conventions," *Liberator,* September 22, 1843; *Liberator,* August 25, 1843; O[restes] K. Hawley to James Monroe, August 1843, Monroe Papers; Gay, *National Anti-Slavery Standard,* September 19, 1843.

207. James Monroe, *Free Labor Advocate,* October 29, 1843.

208. Gay, *Liberator,* October 20, 1843.

209. Fussell, *National Anti-Slavery Standard,* November 2, 1843.

210. Gay, *Liberator,* October 20, 1843.

211. "The Anti-Slavery Convention on the 15th and 16th," *Liberator,* September 22, 1843; "Mr. Monroe's Lectures," *Liberator,* October 13, 1843.

212. Samuel Crothers quoted in Thomas, *Correspondence,* 37–38. See also *New Lisbon Advocate* quoted in "Frederick Douglass," *Liberator,* November 17, 1843.

213. "Humanity," *Liberator,* October 13, 1843. See also Monroe, *Free Labor Advocate,* October 29, 1843; A. J. Gordon, "Testimonials of Respect to C. Lenox Remond," *Liberator,* November 10, 1843.

214. Massachusetts Anti-Slavery Society, *Twelfth Annual Report,* 35.

215. Gay, "The Conventions," *Liberator,* August 17, 1843; Bradburn, *National Anti-Slavery Standard,* September 18, 1843; White, *Liberator,* September 6, 1843.

216. White, *National Anti-Slavery Standard,* August 31, 1843.

217. Massachusetts Anti-Slavery Society, *Twelfth Annual Report,* 36, 37–38.

6 / Itinerant Lecturers in a Fracturing Nation, 1850–1861

1. Josephine S. Griffing, "The Western Field," *Liberator,* April 12, 1861.

2. Holley, *A Life for Liberty,* 62, 94; Massachusetts Anti-Slavery Society, *Twentieth Annual Report, Presented to the Massachusetts Anti-Slavery Society, by Its Board of Managers* (1852; reprint, Westport, CT: Negro Universities Press, 1970), 59, 60.

3. Johnson, *The Liberty Party, 1840–1848,* 251; Watson, "The Anatomy of a Crusade"; "The Berwick Affair, Again," *Galesburg Free Democrat,* April 24, 1856.

4. Massachusetts Anti-Slavery Society, *Nineteenth Annual Report, Presented to the Massachusetts Anti-Slavery Society, by Its Board of Managers* (1851; reprint, Westport, CT: Negro Universities Press, 1970), 59.

5. Sterling, *Ahead of Her Time,* 14, 27, 32, 110, 220, 242, 386; Johnson, *The Liberty Party,* 297, 298.

6. Abby Kelly Foster to Betsy M. Cowles, 28 January 1846, Cowles Papers; B.[etsy] B. Hudson to Betsy Cowles, 27 February 1846, Cowles Papers; Massachusetts Anti-Slavery Society, *Fourteenth Annual Report,* 53; Massachusetts Anti-Slavery Society, *Fifteenth Annual Report, Presented to the Massachusetts Anti-Slavery Society, by Its Board of Managers* (1847; reprint, Westport, CT: Negro Universities Press, 1970), 60.

7. Sterling, *Ahead of Her Time,* 261.

8. Holley, *A Life for Liberty,* 94; Massachusetts Anti-Slavery Society, *Twentieth Annual Report,* 60.

9. Holley, *A Life for Liberty,* 8, 45, 51, 59–60, 62, 65.

10. Sallie Holley, "Anti-Slavery at the West," *Liberator,* September 30, 1853.

11. Lerner, *The Grimké Sisters from South Carolina,* 143–44.

12. Holley, "Anti-Slavery at the West."

13. Helen M. Cowles to Miss A. Y. Hawkins, 3 March 1846, Fletcher Papers.

14. William Lloyd Garrison to Helen Garrison, 15 October 1853, in Garrison and Ruchames, *The Letters of William Lloyd Garrison,* vol. 4, 269–70.

15. Captain Franklin Ellis, *History of Columbia County, New York* (Philadelphia: Everts and Ensign, 1878), 346–47.

16. Kooker, "The Anti-Slavery Movement in Michigan," 173, 175; J. R. Lawler, February 16, 1837; Lillian Drake Avery, ed. *An Account of Oakland County* (Dayton, Ohio: National Historical Association, Inc., 1925), 62. Similar events ensued in 1839. See Kooker, "The Anti-Slavery Movement in Michigan," 285.

17. Stanton, Anthony, and Gordon, *The Selected Papers of Elizabeth Cady Stanton and Susan B. Anthony,* vol. 1, 341, n. 4.

18. Michigan Anti-Slavery Society Daybook, vol. 4.

19. R. Glazier Jr., "Chapter II. From My Note Book," *Liberator,* March 14, 1856.

20. Dillon, *The Abolitionists,* 205.

21. "Border Ruffianism in Monmouth: A Colored Speaker Mobbed." *Galesburg Free Democrat,* March 13, 1856.

22. Ibid., "Eggs vs. Argument," *Galesburg Free Democrat,* March 13, 1856; *Portrait*

and Biographical Album of Warren County, Illinois (Chicago: Chapman Brothers, 1886), 763.

23. "Border Ruffianism in Monmouth: A Colored Speaker Mobbed."

24. Ibid.

25. Still, *The Underground Railroad*, 755–56, 758, 761, 764.

26. Shirley J. Yee, *Black Women Abolitionists: A Study in Activism, 1828–1860* (Knoxville: University of Tennessee Press, 1992), 117.

27. Rhodes, *Mary Ann Shadd Cary*, 131, 221.

28. Olive Gilbert and Frances W. Titus, *Narrative of Sojourner Truth*, The American Negro: His History and Literature (1878; reprint, New York: Arno Press, 1968), ii-iii, 136.

29. Augusta Rohrbach, "Profits of Protest: The Market Strategies of Sojourner Truth and Louisa May Alcott," in *Prophets of Protest*, 251–52.

30. William Hayward, "Pro-Slavery in Indiana," *Liberator*, October 15, 1858.

31. Gwendolyn J. Crenshaw and Indiana Historical Bureau, *"Bury Me in a Free Land,"* 39.

32. Painter, *Sojourner Truth: A Life, a Symbol*, 139–40.

33. Ibid., 142; Gilbert and Titus, *Narrative of Sojourner Truth*, 132–36.

34. T. R. Davis, "Lectures By Miss Watkins," *Liberator*, February 24, 1860.

35. The concept of uplifting the race was common in speeches and writings by middle-class African Americans from the antebellum period and throughout the remainder of the century. Emma Jones Lapsansky, "The World the Agitators Made: The Counterculture of Agitation in Urban Philadelphia," in *The Abolitionist Sisterhood*, 98.

36. Frances Ellen Watkins Harper to Jane E. Hitchcock Jones, 21 September 1860, Green Plain, Ohio, in Ripley, *Black Abolitionist Papers*, vol. 5, 81–82.

37. Marius R. Robinson, "Extract of a Letter from Marius R. Robinson," *Liberator*, February 24, 1860.

38. Michigan Anti-Slavery Society Daybook, vol. 1; Gamble, "Garrisonian Abolitionists in the West," 64.

39. Stebbins, *Upward Steps of Seventy Years*.

40. Dillon, *The Abolitionists*, 214; *Annual Reports of the American Anti-Slavery Society, by the Executive Committee, for the Years Ending May 1, 1857 and May 1, 1858* (New York: American Anti-Slavery Society, 1859), 187–88; *Annual Report Presented to the American Anti-Slavery Society, by the Executive Committee, at the Annual Meeting, Held in New York, May 7, 1856. With an Appendix* (New York: American Anti-Slavery Society, 1856), 52–53.

41. *Anti-Slavery Bugle*, October 23, 1858; Sterling, *Ahead of Her Time*, 310–11, 328.

42. H. Ford Douglas, Speech Delivered at the Town Hall, Salem, Ohio, 23 September 1860; *Anti-Slavery Bugle*, October 6, 1860, in Ripley, *Black Abolitionist Papers*, vol. 5, 88–91.

43. This differs from Nye's and Richards's findings. Richards, *"Gentlemen of Property and Standing,"* 159; Nye, *Fettered Freedom*, 175.

44. Quist, *Restless Visionaries*, 364, 422.

45. Jacob Walton and Catherine A. F. Stebbins, "Michigan Anti-Slavery Convention," *National Anti-Slavery Standard*, February 16, 1861; C. A. F. S., "Pro-Slavery Mob at Ann Arbor," *Liberator*, March 1, 1861; Painter, *Sojourner Truth: A Life, a Symbol*, 144.

46. Stebbins, *Upward Steps of Seventy Years*, 147–149; Nancy A. Hewitt, *Women's Activism and Social Change: Rochester, New York, 1822–1872* (Ithaca, N.Y.: Cornell University Press, 1984), 192.

47. Walton and Stebbins, "Michigan Anti-Slavery Convention."

48. Stebbins, *Upward Steps of Seventy Years*, 115.

49. Walton and Stebbins, "Michigan Anti-Slavery Convention."

50. Parker Pillsbury, "Pro-slavery Mob at Ann Arbor," *Liberator*, February 8, 1861.

51. C. A. F. S., "Pro-Slavery Mob at Ann Arbor."

52. Pillsbury, "Pro-slavery Mob at Ann Arbor"; Richards, *"Gentlemen of Property and Standing,"* 3.

53. C. A. F. S., "Pro-Slavery Mob at Ann Arbor."

54. Ibid.

55. Walton and Stebbins, "Michigan Anti-Slavery Convention."

56. C. A. F. S., "Pro-Slavery Mob at Ann Arbor."

57. Hewitt, *Women's Activism and Social Change*, 131.

58. Walton and Stebbins, "Michigan Anti-Slavery Convention."

59. Curtis, *Free Speech*, 209.

60. Walton and Stebbins, "Michigan Anti-Slavery Convention"; C. A. F. S., "Pro-Slavery Mob at Ann Arbor."

61. Parker Pillsbury, "Convention at Livonia," *Liberator*, February 15, 1861.

62. C. A. F. S., "Pro-Slavery Mob at Ann Arbor." She dated this letter February 8, 1861.

63. Ibid.

64. Josephine S. Griffing, "Letter from Mrs. J. S. Griffing," *Liberator*, February 15, 1861; Pillsbury, "Convention at Livonia," February 15, 1861.

65. Griffing, "Letter from Mrs. J. S. Griffing."

66. Griffing, "The Western Field."

67. Painter, *Sojourner Truth: A Life, a Symbol*, 179.

68. Gilbert and Titus, *Narrative of Sojourner Truth*, 140.

69. Josephine S. Griffing, "Treason in Disguise," *Liberator*, June 21, 1861.

70. Josephine S. Griffing, "Shameful Persecution," *Liberator*, June 28, 1861.

71. Griffing, "Treason in Disguise."

72. Painter, *Sojourner Truth: A Life, a Symbol*, 181

73. Griffing, "Treason in Disguise."

74. Griffing, "Shameful Persecution."

75. Ibid.

76. *National Anti-Slavery Standard*, February 16, 1843.

7 / The Potential for Radical Change: The Turbulent 1850s, the Civil War, and Resilient Racism

1. Finkelman, "The Historical Context of the Fourteenth Amendment," 398.

2. Finkelman, "Race, Slavery, and the Law in Antebellum Ohio," 774–75.

3. Samuel Ringgold Ward, "Speech by Samuel Ringgold Ward," in Ripley, *Black Abolitionist Papers*, vol. 4, 50.

4. John Mercer Langston to Frederick Douglass, *Frederick Douglass' Paper*, April 20, 1855 in Ripley, *Black Abolitionist Papers*, vol. 4, 7, 70, 281. See also Middleton, *The Black Laws: Ohio*, 84, 85; Johnson, *The Liberty Party, 1840–1848*, 255.

5. Jeffrey, *The Great Silent Army of Abolitionism*, 45, 84; Larry Gara, "Slavery and the Slave Power: A Crucial Distinction," *Civil War History* 15 (1969): 6, 9.

6. Augustus C. French, *Message of the Governor of the State of Illinois, to the Seventeenth General Assembly, Convened January 6, 1851* (Springfield: Lanphier & Walker, 1851).

7. Middleton, *The Black Laws: Ohio*, 23, 38, 59; Will Co. Illinois Anti-Slavery Society, *Slave Code*, 10–11.

8. Glasman, "Zebina Eastman," 54–55.

9. "All About the Black Laws," Galesburg *Free Democrat*, January 12, 1854.

10. Gliozzo, "John Jones," 181, 183, 118.

11. Madison, "Race, Law," 46.

12. Marius Robinson, *Anti-Slavery Bugle*, April 4, 1857.

13. Litwack, *North of Slavery*, 61–63, 265.

14. Finkelman, "Slavery, the 'More Perfect Union,' and the Prairie State," 256, 266.

15. Ibid., 256, 268.

16. *Anti-Slavery Bugle*, April 25, 1857; May 16, 1857; Middleton, *The Black Laws: Ohio*, 242, 245.

17. Gliozzo, "John Jones," 182.

18. Mabee, *Black Freedom*; Steven Hahn, *A Nation under Our Feet: Black Political Struggles in the Rural South, from Slavery to the Great Migration* (Cambridge, MA: Belknap Press of Harvard University Press, 2003); Horton and Horton, *In Hope of Liberty*; Howard Holman Bell, "Expressions of Negro Militancy in the North, 1840–1860," *Journal of Negro History* 45, no. 1 (1960).

19. Curry, *The Free Black in Urban America, 1800–1850*, 230.

20. Junger, "'God and Man Helped Those Who Helped Themselves,'" 118.

21. Morris, *Free Men All*, 164–65.

22. Catherine M. Rokicky, *James Monroe: Oberlin's Christian Statesman and Reformer, 1821–1898* (Kent, OH: Kent State University Press, 2002), 41–42; Ellsworth, "Oberlin and the Anti-Slavery Movement up to the Civil War," 136; L. D. Griswold to James Monroe, 2 February 1857, Monroe Papers.

23. Middleton, *The Black Laws: Ohio*, 245.

24. Kooker, "The Anti-Slavery Movement in Michigan," 55–57. The efforts in the Old Northwest to use personal liberty laws to oppose fugitive slave recovery measures were in line with several northeastern states in the mid-1850s, including Massachusetts, Connecticut, Rhode Island, and Maine. In that same time period New York voted against such a law, while Pennsylvania took no such action. Morris, *Free Men All*, 168. The lack of consensus on this issue prevalent in the Old Northwest was also true of other northern states.

25. Gliozzo, "John Jones," 183; Dorothy Sterling, *We Are Your Sisters: Black Women in the 19th Century*, (New York: W.W. Norton, 1984), 147–49.

26. Gliozzo, "John Jones," 183.

27. *Proceedings of the First Convention of the Colored Citizens of the State of Illinois Convened at the City of Chicago, October 6th, 7th, and 8th, 1853*, in *Proceedings of the Black State Conventions, 1840–1865*, ed. Philip Sheldon Foner and George E. Walker, vol. 2 (Philadelphia: Temple University Press, 1986), 59, 61.

28. Ibid., 62.

29. *Proceedings of the State Convention of the Colored Men of the State of Ohio, Held*

in the City of Columbus, January 21st, 22d, and 23d, 1857, in *Proceedings of the Black State Conventions*, vol. 1, 318.

30. Yee, *Black Women Abolitionists*, 144–45; Salerno, *Sister Societies*, 105–6.

31. *Report of the Proceedings of the Colored National Convention, Held at Cleveland, Ohio, 1848*, 12, 17.

32. *Minutes of the State Convention, of the Colored Citizens of Ohio, 1850*, 250; *Minutes of the State Convention of the Colored Citizens of Ohio, Convened at Columbus, Jan. 15th, 16th, 17th, and 18th, 1851*, in *Proceedings of the Black State Conventions*, vol. 1, 266. See also *Proceedings of the State Convention of Colored Men, Held in the City of Columbus, Ohio, Jan. 16th, 17th, and 18th, 1856*, in Ibid., 307.

33. *Proceedings of the National Convention of Colored Men, Held in the City of Syracuse, N.Y., October 4, 5, 6, and 7, 1864; with the Bill of Wrongs and Rights, and the Address to the American People* (Boston: J. S. Rock and Geo. L. Ruffin, 1864), 7, 10.

34. *Proceedings of a Convention of the Colored Men of Ohio. Held in the City of Cincinnati, on the 23rd, 24th, 25th, and 26th Days of November, 1858*, in *Proceedings of the Black State Conventions*, vol. 1, 334, 337.

35. *Proceedings of the National Convention of Colored Men, 1864*, 15, 25.

36. *Proceedings of the Colored Men's Convention of the State of Michigan, Held in the City of Detroit, Tuesday and Wednesday, Sept 12th and 13th, '65, with Accompanying Documents. Also, the Constitution of the Equal Rights League of the State of Michigan*, in *Proceedings of the Black State Conventions*, vol. 1, 200.

37. Rosemarie Zagarri, *Revolutionary Backlash: Women and Politics in the Early American Republic*, Early American Studies (Philadelphia: University of Pennsylvania Press, 2007), 185.

38. Quist, *Restless Visionaries*, 406.

39. Finkenbine, "A Beacon of Liberty on the Great Lakes," 93.

40. Ohio Constitution of 1851, Article 5, in Middleton, *The Black Laws in the Old Northwest*, 12; Ripley, *Black Abolitionist Papers*, vol. 4, 224. These sales did occur, as late as 1863 when officials at Carthage sold six African Americans for living illegally in the state. Arthur Charles Cole, *The Centennial History of Illinois: The Era of the Civil War, 1848–1870*, vol. 3 (Springfield: Illinois Centennial Commission, 1919), 335.

41. Elijah Coffin, Charles Fisher Coffin, and Mary Coffin Johnson, *The Life of Elijah Coffin; with a Reminiscence, by His Son Charles F. Coffin. Edited by His Daughter, Mary C. Johnson. Printed for His Family Only* (Cincinnati?: E. Morgan & Sons, 1863), 78, 80.

42. Gliozzo, "John Jones," 188, 185.

43. Finkelman, "Race, Slavery, and the Law in Antebellum Ohio," 751, 764.

44. Katzman, *Before the Ghetto*, 35–36.

45. "First of August in Columbus, Ohio." *Frederick Douglass' Paper*, August 11, 1854; Frederick Douglass, *Oration, Delivered in Corinthian Hall, Rochester, by Frederick Douglass, July 5th, 1852* (Rochester: Lee, Mann & Co., 1852).

46. Ripley, *Black Abolitionist Papers*, vol. 4, 292.

47. *Proceedings of the Convention, of the Colored Freemen of Ohio, Held in Cincinnati, January 14, 15, 16, 17 and 19, 1852*, in *Proceedings of the Black State Conventions*, vol. 1, 277.

48. *Memorial of John Mercer Langston for Colored People of Ohio to General Assembly of the State of Ohio, June, 1854*, in *Proceedings of the Black State Conventions*, vol. 1, 297.

49. *Proceedings of the State Convention of Colored Men, 1856*, 310–12, 314.

50. Madison, "Race, Law," 45.

51. Pascoe, *What Comes Naturally*, 51.

52. Gliozzo, "John Jones," 185; *Proceedings of the State Convention of Colored Citizens of the State of Illinois, Held in the City of Alton November 13th, 14th, and 15th, 1856*, in *Proceedings of the Black State Conventions*, vol. 2, 71–72.

53. *Proceedings of a Convention of the Colored Men of Ohio, 1858*, 336, 339; *Proceedings of the State Convention of the Colored Men of the State of Ohio, 1857*, 320, 326.

54. Madison, "Race, Law," 43; Thornbrough, *The Negro in Indiana*, 132–33; Indiana General Assembly, *Journal of the Indiana State Senate, During the Called Session of the General Assembly, Commencing Saturday, November 20, 1858* (Indianapolis: Joseph J. Bingham, 1858), 12–13.

55. Gliozzo, "John Jones," 184; Katzman, *Before the Ghetto*, 40; Finkenbine, "A Beacon of Liberty on the Great Lakes," 100.

56. William J. Whipper to Benjamin S. Jones, 15 April 1859, in *Anti-Slavery Bugle*, April 23, 1859, in Ripley, *Black Abolitionist Papers*, vol. 5, 15; William F. Cheek and Aimee Lee Cheek, *John Mercer Langston and the Fight for Black Freedom, 1829–65*, Blacks in the New World (Urbana: University of Illinois Press, 1989), 366. [Italics in original.]

57. Ripley, *Black Abolitionist Papers*, vol. 5, 17.

58. Ibid., 15, 18.

59. Offenses against Lives: Kidnapping and Selling as Slaves, §17–18, Approved July 15, 1838, [Michigan] *Revised Statutes*, in Middleton, *The Black Laws in the Old Northwest*, 356–57.

60. Morris, *Free Men All*, 187–88.

61. Ibid., 216; Finkelman, "Race, Slavery, and the Law in Antebellum Ohio," 769, 773.

62. Dillon, *The Abolitionists*, 237, 240.

63. "The Ohio Republican Platform," *The McKean Citizen*, June 25, 1859.

64. Pascoe, *What Comes Naturally*, 53.

65. Hermann R. Muelder, "Congregationalists and the Civil War," in *A History of Illinois Congregational and Christian Churches*, 156.

66. Dillon, *The Abolitionists*, 258–59.

67. H. Ford Douglas, Speech Delivered at the Town Hall, Salem, Ohio, 23 September 1860, in *Anti-Slavery Bugle*, October 6, 1860, in Ripley, *Black Abolitionist Papers*, vol. 5, 88–91; Ripley, *Black Abolitionist Papers*, vol. 4, 78–79.

68. Eric Foner, *Reconstruction: America's Unfinished Revolution, 1863–1877* (New York: Perennial Classics, 2002), 26–27; Rhodes, *Mary Ann Shadd Cary*, 156.

69. Frederick M. Gittes, "Paper Promises: Race and Ohio Law after 1860," in *The History of Ohio Law*, 783.

70. V. Jacque Voegeli, *Free but Not Equal: The Midwest and the Negro During the Civil War* (Chicago: University of Chicago Press, 1967), 1; McPherson, *The Struggle for Equality*, 31.

71. Katzman, *Before the Ghetto*, 44.

72. McPherson, *The Struggle for Equality*, 225.

73. Madison, "Race, Law," 48; Katzman, *Before the Ghetto*, 44; Voegeli, *Free but Not Equal*, 172, 17–18, 170; Rhodes, *Mary Ann Shadd Cary*, 156.

74. Finkelman, "Race, Slavery, and the Law in Antebellum Ohio," 774–75.

75. Voegeli, *Free but Not Equal*, 17–18.

76. Gittes, "Paper Promises: Race and Ohio Law after 1860," 782.

77. Middleton, *The Black Laws: Ohio*, 247, 251.

78. Voegeli, *Free but Not Equal*, 88–89.

79. Katzman, *Before the Ghetto*, 44; Thomas Buckner et. al., *The Late Detriot Riot* (Detroit: 1863).

80. Gliozzo, "John Jones," 185; Hermann R. Muelder, *A Hero Home from the War: Among the Black Citizens of Galesburg, Illinois, 1860–1880* (Galesburg: Knox College Library, 1987), 8.

81. Eric Foner, *A Short History of Reconstruction, 1863–1877* (New York: Harper & Row, 1990), 8, 9, 10–11, 13, 14.

82. Roberta Sue Alexander, "A Place of Recourse: The Changing Role of the Federal District Court for the Southern District of Ohio," in *The History of Ohio Law*, 279.

83. Ripley, *Black Abolitionist Papers*, vol. 5, 171; Mitchell, *Anti-Slavery Politics in Antebellum and Civil War America*, 207, 210.

84. Madison, "Race, Law," 48; Voegeli, *Free but Not Equal*: 17–18, 170; Rhodes, *Mary Ann Shadd Cary*, 156.

85. Foner, *Reconstruction*, 241; Foner, *A Short History of Reconstruction, 1863–1877*, 8, 9, 10–11, 13, 14.

86. Voegeli, *Free but Not Equal*, 25, 67.

87. Foner, *A Short History of Reconstruction, 1863–1877*, 135, 204.

88. Kusmer, *A Ghetto Takes Shape*, 9.

89. Ripley, *Black Abolitionist Papers*, vol. 5, 171; Mitchell, *Anti-Slavery Politics in Antebellum and Civil War America*, 207, 210.

90. Voegeli, *Free but Not Equal*, 161.

91. Ira Berlin, Joseph P. Reidy, and Leslie S. Rowland, *The Black Military Experience*, vol. 2, Freedom: A Documentary History of Emancipation, 1861–1867 (New York: Cambridge University Press, 1982), 6.

92. J. L. Stevens to Hon. Mr. Cameron, 10 August 1861 in Berlin, Reidy, and Rowland, *The Black Military Experience*, 78-79; Finkenbine, "A Beacon of Liberty on the Great Lakes," 98; G. P. Miller to Simon Cameron, 30 October 1861, in Berlin, Reidy, and Rowland, *The Black Military Experience*, 79; W. T. Boyd and J. T. Alston to Hon. Simon Cameron, 15 November 1861, in Berlin, Reidy, and Rowland, *The Black Military Experience*, 80; Wm. A. Jones to Hon S. Cameron, 27 November 1861, in Berlin, Reidy, and Rowland, *The Black Military Experience*, 80–81.

93. Governor Richard Yates to President Lincoln, 11 July 1862, in Berlin, Reidy, and Rowland, *The Black Military Experience*, 84–85. See also Berlin, Reidy, and Rowland, *The Black Military Experience*, 9.

94. May 22 General Order No. 143, 1863, Orders and Circulars, 1797–1910, Records of the Adjutant General's Office, 1780s–1917, Record Group 94 (National Archives, Washington, DC).

95. Finkenbine, "A Beacon of Liberty on the Great Lakes," 98; Berlin, Reidy, and Rowland, *The Black Military Experience*, 75–76.

96. Ripley, *Black Abolitionist Papers*, vol. 5, 286

97. Ibid., 11, 312.

98. Foner, *Reconstruction*, 286.

99. Gliozzo, "John Jones," 184, 186, 187; John Jones, *The Black Laws of Illinois, and a Few Reasons Why They Should Be Repealed* (Chicago: Tribune Book and Job Office, 1864).

100. *Proceedings of a Convention of the Colored Men of Ohio, Held in Xenia, on the 10th, 11th, and 12th Days of January, 1865; with the Constitution of the Ohio Equal Rights League*, in *Proceedings of the Black State Conventions*, vol. 1, 342, 350.

101. David A. Gerber, *Black Ohio and the Color Line, 1860–1915*, Blacks in the New World (Urbana: University of Illinois Press, 1976), 35.

102. *Proceedings of the First Annual Meeting of the National Equal Rights League, Held in Cleveland, Ohio, October 19, 20, and 21, 1865*, in *Proceedings of the Black National and State Conventions*, vol. 1, 44, 52, 47, 48, 50, 55.

103. Stewart, *Abolitionist Politics and the Coming of the Civil War*, 159.

104. Roediger, *The Wages of Whiteness*, 174–75.

105. Foner, *A Short History of Reconstruction, 1863–1877*, 12; David Montgomery, *Beyond Equality: Labor and the Radical Republicans, 1862–1872* (New York: Knopf, 1967), 83.

106. Illinois General Assembly, *An Act to Repeal Section Sixteen of the Revised Statutes, Entitled "An Act to Prevent the Immigration of Free Negroes into This State," Commonly Known as The "Black Laws"* (February 7, 1865).

107. Gliozzo, "John Jones," 187, 188.

108. Richard Yates, "Message of His Excellency, Richard Yates, Governor of Illinois, to the General Assembly. January 2, 1865," *Chicago Tribune*, January 5, 1865.

109. Middleton, *The Black Laws: Ohio*, 254; Davis, *Black Americans in Cleveland*, 85–86; Montgomery, *Beyond Equality*, 83.

110. Foner, *Reconstruction*, 31; Gittes, "Paper Promises: Race and Ohio Law after 1860," 784, 785.

111. Gliozzo, "John Jones," 188; *Proceedings of the Illinois State Convention of Colored Men, 1866*, 257, 246, 249, 260.

112. *State Convention of the Colored People of Indiana, Indianapolis, October 24, 1865*, in *Proceedings of the Black National and State Conventions*, vol. 1, 186; Indiana General Assembly, *An Act to Amend "An Act in Relation to Witnesses" and to Repeal Section 238 of Article 13, of an Act Entitled an Act to Revise, Simplify, and Abridge the Rules in Cases of the Courts of This State* (December 21, 1865).

113. Middleton, *The Black Laws in the Old Northwest*, 374, 375.

114. Paul Finkelman, "The Promise of Equality and the Limits of Law: From the Civil War to World War II," in *The History of Michigan Law*, 192, 193, 194.

115. Montgomery, *Beyond Equality*, 83.

116. Finkelman, "The Promise of Equality," 199; Finkenbine, "A Beacon of Liberty on the Great Lakes," 102.

117. Litwack, *North of Slavery*, 278–79; Schwalm, *Emancipation's Diaspora*, 177.

118. Gittes, "Paper Promises: Race and Ohio Law after 1860," 787, 788.

119. Richard L. Aynes, "Ohio and the Drafting and Ratification of the Fourteenth Amendment," in *The History of Ohio Law*, 394–95; United States and George P. Sanger, *The Statutes at Large, Treaties, and Proclamations of the United States of America from December 1867, to March 1869*, vol. 15 (Boston: Little, Brown, 1869), 710–11.

120. *Address of the Colored Men's Border State Convention to the People of the*

United States, Baltimore, August 5–6, 1868, in *Proceedings of the Black National and State Conventions*, vol. 1, 323.

121. These states were Maine, Massachusetts, New Hampshire, Rhode Island, and Vermont. Hugh Davis, *We Will Be Satisfied with Nothing Less: The African American Struggle for Equal Rights in the North During Reconstruction* (Ithaca, NY: Cornell University Press, 2011), 40.

122. Ibid., 9.

123. By 1870, Kentucky, Delaware, Maryland, West Virginia, Virginia, Missouri, and Tennessee led the way into "Redemption," as their governments became Democrat dominated. Ibid., 74–75, 94–95, 117; Foner, *Reconstruction*, 421–22. While the situation of Reconstruction-era African American rights in the North was generally bleak, for more on activists' victories in the 1870s and 1880s, see Davis, *We Will Be Satisfied*, 142–48.

124. Middleton, *The Black Laws: Ohio*, 153; Benedict, "Civil Liberty in Ohio," 690.

125. Gittes, "Paper Promises: Race and Ohio Law after 1860," 790, 789.

126. Ibid., 791; Middleton, *The Black Laws: Ohio*, 254; Alexander, "A Place of Recourse," 280.

127. Benedict, "Civil Liberty in Ohio," 686–87.

128. Gliozzo, "John Jones," 188; Charles Branham, "Black Chicago: Accommodationist Politics before the Great Migration," in *The Ethnic Frontier: Essays in the History of Group Survival in Chicago and the Midwest*, ed. Melvin G. Holli and Peter d'Alroy Jones (Grand Rapids: William B. Eerdmans Publishing Company, 1977), 188, 257; Muelder, *A Hero Home from the War*, 12, 15.

129. Madison, "Race, Law," 43, 47, 48–49.

130. Finkelman, "The Promise of Equality," 198, 199; Finkenbine, "A Beacon of Liberty on the Great Lakes," 102.

131. Katzman, *Before the Ghetto*, 37–38; McPherson, *The Struggle for Equality*, 420.

132. Michael Grossberg and Amy Elson, "Family Law in Indiana: A Domestic Relations Crossroads," in *The History of Indiana Law*, 68, 67.

133. Middleton, *The Black Laws in the Old Northwest*, 265.

134. Finkelman, "The Promise of Equality," 198; Finkenbine, "A Beacon of Liberty on the Great Lakes," 102.

135. Middleton, *The Black Laws: Ohio*, 247, 251.

136. Although the state omitted the provisions forbidding interracial marriage from the 1874 volume of the Illinois state legal code, this may have been due to an oversight, and thus sent no definitive message about Illinoisans' views on these laws. It does not represent a repeal, as Pascoe calls it. No records exist that indicate that this was the product of deliberate action, so it is impossible to know whether it was a conscious or overt act. Pascoe, *What Comes Naturally*, 40, 333; David H. Fowler, *Northern Attitudes toward Interracial Marriage: Legislation and Public Opinion in the Middle Atlantic and States of the Old Northwest, 1780–1930* (New York: Garland Publishing, Inc., 1987), 251–52.

137. Muelder, *A Hero Home from the War*, 12.

138. Middleton, *The Black Laws in the Old Northwest*, 161; Voegeli, *Free but Not Equal*, 172, 182.

139. Gittes, "Paper Promises: Race and Ohio Law after 1860," 797–98.

140. Finkenbine, "A Beacon of Liberty on the Great Lakes," 102; Rhodes, *Mary Ann Shadd Cary*, 165, 167; Katzman, *Before the Ghetto*, 24, 33, 35–36, 37.

Conclusion

1. Eric Foner, *A Short History of Reconstruction*, 205, 101–2; William Gillette, *The Right to Vote: Politics and the Passage of the Fifteenth Amendment*, Johns Hopkins University. Studies in Historical and Political Science, Ser. 83, No. 1 (Baltimore: Johns Hopkins Press, 1965), 25–27; Leslie H. Fishel Jr., "Northern Prejudice and Negro Suffrage, 1865-1870," *Journal of Negro History* 39, no. 1 (1954): 15; *Proceedings of the Illinois State Convention of Colored Men, 1866*, 246, 248, 249, 252–53, 254.

2. Paul Finkelman, "The Promise of Equality and the Limits of Law: From the Civil War to World War II," in *The History of Michigan Law*, 198.

3. *Ibid.*, 199; Madison, "Race, Law," 49.

Bibliography

Archival Collections

Abraham Lincoln Presidential Library, Springfield, Illinois

Ichabod Codding Family Papers
Earnest E. East, "History of Peoria," 1946
Albert Hale Letter, 1838
Illinois Anti-Slavery Society Papers
"Journal of the Upper Alton Lyceum"
Elijah Lovejoy Papers
Owen Lovejoy Papers
E. Russell Letter, 1838
Levi Spencer Diaries
State of Illinois, Randolph County, "To the People of the State of Illinois," 1836
Samuel Willard Papers

Bentley Historical Library, University of Michigan, Ann Arbor, Michigan

Guy Beckley Papers
Elizabeth M. Chandler Papers
Laura S. Haviland Papers
Lucian H. Jones Papers
Michigan Anti-Slavery Society Daybook
John Mott Papers
Charles Osborn Letters

Chicago History Museum, Chicago, Illinois

H. O. Wagoner Letter, 1884
Samuel Willard, "The Riot in Alton Ill. Nov. 7. 1837," December 25, 1879

Clements Library, Ann Arbor, Michigan

African-American History Collection
"Michigan Anti-Slavery Society Daybook, Vol. 1," Harriet deGarmo Fuller Collection
"Michigan Anti-Slavery Society Daybook, Vol. 4," 1853–1857, Harriet deGarmo Fuller Collection
Owen Lovejoy Collection
Quaker Collection

Friends Historical Library, Swarthmore College, Swarthmore, Pennsylvania

Dugdale Papers
Rebecca Lewis Fussell Correspondence
Lewis–Fussell Papers

Friends Manuscript Collection, Earlham College, Lilly Library, Richmond, Indiana

Elijah Coffin Papers
Levi Coffin Collection
Robert Nixon Huff Papers
Osborn Family Collection
Pusey Graves Collection

Haverford College, Haverford, Pennsylvania

Coffin Family Letters
Charles H. Moore Papers
William Parker Scrapbook
Updegraff Collection

Indiana Historical Society, Indianapolis, Indiana

James Eastman Letter, 1849
Economy Anti-Slavery Society, "The Economy (Wayne Co.) Anti-Slavery Society, Auxiliary to the Indiana State Anti-Slavery Society, Organized First Month 27th 1840, Minute Book." 1840.
Solomon Fussell Letter, 1843
Oliver N. Huff, "Old Newport: A Paper Read By Dr. O. N. Huff Before the Wayne County Historical Society," August 31, 1900
Society of Friends Collection, "Deer Creek Meeting of Anti-Slavery Friends [Men's Meeting]," 1843–1855

Society of Friends Collection, "Deer Creek Monthly Meeting Of Anti-Slavery Women Friends," 1843–1856

Indiana State Archives, Indianapolis, Indiana

Governor Samuel Bigger: Governors' Correspondence 1840–1843
Governor Morton Correspondence, Civil War Years
Secretary of State Early Petitions
Secretary of State Pardons and Remissions Book, 1830–1854

Indiana State Library, Indianapolis, Indiana

Jacob P. Dunn Papers
George Evans Letters
Minute Book of Neel's Creek Anti-Slavery Society, 1839–1845
"Records of the Henry County Female Anti-Slavery Society," 1841–1849, County Manuscripts Collection
Roberts Settlement Collection: Papers of Roberts Family, Rush, Henry, and Hamilton Counties, 1734–1944

Kent State University, Kent, Ohio

Betsy Mix Cowles Papers, Special Collections

Oberlin College Archives, Oberlin, Ohio

Correspondence, Treasurer
Cowles Papers
Robert S. Fletcher Papers
James Monroe Papers
Hiram Wilson Papers

Ohio Historical Society, Columbus, Ohio

Benjamin Lundy Collection
Rachel M[yers] Letter, c. 1848–1849
Charles Osborn Papers
John Rankin Papers
Benjamin Stanton Correspondence
Wright–Smythe–Condon–Hosack Family Collection

Peoria Public Library, Peoria, Illinois

Samuel H. Davis File, Peoria Public Library Collection
Earnest E. East, "History of Peoria," c. 1950–1965

Southwest Collection, Texas Tech University

Elijah Parish Lovejoy Papers

Western Reserve Historical Society, Cleveland, Ohio

Ashtabula County Female Anti-Slavery Society
Canton Ladies Anti-Slavery Society Records
Marius R. Robinson Papers
Western Anti-Slavery Society Records
White–Ford Family Papers

Newspapers

Anti-Slavery Bugle, Salem, Ohio
Clarion of Freedom, Cambridge and New Concord, Ohio
Evangelist, New York, New York
Frederick Douglass' Paper, Rochester, New York
Free Democrat, Galesburg, Illinois
Free Labor Advocate and Anti-Slavery Chronicle, New Garden, Indiana
Genius of Liberty, Lowell, Illinois
Genius of Universal Emancipation, Mt. Pleasant, Ohio
Liberator, Boston, Massachusetts
Liberty Tree, Chicago, Illinois
National Anti-Slavery Standard, New York, New York
National Era, Washington, DC
Niles' National Register, Baltimore, Maryland
Peoria Register and Northwestern Gazetteer, Peoria, Illinois
Philanthropist, Cincinnati, Ohio
Protectionist, New Garden, Indiana
Richmond Palladium, Richmond, Indiana
Tribune, Chicago, Illinois
Western Citizen, Chicago, Illinois

Printed Primary Sources

An Accompaniment to Mitchell's Reference and Distance Map of the United States. Philadelphia: S. Augustus Mitchell, 1845.

Address of the Colored Men's Border State Convention to the People of the United States, Baltimore, August 5–6, 1868. In *Proceedings of the Black National and State Conventions, 1865–1900*, edited by Philip Sheldon Foner and George E. Walker. Vol. 1, 322–24. Philadelphia: Temple University Press, 1986.

Annual Report Presented to the American Anti-Slavery Society, by the Executive Committee, at the Annual Meeting, Held in New York, May 7, 1856. With an Appendix. New York: American Anti-Slavery Society, 1856.

Annual Reports of the American Anti-Slavery Society, by the Executive Committee, for the Years Ending May 1, 1857 and May 1, 1858. New York: American Anti-Slavery Society, 1859.

Baldwin, Thomas and J. Thomas. *New and Complete Gazetteer of the United States*. Philadelphia: Lippincott, Grambo, and Co., 1854.

Ballance, Charles. *History of Peoria, Illinois.* Peoria: N. C. Nason, 1870.

Barnes, Gilbert Hobbs, and Dwight L. Dumond, eds. *Letters of Theodore Dwight Weld, Angelina Grimké Weld, and Sarah Grimké, 1822–1844.* Vol. 1. 1934. Reprint, Gloucester, MA: Peter Smith, 1965.

Beecher, Lyman. *A Plea for the West.* Cincinnati: Truman and Smith, 1835.

Bell, Howard Holman. *Minutes of the Proceedings of the National Negro Conventions, 1830–1864,* The American Negro: His History and Literature. New York: Arno Press, 1969.

Berlin, Ira, Joseph P. Reidy, and Leslie S. Rowland. *The Black Military Experience.* Vol. 2. Freedom: A Documentary History of Emancipation, 1861–1867. New York: Cambridge University Press, 1982.

Blanchard, Jonathan. *Memoir of Rev. Levi Spencer: Successively Pastor of the Congregational Church at Canton, Bloomington, and Peoria, Illinois.* Cincinnati: American Reform Tract and Book Society, 1856.

Blanchard, Julia. *Blessed Memories: The Life of Mrs. Mary A. Blanchard, by her daughter Julia.* Wheaton: 1890.

Buckner, Thomas, et. al. *The Late Detriot Riot.* Detroit: 1863.

Burnett, Edmund, ed. *The Letters of Members of the Continental Congress.* Vol. 8. Washington, DC: Carnegie Institute of Washington, 1936.

Coffin, Elijah, Charles Fisher Coffin, and Mary Coffin Johnson. *The Life of Elijah Coffin; With a Reminiscence, by His Son Charles F. Coffin. Edited by his Daughter, Mary C. Johnson. Printed for His Family Only.* Cincinnati?: E. Morgan & Sons, 1863.

Coffin, Levi. *Reminiscences of Levi Coffin, the Reputed President of the Underground Railroad.* 1876. Reprint, New York: Arno Press, 1968.

Davis, Mary Brown. *Scenes of Oppression in the Refined Circles of the South; Addressed to the Women of Illinois by Mrs. M. B. Davis*: Peoria County Anti-Slavery Society, 1846.

Davis, Samuel H. *Free Discussion Suppressed in Peoria.* Peoria, IL: Samuel H. Davis, 1843.

Douglass, Frederick. *Oration, Delivered in Corinthian Hall, Rochester, by Frederick Douglass, July 5th, 1852.* Rochester: Lee, Mann & Co., 1852.

Drown, Simeon De Witt. *Drown's Record and Historical View of Peoria from the Discovery by the French Jesuit Missionaries, in the Seventeenth Century, to the Present Time. Also, an Almanac for 1851, Calculated for the Latitude and Longitude of Peoria, Illinois.* Peoria: E. O. Woodcock, 1851.

Eastman, Zebina. "History of the Antislavery Agitation, and the Growth of the Liberty and Republican Parties in the State of Illinois." In *Discovery and Conquests of the Northwest,* edited by Rufus Blanchard. Wheaton: 1879.

Ellsworth, H. L. *Illinois in 1837; A Sketch Descriptive of the Situation, Boundaries, Face of the Country, Prominent Districts, Prairies, Rivers, Minerals, Animal, Agricultural Productions, Public Lands, Plans of Internal Improvement, Manufactures, &c. of the State of Illinois: Also, Suggestions to Emigrants,*

Sketches of the Counties, Cities, and Principal Towns in the State: Together with a Letter on the Cultivation of the Prairies, by the Hon. H. L. Ellsworth. To Which Are Annexed the Letters from a Rambler in the West. Philadelphia: S. Augustus Mitchell, 1837.

Finney, Charles Grandison. *The Original Memoirs of Charles Grandison Finney.* Grand Rapids: Zondervan, 1989.

Foner, Philip Sheldon, and George E. Walker, eds. *Proceedings of the Black National and State Conventions, 1865–1900.* Vol. 1. Philadelphia: Temple University Press, 1986.

———, eds. *Proceedings of the Black State Conventions, 1840–1865.* Vol. 1. Philadelphia: Temple University Press, 1979.

———, eds. *Proceedings of the Black State Conventions, 1840–1865.* Vol. 2. Philadelphia: Temple University Press, 1979.

French, Augustus C. *Message of the Governor of the State of Illinois, to the Seventeenth General Assembly, Convened January 6, 1851.* Springfield: Lanphier & Walker, 1851.

Garrison, William Lloyd, and Walter McIntosh Merrill. *The Letters of William Lloyd Garrison.* Vol. 3. Cambridge: Belknap Press of Harvard University Press, 1971.

Garrison, William Lloyd, and Louis Ruchames. *The Letters of William Lloyd Garrison.* Vol. 4. Cambridge: Belknap Press of Harvard University Press, 1971.

General Order No. 143, May 22, 1863, Orders and Circulars, 1797–1910, Records of the Adjutant General's Office, 1780's-1917, Record Group 94. National Archives, Washington, DC.

Gilbert, Olive, and Frances W. Titus. *Narrative of Sojourner Truth*, The American Negro: His History and Literature. 1878. Reprint, New York: Arno Press, 1968.

Hallowell, Anna Davis, ed. *James and Lucretia Mott: Life and Letters.* Boston: Houghton Mifflin, 1884.

Holley, Sallie, and John White Chadwick. *A Life for Liberty: Anti-Slavery and Other Letters of Sallie Holley.* New York: G. P. Putnam's Sons, 1899.

Illinois Anti-Slavery Convention. *Proceedings of the Illinois Anti-Slavery Convention: held at Upper Alton on the twenty-sixth, twenty-seventh, and twenty-eighth October 1837.* Alton: Parks and Breath, 1838.

Illinois General Assembly. *An Act to Repeal Section Sixteen of the Revised Statutes, entitled "An Act to Prevent the Immigration of Free Negroes into this State," Commonly Known as the "Black Laws."* February 7, 1865.

Illinois Supreme Court. *Decision of the Supreme Court of Illinois in relation to arrest of slaves. Ex parte Thornton. The process by virtue of which the prisoner was arrested, and is now detained, was issued under the provisions of the fifth section of the seventy-fourth chapter of the Revised Statutes.* 1850.

Indiana General Assembly. *An Act to Amend "An Act in Relation to Witnesses" and to repeal Section 238 of Article 13, of an Act Entitled an Act to Revise, Simplify, and Abridge the Rules in Cases of the Courts of this State.* December 21, 1865.

———. *Journal of the Indiana State Senate, During the Called Session of the General Assembly, Commencing Saturday, November 20, 1858.* Indianapolis: Joseph J. Bingham, 1858.

Indiana Yearly Meeting of Friends. *Address to the Citizens of the State of Ohio Concerning What are Called the Black Laws, Issued in behalf of the Society of Friends of Indiana Yearly Meeting, by their Meeting for Sufferings, Representing the Said Yearly Meeting in its Recess [A Large Portion of the Members Reside in the State of Ohio].* Cincinnati: A. Pugh, 1848.

Jones, John. *The Black Laws of Illinois, and a Few Reasons Why They Should Be Repealed.* Chicago: Tribune Book and Job Office, 1864.

Julian, George Washington. *The Rank of Charles Osborn as an Anti-slavery Pioneer.* Indiana Historical Society Publications. Vol. 2, no. 6. Indianapolis: The Bowen-Merrill Company, 1891.

Lincoln, William Sever. *Alton Trials of Winthrop S. Gilman, who was indicted with Enoch Long, Amos B. Roff, George H. Walworth, George H. Whitney, William Harned, John S. Noble, James Morss, Jr., Henry Tanner, Royal Weller, Reuben Gerry, and Theodore B. Hurlbut; for the Crime of Riot, Committed on the Night of the 7th of November, 1837, While Engaged in Defending a Printing Press, from an Attack Made on It at That Time, by an Armed Mob. Written out from Notes of the Trial, Taken at the Time, by a Member of the Bar of the Alton Municipal Court. Also, the Trial of John Solomon, Levi Palmer, Horace Beall, Josiah Nutter, Jacob Smith, David Butler, William Carr, and James M. Rock, Indicted with James Jennings, Solomon Morgan, and Frederick Bruchy; for a Riot Committed in Alton, on the Night of the 7th of November, 1837, in Unlawfully and Forcibly Entering the Warehouse of Godfrey, Gilman, and Co., and Breaking up and Destroying a Printing Press. Written out from Notes Taken at the Time of Trial, by William S. Lincoln, a Member of the Bar of the Alton Municipal Court.* New York: J. F. Trow, 1838.

Lovejoy, Joseph C., and Owen Lovejoy. *Memoir of the Rev. Elijah P. Lovejoy; Who Was Murdered in Defence of the Liberty of the Press, at Alton, Illinois, November 7, 1837.* 1838. Reprint, Freeport, NY: Books for Libraries Press, 1970.

Malvin, John. *North into Freedom: The Autobiography of John Malvin, Free Negro, 1795–1880.* Edited by Allan Peskin. 1879. Reprint, Kent, OH: Kent State University Press, 1988.

———. *Eighteenth Annual Report, Presented to the Massachusetts Anti-Slavery Society, by Its Board of Managers.* 1850. Reprint, Westport, CT: Negro Universities Press, 1970.

———. *Eleventh Annual Report, Presented to the Massachusetts Anti-Slavery Society, by Its Board of Managers.* 1843. Reprint, Westport, CT: Negro Universities Press, 1970.

———. *Fifteenth Annual Report, Presented to the Massachusetts Anti-Slavery Society, by Its Board of Managers.* 1847. Reprint, Westport, CT: Negro Universities Press, 1970.

———. *Fourteenth Annual Report, Presented to the Massachusetts Anti-Slavery Society, by Its Board of Managers.* 1846. Reprint, Westport, CT: Negro Universities Press, 1970.

———. *Nineteenth Annual Report, Presented to the Massachusetts Anti-Slavery Society, by Its Board of Managers.* 1851. Reprint, Westport, CT: Negro Universities Press, 1970.

———. *Twelfth Annual Report, Presented to the Massachusetts Anti-Slavery Society, by Its Board of Managers.* 1844. Reprint, Westport, CT: Negro Universities Press, 1970.

———. *Twentieth Annual Report, Presented to the Massachusetts Anti-Slavery Society, by Its Board of Managers.* 1852. Reprint, Westport, CT: Negro Universities Press, 1970.

Memorial of John Mercer Langston for Colored People of Ohio to General Assembly of the State of Ohio, June, 1854. In *Proceedings of the Black State Conventions, 1840–1865*, edited by Philip Sheldon Foner and George E. Walker. Vol. 1, 297–304. Philadelphia: Temple University Press, 1986.

Michigan State Anti-Slavery Society. *Proceedings of the Second Anniversary of the Michigan State Anti-Slavery Society, Held at Ann Arbor, June 7, 1838.* Detroit: Harsha and Bates, Printers, 1838.

———. *Report of the Meeting of the Michigan State Anti-Slavery Society, June 28, 1837, Being the First Annual Meeting, Adjourned from June 1st, 1837.* Detroit: George L. Whitney, 1837.

Middleton, Stephen. *The Black Laws in the Old Northwest: A Documentary History.* Contributions in Afro-American and African Studies. Westport, CT: Greenwood Press, 1993.

The Minutes and Proceedings of the First Annual Meeting of the American Moral Reform Society, Held at Philadelphia, in the Presbyterian Church in Seventh Street, Below Shippen, from the 14th to the 19th of August, 1837. Philadelphia: Printed By Merrihew And Gunn, No. 7 Carter's Alley, 1837

Minutes of the Fifth Annual Convention for the Improvement of the Free People of Colour in the United States, Held by Adjournment, in the Wesley Church, Philadephia, From the First to the Fifth of June, Inclusive, 1835. Philadelphia: William P. Gibbons, 1835.

Minutes of the State Convention of the Colored Citizens of Michigan. Held in the City of Detroit on the 26th and 27th of October, 1843, for the Purpose of Considering Their Moral and Political Condition as Citizens of the State. Detroit: Printed by William Harsha, 1843.

Minutes of the State Convention of the Colored Citizens of Ohio, Convened at Columbus, Jan. 15th, 16th, 17th, and 18th, 1851. In *Proceedings of the Black State Conventions, 1840–1865*, edited by Philip Sheldon Foner and

George E. Walker. Vol. 1, 257–73. Philadelphia: Temple University Press, 1986.

Minutes of the State Convention, of the Colored Citizens of Ohio, Convened at Columbus, January 9th, 10th, 11th, and 12th, 1850. In *Proceedings of the Black State Conventions, 1840–1865*, edited by Philip Sheldon Foner and George E. Walker. Vol. 1, 241–56. Philadelphia: Temple University Press, 1986.

Mott, Lucretia, Beverly Wilson Palmer, Holly Byers Ochoa, and Carol Faulkner, eds. *Selected Letters of Lucretia Coffin Mott*. Women in American History. Urbana, IL: University of Illinois Press, 2002.

National Convention of Colored Citizens. *Minutes of the National Convention of Colored Citizens: Held at Buffalo, on the 15th, 16th, 17th, 18th, and 19th of August 1843*. New York: Piercy and Reed, 1843.

Ohio Anti-Slavery Society. *Report of the Second Anniversary of the Ohio Anti-Slavery Society held in Mount Pleasant, Jefferson County, Ohio, on the Twenty-Seventh of April, 1837*. Cincinnati: The [Ohio] Anti-Slavery Society, 1837.

Osborn, Charles. *Journal of that Faithful Servant of Christ, Charles Osborn, Containing an Account of Many of His Travels and Labors in the Work of the Ministry, and his Trials and Exercises in the Service of the Lord, and In Defense of the Truth, as it is in Jesus*. Cincinnati: Achilles Pugh, 1854.

Porter, Mary H. *Eliza Chappell Porter, a Memoir*. Chicago: F.H. Revell Company, 1892.

Proceedings of a Convention of the Colored Men of Ohio. Held in the City of Cincinnati, on the 23rd, 24th, 25th, and 26th days of November, 1858. In *Proceedings of the Black State Conventions, 1840–1865*, edited by Philip Sheldon Foner and George E. Walker. Vol. 1, 332–41. Philadelphia: Temple University Press, 1986.

Proceedings of a Convention of the Colored Men of Ohio, Held in Xenia, on the 10th, 11th, and 12th days of January, 1865; With the Constitution of the Ohio Equal Rights League. In *Proceedings of the Black State Conventions, 1840–1865*, edited by Philip Sheldon Foner and George E. Walker. Vol. 1, 342–353. Philadelphia: Temple University Press, 1986.

Proceedings of the Colored Men's Convention of the State of Michigan, Held in the City of Detroit, Tuesday and Wednesday, Sept 12th and 13th, '65, with Accompanying Documents. Also, the Constitution of the Equal Rights League of the State of Michigan. In *Proceedings of the Black State Conventions, 1840–1865*, edited by Philip Sheldon Foner and George E. Walker. Vol. 1, 198–212. Philadelphia: Temple University Press, 1986.

Proceedings of the Convention, of the Colored Freemen of Ohio, Held in Cincinnati, January 14, 15, 16, 17 and 19, 1852. In *Proceedings of the Black State Conventions, 1840–1865*, edited by Philip Sheldon Foner and George E. Walker. Vol. 1, 274–96. Philadelphia: Temple University Press, 1986.

Proceedings of the First Annual Meeting of the National Equal Rights League, Held in Cleveland, Ohio, October 19, 20, and 21, 1865. In *Proceedings of the Black National and State Conventions, 1865–1900*, edited by Philip Sheldon Foner and George E. Walker. Vol. 1, 43–68. Philadelphia: Temple University Press, 1986.

Proceedings of the First Convention of the Colored Citizens of the State of Illinois Convened at the City of Chicago, October 6th, 7th, and 8th, 1853. In *Proceedings of the Black State Conventions, 1840–1865*, edited by Philip Sheldon Foner and George E. Walker. Vol. 2. Philadelphia: Temple University Press, 1986.

Proceedings of the Illinois State Convention of Colored Men, Assembled at Galesburg, October 16th, 17th, and 18th. Containing the State and National Addresses Promulgated by It, With a List of the Delegates Composing It, October 1866. Published by Order of the Convention. In *Proceedings of the Black National and State Conventions, 1865–1900*, edited by Philip Sheldon Foner and George E. Walker. Vol. 1, 248–75. Philadelphia: Temple University Press, 1986.

Proceedings Of The Indiana Convention Assembled To Organize A State Anti-Slavery Society, Held in Milton, Wayne Co., September 12, 1838. Cincinnati: Samuel A. Alley, Printer, 1838.

Proceedings of the National Convention of Colored Men, held in the City of Syracuse, N.Y., October 4, 5, 6, and 7, 1864; with the Bill of Wrongs and Rights, and the Address to the American People. Boston: J. S. Rock and Geo. L. Ruffin, 1864.

Proceedings of the State Convention of Colored Citizens of the State of Illinois, Held in the City of Alton November 13th, 14th, and 15th, 1856. In *Proceedings of the Black State Conventions, 1840–1865*, edited by Philip Sheldon Foner and George E. Walker. Vol. 2. Philadelphia: Temple University Press, 1986.

Proceedings of the State Convention of Colored Men, Held in the City of Columbus, Ohio, Jan. 16th, 17th, and 18th, 1856. In *Proceedings of the Black State Conventions, 1840–1865*, edited by Philip Sheldon Foner and George E. Walker. Vol. 1, 305–17. Philadelphia: Temple University Press, 1986.

Proceedings of the State Convention of the Colored Men of the State of Ohio, Held in the City of Columbus, January 21st, 22d, and 23d, 1857. In *Proceedings of the Black State Conventions, 1840–1865*, edited by Philip Sheldon Foner and George E. Walker. Vol. 1, 318–31. Philadelphia: Temple University Press, 1986.

Purvis, Robert, James Cornish, J. C. Bowers, Robert B. Forten, J. J. G. Bias, James Needham, and John P. Burr. *Appeal of Forty Thousand Citizens, Threatened with Disfranchisement, to the People of Pennsylvania*. Philadelphia: Merrihew and Gunn, 1838.

Report of the Proceedings of the Colored National Convention, Held at Cleveland, Ohio, On Wednesday, September 6, 1848. Rochester: Printed by John Dick, at the North Star Office, 1848.

Reports of Cases Argued and Determined in the Supreme Court of Ohio, Printed by Authority of the General Assembly. Vol. 11. Cincinnati: Robert Clarke and Company, 1873.

Revised Laws Of Indiana in which are Comprised All Such Acts of a General Nature As Are in Force in Said State; Adopted and Enacted by the General Assembly at Their Fifteenth Session. To which are Prefixed the Declaration of Independence, the Constitution of the U. S., the Constitution of the State of Indiana, and Sundry Other Documents, Connected with the Political History of the Territory And State Of Indiana. Arranged and Published by Authority of the General Assembly. Indianapolis: Douglass and Maguire, 1831.

Ripley, C. Peter, ed. *The Black Abolitionist Papers: The United States, 1830–1846.* Vol. 3. Chapel Hill: University of North Carolina Press, 1985.

———, ed. *The Black Abolitionist Papers: The United States, 1847–1858.* Vol. 4. Chapel Hill: University of North Carolina Press, 1985.

———, ed. *The Black Abolitionist Papers: The United States, 1859–1865.* Vol. 5. Chapel Hill: University of North Carolina Press, 1985.

Stanton, Elizabeth Cady, Susan B. Anthony, and Ann D. Gordon. *The Selected Papers of Elizabeth Cady Stanton and Susan B. Anthony.* Vol 1. New Brunswick, NJ: Rutgers University Press, 1997.

State Convention of the Colored People of Indiana, Indianapolis, October 24, 1865. In *Proceedings of the Black National and State Conventions, 1865–1900*, edited by Philip Sheldon Foner and George E. Walker. Vol. 1, 185–86. Philadelphia: Temple University Press, 1986.

Stebbins, Giles Badger. *Upward Steps of Seventy Years. Autobiographic, Biographic, Historic.* New York: United States Book Company, 1890.

Stewart, Maria W. *Maria W. Stewart, America's First Black Political Writer, Essays and Speeches.* Edited by Marilyn Richardson. Bloomington: Indiana University Press, 1987.

Still, William. *The Underground Railroad.* The American Negro: His History and Literature. 1852. Reprint, New York: Arno Press, 1968.

Tanner, Henry. *The Martyrdom of Lovejoy, an account of the life, trials, and perils of Rev. Elijah P. Lovejoy, who was killed by a pro-slavery mob at Alton, Illinois, the night of November 7, 1837. By an eye-witness [Henry Tanner].* 1881. Reprint, New York: Augustus M. Kelley, 1971.

Tappan, Arthur, John Rankin, William Jay, Elizur Wright Jr., Abraham L. Cox, Lewis Tappan, Joshua Leavitt, Samuel E. Cornish, Simeon S. Jocelyn, and Theodore S. Wright. *Address to the Public, Issued by the Executive Committee of the American Antislavery Society, September 3, 1835.* New York.

Thomas, Thomas E., and Alfred A. Thomas. *Correspondence of Thomas Ebenezer Thomas, Mainly Relating to the Anti-Slavery Conflict in Ohio, Especially in the Presbyterian Church.* Dayton, OH: 1909.

United States, and George P. Sanger. *The Statutes at Large, Treaties, and Proclamations of the United States of America from December 1867 to March 1869.* Vol. 15. Boston: Little, Brown, 1869.

Walker, David. *Appeal To the Coloured Citizens of the World.* Edited by Sean Wilentz. 1829. Reprint, New York: Hill and Wang, 1995.

Will Co. Illinois Anti-Slavery Society. *Slave Code of the State of Illinois, Being an Abstract of Those Laws Now in Force in This State, Which Affect the Rights of Colored People, as Such, Both Bond and Free. With Notes*. Juliet, IL: Published by the Will Co. Anti-Slavery Society, 1840.

Secondary Sources

Alexander, Roberta Sue. "A Place of Recourse: The Changing Role of the Federal District Court for the Southern District of Ohio." In *The History of Ohio Law*, edited by Michael Les Benedict and John F. Winkler. Vol. 1, 267–338. Athens: Ohio University Press, 2004.

Anderson, Benedict R. O. *Imagined Communities: Reflections on the Origin and Spread of Nationalism*. London: Verso, 1983.

Aptheker, Herbert. *Abolitionism: A Revolutionary Movement*, Social Movements Past and Present. Boston: Twayne Publishers, 1989.

Ashworth, John. *'Agrarians' and 'Aristocrats': Party Political Ideology in the United States, 1837–1846*. New Jersey: Humanities Press Inc., 1983.

Avery, Lillian Drake, ed. *An Account of Oakland County*. Dayton, OH: National Historical Association, Inc., 1925.

Aynes, Richard L. "Ohio and the Drafting and Ratification of the Fourteenth Amendment." In *The History of Ohio Law*, edited by Michael Les Benedict and John F. Winkler. Vol. 1, 370–401. Athens: Ohio University Press, 2004.

Baker, H. Robert. *The Rescue of Joshua Glover: a Fugitive Slave, the Constitution, and the Coming of the Civil War*, Ohio University Press Series on Law, Society, and Politics in the Midwest. Athens: Ohio University Press, 2006.

Ballance, Charles. *History of Peoria, Illinois*. Peoria: N. C. Nason, 1870.

Barnhart, John D. "The Southern Influence in the Formation of Illinois." *Journal of the Illinois State Historical Society* 32 (1939): 358–78.

Baumann, Roland M. *The 1858 Oberlin-Wellington Rescue: A Reappraisal*. Oberlin: Oberlin College, 2003.

Baumgartner, Sandra Anne. "The Legal Status of the Negro in Illinois as Determined by State Legislation and State Supreme Court Decisions, 1818–1853." Master's thesis, Southern Illinois University, 1966.

Bell, Howard Holman. "Expressions of Negro Militancy in the North, 1840–1860." *Journal of Negro History* 45, no. 1 (1960): 11–20.

Bender, Thomas, John Ashworth, David Brion Davis, and Thomas L. Haskell. *The Antislavery Debate: Capitalism and Abolitionism as a Problem in Historical Interpretation*. Berkeley: University of California Press, 1992.

Benedict, Michael Les. "Civil Liberty in Ohio." In *The History of Ohio Law*, edited by Michael Les Benedict and John F. Winkler. Vol. 2, 675–747. Athens: Ohio University Press, 2004.

Bennett, Lerone. *Forced Into Glory: Abraham Lincoln's White Dream*. Chicago: Johnson Publishing Company, 2000.

Berthoff, Rowland. "Conventional Mentality: Free Blacks, Women, and Business

Corporations as Unequal Persons, 1820–1870." *Journal of American History* 76, no. 3 (1989): 753–84.

Berwanger, Eugene H. *The Frontier Against Slavery: Western Anti-Negro Prejudice and the Slavery Extension Controversy.* Urbana: University of Illinois Press, 1967.

Biographical Encyclopaedia of Illinois of the Nineteenth Century. Philadelphia: Galaxy Publishing Company, 1875.

Blackmore, Josiah H., II. "Not from Zeus's Head Full-Blown: The Story of Civil Procedure in Ohio." In *The History of Ohio Law*, edited by Michael Les Benedict and John F. Winkler. Vol. 1, 441–65. Athens: Ohio University Press, 2004.

Blight, David W. *Frederick Douglass' Civil War: Keeping Faith in Jubilee.* Baton Rouge: Louisiana State University Press, 1989.

Blue, Frederick J. *No Taint of Compromise: Crusaders in Antislavery Politics.* Baton Rouge: Louisiana State University Press, 2005.

Bogin, Ruth, and Jean Fagan Yellin. "Introduction." In *The Abolitionist Sisterhood: Women's Political Culture in Antebellum America*, edited by Jean Fagan Yellin and John C. Van Horne, 1–19. Ithaca: Cornell University Press, 1994.

Bond, James O. *Chickamauga and the Underground Railroad: A Tale of Two Grandfathers.* Baltimore: Gateway Press, 1993.

Branham, Charles. "Black Chicago: Accommodationist Politics Before the Great Migration." In *The Ethnic Frontier: Essays in the History of Group Survival in Chicago and the Midwest*, edited by Melvin G. Holli and Peter d'Alroy Jones, 211–62. Grand Rapids: William B. Eerdmans Publishing Company, 1977.

Burke, Diane Mutti. *On Slavery's Border: Missouri's Small-Slaveholding Households, 1815–1865*, Early American Places. Athens: University of Georgia Press, 2010.

Calhoun, Craig J. *Habermas and the Public Sphere*, Studies in Contemporary German Social Thought. Cambridge, MA: MIT Press, 1992.

Cashin, Joan E. "Black Families in the Old Northwest." *Journal of the Early Republic* 15, no. 3 (1995): 449–75.

Cayton, Andrew R. L. "Law and Authority in the Northwest Territory." In *The History of Ohio Law*, edited by Michael Les Benedict and John F. Winkler. Vol. 1, 13–39. Athens: Ohio University Press, 2004.

Chardavoyne, David G. "The Northwest Ordinance and Michigan's Territorial Heritage." In *The History of Michigan Law*, edited by Paul Finkelman and Martin J. Hershock, 13–36. Athens: Ohio University Press, 2006.

Cheek, William F., and Aimee Lee Cheek. *John Mercer Langston and the Fight for Black Freedom, 1829–65*, Blacks in the New World. Urbana: University of Illinois Press, 1989.

Cole, Arthur Charles. *The Centennial History of Illinois: The Era of the Civil War, 1848–1870.* Vol. 3. Springfield: Illinois Centennial Commission, 1919.

Cook, James H. "Fighting with Breath, not Blows: Frederick Douglass and Antislavery Violence." In *Antislavery Violence: Sectional, Racial, and Cultural Conflict in Antebellum America*, edited by John R. McKivigan and Stanley Harrold, 128–63. Knoxville: University of Tennessee Press, 1999.

Cord, Xenia E. "Black Rural Settlements in Indiana before 1860." In *Indiana's African-American Heritage: Essays From Black History News & Notes*, edited by Wilma L. Gibbs, 99–110. Indianapolis: Indiana Historical Society, 1993.

Corfield, Justin. "Indiana." In *Encyclopedia of U.S. Campaigns, Elections, and Electoral Behavior*, edited by Kenneth F. Warren, 322–25. Thousand Oaks: Sage, 2008.

———. "Michigan." In *Encyclopedia of U.S. Campaigns, Elections, and Electoral Behavior*, edited by Kenneth F. Warren, 407–9. Thousand Oaks: Sage, 2008.

———. "Ohio." In *Encyclopedia of U.S. Campaigns, Elections, and Electoral Behavior*, edited by Kenneth F. Warren, 470–73. Thousand Oaks: Sage, 2008.

Cott, Nancy. *The Bonds of Womanhood: "Woman's Sphere" in New England, 1780–1835*. New Haven: Yale University Press, 1977.

Cramer, Clayton E. *Black Demographic Data, 1790–1860: A Sourcebook*. Westport, CT: Greenwood Press, 1997.

Crenshaw, Gwendolyn J., and Indiana Historical Bureau. *"Bury Me in a Free Land": The Abolitionist Movement in Indiana, 1816–1865: The Catalog*. Indianapolis: Indiana Historical Bureau, 1986.

Cruz, Barbara C., and Michael Berson. "The American Melting Pot? Miscegenation Laws in the United States." *OAH Magazine of History* 15, no. 4 (2001): 80–84.

Curry, Leonard P. *The Free Black in Urban America, 1800–1850: The Shadow of the Dream*. Chicago: University of Chicago Press, 1981.

Curtis, Michael Kent. *Free Speech, "The People's Darling Privilege": Struggles for Freedom of Expression in American History*. Durham: Duke University Press, 2000.

Cyr, Mark Allen. "'I Would Not Be a Master': Democracy and the Political Culture of Mastery in Illinois, 1837–1858." PhD diss., Washington University, 2003.

Dailey, Jane Elizabeth. *Before Jim Crow: The Politics of Race in Postemancipation Virginia*. Gender and American Culture. Chapel Hill: University of North Carolina Press, 2000.

Davis, Hugh. *We Will Be Satisfied with Nothing Less: The African American Struggle for Equal Rights in the North during Reconstruction*. Ithaca: Cornell University Press, 2011.

Davis, James Edward. *Frontier Illinois*. Bloomington: Indiana University Press, 1998.

Davis, Russell H. *Black Americans in Cleveland from George Peake to Carl B. Stokes, 1796–1969*. Washington: Associated Publishers, 1972.

DeBlasio, Donna M. "'The Greatest Woman in the Reserve': Betsy Mix Cowles, Feminist, Abolitionist, Educator." *The Old Northwest* 13 (1987): 223–36.

Deskins, Donald Richard, Hanes Walton, and Sherman C. Puckett. *Presidential Elections, 1789–2008: County, State, and National Mapping of Election Data*. Ann Arbor: University of Michigan Press, 2010.

Dillon, Merton Lynn. *The Abolitionists: The Growth of a Dissenting Minority*. Minorities in American History. DeKalb: Northern Illinois University Press, 1975.

———. "Elizabeth Chandler and the Spread of Anti-Slavery Sentiment to Michigan." *Michigan History* 39, no. 4 (1955): 481–94.

———. *Slavery Attacked: Southern Slaves and Their Allies, 1619–1865*. Baton Rouge: Louisiana State University Press, 1990.

Dixon, Chris. *Perfecting the Family: Antislavery Marriages in Nineteenth Century America*. Amherst: University of Massachusetts Press, 1997.

Donaldson, Charles Robert. "The Antislavery Career of Marius Robinson, 1834–1861." Master's thesis, The Ohio State University, 1970.

Dykstra, Robert R. *Bright Radical Star: Black Freedom and White Supremacy on the Hawkeye Frontier*. Cambridge: Harvard University Press, 1993.

Edwards, Laura. *Gendered Strife and Confusion: The Political Culture of Reconstruction*. Chicago: The University of Illinois Press, 1997.

Ellis, Captain Franklin. *History of Columbia County, New York*. Philadelphia: Everts and Ensign, 1878.

Ellsworth, Clayton Sumner. "Oberlin and the Anti-Slavery Movement up to the Civil War." PhD diss., Cornell University, 1930.

Feldberg, Michael. *The Turbulent Era: Riot and Disorder in Jacksonian America*. New York: Oxford University Press, 1980.

Ferguson, Earline Ray. "In Pursuit of Full Enjoyment of Liberty and Happiness: Blacks in Antebellum Indianapolis, 1820–1860." In *Indiana's African-American Heritage: Essays From Black History News & Notes*, edited by Wilma L. Gibbs, 121–35. Indianapolis: Indiana Historical Society, 1993.

Fields, Barbara. "Slavery, Race, and Ideology in the United States of America." *New Left Review* 181 (1990): 95–118.

Finkelman, Paul. "The Historical Context of the Fourteenth Amendment." *Temple Political and Civil Rights Law Review* 13, no. 2 (2004): 389–409.

———. "The Promise of Equality and the Limits of Law: From the Civil War to World War II." In *The History of Michigan Law*, edited by Paul Finkelman and Martin J. Hershock, 187–213. Athens: Ohio University Press, 2006.

———. "Race, Slavery, and the Law in Antebellum Ohio." In *The History of Ohio Law*, edited by Michael Les Benedict and John F. Winkler. Vol. 2, 748–81. Athens: Ohio University Press, 2004.

———. "Slavery and the Northwest Ordinance: A Study in Ambiguity." *Journal of the Early Republic* 6, no. 4 (1986): 343–70.

———. "Slavery, the 'More Perfect Union,' and the Prairie State." *Illinois Historical Journal* 80, no. 4 (Winter 1987): 248–69.

Finkelman, Paul, and Martin J. Hershock. "Introduction." In *The History of Michigan Law*, edited by Paul Finkelman and Martin J. Hershock, 1–12. Athens: Ohio University Press, 2006.

Finkenbine, Ray E. "A Beacon of Liberty on the Great Lakes: Race, Slavery, and the Law in Antebellum Michigan." In *The History of Michigan Law*, edited by Paul Finkelman and Martin J. Hershock, 83–107. Athens: Ohio University Press, 2006.

Fishel, Leslie H., Jr. "Northern Prejudice and Negro Suffrage, 1865–1870." *Journal of Negro History* 39, no. 1 (1954): 8–26.

Foner, Eric. *Free Soil, Free Labor, Free Men: The Ideology of the Republican Party Before the Civil War*. New York: Oxford University Press, 1994.

———. *Reconstruction: America's Unfinished Revolution, 1863–1877*. New York: Perennial Classics, 2002.

———. *A Short History of Reconstruction, 1863–1877*. New York: Harper & Row, 1990.

Forkner, John L., and Byron H. Dyson. *Historical Sketches and Reminiscences of Madison County, Indiana: A Detailed History of the Early Events of the Pioneer Settlement of the County, and Many Happenings of Recent Years, as Well as a Complete History of Each Township, to Which is Added Numerous Incidents of a Pleasant Nature, in the Way of Reminiscences and Laughable Occurrences*. Anderson, IN: J.L. Forkner, 1897.

Fowler, David H. *Northern Attitudes toward Interracial Marriage: Legislation and Public Opinion in the Middle Atlantic and States of the Old Northwest, 1780–1930*. New York: Garland Publishing, Inc., 1987.

Freehling, William W. *The Road to Disunion Volume Two, Secessionists Triumphant: 1854–1861*. New York: Oxford University Press, 2007.

Friedman, Lawrence J. "Antebellum American Abolitionism and the Problem of Violent Means." *Psychohistory Review* 9 (1980): 23–58.

Galbreath, Charles. "Anti-Slavery Movement in Columbiana County." *Ohio Archaeological and Historical Quarterly* 30, no. 4 (1921): 355–95.

Gamble, Douglas A. "Garrisonian Abolitionists in the West: Some Suggestions for Study." *Civil War History* 23, no. 1 (1977): 52–68.

———. "Moral Suasion in the West: Garrisonian Abolitionism, 1831–1861." PhD diss., Ohio State University, 1974.

Gans, Laura B. "Hudson Finding Aid: Hudson Family Papers, 1807–1963." Accessed May 30, 2011. http://asteria.fivecolleges.edu/findaids/umass/mu89.html.

Gara, Larry. "Slavery and the Slave Power: A Crucial Distinction." *Civil War History* 15, (1969): 5–18.

Garman, Mary Van Vleck. "'Altered Tone of Expression': The Anti-Slavery Rhetoric of Illinois Women, 1837–1847." PhD diss., Northwestern University, 1989.

Geary, Linda L. *Balanced in the Wind: A Biography of Betsey Mix Cowles*. Lewisburg: Bucknell University Press, 1989.

Gerber, David A. *Black Ohio and the Color Line, 1860–1915*. Blacks in the New World. Urbana: University of Illinois Press, 1976.

Gertz, Elmer. "The Black Laws of Illinois." *Journal of the Illinois State Historical Society* 61, no. 3 (1963): 454–73.

Gibson, Campbell. "Population of the 100 Largest Cities and Other Urban Places in the United States: 1790 to 1990." Washington, DC: US Bureau of the Census, 1998.

Gienapp, William E. "'Politics Seem to Enter into Everything': Political Culture in the North, 1840–1860." In *Essays on American Antebellum Politics, 1840–1860*, edited by Stephen E. Maizlish and John J. Kushma, 15–69. Arlington: University of Texas at Arlington Press, 1982.

Gilje, Paul A. *Rioting in America*. Bloomington: Indiana University Press, 1996.

Gill, John. *Tide Without Turning: Elijah P. Lovejoy and Freedom of the Press*. Boston: Starr King Press, 1958.

Gillette, William. *The Right to Vote: Politics and the Passage of the Fifteenth Amendment*, Johns Hopkins University. Studies in Historical and Political Science, ser. 83, no. 1. Baltimore: Johns Hopkins Press, 1965.

Ginzberg, Lori D. *Women and the Work of Benevolence: Morality, Politics, and Class in the Nineteenth-Century United States*. New Haven: Yale University Press, 1990.

Gittes, Frederick M. "Paper Promises: Race and Ohio Law after 1860." In *The History of Ohio Law*, edited by Michael Les Benedict and John F. Winkler. Vol. 2, 782–833. Athens: Ohio University Press, 2004.

Glasman, Paula. "Zebina Eastman, Chicago Abolitionist." Master's thesis, University of Chicago, 1968.

Glickman, Lawrence B. "'Buy for the Sake of the Slave': Abolitionism and the Origins of American Consumer Activism." *American Quarterly* 56, no. 4: 889–912.

Gliozzo, Charles A. "John Jones: A Study of a Black Chicagoan." *Illinois Historical Journal* 80, (1987): 177–88.

Goerler, Raimund Erhard. "Family, Self, and Anti-Slavery: Sydney Howard Gay and the Abolitionist Commitment." PhD diss., Case Western University, 1975.

Goodman, Paul. *Of One Blood: Abolitionism and the Origins of Racial Equality*. Berkeley: University of California Press, 1998.

Gossett, Thomas F. *Race: The History of an Idea in America*. New ed., Race and American Culture. New York: Oxford University Press, 1997.

Greve, Charles Theodore. *Centennial History of Cincinnati and Representative Citizens*. Chicago: Biographical Publishing Company, 1904.

Griffler, Keith P. *Front Line of Freedom: African Americans and the Forging of the Underground Railroad in the Ohio Valley*. Lexington: University of Kentucky Press, 2004.

Grimsted, David. *American Mobbing, 1828–1861: Toward Civil War*. New York: Oxford University Press, 1998.

Grossberg, Michael, and Amy Elson. "Family Law in Indiana: A Domestic Relations Crossroads." In *The History of Indiana Law*, edited by David J. Bodenhamer and Randall T. Shepard, 60–89. Athens: Ohio University Press, 2006.

Hagaman, Ardath. "Women of the Old Northwest in the Antislavery Movement." Unpublished paper, University of Michigan Department of History Student Papers, Manuscript Collection, Bentley Historical Library, University of Michigan, Ann Arbor, Michigan, 1941.

Hahn, Steven. *A Nation under Our Feet: Black Political Struggles in the Rural South, from Slavery to the Great Migration*. Cambridge: Belknap Press of Harvard University Press, 2003.

Hamm, Thomas D. *The Anti-Slavery Movement in Henry County, Indiana: A Study of the Local Abolitionists*. Henry County Historical Society Inc., 1975.

———. *God's Government Begun: The Society for Universal Inquiry and Reform, 1842–1846*. Religion in North America Series. Bloomington: Indiana University Press, 1995.

Hamm, Thomas D., David Dittmer, Chedna Fruchter, Ann Giordano, Janice Mathews, and Ellen Swain. "Moral Choices: Two Indiana Quaker Communities and the Abolitionist Movement." *Indiana Magazine of History* 87 (June 1991): 117–54.

Harris, L. M. "From Abolitionist Amalgamators to 'Rulers of the Five Points': The Discourse of Interracial Sex and Reform in Antebellum New York City." In *Sex, Love, Race: Crossing Boundaries in North American History*, edited by Martha Hodes, 191–212. New York: New York University Press, 1999.

Harris, Norman Dwight. *The History of Negro Servitude in Illinois and of the Slavery Agitation in that State, 1719–1864*. 1904. Reprint, Ann Arbor: University Microfilms, 1968.

Harrold, Stanley. *Border War: Fighting over Slavery before the Civil War*. Civil War America. Chapel Hill: University of North Carolina Press, 2010.

———. "John Brown's Forerunners: Slave Rescue Attempts and the Abolitionists, 1841–51." *Radical History Review* 55 (1992): 89–110.

———. *The Rise of Aggressive Abolitionism: Addresses to the Slaves*. Lexington: University Press of Kentucky, 2004.

———. *Subversives: Antislavery Community in Washington, D.C., 1828–1865*, Antislavery, Abolition, and the Atlantic World. Baton Rouge: Louisiana State University Press, 2003.

Heighway, David. "Micajah C. White: A Forgotten Victim of the Assault on Frederick Douglass." *Preserving Indiana* (2001): 1, 5.

Hendrickson, Thomas A. "Sheltering a Famous Fugitive Slave, Part 1." *Black History News and Notes* (2001): 1–7.

Hersh, Blanche Glassman. "'Am I Not A Woman and a Sister?' Abolitionist Beginnings of Nineteenth Century Feminism." In *Antislavery Reconsidered: New Perspectives on the Abolitionists*, edited by Louis Perry and

Michael Fellman, 252–83. Baton Rouge: Louisiana State University Press, 1979.

———. *The Slavery of Sex: Feminist-Abolitionists in America*. Urbana: University of Illinois Press, 1978.

Hewitt, Nancy A. "On Their Own Terms: A Historiographical Essay." In *The Abolitionist Sisterhood: Women's Political Culture in Antebellum America*, edited by Jean Fagan Yellin and John C. Van Horne, 23–30. Ithaca: Cornell University Press, 1994.

———. "The Social Origins of Antislavery Politics in Western New York." In *Crusaders and Compromisers: Essays on the Relationship of the Antislavery Struggle to the Antebellum Party System*, edited by Alan M. Kraut. Westport, CT: Greenwood Press, 1983.

———. *Women's Activism and Social Change: Rochester, New York, 1822–1872*. Ithaca, N.Y.: Cornell University Press, 1984.

Hill, Tony L. "Illinois." In *Encyclopedia of U.S. Campaigns, Elections, and Electoral Behavior*, edited by Kenneth F. Warren, 312–14. Thousand Oaks: Sage, 2008.

History of Madison County, Illinois. Illustrated. With Biographical Sketches of Many Prominent Men and Pioneers. Edwardsville, IL: W. R. Brink and Co., 1882.

History of Peoria County Illinois. Chicago: Johnson and Company, 1880.

Holland, Frederic May. *Frederick Douglass: The Colored Orator*. Edited by Carlos Martyn, American Reformers. New York: Funk and Wagnalls, 1895.

Holt, Michael F. *Political Parties and American Political Development: From the Age of Jackson to the Age of Lincoln*. Baton Rouge: Louisiana State University Press, 1992.

Horton, James Oliver, and Lois E. Horton. *In Hope of Liberty: Culture, Community, and Protest Among Northern Free Blacks, 1700–1860*. New York: Oxford University Press, 1997.

Humphrey, Carol Sue. *The Press of the Young Republic, 1783–1833*. The History of American Journalism. Westport, CT: Greenwood Press, 1996.

Isenberg, Nancy. *Sex and Citizenship in Antebellum America*. Chapel Hill: University of North Carolina Press, 1998.

Jacobi, Lori B. "More Than a Church: The Educational Role of the African Methodist Episcopal Church in Indiana, 1844–1861." In *Indiana's African-American Heritage: Essays From Black History News & Notes*, edited by Wilma L. Gibbs, 3–17. Indianapolis: Indiana Historical Society, 1993.

Jeffrey, Julie Roy. *The Great Silent Army of Abolitionism: Ordinary Women in the Antislavery Movement*. Chapel Hill: University of North Carolina Press, 1998.

Johnson, Reinhard O. *The Liberty Party, 1840–1848: Antislavery Third-Party Politics in the United States*. Antislavery, Abolition, and the Atlantic World. Baton Rouge: Louisiana State University Press, 2009.

Junger, Richard. "'God and man helped those who helped themselves:' John and Mary Jones and the Culture of African American Self-Sufficiency in Mid-Nineteenth Century Chicago." *Journal of Illinois History* 11 (Summer 2008): 111–32.

Katzman, David M. *Before the Ghetto: Black Detroit in the Nineteenth Century.* Blacks in the New World. Urbana: University of Illinois Press, 1973.

Kerber, Linda K. *No Constitutional Right to Be Ladies: Women and the Obligations of Citizenship.* New York: Hill and Wang, 1998.

———. "Separate Spheres, Female Worlds, Woman's Place: The Rhetoric of Women's History." *Journal of American History* 75 (1988): 9–39.

———. *Women of the Republic: Intellect and Ideology in Revolutionary America.* Chapel Hill: Published for the Institute of Early American History and Culture by the University of North Carolina Press, 1980.

Kloppenberg, James T. *The Virtues of Liberalism.* New York: Oxford University Press, 1998.

Kooker, Arthur Raymond. "The Anti-Slavery Movement in Michigan, 1796–1840: A Study in Humanitarianism." PhD diss., University of Michigan, 1941.

Kraditor, Aileen S. *Means and Ends in American Abolitionism: Garrison and His Critics on Strategy and Tactics, 1834–1850.* New York: Pantheon Books, 1969.

Kusmer, Kenneth L. *A Ghetto Takes Shape: Black Cleveland, 1870–1930.* Blacks in the New World. Urbana: University of Illinois Press, 1978.

Lapsansky, Emma Jones. "The World the Agitators Made: The Counterculture of Agitation in Urban Philadelphia." In *The Abolitionist Sisterhood: Women's Political Culture in Antebellum America,* edited by Jean Fagan Yellin and John C. Van Horne, 91–99. Ithaca: Cornell University Press, 1994.

Le Beau, Bryan. "1990 MAASA Presidential Address: 'Saving the West from the Pope': Anti-Catholic Propaganda and the Settlement of the Mississippi River Valley." *American Studies* 31, no. 1 (1991): 101–114.

Lerner, Gerda. *The Grimké Sisters from South Carolina: Pioneers for Women's Rights and Abolition.* New York: Oxford University Press, 1998.

———. *The Majority Finds Its Past: Placing Women in History.* New York: Oxford University Press, 1979.

Lersch, Arthur D. "Marius Racine Robinson: The Life and Beliefs of a Radical Abolitionist." Master's thesis, Kent State University, 1988.

Lesick, Lawrence Thomas. *The Lane Rebels: Evangelicalism and Antislavery in Antebellum America.* Studies in Evangelicalism no. 2. Metuchen, NJ: Scarecrow Press, 1980.

Lidsky, Lyrissa Barnett, and R. George Wright. *Freedom of the Press: A Reference Guide to the United States Constitution.* Westport, CT: Praeger, 2004.

Litwack, Leon F. *North of Slavery: The Negro in the Free States, 1790–1860.* Chicago: University of Chicago Press, 1961.

Lindquist, Charles N. *The Antislavery-Underground Railroad Movement in Lenawee County, Michigan, 1830–1860*. Adrian, Michigan: Lenawee County Historical Society, 1999.

Lumpkin, Katherine DuPre. "'The General Plan Was Freedom': A Negro Secret Order on the Underground Railroad." *Phylon* 28, no. 1 (1967): 63–77.

Lyda, John W. *The Negro in the History of Indiana*. Terre Haute, IN: 1953.

Mabee, Carleton. *Black Freedom: The Nonviolent Abolitionists from 1830 Through the Civil War*. New York: Macmillan, 1970.

Madison, James H. "Race, Law, and the Burdens of Indiana History." In *The History of Indiana Law*, edited by David J. Bodenhamer and Randall T. Shepard, 37–59. Athens: Ohio University Press, 2006.

Maier, Pauline. *American Scripture: Making the Declaration of Independence*. New York: Knopf, 1997.

Mangin, Michael. "Freemen in Theory: Race, Society, and Politics in Ross County, Ohio, 1796–1850." PhD diss., University of California at San Diego, 2002.

Marshall, Nicholas. "The Rural Newspaper and the Circulation of Information and Culture in New York and the Antebellum North." *New York History* (Spring 2007): 133–51.

Mason, Matthew. *Slavery and Politics in the Early American Republic*. Chapel Hill: University of North Carolina Press, 2006.

McCarthy, Timothy Patrick, and John Stauffer. *Prophets of Protest: Reconsidering the History of American Abolitionism*. New York: New Press, 2006.

McCulloch, David, ed. *History of Peoria County*. Chicago: Munsell Publishing Company, 1901.

McDermott, Stacy Pratt. "'Black Bill' and the Privileges of Whiteness in Antebellum Illinois." *Journal of Illinois History* 12, no. 1 (Spring 2009): 2–26.

McPherson, James M. *The Struggle for Equality: Abolitionists and the Negro in the Civil War and Reconstruction*. Princeton: Princeton University Press, 1964.

Melish, Joanne Pope. "The 'Condition' Debate and Racial Discourse in the Antebellum North." *Journal of the Early Republic* 19, no. 4 (1999): 651–72.

———. *Disowning Slavery: Gradual Emancipation and "Race" in New England, 1780–1860*. Ithaca: Cornell University Press, 1998.

———. Middleton, Stephen. *The Black Laws: Race and the Legal Process in Early Ohio*. Athens: Ohio University Press, 2005.

Miller, William Lee. *Arguing about Slavery: The Great Battle in the United States Congress*. New York: A. A. Knopf, 1996.

Mitchell, Thomas G. *Anti-Slavery Politics in Antebellum and Civil War America*. Westport, CT: Praeger Publishers, 2007.

Montgomery, David. *Beyond Equality: Labor and the Radical Republicans, 1862–1872*. New York: Knopf, 1967.

Morris, Thomas D. *Free Men All: The Personal Liberty Laws of the North, 1780–1861*. Baltimore: The Johns Hopkins University Press, 1974.

Morse, O. E. "Sketch of the Life and Work of Augustus Wattles." *Collections of the Kansas State Historical Society* 17 (1928): 290–99.

Muelder, Hermann R. "Congregationalists and the Civil War." In *A History of Illinois Congregational and Christian Churches*, edited by Matthew Spinka, 139–158. Chicago: The Congregational and Christian Conference of Illinois, 1944.

———. *Fighters for Freedom: The History of Anti-slavery Activities of Men and Women Associated with Knox College*. New York: Columbia University Press, 1959.

———. *A Hero Home from the War: Among the Black Citizens of Galesburg, Illinois, 1860–1880*. Galesburg: Knox College Library, 1987.

Muelder, Owen W. *The Underground Railroad in Western Illinois*. Jefferson, NC: McFarland & Co., 2008.

Myers, John L. "American Antislavery Society Agents and the Free Negro, 1833–1838." *Journal of Negro History* 52, no. 3 (1967): 200–219.

Nation, Richard Franklin. *At Home in the Hoosier Hills: Agriculture, Politics, and Religion in Southern Indiana, 1810–1870*. Midwestern History and Culture Series. Bloomington: Indiana University Press, 2005.

Nelson, Jacquelyn S. *Indiana Quakers Confront the Civil War*. Indianapolis: Indiana Historical Society, 1991.

Nerone, John C. *Violence Against the Press: Policing the Public Sphere in U.S. History*. New York: Oxford University Press, 1994.

Newman, Richard S. *The Transformation of American Abolitionism: Fighting Slavery in the Early Republic*. Chapel Hill: University of North Carolina Press, 2002.

Norman, Matthew. "From An 'Abolition City' to the Color Line: Galesburg, Knox College, and the Legacy of Antislavery Activism." *Journal of Illinois History* 10, no. 1 (Spring 2007): 2–26.

Nuermberger, Ruth Ketring. *The Free Produce Movement: A Quaker Protest Against Slavery*. Historical Papers of the Trinity College Historical Society. Series 25. Durham: Duke University Press, 1942.

Nye, Russel Blaine. *Fettered Freedom: Civil Liberties and the Slavery Controversy, 1830–1860*. East Lansing: Michigan State University Press, 1964.

Oberlin College Archives. "Betsy Mix Cowles." In *Papers of Other Individuals (Group 30)*. Accessed May 30, 2011. http://www.oberlin.edu/archive/resources/women/group30.html.

Painter, Nell Irvin. *Sojourner Truth: A Life, a Symbol*. New York: W.W. Norton, 1996.

Pascoe, Peggy. "Miscegenation Law, Court Cases, and Ideologies of 'Race' in Twentieth-Century America." *Journal of American History* 83, no. 1 (1996): 44–69.

———. "Race, Gender, and Intercultural Relations: The Case of Interracial Marriage." *Frontiers: A Journal of Women Studies* 12, no. 1 (1991): 5–18.

———. *What Comes Naturally: Miscegenation Law and the Making of Race in America*. Oxford: Oxford University Press, 2009.

Pasley, Jeffrey L. *"The Tyranny of Printers": Newspaper Politics in the Early American Republic.* Charlottesville: University Press of Virginia, 2001.

Pease, Jane H., and William H. Pease. "Antislavery Ambivalence: Immediatism, Expediency, Race." *American Quarterly* 17, no. 4 (1965): 682–95.

———. *They Who Would Be Free: Blacks' Search for Freedom, 1830–1861.* Blacks in the New World. Urbana: University of Illinois Press, 1990.

Perry, Lewis. *Boats Against the Current: American Culture Between Revolution and Modernity, 1820–1860.* New York: Oxford University Press, 1993.

Pirtle, Carol. *Escape Betwixt Two Suns: A True Tale of the Underground Railroad in Illinois.* Carbondale: Southern Illinois University Press, 2000.

Portnoy, Alisse. *Their Right to Speak: Women's Activism in the Indian and Slave Debates.* Cambridge: Harvard University Press, 2005.

Portrait and Biographical Album of Warren County, Illinois. Chicago: Chapman Brothers, 1886.

Quarles, Benjamin. *Black Abolitionists.* New York: Oxford University Press, 1969.

Quist, John W. *Restless Visionaries: The Social Roots of Antebellum Reform in Alabama and Michigan.* Baton Rouge: Louisiana State University Press, 1998.

Rhodes, Jane. *Mary Ann Shadd Cary: The Black Press and Protest in the Nineteenth Century.* Bloomington: Indiana University Press, 1998.

Rice, James M. *Peoria City and County Illinois, A Record of Settlement, Organization, Progress, and Achievement, Illustrated.* Chicago: The S. J. Clarke Publishing Company, 1912.

Richards, Leonard L. *"Gentlemen of Property and Standing": Anti-Abolition Mobs in Jacksonian America.* New York: Oxford University Press, 1970.

Riker, Dorothy, and Gayle Thornbrough. *Indiana Election Returns, 1816–1851.* Indiana Historical Collections. Indianapolis: Indiana Historical Bureau, 1960.

Robertson, Stacey. *Hearts Beating For Liberty: Women Abolitionists in the Old Northwest.* Chapel Hill: University of North Carolina Press, 2010.

Rodgers, Daniel T. "Rights Consciousness in American History." In *The Bill of Rights in Modern America After 200 Years,* edited by David J. Bodenhamer and James W. Ely, 3–17. Bloomington: Indiana University Press, 1993.

Roediger, David R. *The Wages of Whiteness: Race and the Making of the American Working Class,* rev. ed. New York: Verso, 1999.

Rohrbach, Augusta. "Profits of Protest: The Market Strategies of Sojourner Truth and Louisa May Alcott." In *Prophets of Protest: Reconsidering the History of American Abolitionism,* edited by Timothy Patrick McCarthy and John Stauffer, 235–55. New York: New Press, 2006.

Rokicky, Catherine M. *James Monroe: Oberlin's Christian Statesman and Reformer, 1821–1898.* Kent, OH: Kent State University Press, 2002.

Rotundo, E. Anthony. *American Manhood: Transformations in Masculinity from the Revolution to the Modern Era.* New York: BasicBooks, 1993.

Rugh, Susan Sessions. *Our Common Country: Family Farming, Culture, and*

Community in the Nineteenth-Century Midwest. Midwestern History and Culture. Bloomington: Indiana University Press, 2001.

Ryan, Mary P. "Civil Society as Democratic Practice: North American Cities during the Nineteenth Century." In *Patterns of Social Capital: Stability and Change in Historical Perspective,* edited by Robert I. Rotberg, 221–46. New York: Cambridge University Press, 2001.

———. "Gender and Public Access: Women's Politics in Nineteenth-Century America." In *Feminism, the Public and the Private,* edited by Joan B. Landes. New York: Oxford University Press, 1998.

Salerno, Beth A. *Sister Societies: Women's Antislavery Organizations in Antebellum America.* DeKalb: Northern Illinois University Press, 2005.

Salstrom, Paul. *From Pioneering to Persevering: Family Farming in Indiana to 1880.* West Lafayette: Purdue University Press, 2007.

Sarchet, Cyrus Parkinson Beatty. *History of Guernsey County, Ohio.* Vol. 1. Indianapolis: B.F. Bowen & Company, 1911.

Schudson, Michael. *Discovering the News: A Social History of American Newspapers.* New York: Basic Books, 1978.

Schwalm, Leslie A. *Emancipation's Diaspora: Race and Reconstruction in the Upper Midwest.* John Hope Franklin Series in African American History and Culture. Chapel Hill: University of North Carolina Press, 2009.

Scott, Donald M. "Print and the Public Lecture System, 1840–1860." In *Printing and Society in Early America,* edited by William L. Joyce, David D. Hall, Richard D. Brown, and John B. Hench, 278–99. Worcester, MA: American Antiquarian Society, 1983.

Scott, James C. *Domination and the Arts of Resistance: Hidden Transcripts.* New Haven: Yale University Press, 1990.

Sellers, Charles. *The Market Revolution: Jacksonian America, 1815–1846.* New York: Oxford University Press, 1991.

Sewell, Richard H. *Ballots for Freedom: Antislavery Politics in the United States, 1837–1860.* New York: Oxford University Press, 1976.

Shoemaker, Rebecca S. "The Indiana Bill of Rights: Two Hundred Years of Civil Liberties History." In *The History of Indiana Law,* edited by David J. Bodenhamer and Randall T. Shepard, 193–212. Athens: Ohio University Press, 2006.

Simmons, William J. *Men of Mark: Eminent, Progressive and Rising.* Cleveland: Geo. M. Rewell and Co., 1887.

Simon, Paul. *Freedom's Champion: Elijah Lovejoy.* Carbondale: Southern Illinois University Press, 1994.

Sklar, Kathryn Kish. *Catharine Beecher: A Study in American Domesticity.* New York: Norton, 1976.

Smith, Theodore C. *Liberty and Free Soil Parties in the Northwest.* New York: Longmans, Green, and Co., 1897.

Spinka, Matthew. "Organization of the General Association and After, 1844–1865." In *A History of Illinois Congregational and Christian Churches,* edited by Matthew Spinka, 91–138. Chicago: The Congregational and Christian Conference of Illinois, 1944.

Stanton, William Henry. *Our Ancestors the Stantons.* Philadelphia: Innes and Sons, 1922.

Stauffer, John. *The Black Hearts of Men: The Radical Abolitionists and the Transformation of Race.* Cambridge: Harvard University Press, 2002.

Sterling, Dorothy. *Ahead of Her Time: Abby Kelley and the Politics of Anti-Slavery.* New York: W.W. Norton, 1991.

———. *We Are Your Sisters: Black Women in the 19th Century.* New York: W.W Norton, 1984.

Stewart, James Brewer. *Abolitionist Politics and the Coming of the Civil War.* Amherst: University of Massachusetts Press, 2008.

———. *Holy Warriors: The Abolitionists and American Slavery.* New York: Hill and Wang, 1976.

———. "Modernizing 'Difference': The Political Meanings of Color in the Free States, 1776–1840." *Journal of the Early Republic* 19, no. 4 (1999): 691–712.

Stewart, James Brewer, et al. "The Emergence of Racial Modernity and the Rise of the White North, 1790–1840." *Journal of the Early Republic* 18 (1998): 181–236.

Taylor, Agnes Longstreth. *The Longstreth Family Records, Revised and Enlarged by Agnes Longstreth Taylor.* Philadelphia: Press of Ferris & Leach, 1909.

Taylor, Nikki Marie. *Frontiers of Freedom: Cincinnati's Black Community, 1802–1868.* Ohio University Press Series on Law, Society, and Politics in the Midwest. Athens: Ohio University Press, 2005.

Terzian, Barbara A. "Ohio's Constitutional Conventions and Constitutions." In *The History of Ohio Law*, edited by Michael Les Benedict and John F. Winkler, 40–87. Athens: Ohio University Press, 2004.

Thornbrough, Emma Lou. *The Negro in Indiana: A Study of a Minority.* Vol. 37, Indiana Historical Collections. Indianapolis: Indiana Historical Bureau, 1957.

United States Bureau of the Census. *Historical Statistics of the United States, Colonial Times to 1870, Part 1.* Bicentennial ed. Washington, DC: Government Printing Office, 1975.

Van Broekhoven, Deborah Bingham. "'Let Your Names Be Enrolled:' Method and Ideology in Women's Antislavery Petitioning." In *The Abolitionist Sisterhood: Women's Political Culture in Antebellum America*, edited by Jean Fagan Yellin and John C. Van Horne, 179–200. Ithaca: Cornell University Press, 1994.

Varon, Elizabeth R. *We Mean to be Counted: White Women and Politics in Antebellum Virginia.* Gender and American Culture. Chapel Hill: University of North Carolina Press, 1998.

Vlach, John Michael. "Above Ground on the Underground Railroad: Places of Flight and Refuge." In *Passages to Freedom: the Underground Railroad in History and Memory*, edited by David W. Blight, 95–115. Washington:

Smithsonian Books in Association with the National Underground Railroad Freedom Center, 2004.

Voegeli, V. Jacque. *Free but Not Equal: The Midwest and the Negro During the Civil War.* Chicago: University of Chicago Press, 1967.

Volpe, Vernon L. *Forlorn Hope of Freedom: The Liberty Party in the Old Northwest, 1838–1848.* Kent, OH: Kent State University Press, 1990.

———. "Theodore Dwight Weld's Antislavery Mission in Ohio." *Ohio History* 100 (1991): 5–18.

Waldrep, Christopher. *Lynching in America: A History in Documents.* New York: New York University Press, 2006.

———. *The Many Faces of Judge Lynch: Extralegal Violence and Punishment in America.* New York: Palgrave, 2002.

Walker, Juliet E. K. *Free Frank: A Black Pioneer on the Antebellum Frontier.* Lexington: University Press of Kentucky, 1983.

Walters, Ronald G. *American Reformers, 1815–1860.* American Century Series. New York: Hill and Wang, 1978.

———. *The Antislavery Appeal: American Abolitionism After 1830.* Baltimore: Johns Hopkins University Press, 1976.

———. "The Boundaries of Abolitionism." In *Antislavery Reconsidered: New Perspectives on the Abolitionists,* edited by Louis Perry and Michael Fellman, 3–23. Baton Rouge: Louisiana State University Press, 1979.

Watson, Robert Meredith. "The Anatomy of a Crusade: A Western Reserve Township and the War Against the Slaveholders, 1831–1865." PhD diss., Memphis State University, 1978.

Weiner, Dana Elizabeth. "Racial Radicals: The Antislavery Movement in the Old Northwest, 1830–1861." PhD diss., Northwestern University, 2007.

Wheeler, Adade Mitchell. *The Roads They Made: Women in Illinois History.* Chicago: Charles H. Kerr Publishing Company, 1977.

Wilentz, Sean. *The Rise of American Democracy: Jefferson to Lincoln.* New York: Norton, 2005.

Wirls, Daniel. "'The Only Mode of Avoiding Everlasting Debate': The Overlooked Senate Gag Rule for Antislavery Petitions." *Journal of the Early Republic* 27, no. 1 (2007): 115–38.

Yee, Shirley J. *Black Women Abolitionists: A Study in Activism, 1828–1860.* Knoxville: University of Tennessee Press, 1992.

Zaeske, Susan. *Signatures of Citizenship: Petitioning, Antislavery, and Women's Political Identity.* Chapel Hill: University of North Carolina Press, 2003.

Zagarri, Rosemarie. *Revolutionary Backlash: Women and Politics in the Early American Republic.* Early American Studies. Philadelphia: University of Pennsylvania Press, 2007.

Index

Page numbers in italics refer to maps.

Lightning Source UK Ltd.
Milton Keynes UK
UKHW040744290919
350631UK00003B/153/P

9 780875 804576